MARY WOLLSTONECRAFT

A Social Pioneer

MARY WOLLSTONECRAFT
A Social Pioneer

Margaret Tims

And we are put on earth a little space,
That we may learn to bear the beams of love.
William Blake

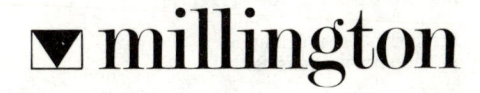

▼ millington

For F.A.L.

Copyright © 1976 by Margaret Tims
All rights reserved
ISBN 0 86000 034 6

First published 1976 by
Millington Books Ltd
109 Southampton Row
London WC1B 4HH
also
Wessex House, Blandford Heights
Blandford Forum, Dorset DT11 7TS

Printed in Great Britain
at The Pitman Press, Bath

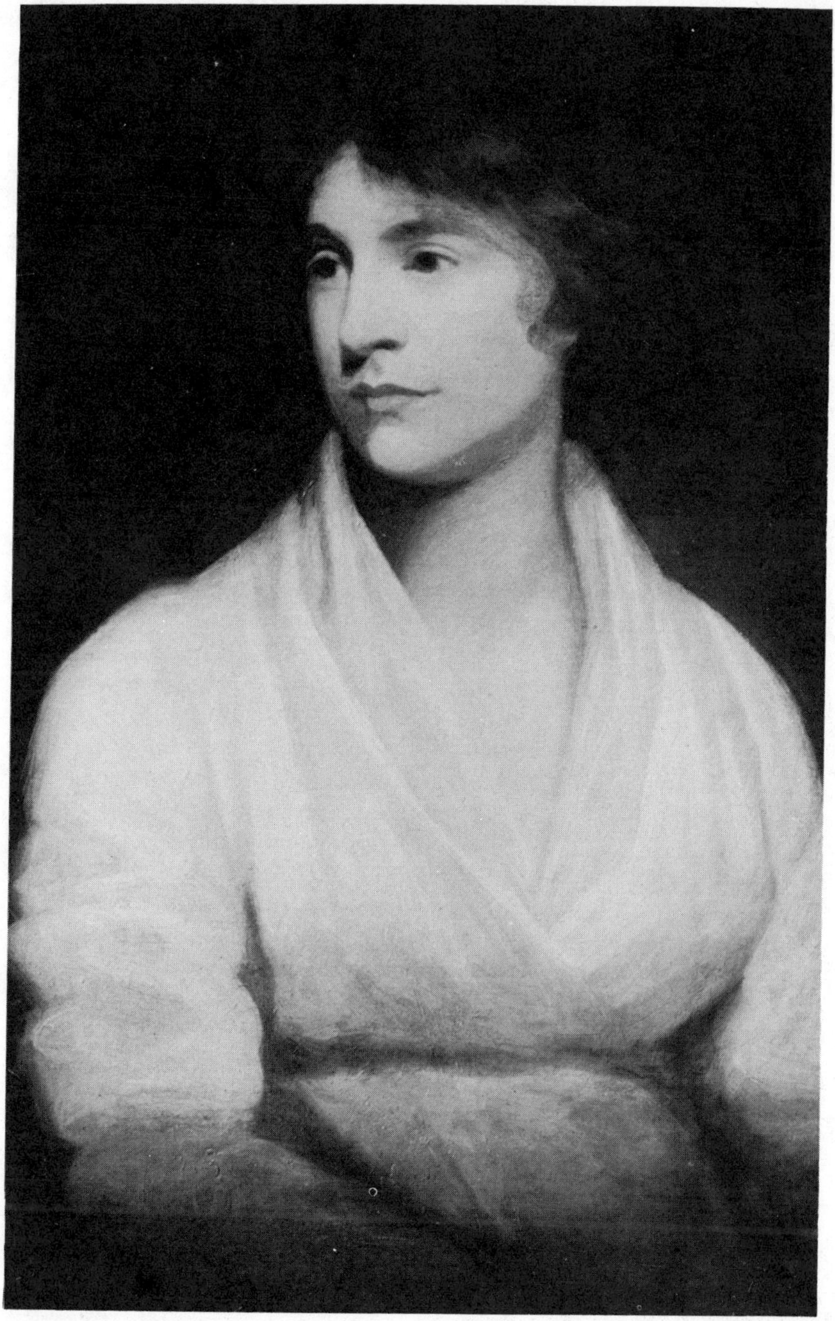

Contents

Preface ix

Acknowledgments xi

PART ONE: The School of Adversity
1. First Lessons: 1759–78   3
2. On Probation: 1778–84   13
3. Graduation: 1784–5   30
4. End of a Career: 1786–7   41
5. Report in Triplicate   60

PART TWO: The Social Challenge
6. A Journalist in London: 1788–90   81
7. The Radical Revolt: 1789–90   103
8. Women's Liberation: 1792   121
9. Life and Art: 1791–2   147

PART THREE: The Romantic Nightmare
10. Paris in the Spring: 1793   171
11. Midsummer Madness: 1793   185
12. Terror and Despair: 1793–4   199
13. A Revolution and its Aftermath: 1794–5   231
14. Journey's End: 1795   249

PART FOUR: Towards Humanity

15. Death of a Romantic: 1795–6	273
16. The Consummation of Compromise: 1796–7	289
17. Femme Godwin: 1797	318
18. Post-mortem	339
Notes	358
Bibliography	370
Index	372

Preface

By coincidence, and after many vicissitudes, this book goes to press in International Women's Year. It is therefore appropriate to ask: has Mary Wollstonecraft a message for today—and tomorrow? The answer must surely be Yes. Many thousands of words have been, are being and will be written on the theme of women's liberation. It is an inexhaustible topic, as old as Eve and as new as next year's trend. Yet few of these words, we may predict, will be read in two hundred years' time, as Mary Wollstonecraft is read today. The spate of recent biographies testifies to her relevance.

So why another book? Every author seeks to present a unique point of view, and with such a subject there is always something fresh to say. The purpose of this study is to present the life of a woman who has 'thinking powers' (as Mary Wollstonecraft described her own heroine in *Mary: a Fiction*)—and who 'thinks' not in intellectual abstractions but in terms of personal rights and corporate responsibility. The result is a social philosophy which we have scarcely yet begun to comprehend.

Mary Wollstonecraft lived and wrote as a woman in eighteenth-century England; but she had also the kind of universal consciousness which is perhaps a hallmark of genius. The conclusions she drew from that society, and her own predicament in it, transcend her own life and may be extended to both sexes, at all times, and in any country. In her vision of human progress, Mary Wollstonecraft is still a woman of the future.

Acknowledgments

All biographers must be indebted to their predecessors in the same field, and especially so where historical research is required. Published works which have contributed to this study are listed in the Bibliography.

The primary source for any biography of Mary Wollstonecraft must be the *Memoirs* of his wife published by William Godwin in the year after her death; but on many points of detail Godwin was vague and sometimes misleading. Valuable new material was included in the 1927 edition of the *Memoirs* which was edited with an introduction and supplement by W. Clark Durant. More recently, Ralph M. Wardle's *Mary Wollstonecraft: a critical biography*, published in 1951, was by far the most comprehensive to date, and I am greatly indebted to this source. Since then more information has come to light through the researches of the Carl Pforzheimer Library in New York, in particular the hitherto untraced letters to Jane Arden which are included in *Shelley and his Circle,* vol. II, 1961. Other new information is contained in the most recent biographies by Eleanor Flexner (1972) and Claire Tomalin (1974).

In the search for out-of-print and unpublished material libraries and record offices have given indispensable service, amongst them the British Museum; Bodleian Library, Oxford; Fawcett Library, London; Guildhall Library, London; Essex Record Office; London Record Office; Middlesex Record Office. Helpful service has been received from public libraries in Beverley,

Fulham, Jersey, Liverpool and Pembrokeshire, with special thanks to the staff of Ealing central reference library.

Thanks are also due to Lord Abinger for directing me to the microfilm copies of the Shelley family papers in the Abinger collection at the Bodleian Library, the source of most of the surviving letters of Mary Wollstonecraft and her sisters; to Miss Olive Arden of Beverley and Mr C. R. Arden for information on their family history; and to the vicars and vergers who have opened up their parish registers for inspection. Last but not least, I am grateful to the friends and associates who have given practical help, advice and encouragement over a long period of writing.

M.T.

CHAPTER ONE

First Lessons: 1759–1778

Mary Wollstonecraft, still remembered after two hundred years as the author of *A Vindication of the Rights of Woman*, was born and died a feminist although she did not always live as one. So rich and original a character could not easily be contained in any one mould. Mary was a 'feminist' by force of circumstance—both personal and historical—rather than from any natural inclination of temperament, as her life-pattern clearly demonstrates.

As the eldest daughter of a drunken, brutish father and a weak but harsh mother she was made painfully aware of the 'wrongs of woman' at a much too tender age. This early wound to her sensibility never healed, and much of the tribulation of her adult life may be seen to have stemmed from it. Add to these personal scars the historical fact that the status of women in England fell to a nadir in the early eighteenth century; and that the winds of revolution were buffeting these islands both easterly from America and westerly from France—and the recipe for a declaration of the 'rights of woman' was timely and complete.

Complete, that is, except for the force of character without which no force of circumstance would budge the lowliest molehill, let alone those peaks of ignorance and prejudice which Mary Wollstonecraft attacked single-handedly: only to collapse, exhausted, at the summit. In a life punctuated by tragic ironies it was the cruellest irony of all that this pioneer of female emancipation should have died, at the age of thirty-eight, as a result of childbirth.

Mary was born at Primrose Street, Spitalfields, on 27th April 1759, and baptised at St Botolph's Bishopsgate, on 20th May. Her parents already had a son, Edward, and five more children were to follow her: Henry (who died in infancy)[1], Eliza, Everina, James and Charles. Mary's concern and sense of responsibility for her younger sisters and brothers, which developed quite soon, foreshadowed the wider concerns of her adult life. This quality of concern, which was so marked a feature of her character, invalidates the concept of Mary Wollstonecraft as a dedicated liberationist who had discarded the 'shackles' of emotion; nothing could be further from the truth. Her whole life, indeed, was for this very reason a struggle to achieve a proper balance between the claims of personal feeling and social justice (including justice to women); she passionately believed that if either claim were abandoned in the interest of the other, the battle was lost. It was this dualism, rather than a single-minded feminism, that constituted Mary's original contribution to the history of human progress. There was little to sustain her in this doctrine in her own family circumstances, but sustain it she did.

The Wollstonecrafts had been for two generations silk-weavers in Spitalfields, although the name suggests a north of England origin, and through the diligence of Mary's paternal grandfather the family had prospered. But his son, Edward John Wollstonecraft—Mary's father—proved incapable of building on these foundations. He has often been portrayed, in the darkest terms, as no more than a drunken wastrel; but he was not without some talents, as is shown in his multiplicity of schemes for making a livelihood. His natural gifts, however, were far outweighed by his defects of character. It was from her grandfather that Mary must have inherited the positive qualities that drove her forward through years of adversity. This Edward Wollstonecraft had built up a substantial manufacturing business and acquired land and property in and around London. There is a record of the transfer of land and buildings at Pinner in Middlesex from Edward Wollstonecraft 'citizen and weaver of London'[2] in 1745; and the row of houses in Primrose Street where Mary was born was owned by the family. At his death in 1765 Edward bequeathed to his son Edward John a sum in the region of £10,000: no mean fortune in those days[3]. In theory, therefore, Mary had a good start in life. It must have been at about this time that the family moved out of London to a farm on the edge of Epping Forest, where Mr Wollstonecraft may have had visions of establishing himself as a gentleman farmer. But it seems clear that it was after receiving his inheritance that his downward slide began. The sight of her father's decline may have influenced Mary in her later attacks on the laws of inheritance and the evil effects of wealth on the character of the heirs.

No doubt, having moved up in society after his father's death, Edward John Wollstonecraft began to live above his means. He had a young and growing family to support, a second daughter having been born in 1763 (baptised Elizabeth at St Botolph's on 24th July) and a third was to follow two years later (Everina, baptised at Romford on 10th November 1765). The family had by this time moved to another farm in Essex, which was described as being 'near the Whalebone a little way out of the Chelmsford Road'[4]. But this venture seems to have been no more successful than the first, and only a year after Everina's birth the family moved again to Barking, then a busy port and fishing village. Here their near neighbours were the wealthy landowners Bamber and Joseph Gascoyne. Bamber, a Member of Parliament, was absent much of the time, but Joseph and his family were said to have been 'in habits of the most frequent intercourse'[5] with Mary's family. This would seem to indicate that the Wollstonecrafts were still in a fairly substantial position. There were now four children and a fifth child, James, was baptised at St Margaret's Church, Barking, on 23rd February 1768.

As the family increased in size, however, its fortunes steadily declined. Edward Wollstonecraft had neither the strength of will to husband his resources nor the experience to husband his land. Essex was at that time one of the most prosperous regions of England, supplying the needs of the rapidly-growing population of London from its cloth-making and market-gardening industries and just becoming popular as a fashionable place of residence for the emerging gentry. Though the enclosure acts of 1760 and 1782 were soon to send up land prices and squeeze out the peasant farmer, Edward Wollstonecraft was hardly in that category. The Georgian period has been described as a 'golden age'[6] for Essex farming and there was little excuse for failure outside a man's own character. Edward's farms obstinately refused to prosper and it was during these years in Essex that the vicious circle of failure, drink and debt must have been set in rotation.

At Michaelmas in 1768 he took a major decision, uprooting himself from the hostile soil of a southern gentry to try his luck in the north country. Still intent on farming, he settled his family at Walkington, three miles from Beverley in east Yorkshire. This was by no means a banishment from civilisation. A thriving town which had not only a prosperous agriculture but a certain rugged elegance, Beverley supported a lively culture with its own theatre and scientific societies. It had a liberal tradition and girls were admitted to the grammar school even in the eighteenth century. The Wollstonecrafts remained at Beverley for six years, the longest time Mary spent at any one place in her whole brief, restless life. Here her youngest brother Charles was born, and baptised at the ancient and beautiful Minster on 23rd June 1770[7]. Here she had most of her schooling, although it is not known how regular this was nor which school she attended. The length of their stay was probably determined by some family connections in the neighbourhood rather than by any new-found stability on the part of Mr Wollstonecraft. There is a record of one Henry Woodstock Wollstonecraft, son of David John Wollstonecraft (gent.) being apprenticed to Marmaduke Hewitt (surgeon and apothecary) in 1775[8].

Apart from the domestic crises caused by her father's vagaries of temper, Mary's years at Beverley were not unhappy and she later looked back on this period with nostalgia. She had congenial friends in the town and a beautiful countryside to explore. The one great joy of her childhood was the freedom to run wild in the open air, a circumstance which contributed both to her independence of spirit and her sensitivity to natural beauty. The family farm at Walkington—possibly on the site of the present Broadgate farm adjoining Westwood common—was separated from the town by a stretch of woodland, and in a letter to her Beverley friend Jane Arden she speaks of her longing for 'a walk in my darling Westwood'[9]. Jane was the daughter of John Arden, a noted astronomer and lecturer on experimental philosophy, and Mary was one of his pupils. As she grew into adolescence her thoughts and feelings jostled for expression. Mary had to confide them to somebody, and she chose as her confidante Jane Arden.

The series of letters written by Mary to Jane between 1773 and 1780[10] throws new light on her early development. She wrote at first as a child, a little in awe of her friend yet also jealous of her more privileged situation. She was already conscious of the drawbacks arising from her own family's deficiencies. 'I have not the advantage of a Master as you have,' she wrote in apology for her own ill-written letter, 'and it is with great difficulty to get my brother to mend my pens'. Jane was at this time away visiting friends in Hull, and Mary could not help envying her greater social freedom. Again, in her third letter, she was apologising for its illegibility: 'I am afraid you cannot read this as all the children are plaguing me.' As the eldest girl in the family, Mary no doubt had more than her fair share of drudgery. She had to content herself with vicarious enjoyment through Jane's letters: '... you could not more oblige me than your description of Miss C— and her lover (lovers you know we are to call them) as it is my greatest pleasure to read odd characters', she remarked, and begged Jane to write again and to return as soon as possible.

If Mary's childhood was not wholly so dark as she painted it in recollection, there is no doubt that she was emotionally damaged by her parentage. She suffered not only from her father's weaknesses of character but also from a lack of affection in her mother, which in the long term was perhaps the worse deprivation. Mrs Wollstonecraft (née Elizabeth Dixon, with ancestry from Ballyshannon, Donegal) was quite inadequate to meet the demands made on her: as incapable of withstanding her tyrannical husband as she was of governing her children with equity and love. Whilst the eldest son was favoured to the point of spoiling him, Mary as the second child was both rebuffed and exploited: the worst possible treatment for a girl whose hunger for affection was only equalled by her passion for justice. Later, Mrs Wollstonecraft saw the error of this treatment and used her younger daughters more generously—but by that time the damage was done. William Godwin described the situation in his *Memoirs* of Mary[11]:

> She experienced in the first period of her existence, but few of those indulgences and marks of affection, which are principally calculated to sooth the subjection and sorrow of our early days. She was not the favourite either of her father or mother. Her father was a man of a quick, impetuous disposition, subject to alternate fits of kindness and cruelty. In his family he was a despot, and his wife appears to have been the first, and

most submissive of his subjects. The mother's partiality was fixed upon the eldest son, and her system of government relative to Mary was characterized by considerable rigour.

Not to be the favourite child of either parent must have wounded Mary to the quick. The lack of affection at home made her the more demanding of her friends: 'I must have the first place or none,' she declared to Jane Arden in the course of a girlish quarrel. When love failed Mary was always quick to take offence; yet she never bore malice, and she showed none towards her mother. Her first impulse was to defend the weak; and when her mother needed defending Mary was there, before her brothers, interposing her own person between the oppressor and the oppressed. Mary endured chastisement from her mother with humility and violence from her father with contempt; but violence towards a third party she could not accept on any terms. In Godwin's words:

> The quickness of her father's temper led him sometimes to threaten similar violence towards his wife. When that was the case, Mary would throw herself between the despot and his victim, with the purpose to receive upon her own person the blows that might be directed against her mother. She has even laid whole nights upon the landing-place near their chamber-door, when, mistakenly or with reason, she apprehended that her father might break out into paroxysms of violence.

Nor could Mary tolerate cruelty towards animals. Mr Wollstonecraft was the sort of man who would fondle his dogs at one moment and kick them away the next. When this happened, Mary described her abhorrence as having 'risen to agony'.

This agony of sensibility was to cause Mary considerable heartbreak. The slightest breath of coldness could overshadow her happiness, as she tried to explain to Jane Arden in making amends for her previous touchiness: 'I have a heart too susceptible for my own peace'. She admitted that she had been at fault in provoking the quarrel and admitted the cause: 'Love and jealousy are twins'. But to identify the cause did not heal the wound: 'There is some part of your letter so cutting,' she continued, 'I cannot comment upon it'; and she went on to extol the virtues of a friendship 'founded upon virtue Truth and love'. Strange words from a girl of fifteen, but she may have been echoing the sentiments of a rather florid essay on the subject which Dr Arden had given her to read.

The final letter in this series to Jane Arden, and the only one precisely dated, was written on 16th November 1774. It is short and cheerful. The quarrel was over and the two girls were still friends. Mary was recommending Jane to read Goldsmith's *Citizen of the World*: 'letters from a Chinese Philosopher residing in London to his friends in the East'. This led her to think of the Beverley philosopher, Dr Arden:

> Pray tell the worthy Philosopher, the next time he is so obliging as to give me a lesson on the globes, I hope I shall convince him I am quicker than his daughter at finding out a puzzle, tho' I can't equal her at solving a problem.

There may have been no 'next time'. Shortly afterwards the Wollstonecrafts left Beverley—under a cloud of disgrace. Mary gave some inkling of this when she resumed her correspondence with Jane, under very different circumstances, three and a half years later. In the second of these letters[12] she wrote:

> It is almost needless to tell you that my father's violent temper and extravagant turn of mind, was the principal cause of my unhappiness and that of the rest of my family.—
>
> The good folks of Beverley (like those of most Country towns) were very ready to find out their Neighbours' faults, and to animadvert on them;—Many people did not scruple to prognosticate the ruin of the whole family, and the way he went on, justified them for so doing.

This crisis in the family fortunes had a profound effect on Mary's development and coloured her whole future. It could not have come at a worse time, coinciding as it did with the natural strains and stresses of adolescence, and she never fully recovered from the shock and disillusionment of the upheaval. As a result of her father's 'ungovernable temper', she told Jane, 'my health is ruined, my spirits broken'. In fact, so badly had Mr Wollstonecraft managed his affairs that not only had he lost his own capital but was 'obliged to take the fortune that was settled on us children'. Mary 'very readily' gave up her part, she said, although she knew that with it she forfeited her one hope of independence.

According to Godwin's account of these years the family moved from Beverley to Hoxton in north London, and then to Laugharne in South Wales. But in her letter to Jane Arden Mary reversed this order:

—a pretended scheme of economy induced my father to take us all into Wales,—a most expensive and troublesome journey that answered no one good end.—Business or pleasure took him often to London, and at last obliged him once more to fix there.

In Wales Mary became acquainted with the daughters of John Bartlett Allen at Cresselly. Two of the nine daughters later married the two elder sons of Josiah Wedgwood, and the Allens have been described as 'a family distinguished by good looks, character and breeding'[13]. So in spite of the débacle at Beverley the Wollstonecrafts must still have been socially accepted by the 'gentry'. When the family returned to London Mary spent much of her time in the home of a clergyman, Mr Clare, and his wife: 'a very amiable Couple,' she told Jane. The Clares took a great interest in Mary and encouraged her education, which had been interrupted by the family upheaval. 'I should have lived very happily with them,' Mary continued, 'if it had not been for my domestic troubles, and some other painful circumstances, that I wish to bury in oblivion.' The 'painful circumstances' are not explained, but may have arisen out of an absorbing new friendship which now claimed her attention:

> I could dwell for ever on her praises, and you wod. not wonder at it, if you knew the many favours she has conferred on me, and the many valuable qualifications she possesses:— She has a masculine understanding, and sound judgment, yet she has every feminine virtue.

Fanny Blood, the subject of this eulogy, was the eldest daughter of a family to whom Mary was introduced by Mrs Clare. The Bloods lived at Newington Butts, Southwark, and it was here that she visited them. Godwin said that the Clares lived in Queen's Row, Hoxton, as neighbours of the Wollstonecrafts, but Mary told Jane that she enjoyed Fanny's society at the Clares' house, which would seem to suggest that they too lived in Southwark. (No Queen's Row is shown on maps of Hoxton, but there was a street of this name in Walworth quite close to Newington Butts.) The girls must have seen each other frequently to have formed such a close attachment. For this was no commonplace friendship. Writing some two years after their first meeting, Mary confided to Jane Arden that she loved Fanny 'better than all the world'.

Mary's feeling for Fanny should not be dismissed as a sentimental, schoolgirl 'crush' or regarded as an unnatural fixation resulting from the emotional starvation of her early years. For Mary loving was as natural as breathing; to give and receive affection the deepest need of her being. Yet such was her nature that she could not love what she did not also esteem. She had found little to esteem within her own family, which should have been the natural repository of affection; nor, thanks to their unsettled circumstances, could she make lasting relationships outside it—her continued correspondence with Jane Arden witnesses to this lack. Now for the first time, in Fanny Blood, the ideal was made flesh; and Mary did not mean to let it go. Nothing would do now but to live with Fanny and share her life. This, she told Jane, was the 'most rational' wish she could make; for she found Fanny's company not only agreeable but improving. This was not a delusion on Mary's part. Fanny Blood, according to Godwin, was 'a young woman of extraordinary accomplishments'. She played and sang well and had a particularly fine skill in drawing, even earning money from this talent. Mary, at this stage, was more skilled at running and tumbling with her brothers than in the gentler arts; she must have felt herself, by comparison, an uncouth, Yorkshire hoyden. She viewed her friend, as Godwin described it, 'with sentiments of inferiority and reverence'. She was so conscious of her limitations that she even requested Fanny to instruct her in spelling and composition.

For the time being, Mary had to be content with this unequal friendship. Her family still claimed her greater attention. Their sojourn at Hoxton—whether before or after the temporary removal to Wales—must have been a brief one, for in 1777 Mary prevailed upon her father to take a house at Walworth. Here she could be close to Fanny, while helping her mother with the younger children and pursuing her own studies as best she could. But the affairs of the family continued to deteriorate. Mr Wollstonecraft had by now given up all semblance of an occupation and resigned himself to living off his remaining property, whilst her mother grew increasingly ailing and fretful. The eldest son, Edward, had been articled to an attorney at Tower Hill and was living in the city[15]. After his departure the demands on Mary became intolerable: with both parents in decline she was virtually the head of the house. But how could she fulfil her responsibilities towards her younger sisters and brothers with no means of support? At the same time, Godwin said, she was struggling to educate herself, and she demanded a room of her own as a study. Her ascendancy in the family was now 'considerable'. But responsibility without power was a hollow mockery. No one could have been more conscious than Mary of her duty to her family. Yet above all she saw that the first need was to establish her own independence, and to this end she bent all her determination.

To determine to be independent was one thing: to find the means of achieving it, quite another. There were few ways open to a girl in Mary's position. She was nineteen years old, untrained and untried; as ignorant of life outside the forcing-house of the family as she was confident of her ability to deal with it. Endowed equally with passion and intelligence, and almost totally frustrated in both, her bubbling and baffled energies were channelled into a fierce and incorruptible idealism. Contemptuous and uncompromising, with a mind of steel and a heart as fragile as eggshell, the new woman of 1778 stepped out to freedom—as a lady's companion in Bath.

CHAPTER TWO

On Probation: 1778–1784

Mrs Dawson, the daughter of a Canon of Windsor and widow of a wealthy merchant, was living at Milsom Street, Bath, when Mary presented herself in the spring of 1778. She had a reputation for being difficult and had given short shrift to her succession of 'companions'. How soon, one may speculate, did she regret having engaged Mary Wollstonecraft in this unlikely capacity? The new companion made it clear from the start that she had no intention of being dominated by her employer. The Wollstonecrafts, though in straitened circumstances, belonged by heritage in the rank of society to which their father's fortune, in more prudent hands, would naturally have entitled them; and Mary was acutely conscious of this. She had not yet evolved her egalitarian philosophy. It was the artificialities and hypocrisies of society, rather than its injustices, that mortified her. Nevertheless, she accepted her first chance of employment, unsatisfactory as it was, as a challenge to carry out her duties with scrupulous conscientiousness whilst at the same time maintaining her own dignity and self-respect. These tactics must have achieved some success and won a grudging approval from Mrs Dawson, who acknowledged that Mary was the only one of her companions in whose treatment 'she had felt herself under any restraint'[1].

Mary remained at Bath for two years, enduring rather than enjoying her situation. The fashionable spa, with its elegant women and rakish bucks, its self-conscious culture and pretentious intellectualism, represented all the values she most despised.

Her lack of responsiveness to this glittering scene must have exasperated Mrs Dawson when she attempted to draw her companion into her own round of social diversions. The consolations for Mary were that Bath was a beautiful city; that she was at least experiencing a more gracious and cultivated style of life than she could ever hope to find in her own family; and that she had achieved, in however small a degree, some measure of independence. One unexpected blessing, too, had been her discovery some months after her arrival that her friends the Ardens were staying in the city, where Dr Arden was giving a course of lectures. Jane, however, was not with them: like Mary she had taken her first situation and was acting as governess to the six daughters of Sir Mortdant Martin at Burnham in Norfolk. On hearing this news Mary wrote to Jane[2], expressing her pleasure that 'the family you are with, are of a kind to set a value on merit, for generally speaking to deserve and gain esteem, are two very different things'. Her description in this letter of her own experiences is a less happy one: 'Pain and disappointment have constantly attended me since I left Beverley'. Her troubles had an emotional as well as a material basis which she now revealed more explicitly:

> Tho' I talk so philosophically now, yet I must own, under the pressure of afflictions, I did not think so rationally; my feelings were then too acute, and it was not 'till the Storm was in some measure blown over, that I could acknowledge the justness of it:—Young people generally set out with romantic and sanguine hopes of happiness, and must receive many stings before they are convinced of their mistake, and that they are pursuing a mere phantom; an empty name.

To have been so disillusioned at the age of nineteen—even though some of the 'stings' may have been more imaginary than real—was an affliction that Mary never overcame. To have an old head on young shoulders may often be deemed a blessing; to carry the burden of an 'old heart' so young could only be a curse.

But Mary was not always so depressed. She had the resilience of youth, as well as its vulnerability. In a letter to Jane Arden written in October 1778[3], after a summer holiday by the sea at Southampton, she was in much more cheerful spirits:

> I have spent a very agreeable summer. S—n is a very pleasant place in every sense of the word.—The situation is delightful;

and, the inhabitants polite, and hospitable. I received so much civility that I left it with regret, I am apt to get attached to places—and so interested in the happiness of mere acquaintances, that it is the source of much pain to me.

Despite her own reserve, Mary never failed to establish friendships after even the briefest acquaintance and here she reveals the secret: having (as she believed) little hope of happiness for herself, she was all the more concerned with the happiness of others. This spontaneous concern was no doubt more appreciated by the unsophisticated Hampshire people than in the artificial society of Bath, from which Mary was thankful to escape. It is not clear whether she was taken to Southampton by Mrs Dawson or went on a private visit, but from the tone of this letter the latter seems more likely. She may well have been staying with relatives, and there is some evidence for this in the record of the death of an Edward Bland Wollstonecraft 'at his home in Gloucester-square, Southampton' in 1795[4]. Although born in London, Mary regarded herself as a country girl, and the closer she came to nature the higher her spirits soared. She acknowledged to Jane that Bath, which her friend greatly admired, was 'a most delightful place' and its buildings 'the most regular and elegant I have ever seen'. Nevertheless, 'I cannot say that I should chuse a large town for my constant residence, if I was my own mistress ...' This, of course, Mary was not; though she did concede now that there were some advantages to be gained from her present situation:

The family I am with here is a very worthy one, Mrs Dawson has a very good understanding—and she has seen a great deal of the world. I hope to improve myself by her conversation, and I endeavour to render a circumstance (that at first was disagreeable) useful to me.

Her reference to a 'family' is a little puzzling. Godwin described Mrs Dawson as a widow with one grown-up son, presumably the 'William Dawson Esq.' care of whom Mary requested her letters to be addressed at Milsom Street. The 'family' was no doubt extended to include the comings and goings of relatives outside the immediate circle.

In January 1779 Mary wrote again to Jane Arden[5]. Though she put a brave face on things, it is clear that despite the kindness of Mrs Dawson she would never feel at home there. For all their shortcomings, she missed her own family; and she was living in a thoroughly alien society. 'I am detained here only by prudential motives,' she told Jane, 'if I was to follow the bent of my inclination I shod haste away.—You will not wonder at this,—when you consider I am among Strangers, far from all my former connexions'. What was she doing with her life, she must have wondered? She could find no place for herself in Bath, with its 'Balls & plays without end or number':

> I seldom go into public;—I have been but twice at the rooms;—I am quite a piece of still life, not but that I am a friend to mirth and cheerfulness; but I would move in a small circle;—I am fond of domestic pleasures and have not spirit sufficient to bustle about.

But whatever her private inclinations, so long as she remained with Mrs Dawson Mary could not entirely cut herself off from society—which, at her age, was not altogether a bad thing. However much she disliked it, she was acquiring a knowledge of the ways of the world which she could have obtained by no other means; a knowledge which reinforced her later rejection of conventional values.

Nor was the learning process without some pleasurable compensations. The following spring found Mary with Mrs Dawson on a prolonged visit to Windsor. Despite her reluctance to 'bustle about', she had to admit that she enjoyed the change of scene. 'Windsor is a most delightful place,' she wrote to Jane[6], 'and I long to live in the forest every time we ride through it'. But the town had the same fault as Bath: it was 'too gay'. Mrs Dawson's sister—although a daughter of the Church—erred in this respect. She was 'pleasant and entertaining' and behaved 'in the politest manner' to Mary, but: 'She is rather too fond of dissipation and brings up her daughters in a stile I dont approve of—that is, she seems to wish rather to make them accomplished and fashionable than good and sensible, in the true sense of the word'. Mrs Dawson could hardly have disapproved if Mary preferred visiting the Cathedral to making social calls, though she may have been surprised by her young companion's tastes: 'I go constantly...,' Mary wrote, 'I am very fond of the Service'. No doubt because of the presence of the Court, the great preoccupation in Windsor was fashion. 'You cannot imagine how amazingly they dress here, she told Jane, '... I believe I am thought a very poor creature, but to dress violently neither suits my inclination, nor purse.'

Nevertheless, her proximity to the King and the Prince of Wales gave Mary an opportunity to study them with some care. The Prince, she reported, was 'the principal beau here'—though not, of course, for Mary. 'You can have no idea,' she observed scornfully, 'of the commotion he throws the good ladies into; he certainly keeps both envy & vanity alive.' To George III she was much more charitable:

> The King is quite a domestic man and it is pleasing to see him surrounded by his children:—he is a most affectionate father, but his love seems to be confined to a very narrow circle, at least I am sure his humanity is:—to tell you the truth, he is out of favor with me, and you will not wonder at it when I inform you that he killed three horses the other day riding in a hurry to pay a visit; this has lost him my warm heart;—I cannot bear an unfeeling mortal.

If this tells us as much about Mary as about the King, it was all the same a perceptive observation.

In another letter to Jane Arden from Windsor[7] Mary repeated with even greater emphasis her dislike of 'genteel life' and its 'unmeaning civilities'. She was in low spirits; indeed, so world-weary that she looked forward to meeting her friend in 'that abode of peace' where 'the follies and weaknesses' of this life would be no more. Jane's sister was planning to open a school in Bath and Jane was considering whether to join her. Mary strongly approved of this plan:

> —let not some small difficulties intimidate you, I beseech you;—struggle with any obstacle rather than go into a state of dependance:—I speak feelingly.—I have felt the weight, and wod have you by all means avoid it.

She then disclosed that, despite her depression, she was making some plans of her own. She had recently been to London and visited Fanny Blood, whose health had been causing anxiety:

> To my great satisfaction, I found Miss Blood in better health than I expected from the accounts I have had of her.—She received me as she ever has done in the most friendly manner, and we passed a comfortable week together, which knew no other alloy than what arose from the thoughts of parting so soon. —The next time we meet, it will be for a longer continuance, and to that period I look, as to the most important one of my life.

Mary had decided, in short, to give up her post and go to live with Fanny. This had been in her mind for some time, and in her previous letter she had observed: '... the prospect of living with my ffanny gladdens my heart:—You know not how I love her'. She felt obliged to offer Jane some explanation for this decision:
> I know this resolution may appear a little extraordinary, but in forming it I follow the dictates of reason as well as the bent of my inclination; for tho' I am willing to do what good I can in my generation, yet on many accounts I am averse to any matrimonial tie.—

From her experience of the tyrannies and injustices in her own family, and the insincerities and inanities in Mrs Dawson's, Mary had already resolved at the age of twenty-one that she did not wish to marry.

Mary made no mention of her own family in this letter, but if they knew of her plan it is hardly likely that they would approve of it. A letter written to Eliza from Windsor on 17th August 1780—the only one surviving from this period[8]—suggests some strain in their relations. Her family may well have resented the attention she was giving to Fanny, rather than to them:
> You don't do me justice in supposing I seldom think of you—the happiness of my family is nearer my heart than you imagine—perhaps, too near for my own health or peace—For my anxiety preys on me, and is of no use to you. You don't say a word of my mother. I take it for granted she is well—tho' of late she has not even desired to be remembered to me. Some time or the other, in this world or a better, she may be convinced of my regard—and then may think I deserve not to be thought so harshly of. But enough on this subject. Love me but as I love you, and I'll be contented.

Since Mary left home the family had undergone yet another move and were now living at Chase-side, Enfield. When she wrote to Jane Arden from Bath in the summer of 1779 they were probably still at Walworth, since she mentioned that her sisters were at school in Chelsea. She also expressed the hope that her father would 'act more prudently in future, and then my mother may enjoy some comfort'. This hope was not to be fulfilled. In her letter to Eliza Mary had foreseen the future. Before the year was out an urgent summons came for her to return home immediately as her mother was feared to be dying. Although this meant a postponement of her own cherished plans, she did not hesitate to answer the call of duty. As a moth to the candle, Mary was always irresistibly impelled towards any human being in distress—and this was her own mother, whom she loved with a generosity that could ignore her own wounds when a greater suffering was calling for alleviation.

Now at any rate the mother appreciated her daughter's quality. Mary nursed her with devotion and forbearance over many painful months. She disclosed the details when she wrote again to Jane Arden the following year: 'my poor mother was confined to her room, and had been so a long while:—her disorder was a dropsy attended with many other disagreeable complaints, which at last ended in her death'[9]. Before this release came, Mary had endured almost as much distress herself. In Godwin's words:

Mary was assiduous in her attendance upon her mother. At first, every attention was received with acknowledgments and gratitude; but, as the attentions grew habitual, and the health of the mother more and more wretched, they were rather exacted, than received. Nothing would be taken by the unfortunate patient, but from the hands of Mary; rest was denied night or day, and by the time nature was exhausted in the parent, the daughter was qualified to assume her place, and become in turn a patient.

Only in dying did Mrs Wollstonecraft achieve a little of the dignity that was denied to her in life: 'A little patience,' she murmured, 'and all will be over'. Mary was so impressed by this simple valediction that she was to repeat it, many years later, in the book she was writing at the time of her own death.

The Wollstonecrafts' residence at Enfield must have been a brief one. The poor rate book shows an entry for Edward John Wollstonecraft in the first and second quarter of 1780; by 1781, his property was listed as 'empty'[10]. There is no record in the parish of Elizabeth Wollstonecraft's burial in this period[11]. In any event, her death marked the break-up of the family. Mr Wollstonecraft seems to have returned to Laugharne soon afterwards and to have remained there. He quickly acquired a substitute for his unfortunate wife—a woman named in the family letters as 'Lydia'—and it appears that he eventually re-married[12]. Eliza and Everina may still have been at school in Chelsea when their mother died. It is possible that Eliza stayed on for a time as a pupil teacher, while Everina soon afterwards went to live with her eldest brother Edward, who was already married and established as a lawyer in the city. James was sent to sea, while the youngest boy Charles returned with his father to Wales. The following year Eliza's future seemed assured when she became betrothed to Meredith Bishop, a ship-builder in business with his father at Rotherhithe; they were married at St Katherine's-by-the-Tower on 20th October 1782.

As for Mary, she did not need to think twice where she should go. With some relief, it may be presumed, she put behind her the painful memories of her own home to join her fortunes with those of the Blood family, now living at No. 1 King's Row, Walham Green[13]. Apart from the presence of Fanny, however, Mary must soon have begun to ask herself if she had not jumped out of the frying pan only to land in the fire. The Bloods, too, were beset with financial difficulties and domestic discord. Mr Blood, like Mr Wollstonecraft, was a man of violent temper, given to bouts of drunkenness and with the same sorry record of failure in business. Mrs Blood was down-trodden and ineffectual. Much of the responsibility for maintaining the family devolved on the eldest daughter, Fanny, whose income from her drawings was their main means of support. But this burden was already proving too heavy for her delicate constitution. In addition, the female members of the family, amongst whom Mary was now counted, took in sewing and sat up half the night working to obtain a little extra money. There were several younger brothers and sisters to be supported, and Mary was soon at home with them. She was particularly fond of young George Blood, who in turn became very much attached to the Wollstonecraft sisters.

Mary was to remain at Walham Green for nearly two years. She must soon have realised that in fulfilling her ambition to share Fanny's home she had achieved practically nothing for herself. Life with the Bloods offered little more scope for the exercise of her own abilities than she had found in her previous situation. Whilst her affections had found some repose in Fanny, her intellect was still frustrated; she was now as effectually barred from further progress by poverty as she had earlier been held back by an uncongenial background. In addition, she was no longer a child but an adult: what was her role in life to be? Writing to Jane Arden during this phase[14], she does not give the impression that she had found the answer. After excusing herself for her long silence on account of her mother's illness, she then admitted that the real reason she had not written sooner was that she had nothing to write about: 'I was some time before I could rouse myself to tell you that I am alive, for I send this merely to convince you that I am in the land of the living'. She recalled their 'merry days' together at Beverley, adding: 'You are a laugher still, but I am a stupid creature, and you would be tired to death of me, if you were to be with me a week'. She envied Jane a trip to Ireland: 'of all the places in the world, I long to visit Ireland,' she wrote—as it turned out, a dire prophecy—and warned her friend against flirtatious Irishmen: 'take care of your heart, and don't leave it in one of the Bogs'. Despite her declared intention not to marry, Mary must have learned by now of her own susceptibilities in this respect. She must also have realised that, among the kind of men she had so far encountered, an insipid woman would be preferred. She assured Jane, however, that her amiable nature would attract admirers 'that will have sense enough to prefer such good qualities to a baby face'. For herself, Mary had already given up hope. Her early struggles, she believed, had marked her for life: 'I have already got the wrinkles of old age, and so, like a true woman, rail at what I don't possess'.

Mary's prospects were indeed dim at this time. Within her present limited milieu she could not hope to find either a suitable marriage-partner or a worthy career, and she was not prepared to lower her critical standards in order to accept a second-best. Her younger sister's early marriage could only have depressed her the more, and she would not have been human if she had not resented it a little—even though it was not what she wanted for herself. It was galling to her pride that, by the mere fact of being married, Eliza's status was dramatically improved, regardless of her actual circumstances. There was a sour note in her letter to Jane Arden breaking this news[15]:

> You remember Bess; she was a mere child when we were together, and it would have hurt our dignity to have admitted her into our Parties, but she must now take place of us, being of the honourable order of matrons.

Jane's sister too had recently married, and Mary was hard put to congratulate her on the event. She made little attempt to hide her own sense of disillusionment with the whole business of matrimony:

> The joy, and all that, is certainly over by this time, and all the raptures have subsided, and the dear hurry of visiting and figuring away as a bride, and all the rest of the delights of matrimony are past and gone and have left no traces behind them, except disgust:—I hope I am mistaken, but this is the fate of most married pairs.

She rather spoiled the effect of this quite genuine observation on the horrors of a loveless marriage—which she was to develop later as a major theme—by an unconvincing, and false, declaration of her own intention not to marry: 'I don't want to be tied to this nasty world, and old maids are of so little consequence'. What she really meant was not that she did not wish to be tied to the world but that she did not wish to be tied down by a family, as she now made clear:

> It is a happy thing to be a mere blank, and to be able to pursue one's own whims, where they lead, without having a husband and half a hundred children at hand to teaze and controul a poor woman who wishes to be free.

Mary was still in a state of confusion about her own desires and ambitions. It was certainly true that she wished to be 'free', but quite untrue that she could ever be happy as a 'mere blank' or that she would use her freedom in pursuit of a whim. She knew that she must have freedom, but did not know for what purpose. This is not surprising, since the first requisite of freedom was to discover her true 'self'.

Another year went by with no significant change in Mary's circumstances. It was a time of recuperation and preparation rather than of positive achievement. But preparation for what? Though she assumed increasing responsibilities in the Blood family, as she had done in her own, this comparatively minor role could not suffice for much longer to contain her restless spirit. Then, towards the end of 1783, the problem of her immediate future was suddenly resolved by another family crisis.

Mary's forebodings about the married state seem to have been amply justified in the case of her sister Eliza. 'Bess', as she was familiarly called, had now been a wife for more than a year and in August 1783 had given birth to a baby girl (christened Elizabeth Mary Frances at the Church of St Mary Magdalene, Bermondsey). But things had not gone well in the marriage. Eliza had married almost from the schoolroom, probably as much to escape from her father's household as for any deeper reason. She had only succeeded in exchanging one evil for another. Her husband, it seemed, was as brutal and dominating as her father—or perhaps he was just the average man of his time, who viewed his wife as his chattel and gave scant consideration to her feelings. Whatever the rights and wrongs of the case—and there is little firm evidence by which to judge Meredith Bishop's character—Bess was totally unprepared for the wifely role that was expected of her. Not surprisingly, her happiness was short-lived; and the birth of a baby only seemed to make matters worse. By November, when Mary was summoned, she was in a dangerously morbid state. The exact nature of her malady is unknown, but it seems likely that the unfortunate girl had suffered an acute attack of post-natal depression which, without proper treatment or understanding, had now reached the point of derangement. It is not unusual, in such cases, for a young wife to turn against her husband and blame him for all her pain and distress. 'Deliver me from this monster!' Eliza must have cried—and the dragon-slayer was of course at hand. Abandoning the Bloods to their penury, Mary came flying to her aid.

Her motives in mounting this rescue-operation must be viewed with a little suspicion. As we have seen, she had resented Eliza's marriage, and one cannot help feeling that she seized on this crisis as a pretext for ending it—whether justifiably is a matter for conjecture. As the little drama unfolds—not without the touch of melodrama that seemed inseparable from all Mary's escapades—it is difficult to know which character to pity the more: the distracted wife crying out to be rescued or the bewildered husband pleading for a reconciliation. Let Mary tell the story in her own words, as she described it to Everina soon after her arrival at the Bishops:

> I cannot yet give any certain account of Bess ... She has not had a violent fit of frenzy, since I saw you, but her mind is in a most unsettled state and attending to the constant fluctuation of it is far more harassing than watching those raving fits that had not the least tincture of reason ... She seems to think she has been very ill-used, and, in short, till I see some more favourable symptoms, I shall only suppose that her malady has assumed a new and more distressing appearance.

These fears were well-founded, for a month later things had taken a sharp turn for the worse:

> I don't know what to do. Poor Eliza's situation almost turns my brain. I can't stay and see this continual misery, and to leave her to bear it by herself without any one to comfort her is still more distressing. I would do anything to rescue her from her present situation.

Mary was even prepared to turn to her brother for help:

> Do you think Edward will receive her? Do speak to him, or if you imagine that I should have more influence on his mind, I will contrive to see you, but you must caution him against expostulating with or even mentioning the affair to Bishop, for it would only put him on his guard and we should have a storm to encounter that I tremble to think of.

It is clear that Mary was already plotting, without consulting Bishop, to take Eliza away; and in this same letter she threw out a hint of what was in her mind: 'I am convinced that this is the only expedient to save Bess, and she declares that she would rather be a teacher than stay here....'

While it is obvious that in order to be cured Eliza would need a period of complete rest, the idea of a temporary separation from her husband does not seem to have occurred to Mary; although, unless he were as demented as Eliza herself, Bishop could hardly have objected to that. It is evident that Mary did not want a reconciliation, and her own behaviour in the affair was not entirely rational. When Edward declined to be involved in his sister's misfortunes, Mary turned to her only other source of support, Fanny Blood. But Fanny herself was something of a broken reed. With her health already undermined by overwork, she was also under emotional strain: she had 'suffered a disappointment', said Godwin, 'which preyed on her mind'. There is some mystery about this 'romance', to which much of Fanny's ill-health has been attributed. She is said to have been affected by the long dalliance of her suiter, Hugh Skeys, but (as will be seen later) this was by no means certain and her early disappointment probably originated elsewhere. Skeys was an Irishman from Dublin whose business took him to Lisbon. The Skeys, like the Bloods and the Wollstonecrafts, had numerous Irish connections and the families were all acquainted. In surviving correspondence, the name is first mentioned by Mary in her next letter to Everina. 'Misery haunts this house,' she wrote in January 1784:

My spirits are hurried (sic) with listening to pros and cons, my head is so confused that I sometimes say no when I ought to say yes. My heart is almost broken with listening to B while he reasons the case. I cannot insult him with advice, which he would never have wanted if he was capable of attending to it ... I expect Fanny next Thursday, and she will stay with us but a few days. Bessie desires to give her love; she grows better, and of course, more sad.

If Eliza was really recovering, as this letter suggests, she might well decide that her situation was bearable after all. Bishop, too, from Mary's report, would seem to have become more cooperative. If Mary's own scheme was to succeed, she knew she must act quickly; and if Fanny had realised what her intrepid friend was planning, it is probable that she would never have consented to come. For what Mary now proposed, with Fanny's help, was to steal Eliza from the house in secret and take her into hiding: a course of action that was not only irrational, but illegal. Had Bishop been half the tyrant he was painted, all parties to the action could have been severely punished.

Yet the coup succeeded. Seizing the opportunity of Bishop's temporary absence from home, Mary executed her plan with all the dash of a military operation. Eliza's belongings were hastily gathered up and despatched with Fanny in one coach, while the two sisters took another carriage to a lodging in Hackney which Mary had already reserved. So far, so good. But how would Bishop react? She poured out her fears to Everina (or 'Averina', as she mis-spelt her name):

Here we are, Averina, but my trembling hand will scarce let me tell you so. Bess is much more composed than I expected her to be. To make my trial still more dreadful I was afraid in the coach that she was going to have one of her flights, for she bit her wedding ring to pieces. When I can recollect myself I will send you particulars; but at present my heart beats time with every carriage that rolls by and a knocking at the door almost throws me into a fit. I hope B. will not discover us, for I could sooner face a lion. The door never opens but I expect to see him panting for breath. Ask Ned how we are to behave if he should find us out, for Bess is determined not to return. Can he force her?—but I'll not suppose it, yet I can think of nothing else.

Strangely enough, it was Mary rather than Eliza who was afraid to face Bishop, as she now admitted: 'Bess does not dread him now as much as I do'. Again she urged Everina to write (and, presumably, to let her have Edward's opinion as a lawyer), 'as Bishop's behaviour may silence my fears'.

With hindsight, the episode has not only the ingredients of melodrama but even a hint of farce. Truth is difficult to distinguish from fantasy: Bess is 'determined not to return', yet she does not 'dread' Bishop as much as Mary herself; at the same time Mary did not wish to encounter the irate husband in case he may 'silence' her fears—as if these were not well-founded. Could it be that the real cause of her misgiving—in so far as it was genuine and not a rationalisation of her own ambivalent attitude to Eliza's marriage—was not so much the behaviour of Bishop as her knowledge of her own sister's mental instability? To have 'bit her wedding ring to pieces' was no mean feat, suggesting an abnormal deflection of energy; and if this was a sign of 'one of her flights', it was evidently not an isolated incident. Caught between the devil of Bishop's domination and the deep of Eliza's *malaise*, Mary was almost distracted herself. She added a postscript to this letter which showed how near to breaking-point she was.

> She looks now very wild. Heaven protect us! I almost wish for a husband, for I want some one to support me.

This was a curious wish, at a moment when she had just successfully separated a wife from her husband; and when, if her account of the situation was correct, the word 'husband' must have seemed synonymous with 'tyrant' rather than 'support'.

As was to be expected, Bishop demanded of Everina that his wife should come home immediately. There was not only himself to be considered but also the baby; and Mary's attitude in this respect is the oddest thing of all in an altogether odd affair. She replied to Everina:

> The plea of the child occurred to me and it was the most rational thing he could complain of. I know he will tell a plausible tale and the generality will pity him and blame me, but, however, if we can snatch Bess from extreme wretchedness, what reason shall we have to rejoice. It was indeed a very disagreeable affair and if we had stayed a day or two longer I believe it would never have been effected, for Bess's mind was so harassed for fear of being discovered and by the thought of

leaving the child that she could not have stood it long.
Did Mary really imagine that she was setting her sister's mind at
rest by snatching her away from her child? And that in doing so
she was acting in Eliza's interest rather than her own? The sheer
callousness of her next remark to Everina can only be excused by
the stress under which her own mind was labouring: 'Well, all this
may serve to talk about and laugh at when we meet but it was no
laughing matter at the time.' Nor was Mary quite devoid of concern for the abandoned baby:
> Bess is tolerably well; she cannot help sighing about little Mary
> whom she tenderly loved; and on this score I both love and pity
> her. The poor brat! it had got a little hold on my affections,
> sometime or other I hope we shall get it ...

She evidently had it in mind that, when things had settled down, by fair means or foul the baby could be reunited with her mother[16]. Meanwhile, however, she was adamant that Eliza should not return: 'Tell my brother,' she informed Everina, 'that Bess is fixed in her resolution of never returning ... And if a separate maintenance is not to be obtained, she'll try to earn her own bread.' Poor Eliza, it seemed, was not deemed capable of speaking for herself and was to be made the guinea-pig for Mary's theories of female independence! She now spelt out what this would mean:

> With economy we can live on a guinea a week, and that we can
> with ease earn. The lady who gave Fanny five guineas for two
> drawings will assist us and we shall be independent ... If Ned
> makes us a little present of furniture it will be very acceptable,
> but if he is prudent we must try to do without if.

Edward was possibly the only member of the Wollstonecraft family who could justly be termed 'prudent'; Mary herself certainly was not. As she now admitted to Everina, her behaviour had thoroughly shocked all their friends:

> I knew I should be the shameful incendiary in this shocking
> affair of a woman leaving her bedfellow, they thought the
> strong affections of a sister *might* apologise for my conduct,
> but that the scheme was by no means a good one. In short, 'tis
> contrary to all the rules of conduct that are published for the
> benefit of newly married ladies... Mrs. Clare, too, with
> cautious words disapproved of our conduct, and were she to
> see Bishop might advise a reconciliation.

Here is the first hint of Mary's capacity for rebellion against 'all the rules of conduct', when she believed the rules to be wrong. On this occasion she had taken up the cudgels ostensibly on her sister's behalf; in future it would be for herself. This must have been a relief to Eliza, who at best was a reluctant pioneer; and Mary shows something of the blindness of the fanatic to other people's feelings as she describes to Everina their sister's state of mind:

> Last night she was very restless and terrified me for when I spoke to her she said she was sufficiently tried—and today she has been deaf—this was the forerunner of her malady so what will be the issue of this affair tis impossible to say—but I am cheered with the hope that our poor girl will never again be in this man's power—Had he been only *unhappy* I should have felt some pain in acting with firmness for I hold the marriage vow sacred—but now I am not much disturbed by compassion.

Mary is shown here at her worst. It is quite clear that she had exerted a dominating influence over her weaker sister and allowed her judgment to be warped by her own dislike of Eliza's husband. She was, of course, quite unconscious of any ulterior motive and sincerely believed that she was acting for the best. Mary had never been committed in love herself and did not understand the complexities and contradictions of marriage. She believed in the 'marriage vow', she said; but she could not accept its consequences. Mary was still very much a probationer in affairs of the heart.

The episode of Eliza's abduction is strangely glossed over by Godwin in his *Memoirs*. His account is surely somewhat disingenuous, for he must have been acquainted with the true situation:

> Mary was ever ready at the call of distress, and, in particular, during her whole life was eager and active to promote the welfare of every member of her family. In 1780 she attended the deathbed of her mother; in 1782 she was summoned by a not less melancholy occasion, to attend her sister Eliza, married to a Mr Bishop, who, subsequently to a dangerous lying-in, remained for months in a very afflicting situation. Mary continued with her sister without intermission, to her perfect recovery.

Godwin did not even get the year right, and his error has been perpetuated—with the consequence that Eliza's baby was assumed to have been born in the same year as her marriage[17]. His natural bias in favour of Mary also tended to cast her sisters in a less favourable light. But it is worth remembering that a genius in the family is not the easiest thing for the other members to live with. All three sisters were soon to learn that their difficulties were only just beginning.

CHAPTER THREE

Graduation: 1784–1785

Mary had asserted with her usual confidence that 'with economy we can live on a guinea a week, and that we can with ease earn'. Fanny, with more practical experience of earning a living, was less sure. Having fulfilled her part in Eliza's escapade she had returned to her own home at Walham Green. From here she wrote to Everina[1] on 18th February 1784 in some alarm:

The situation of our two poor girls grows more and more desperate. My mind is tortured about them because I cannot see any possible resource they have for a maintenance. The letter I last night received from Mary disturbed me so much that I have never since closed my eyes and my head is this morning almost distracted.

Fanny's anxiety was not only due to concern about her friends. She was also alarmed by her own involvement in Mary's schemes:

I find she wrote to her brother informing him that it was our intention to live all together and earn our bread by painting and needlework, which gives me great uneasiness as I am convinced that he will be displeased at his sisters being connected with me, and their forfeiting his favour at this time is of the utmost consequence... The very utmost I can earn one week from another, supposing I have uninterrupted health, is half a guinea a week, which would just pay for furnished lodgings for *three* persons to pig together. As for needlework, it is utterly impossible they could earn more than half a guinea a week between them supposing they had constant employment, which is of all things most uncertain ... I own with sincere sorrow that I was greatly to blame for ever mentioning such a plan before I had maturely considered it.

After being temporarily carried away by Mary's enthusiasm, Fanny was evidently having serious misgivings about the whole business. The grounds for Edward Wollstonecraft's disapproval of her are not clear, since she would seem to have been of exemplary character as well as an economic asset. She now put forward the alternative suggestion that Edward might be prevailed on to set up his sisters in a small haberdashery business, a plan that was also favoured by their friend Mrs Clare. But Edward would have no part in what he no doubt regarded as another of Mary's mad schemes.

Mary herself had other plans. Haberdashery, after all, was hardly her true métier. She had long held the conviction that the way to independence was through education and cherished a dream that one day she might open a school of her own.* Now, with the urgent necessity to find a home and a livelihood, the opportunity had surely come? Not only for herself and Eliza but also for Fanny the future was uncertain. By uniting their talents and resources, their precarious 'independence' could be placed on a sounder footing. Other friends were ready to help, and Fanny was finally persuaded that this new plan was a practical proposition. The change in her relationship with Mary since their early friendship had been considerable, and the roles of teacher and pupil were by now reversed. Mary had clearly become the dominant influence.

Later that same year, accordingly, she leased a house in Islington as premises for a modest day-school. Here she took the complaisant Eliza and was soon joined by Fanny. The stage was set, the cast assembled, and they waited hopefully for the action to begin. But pupils were slow to take their cue, and few children appeared to test the quality of the teachers. Perhaps the house was unsuitable or in an undesirable location; in taking it Mary had no doubt been guided by economy rather than convenience. But she was determined to succeed. A few months later, undaunted by this first setback, she moved to a larger house in the more fashionable neighbourhood of Newington Green[2]. At once the school's fortunes dramatically improved. Soon not only were the day classes filled to capacity but Mary was taking boarding pupils

* Mary Wollstonecraft's lack of formal qualifications as a teacher placed her in no worse position than any of her contemporaries who seized on this form of livelihood. It was not expected that the pupils would progress far beyond reading and writing, plus a little accomplishment in drawing, music and fine sewing. Mary, we may be sure, could do better than this; and Fanny must have brought distinction to the 'art' department.

as well. At Newington Green she was ideally situated for this venture. The Green, which was already developed as an urban square, had a lively intellectual life centred around the noted dissenting minister Dr Richard Price, whose Presbyterian chapel stood (and still stands) at the north side. Another resident was the widow of James Burgh, who had achieved some fame as the author of *Political Disquisitions* (1775), in which amongst other things he advocated the admission of women to Parliament. Mrs Burgh for a time had her own school on the Green, and Mary may even have taken this over; according to Everina it was on Mrs Burgh's advice that they decided to open the school there[3]. At Newington Green, for the first time Mary found herself living in a congenial environment amongst her intellectual peers, by whom she was treated as an equal. At last, she must have felt, she was on the high road to life and liberty.

Only one cloud darkened the horizon: Fanny's health. Scarcely was the school established than this began to cause serious concern. Symptoms of suspected consumption were confirmed, and the only hope of a cure was to get her into a warmer climate without delay. This was a blow to Mary's plans, but as in the case of Eliza she did not hesitate to act as she thought best. This time, however, she became not a match-breaker but a match-maker. Hugh Skeys was in Lisbon and, by miraculous coincidence, at this time 'paid his addresses' to Fanny[4], culminating in a proposal of marriage. There is little doubt that the miracle was woman-made. As Godwin observed[5]: 'The advice of Mary in this instance, though dictated by the sincerest anxiety for her friend's welfare, is scarcely entitled to our approbation'. He does not explain this remark. Did he feel that Skeys had been cheated, or Fanny subjected to intolerable strain? Yet it was her own need that dictated the journey; in the circumstances Mary had little choice but to facilitate it. Fanny duly sailed for Portugal and was married to Skeys on 24th February 1785.

But what of the love-sick maiden? In a letter to Eliza and Everina on 30th March she spoke of her state of depression since arriving in Lisbon. Nor was she at all enthusiastic about her husband, conceding merely that he was 'a good sort of creature, and has sense enough to let his cat of a wife follow her own inclination in *almost* everything'. The passage following goes even further, suggesting not only that this was a marriage of convenience rather than a love-match but even that the partners were hitherto unacquainted:

> Skeys's picture was more like him than pictures in general are—but he is much fatter, and looks at least ten years older than it. He has been a dreadful flirt among the damsels here, some of whom I could easily perceive were disappointed by his marriage—but I have completely metamorphosed him into a *plain* man—and I am sorry to add that he is too much inclined to pay more attention to his wife than any other woman—but 'tis a fault that a little time, no doubt, will cure.

The apparent cynicism of the final remark, if not due to an error in composition, may perhaps be explained by the coyness of a young bride. But the general tone of the letter destroys the theory that Fanny's illness was caused by grief for this absent lover. Fanny may have been pining away—but not, it seems, for Hugh Skeys!

In despatching Fanny to Portugal Mary could not be accused of acting from self-interest, as might have been the case with Eliza. Now she had lost not only a friend but a valuable colleague. Fanny's place in the school was taken by Everina, who could scarcely have been an adequate substitute: at the time of Fanny's departure she was still only nineteen. The main burden of teaching must therefore have been shouldered by Mary herself. But she had overcome worse difficulties than this, and she was determined to succeed. She was helped, no doubt, by the presence of congenial neighbours and the stimulus of an intellectual challenge far greater than anything she had so far experienced. Dr Price was counted amongst the giants of his generation. A noted mathematician as well as a preacher, he was a member of the Royal Society and a friend of the famous Dr Joseph Priestley. He was not only a religious dissenter but a political radical, who had so far identified himself with the cause of American independence that he was made an honorary doctor of law by Yale University, together with George Washington. His international reputation had extended to France, and he was in correspondence with many of the men who even then were laying the foundations for the French Revolution. These activities were to bring him under fierce attack from the English 'establishment' as the fear of revolution mounted.

Price's influence on Mary Wollstonecraft must have been enormous. His ideas were perfectly in tune with her own awakening radicalism. His notable circle of acquaintans, to whom she was soon introduced, extended her awareness from personal to national issues and guided her mode of thinking from the intuitive to the analytical. With Price and his friends her still captive spirit was released in the excitement of feeling herself part of a 'movement'. On his side too, Price was not slow to recognise the calibre of his new neighbour. The regard they felt for each other, said Godwin, was mutual and 'partook of a spirit of the purest attachment'. The fact that Mary was still a practising member of the Church of England made little difference. Tolerance was the order of the day, and Price's own wife remained an Anglican while he battled in the forefront of dissent. It is perhaps more surprising that Mary herself continued to attend Anglican services regularly at least until 1787.

She may have influenced in this by her friendship with an Anglican preacher, Rev. John Hewlett, who kept a school at Hackney. Although three years her junior he was already a biblical scholar and his *Sermons* were published in 1786. It was possibly Hewlett who arranged for Mary to visit the awesome Dr Samuel Johnson shortly before his death: 'The doctor treated her with particular kindness and attention,' wrote Godwin, 'had a long conversation with her, and desired her to repeat her visit often'. Unfortunately the onset of Dr Johnson's final illness prevented this. Of more lasting importance was Hewlett's introduction of Mary to his publisher, Joseph Johnson, who was to play a crucial part in her later fortunes. He may also have introduced her to a fellow-clergyman, Joshua Waterhouse, who is believed to have affected her development in other ways.

Evidence has been offered that Waterhouse was the first man to win Mary's love[6]; an alternative theory is that the courtship was initiated on his side but was not reciprocated. From the information available, he does not seem to have been a likely candidate for her affections and her connection with him is full of question-marks. The indisputable fact remains, however, that she did write a number of letters to him which were found, in bizarre circumstances, after his death. After studying theology at Cambridge (where Hewlett also studied), Waterhouse became a fellow of St Catherine's College and in 1788 acquired the college 'living' at the village of Coton. At the same time, being a young man of some means, he was enjoying a gay bachelor existence and is known to have frequented the fashionable society of Bristol and

Bath in the company of his friend Sir John Danvers. This suggests another possible point of contact with Mary during her time at Mrs Dawson's. Whether she ever took his attentions seriously, however, is by no means certain. Since coming to Newington Green she had opportunities to make many more stimulating contacts. Yet she continued to suffer from a chronic depression for which there was no obvious cause. Nor did she make life any easier for herself by taking on other people's troubles to add to her own; but that was always Mary's way.

No sooner was Fanny's problem off her hands than she was involving herself in the affairs of the rest of the Blood family. Mr Blood was out of employment and must be found a job. Then George fell into worse trouble. Fanny's brother had been articled to an attorney who turned out to be dishonest, and at this point the man was arrested for forgery. George, whether or not he could be held responsible for his employer's misdemeanours, arrived at Newington Green asking for refuge. From there, with Mary's help, he fled to Dublin: and then the balloon went up with a vengeance. George, it appeared, was wanted by the police himself—not on his employer's account, but to face a charge of bastardy by a servant-girl. Loyally and imprudently, Mary stood by him in the face of evidence which if not conclusive was at least ambiguous. George alleged that his employer was blaming him for his own sins; but his reputation was none too sound. Mary wrote to him on 3rd July 1785, soon after his departure, that malicious gossip about his 'vices' and her 'encouragement' of them had spread all over the Green[7].

This scandal could have done no good to the school. Financial worries, the loss of Fanny, the trouble over George: all these, and perhaps other causes, now reduced Mary to one of her nadirs of despair. 'I have been very ill,' she continued in the same letter, 'have been bled and blistered, yet still am not well . . . I have lost all relish of life and my almost broken heart only cares for the prospect of death'. This was strong stuff indeed. Was Waterhouse really at the root of it, or could it have been George Blood himself? She gave some inkling of her feeling for him in this same letter:

I feel that I love you better than I ever supposed that I did . . .
Adieu to the village delights. I almost hate the Green, for it seems the grave of all my comforts. Shall I ever again see your

honest heart dancing in your eyes?

That Mary cherished a strong affection for George is not in doubt. But in general her attitude to him suggests that of an elder sister rather than a sweetheart. The real basis of her affection was the fact that he was Fanny's brother and in her absence, the next best thing. Since Fanny's marriage he had become Mary's chief confidant. She wrote to him constantly, not only about Fanny's progress in Lisbon—which was at first encouraging—but about his prospects in Ireland and her own increasingly miserable condition. 'I have a motherly tenderness for you,' she assured him on 21st July. She was hopeful that Mr Blood would soon get 'the emplacement in the India house that has been so long talked of', thanks to the efforts on his behalf of 'friendly Church'. Church, whose name occurs frequently and with some warmth in Mary's letters of this time, was a nephew of Mrs Burgh. She spoke of him again:

I am incapable of joy—nothing interests me.—yes, I forgot, *humane*, rational Church can please me—but business and many other things prevents his calling often, and when he does, I seldom enjoy his company, we have so many tattling females—

The real source of Mary's depression seems likely to have been her sense of isolation, rather than her allegedly broken heart. Her problem was to find some fellow creature with whom she could commune on equal terms; none so far, with the possible exception of Fanny Blood, had appeared: 'I have no creature to be unreserved to,' she cried to George:

Eliza and Everina are so different that I could as soon fly as open my heart to them. How my social comforts have dropped away. Fanny first, and then you went over the hills and far away. I am resigned to my fate, that gloomy kind of resignation tinged with despair. My heart—my affection cannot fix here and without some one to love the world is a desert to me.

Mary's longing for a worthy object to love was only equalled by her longing for understanding. Try as she would to make them 'independent' women like herself, Eliza and Everina were never really in sympathy with her aspirations. 'Eliza still turns up her nose and ridicules,' she observed to George, 'and as to Everina I can neither *love* nor *hate* her—or to use a softer word, be indifferent to her'. Only with Fanny and George, it seemed, had

Mary ever been able to express something of her inner self and know that it would be taken seriously. The 'desart' was the core of loneliness, a desert of the heart. Already she had discovered that intellectual stimulus alone was not enough. There was a vacuum at the centre that could not be wished away.

Another burden was added to Mary's already heavy spirits. With some bitterness she wrote again to George on 25th July that the news of Fanny's health was 'far from pleasing'; and she blamed Skeys for this.

Despite her encouragement of the marriage, Mary did not like Hugh Skeys any more than she had liked Meredith Bishop. One cannot help feeling that she nourished a certain resentment against husbands in general, and there was no doubt an element of jealousy in this. Now she accused Skeys of jeopardising Fanny's health by his philandering:

Skeys has received congratulatory letters from most of his friends and relations in Ireland, and he now regrets that he did not marry sooner. All his mighty fears had no foundation, so that if he had had courage to have braved the world's dread laugh and ventured to have acted for himself, he might have spared Fanny many griefs, part of which will never be obliterated. Nay, more. If she had gone a year or two ago her health might have been perfectly restored, which I do not think now will ever be the case... How Hugh could let Fanny languish in England while he was throwing money away in Lisbon, is to me inexplicable if he had a passion that did not require the fuel of seeing the object.

This letter is further evidence that Fanny's betrothal to Skeys was based on material rather than emotional considerations. Mary accuses him of 'throwing money away' in Lisbon while Fanny languished at home. The 'languishing' may have referred to her state of health rather than her heart. Why should Skeys have feared 'the world's dread laugh' unless his marriage was to some extent an arranged one between the families? The only explanation—and a likely one—is that the Bloods were very much his inferiors.

Skeys was certainly expected to be the universal provider. Since her marriage Fanny had been pressing him to find a situation for George in Lisbon. Now at last some prospect of this seemed to be opening up, and Mary cautioned George about his conduct: 'do not be so familiar with Skeys as to let him discover your weaknesses ... he is so little conversant with his own heart and of course so little acquainted with human nature—that he can't make allowances for the infirmities that are often found in the best characters'. She seems here to be defending George in spite of her own knowledge of his faults, so as to justify her regard for him, while poor Hugh Skeys is scarcely acknowledged to be human. In another letter two weeks later, dated 11th August, Mary's hope that George would soon be in Lisbon was shadowed by her concern for Fanny's deteriorating health. She was now doubly anxious, having recently heard that her friend was pregnant. Her own news continued to be depressing. Mr Blood was still unemployed. As for herself:

> I now seldom see Church or any other rational creature who I can love—Labour and sorrow fill up my time and so I trail through this vale of tears—and all this leads to an end which will be happy if I faint not.

Portions of this letter have been blotted out. Mary signed herself 'Your ever affectionate friend', and reinforced the sentiment in a postcript of which the final words have also been obliterated: 'This letter is proof of my affection to you for spite of languor and sickness of heart I have forced myself to write ...' Again, it seems as if Mary was more distressed by George's absence than by anything the elusive Waterhouse might have done. Yet her unrelieved depression is puzzling. Surely Dr Price was a 'rational creature', who could afford some solace to her spirit? The drawback about him, perhaps, was that he was old enough to be her father.

When George Blood's appointment in Lisbon was confirmed by Skeys the following month, Mary roused herself to take a decision that had been nagging at her ever since she heard about Fanny's present condition. She resolved that, whatever the cost, she too would make the journey to Portugal. She hoped to be in Lisbon, she told George, 'before the end of the year'. She was not, of course, going on his account—though his presence there may have strengthened her resolve—but in order to attend Fanny at her confinement. She was well aware what this would mean in financial terms. 'Church tells me,' she commented ruefully, 'I shall never thrive in the world—and I believe he is right'. Cost, however, was something that Mary Wollstonecraft never learned

Graduation: 1784–5

to count. She had no spare money and the school would undoubtedly suffer in her absence. Her friends at Newington Green—and for all her protestations, she had some staunch ones—tried hard to dissuade her from the journey; and then, having failed, raised the money for her fare by means of an anonymous loan from Dr Price. In November 1785 Mary sailed for Lisbon: the first in a succession of journeys that were to be always dramatic, usually dangerous and often fraught with tragedy. On this occasion, all three elements were present.

Crossing the Bay of Biscay in a sailing boat was a hazardous undertaking. The voyage out took thirteen days—and this was mercifully quick, the average duration being three weeks. Mary described the experience in a letter to her sisters soon after her arrival:

... I could not write to you on shipboard, the sea was so rough and we had such hard gales and winds that the captain was afraid we should be dismasted.

Two days later, she had time to sit down and fill in the details:

The wind was so high and the sea so boisterous the water came in at the cabin windows and the ship rolled about in such a manner it was dangerous to stir. The women were seasick the whole time and a poor invalid so oppressed by his complaints I never expected he would live to see Lisbon. I supported him for hours together gasping for breath, and at night, if I had been inclined to sleep, his dreadful cough would have kept me awake...

How typical it was of Mary that she did not include herself with 'the women' who were seasick and that she devoted herself to the care of an invalid!

But other and worse fears were occupying her mind now. Four hours after her arrival at Lisbon Fanny had given birth to a son. The child, she reported, was 'alive and well'; but the mother's state was so low that 'her recovery would be almost a resurrection'. 'My reason,' Mary added, 'will scarcely allow me to think this possible.' Her forebodings were justified. The 'resurrection' did not take place and Fanny died in her arms on 29th November. Before she left Portugal three weeks later, the baby too was dead. Fanny's brief marriage had ended in a tragedy of waste. Did Mary feel some compunction, as well as grief, for her part in bringing it about? During this unhappy time George Blood's presence in Lisbon must have given her a little comfort; and that she had some opportunities for going out into the society of the city is confirmed by Godwin's remark that 'She was admitted to the best company the English factory afforded'. Her normally acute observation was not blurred by grief. She stored up some 'profound observations on the character of the natives, and the baleful effects of superstition'[8]. One of these 'baleful effects' was the necessity to carry out Fanny's Protestant burial, in this Roman Catholic country, 'by stealth and in darkness': an episode that reinforced Mary's generally unfavourable impression of the state of Portugal at that time.

During the melancholy journey home Mary's spirits must have sunk to their lowest depths. Her thoughts may have dwelt once more, as they had so often, on the 'wrongs of woman': a mother harried by tyranny into an early grave; a sister deranged by childbirth; and now Fanny, in whom nature's work had only completed the destruction of a constitution already weakened beyond repair by sweated labour and a suitor's indifference. Was her own fate to be no better? Surely, she must have prayed, 'independence' would save her from this! Independence must hold the key to salvation; even though in fighting to gain independence, she was in large measure fighting against herself.

Stormed-tossed though she was—by her own anguish no less than by the tempests that again lashed the ship on a journey which this time took four weeks at sea—neither her courage nor her compassion forsook her. Godwin described one incident during the voyage, when a French ship hailed them in distress. The captain was reluctant to take the French crew on board, because his own provisions were in short supply:

> Mary, shocked at his apparent insensibility, took up the cause of the sufferers, and threatened the captain to have him called to a severe account, when he arrived in England. She finally prevailed, and had the satisfaction to reflect, that the persons in question possibly owed their lives to her interposition.

After a safe landing, Mary was still to need all her courage for fresh storms that lay ahead.

CHAPTER FOUR

End of a Career: 1786–1787

Mary arrived back at Newington Green in January 1786 to find her school on the verge of collapse. Her sisters had been unable to maintain her own successful management of the children and their parents. As Godwin charitably expressed it: 'It can be little reproach to any one, to say that they were found incapable of supplying her place'[1]. Pupils were leaving as fast as debts were piling up. The rent of the house was due and there was not enough money coming in to meet it. What was to be done? In taking on the school Mary had assumed responsibility for her sisters as well as for herself. It was unthinkable that they should be turned out on the world with no means of support. At the same time she was concerned about the Blood family. Since the departure of their frail bread-winner to Portugal they had sunk to an even lower ebb. Now, with Fanny dead and little hope of making an income in England—Mr Blood's promised jobs never materialised—the parents were anxious to move to Ireland. George had already returned to Dublin from Lisbon and obtained a situation there. Mary wrote to him[2] on 5th February in deepest gloom:

> The school dwindles to nothing and we shall soon lose our last boarder, Mrs Disney. She and the girls quarrelled while I was away, which contributed to make the house very disagreeable. Her sons are to be whole boarders at Mrs Cockburn's ... I have too many debts. I cannot think of remaining any longer in this house, the rent is so enormous ... Where to go, without friends and money, who can point out? My eyes are very bad

41

and my memory gone. I cannot think of any situation, and as for Eliza I don't know what will become of her. My constitution is impaired. I hope I shan't live long, yet I may be a tedious time dying...

This was a gross exaggeration, of course. Though Mary was often desperately short of money she never lacked friends; and her fears about her health were largely imaginary. The situation only seemed blacker than it was because she had no one to share the burden. Her only relief was in writing to George; and the mere act of writing helped to raise her spirits. By the time she reached the postscript she was already more cheerful:

Well, I am too impatient. The Will of Heaven be done. I will labour to be resigned... I long to hear that you are settled. This is the only quarter from which I can reasonably expect any pleasure.

She then turned to other matters. The Bloods had evidently expected to receive some help from Hugh Skeys, but this was not forthcoming:

I have received a very short, unsatisfactory letter from Lisbon. It was written to apologise for not sending the money to your father which he promised. It would have been particularly acceptable at this time; but he is prudent and will not run any hazards to serve a friend.

How different from Mary herself! It was no wonder that she so disliked Skeys.

No wonder, either, that she was fond of George Blood. His response was very different. He suggested, in effect, that she should cut her losses and join him in Dublin. But such a course of action, tempting as it may have been, was quite repugnant to Mary. She replied on 27th February:

I am indeed very much distressed at present, and my future prospects are still more gloomy—yet nothing should induce me to fly from England. My creditors have a right to do what they please with me, should I not be able to satisfy their demands.

Characteristically, she was more worried by the effect on others than on herself if she should be forced to close the school:

Should our present plan fail, I cannot even guess what the girls will do. My brother, I am sure, will not receive them, and they are not calculated to struggle with the world. Eliza, in particular, is very helpless. Their situation has made me very uneasy—and as to your father and mother, they have been a continual weight on my spirits. You have removed part of the load, for I now hope you would be able to keep them from perishing, should my affairs grow desperate,—and this hope has made me very grateful—for often when I have thought of death as the only end of my sorrows and cares, I earnestly wished to see them settled before I went to *rest*.

Mary was now not only depressed but morbid in her fears. She could not face the challenge which her own actions—both in starting the school and in deserting it to go to Lisbon—had created. She blamed her state of health for this inertia, and there must certainly have been some physical cause for her low spirits:

Indeed I am very far from being well. I have a pain in my side, and a whole train of nervous complaints, which render me very uncomfortable. My spirits are very very low, and [I] am so opprest by continual anxiety 'tis a labour to me to [do] anything. My former employments are quite irksome to me. If something decisive was to happen I should be better; but 'tis this suspense, this dread of I cannot tell what, which harrasses me.

Here, in this almost classic confession of *angst*, was a new element in the situation. The school was in danger of failing not only on financial grounds but because Mary had lost her enthusiasm for it; she no longer cared whether it succeeded or not. She had all the will-power and all the intelligence necessary to put the school on its feet again if she had really wanted to do so. But as she here admitted, her duties had become 'quite irksome'; so much so, in fact, that she was almost hoping for the worst to happen—'something decisive'—to get her off the hook.

Then, miraculously, a new way did open up which offered some chance of an alternative. It was a small beginning, but one from which enormous consequences were to flow. It could not have escaped Mary's notice at Newington Green that she was surrounded by men who were making their reputations—and, of more immediate importance, their money—by the practice of letters. Amongst them was her friend John Hewlett; and it was Hewlett now who encouraged her to profit from her experience as a teacher by writing down her thoughts on the subject. Here was the spur to goad her into action again and she set to work with a will. Her intention was admittedly to produce a quick 'pot-boiler';

as Godwin drily observed, 'what she desired in a pecuniary view, she was ready to take on herself to effect'. The result was a 'pamphlet', as Godwin describes it, of 160 pages entitled *Thoughts on the Education of Daughters*. Hewlett duly submitted this on Mary's behalf to his publisher Joseph Johnson and obtained a sum of ten guineas for the copyright. It was a modest return, but sufficient to pay the Bloods' fare to Ireland. Though she gained nothing for herself, that was one load off Mary's mind; and she had other rewards than the purely financial one. In the process of committing her thoughts to paper she had discovered an unsuspected new talent, for it is doubtful if Mary had ever previously thought of herself as being in any sense 'a writer'. She had no literary education and her early letters are full of apologies for her poor style and spelling—with some reason, though she was not alone in this.* But Mary was on the brink of discovering that a writer who was capable of thinking for herself could create her own style and make it acceptable.

Meanwhile, however, the problem of securing an immediate livelihood for herself and her sisters remained unsolved. The problem was not only a financial one, as we have seen. More and more Mary was coming to realise her mistake in attempting to set up this household of self-supporting women. 'Experience impressed upon her a rooted aversion to that sort of co-habitation with her sisters, which the project of the school imposed,' said Godwin:

> The activity and ardent spirit of adventure which characterized Mary, were not felt in an equal degree by her sisters, so that a disproportionate share of every burthen attendant upon the situation, fell to her lot.

She was now twenty-seven years old. She had made her bid for independence and proved that independence was possible—so long as things went well. Yet so small were her reserves, not only of capital but also—she now discovered—of commitment, that one major setback could send her whole world crashing. Independence was a hollow mockery, and freedom a delusion, when she did not know which way to turn. She knew only that the next step meant a parting from her sisters; and her sense of isolation again overwhelmed her. Her grief for Fanny was still unassuaged, as she wrote to George on 1st May 1786:

> She was indeed George my best earthly comfort—and my

---

* In commending Dr Johnson's famous *Dictionary* of 1775 Lord Chesterfield (quoted by Boswell) described the English language as being 'in a state of anarchy'.

poor heart still throbs with *selfish* anguish—it is formed for friendships and confidence—yet how often is it wounded...
Parts of this letter have been obliterated. No doubt she was dwelling at length, and with excessive emotion, on the causes of her melancholy. In the next legible portion she was saying:
I am too apt to be attached with a degree of warmth that is not consistent with a probationary state, I have leaned (sic) on earth and have been sorely hurt.

Mary evidently still saw herself as a 'probationer'; and one source of her dissatisfaction was her knowledge that she was not yet ready to give or receive the 'degree of warmth' for which she pined. 'My heart would fain hold all the human race,' she wrote in this same letter, 'and every new affection would add to its comfort—but for the bitter alloy which will mix itself with everything here'.

George now suggested again that Mary and her sisters should all come to Ireland and start a school there; again Mary refused to leave England whilst her debts were unpaid. In any case, this was not what she wanted. She was already making plans for the sisters to go their separate ways. 'Averina and Eliza are both endeavouring to go out into the world,' she wrote on 22nd May, 'the one as a companion, and the other as a teacher.' With her sisters off her hands, Mary believed that she might manage to support herself in a modest way by teaching. She would remain on the Green, she said, 'taking a little cheap lodging and living without a servant. The few scholars I have will maintain me.' But this modest scheme would never have sufficed to meet the demands of her creditors. Mary was forced to move in with her neighbour, Mrs Cockburn. Mrs Burgh again came to the rescue and found a post for Eliza in a boarding-school at Market Harborough, while Everina was obliged to return to her brother's house at No. 1 St Katherine Street in the city of London.

As for Mary herself, her situation was still precarious. Then an opening was suggested by friends of Dr Price, the Rev. and Mrs John Prior of Eton, who were willing to recommend her for the post of governess to the three daughters of Lord Kingsborough at Mitchelstown, County Cork. This was a chance that many young women in her position would have jumped at, but Mary wrote to George Blood on 3rd July with little enthusiasm for the plan:
Lady Kingsborough has written about me to Mrs Prior and I

wait for further particulars before I give my final answer. Forty pounds a year were the terms mentioned, and half of the sum I could spare to discharge my debts, and afterwards to assist Eliza. I by no means like the proposal of being a governess ... But what else, in fact, could she do? To make a livelihood out of writing was still a dream. She knew she had really no option but to accept, although to George she continued to maintain the fiction of a choice: '*Duty* impels me to consider about it and not too hastily reject it,' she wrote the same month, 'and yet only duty would influence me if [I] accepted of it'. She still owed 'near eighty or ninety pounds', she confessed: an impossible sum for her to find out of her own resources. By August the decision was made. Mary would go to Mitchelstown. According to Godwin she intended to stay in the post only long enough to enable her to pay off her debts and start saving again, so that she could pursue a 'literary occupation'.

In her letter of 3rd July already quoted, Mary added a cryptic message which has given rise to some speculation:

Give my love to your father and mother—and you may give the same to Neptune, I have done with all resentments—and perhaps I was as much to blame in expecting too much as he was in doing too little—I looked for what was not to be found.

From this allusion a previous biographer has deduced that 'Neptune' was none other than the Rev Joshua Waterhouse, on no other evidence than the possible pun on his name[3]. Yet it seems highly unlikely that the fashionable cleric had any intimate connection with the impoverished Bloods, as this letter implies. 'Neptune' might equally have been a nickname for some other member of the family or some mutual acquaintance; the Irish ramifications of the Bloods, the Wollstonecrafts and the Skeys went far and wide.

By the end of September 1786, with the aid of a loan from the faithful Mrs Burgh, Mary had wound up her affairs and was ready to leave Newington Green. From there she travelled to Eton, where her future charges were to join her before embarking for Ireland. By a strange coincidence Dr Price was also moving at that time, following the death of his wife. Mary wrote to Eliza on 29th September, after her arrival at the Priors: 'Dr P. intends soon leaving the Green. He has been uncommonly friendly to me! I have the greatest reason to be thankful—for my difficulties appeared unsurmountable.' No doubt he had given Mary financial as well as moral support. Her time at Eton hung heavily, and she waited a whole month for the King girls to join her before it was decided that she should travel to Ireland alone. In the interim she stored up some highly critical impressions of life in a boys' public school. (Mr Prior was at that time an assistant master at Eton College.) Mary wrote to Everina on 9th October: 'I could not live the life they lead at Eton; nothing but dress and ridicule going forward ... witlings abound—and *puns* fly about like crackers'. The social life was evidently very similar to that she had experienced at Windsor with Mrs Dawson: 'Vanity in one shape or another reigns triumphant'. The headmaster of the college at that time, Dr Jonathan Davies, has been described as 'a noted *bon-vivant*, and a friend of the Prince of Wales'[4].

Mary used this waiting time as best she could by studying French in preparation for her future duties. She was a little encouraged by Lady Kingsborough's complaint to Mrs Prior that her daughters' previous governess had 'neglected their minds and only attended to the ornamental part of their education'. Mary would certainly change all that. As she wrote to Everina: 'These sentiments prejudice me in her favour more than anything I have heard of her.' She could not pretend, however, that she viewed her new situation as anything more than a necessary evil to provide a roof over her head and some kind of 'home'—though 'how unlike the one I have in my "mind's eye" ', she confessed to her sister. For Mary there was always something missing: 'A mind that has once felt the pleasure of loving and being beloved cannot rest satisfied with any inferior gratification'. She may have been thinking here of Fanny Blood, or of her intellectual friendships at Newington Green; though neither had given her quite the gratification she endowed them with in recollection.

Mary was not alone in this dissatisfaction with her lot. Her intervention in her sister's affairs had not produced much amelioration for 'poor Bess'. Eliza had now settled into her post at Market Harborough, and from here she wrote to Everina on 17th August. There is nothing in her long and fluently-expressed letter to indicate that this was the 'weak-minded' member of the family. Eliza revealed an acuteness of observation that is akin to Mary's own. She was evidently quite recovered from the breakdown that had wrecked her marriage. She teased Everina for neglecting her in favour of more pressing interests: 'I could almost wish you may not see Lothario, for many a day'. It was Everina, rather than Eliza, who was the 'flighty' sister; and the Wollstonecraft fondness for nicknames has not made the elucidation of their tangled affairs any easier. Eliza had no such diversions: 'I can no longer indulge the delusions of fancy, and the phantoms of hope are for ever, ever flown,' she wrote in terms oddly reminiscent of Mary herself. With a broken marriage behind her, the luckless Bess had real grounds for feeling so. She had also to face alone the disapproval of society: 'The idea of parting from a *husband* one could never make them comprehend; I could much sooner persuade them, that a stone might speak'. But she did not recommend Everina to follow her example: 'Oh! that you had a good *Husband*, to screen thee from those heart-breaking disagreeables'. Eliza's employers were strict Presbyterians, with little sympathy for her predicament. She was depressed too by the monotonous Leicestershire landscape, dotted with mud cottages, though her description of it is both graphic and entertaining. Eliza was certainly not the witless, helpless creature that legend—influenced, no doubt, by Mary's dominance—has created.

Mary's journey to Ireland was calm and uneventful. As usual on her travels she made a friend during the voyage, this time a young clergyman, Henry Gabell. On arrival Mary stayed briefly in Dublin to visit the Bloods and arranged for the faithful George to act as her postman. 'Direct your letters to Brabt. Noble's Esq.,' she instructed Everina, 'and George will get franks and forward them to me'. Mr Noble was evidently George's employer at this time, with whom he resided at No. 96 Britain Street, Dublin. But the pile of Mitchelstown Castle loomed ahead of her; and on passing through the gates it seemed, she wrote to Everina on 30th October, like 'going into the Bastille'.* Gloom descended and enveloped her like a shroud:

> I have been so very low-spirited for some days past that I could not write. All the moments I could spend in solitude were lost in sorrow and unavailing tears. There was such an air of solemn stupidity about this place that froze my very blood.

Nevertheless, Mary knew she had to try and reconcile herself to a state 'which is contrary to every feeling of my soul'. Materially, at least, her position must have been easier than for many months past. The castle was set in magnificent, mountainous country on

---

* Mary evidently subscribed to the eighteenth-century view of the Bastille as a symbol of oppression. In fact the prison was used mainly for the detention of aristocratic victims of court intrigues by order of the monarch's *lettres de cachet*.

the borders of Cork and Tipperary. Lord Kingsborough was an amiable employer and, by the standards of his age and class, an enlightened landowner[5]. He had employed as his manager some years earlier that noted agriculturist Arthur Young, who had surveyed the Essex farmlands during the time of the Wollstonecrafts' residence there. Mary admitted in a letter to George Blood on 7th November that she had 'no reason to complain with respect to the treatment I meet with'.

Her greatest disappointment was in the character of Lady Kingsborough, whom she had come prepared to respect and eager to serve in the education of her daughters. But on closer acquaintance she proved to be a conventional 'lady of quality', living a vapid and parasitical life surrounded by women as foolish as herself—'a *host* of females,' as Mary described them; and she damned herself for ever in the eyes of her governess by appearing to give more attention to her dogs than her children. It was the children who provided Mary's chief solace. However dissatisfied she may have felt with her mode of life, it is clear that as a governess she was an outstanding success—so much a success, said Godwin, that Lady Kingsborough became uneasy 'lest the children should love their governess better than their mother'. Mary had made her position clear from the start: she would be treated as a gentlewoman, not as a sort of upper servant, and she would follow her own methods of teaching. She swept away the repressive prohibitions by which their mother had sought to control the children and undertook 'to govern them by their affections only'. This revolutionary approach must have been regarded with some scepticism by the adult members of the household, but the response of the children was overwhelming. They were soon devoted to the new governess—who was so much more than a governess—and a warm bond of friendship was established between Mary and the eldest daughter Margaret, then aged fourteen.

But the 'teacher' in Mary Wollstonecraft was already waning. She had established her principles, proved their worth in practice, written down her conclusions in a book—and now was only repeating the same well-rehearsed lessons. She still had much to give as a teacher, but little more to learn. It was her passion for independence that had originally led her into teaching. She found now that her relationship with children touched her at a deeper level. She was playing the part less of a governess than of a substitute-mother. She had been engaged to teach the three elder daughters of the Kingsboroughs, but it is evident that she was soon taking on herself the welfare of the younger children too. As she wrote to Everina in January 1787:

> I go to the nursery. *Something like* maternal fondness fills my bosom. The children cluster about me. One catches a kiss, another lisps my long name—while a sweet little boy, who is conscious that he is a favourite, calls himself my Tom. At the sight of their mother they tremble and run to me for protection. This renders them dear to me—and I discover the kind of happiness I was formed to enjoy.

The state in which Mary found herself was not, as she described it to Everina, 'contrary to every feeling of my soul': in protecting the weak and helpless she was in her element. It was her own position in this situation that was at fault. She knew now that she should herself have been the mother of such a family of children.

Yet this maternal longing represented only one side of her nature. In other moods she was more conscious of the frustration of her own self-development. She could not become a mother until she had first become a whole woman, and this she was still far from achieving. She continued to be racked by depression and morbid fancies, which were exacerbated by her isolation in an alien society. Past griefs mingled with present dissatisfactions to bring her close to despair. She summed up her dilemma in a letter to George Blood on 4th December 1786: 'bitter recollections wound my poor heart which cannot be filled by mere common placed affections—yet every thing which humanity dictates is thought for me'. Mary knew that her limitless capacities for giving affection and sympathy fitted her for almost any role, however humble; but she also knew that her intellectual capacities destined her for something beyond the common run of man—or woman. 'This warfare will in time be over,' she continued, '—and my soul will not vainly pant after happiness—or doubt in what it consists'. Writing the next day to Joseph Johnson—the first extant letter to her publisher[6]—Mary seemed resigned to the annihilation of all her hopes:

> I have most of the negative comforts of life, yet when weighed with liberty they are of little value. In a christian sense I am resigned—and contented; but it is with pleasure that I observe

my declining health, and cherish the hope that I am hastening to the land where all these cares will be forgotten.
To the caged bird, even death represents an escape to freedom. Although it should not be overlooked that Mary had tasted liberty at Newington Green and by her own impetuosity had thrown it away.

Mary's depression could certainly not be attributed solely to her circumstances. She was suffering from some deep emotional *malaise*, which may or may not have been bound up with the mysterious 'Neptune'. When the Kingsboroughs proposed that she and the children should accompany them to their town house in Dublin in February 1787 she wrote to George Blood: 'Is Neptune still in Dublin?—Let me know directly'. She concluded this letter: 'Life is but a frightful dream—I long to go to sleep—with my friend in the house appointed for all living!' When present realities became too unpleasant Mary sought refuge in memories of Fanny. She seems to have been oscillating between the ideal of love that can only be found in death and the more complex demands of the living. With George, however, she had evidently established a mutually satisfactory relationship. She wrote to Everina on 12th February 1787:

> George is still the same. His understanding soon arrived at maturity. He has made me a very acceptable present—Shakespeare's plays, the new edition.

Although George Blood may sometimes have given the impression of being a weak and unreliable character, he had qualities of sensibility and loyalty which enabled him to recognise Mary's worth and at the same time to accept that her destiny must take a different path from his own.

The move to Dublin temporarily dispelled Mary's gloom. Despite herself she was drawn into the social life of this 'most hospitable city', as she later described it[7]: attending a festival of Handel's music, accompanying the Kingsboroughs to parties and balls, and taking part in a masquerade. But these frivolous activities seemed to her the shadow rather than the substance of life. 'I think, and think,' she wrote to Everina in March, 'and these reveries do not tend to fit me for enjoying the *common* pleasures of this world'. But the explanation she gave for her 'reveries' suggests an excess of feeling rather than thought: 'Certainly I must be in love—for I am grown "thin and lean, pale and wan" '.

Whatever the reason, her low condition finally alarmed Lady Kingsborough who called in the family physician to examine her governess. He diagnosed 'a constant nervous fever', she reported to Everina—not without a certain relish. If Mary could enjoy nothing else, she was obviously enjoying her ill-health:

> Indeed it is impossible to enumerate the various complaints I am troubled with; and how much my mind is harassed by them. I know they all arise from disordered nerves, that are injured beyond a *possibility* of receiving any aid from medicine. There is no cure for a broken heart!

Mary could diagnose her own ills better than any physician; and she was right that no medicine could cure them. Only she could do that but not while she persisted in perpetuating the myth of her 'broken heart'. In a postscript to Everina she comes near to acknowledging this, with a touch of wry humour:

> I am like a *lilly* drooping. Is it not a sad pity that so sweet a flower should waste its sweetness on the *Desart* (Dublin) air, and that the Grave should receive to *untouched* horrors Yours an Old Maid . . .

Yet she refused to lower her exacting standards. It is not to be supposed that Mary Wollstonecraft could not easily have married on what she would have called 'common place' terms. But she knew that only a man of unusual qualities—her idea of a 'genius'—could offer her any hope of an equal union. Mary's problem—and tragedy—was not the alleged 'inferiority' of women, but her own superiority to the average human being of either sex. It is true that she had met a number of men with some claim to distinction, from Dr Price downwards, but they were inevitably her seniors in age and already established in society. Poor Mary gave the impression now of reviewing her male acquaintances, a little desperately, in the hope of filling the aching emptiness of a loveless existence.

It was not easy. She continued to harp on her 'broken heart', plucking the strings in an ecstasy of misery that approaches masochism. Or was this just for the record? She wrote, after all, in the style of her time, and this was the Age of Sensibility *par excellence*. So she takes her harp to the party and plays her melancholy tune, while the truth is that she was never short of masculine admirers. She had noted with satisfaction, on coming to Dublin, that she now had 'a parlour to receive my *male* visitors in'. Her heart was not so much broken as congealing for lack of a worthy protagonist. None had so far appeared, though this was not for any want of looking on her part. Mary was all too prone to seek 'what was not to be found'. Her first thought about Dublin had been to enquire from George Blood whether 'Neptune' would be there. Evidently he was, but his presence brought little comfort. She wrote to Everina on 11th May 1787 that he had enquired after her—'yet could not find time to visit me'. But when she met him by chance one evening at a social gathering in the Rotunda and he attempted to speak to her, she told Everina that 'I *would* not see him—and from the corner of my eye he might have caught a look of ineffable contempt'. This was the language of coquetry rather than of love, and leads one to suppose that Neptune need not be placed too high in the catalogue of Mary's affections. Only three days later she was writing to Everina about another of her old acquaintances: 'Pray remember me in a most affectionate manner to *Hewlett*—Tis a pity that *such* a man should be thrown away!!!' In the same letter she makes references to Church and to Skeys, whom she describes without enthusiasm as 'still the same *prudent* creature'. 'I must not forget to tell you that you have rivalled the princess—George talks continually of you and *blushes* when he mentions your name'. The 'princess' was of course Mary herself, and she gave an impression of trying to divert George's admiration in the direction of her sister. She was very fond of George, but she could not take him seriously as a suitor. He was in any case several years her junior, and Mary was more attracted by older men.

One such, with whom she became acquainted in Ireland, was the Member of Parliament for Wexford, George Ogle. In Godwin's words:

> She held his talents in very high estimation; she was strongly prepossessed in favour of the goodness of his heart; and she always spoke of him as the most perfect gentleman she had ever known.

Ogle, a close friend of Lord Kingsborough, was undoubtedly a man of high abilities and rose to be governor of Wexford in 1796. He also won renown as a facile versifier and was something of a philanderer. Faced with this formidable combination of intellect, wit and charm, Mary's romantic idealism outran her commonsense. Writing to Everina in March 1787 she described Ogle as 'a genius—and *unhappy*'; and she was well aware of her own susceptibility: 'such a man, you may suppose, would catch your sister's eye'. She was aware too of the unstable state of her imagination, which was in danger of running wild for want of an adequate focus. She described this state in her letter to Everina of 11th May, already quoted:

"That vivacity which increases with age is not far from madness," says Rochefoucault. I then am mad—deprived of the only comforts I can relish, I give way to whim.

What she described was indeed close to hysteria: 'sprightly sallies' are followed by tears and sighs; her eyes roll 'in the wild way you have *seen* them'; a 'deadly paleness' alternates with 'the most painful suffusion'. But Mary was not a hysteric. Even in the most storm-tossed state of emotion her intellect remained cool and analytical, and she could give a rational explanation for her apparently irrational responses:

You know not, my dear Girl, of what materials this strange inconsistent heart of mine is formed, and how alive it is to tenderness and misery. Since I have been here I have turned over several pages in the vast volume of human nature, and what is the amount? Vanity and vexation of spirit—and yet I am *tied* to my fellow-creatures by partaking of their weaknesses. I rail at a fault—sicken at the sight—and find it stirring within me. New feelings and sympathies *start* up. I know not myself.—"Tis these whims," Mr Ogle tells me, "render me interesting"—and Mrs Ogle with a placid smile quotes some of my own sentiments—while I cry the physician *cannot* heal himself.

If self-knowledge could have cured her conflicts, Mary would have been in perfect spiritual health. But self-knowledge alone was not enough; indeed, by increasing her self-consciousness it only made the inner conflict more painful. It was not true, as Mary said, that 'I know not myself'. What she did not know was how to be reconciled to the 'self' that she knew all too well; and her intellect could not give her the answer.

Some of these doubts and difficulties were voiced in correspondence with her new acquaintance, Henry Gabell. Two letters, both dated 16th April 1787, have recently been published[8]. The first is no more than a covering note to accompany a copy of her newly-published book, *Thoughts on the Education of*

Daughters. The second, a much longer letter, is of interest in showing how Mary's intellectual development was beginning to collide with her religious beliefs; but at this stage it was her intellect that she doubted, rather than her faith. Her own thinking had so far been counter-productive, in that it only increased her dissatisfaction. If one wished to enjoy 'the common pleasures of this life', she observed, it was better not to think. Yet she could not believe that God would have given her a brain if he did not intend her to use it:

> Why have we implanted in us an irresistible desire to think—if thinking is not in some measure necessary to make us wise unto salvation? Indeed intellectual and moral improvement seem to me so connected—I cannot, even in thought, separate them.

She acknowledged that she had thought, and felt, too much. Sensibility, like thinking, brought more pain than pleasure, and for no apparent good—yet it too must have some purpose in the world: 'Surely,' she cried, '*peculiar* wretchedness has something to balance it!' In searching for this compensating balance, and failing to find it, Mary had driven herself to the limit of her endurance:

> My reason has been too far stretched, and tottered almost on the brink of madness—no wonder then, if I humbly hope, that the ordeal trial answered some end, and that I have not suffered in vain.

Mary was surely right to argue that her faculties of mind and heart, implanted in her by God or nature, were intended to be used. Where she went wrong, perhaps, was in trying to solve what was essentially an emotional problem by intellectual means. The brain, given time, can solve its own problems; it cannot solve those of the heart. In realistic, human terms, this means that intellect cannot be a substitute for sense. Mary was very much a creature of sense, as well as of sensibility and of intellect; but the conventions of society forbade her to acknowledge it, even within her own consciousness. It was in this 'sense', and this alone, that she was ignorant of herself. In the realm of sensation the rationalist Dr Price could not give her an answer, any more than the devout Mr Gabell; nor could *l'homme moyen sensuel*—represented perhaps by 'Neptune' or George Blood or Hugh Skeys—who was content with sensation as an end in itself. Mary needed to be reconciled at all three levels of her being; and now a new consciousness was stirring that brought the first glimmer of a solution. In Dublin, though scarcely aware of it, Mary Wollstonecraft became a Romantic.

'I am now reading Rousseau's *Emile*,' she wrote to Everina in March 1787, 'and love his paradoxes'. In Rousseau, at last, Mary had discovered a kindred spirit:

> ... he rambles into that chimerical world in which I have too often wandered, and draws the usual conclusion that all is vanity and vexation of spirit. He was a strange, inconsistent, unhappy, clever creature, yet he possessed an uncommon portion of sensibility and penetration.

Her description of Rousseau could as well be applied to herself. Yet she did not admire him unreservedly; it was a 'love-hate' relationship from the start. The affinity lay in their weaknesses rather than their strengths; and, though she could never entirely escape it, became increasingly distasteful to Mary. Rousseau might help to explain her conflicts, but he could not resolve them.

Mary expressed her present discontent in another letter to Joseph Johnson in April[9]:

> I feel all of a mother's fears for the swarm of little ones which surround me, and observe disorders, without having power to apply proper remedies. How can I be reconciled to life, when it is always a painful warfare, and when I am deprived of all the pleasures I relish?—I allude to rational conversations, and domestic affections. How alone, a poor solitary individual in a strange land, tied to one spot, and subject to the caprice of another can I be contented?

Mary's recipe for happiness was a modest one, but it had so far eluded her. 'Rational conversations' could only be enjoyed between equals, and she was still 'subject to the caprice of another'. 'Domestic affections' depended on an emotional equilibrium which she had similarly failed to achieve. She needed to change both her circumstances and her attitudes; and the former change would be largely determined by the latter. The result of all this heart-searching and mind-stretching was only to complete her alienation from the role of the schoolmistress and the governess. She had reached the end of that road.

By the summer of 1787 Mary's relationship to her employers had markedly changed. As with her own family, with Mrs Dawson and with the Bloods, she had progressed from a position of subservience to one of near-domination. At Mitchelstown, the surprising discovery that (however much she despised society) she was a social success, seems to have gone to her head a little. The governess was undoubtedly getting above herself! She even wrote to Everina that Lady Kingsborough was 'afraid of me', continuing: 'Why she wishes to keep me I cannot guess—for she cannot bear that any one should take notice of me'. It was doubtless a relief to all parties when the Kingsboroughs decided to spend the summer at the Bristol Hot-wells, and then possibly to visit the Continent. It is not difficult to detect the hand of Mary in this congenial plan. 'I am trying to persuade Lady K. to go to the Continent,' she wrote to Everina on 12th May, 'but I am afraid she will not. I wish to take in some *quite* new objects—'. As usual Mary got her way, and the next month saw her in England again. Leaving Ireland was in itself a stimulus to her spirits. 'I do not *admire* the Irish', she had confided to Everina in the spring, '. . . I should not chuse this Kingdom for my residence, if I could subsist anywhere else.' She could not have guessed then that she was never to return.

From Bristol, writing to Eliza on 27th June, she fabricated another of her little mysteries:

I have every reason to think I shall be able to pay my debts before I again leave the Kingdom. *A friend* whose name I am not *permitted* to mention has insisted on lending me the money.

The Wollstonecraft charm had evidently worked another miracle. Mary could not resist telling Eliza the real truth: the money was not a loan but a gift. 'I could have no scruple,' she assured her sister, 'and I rejoiced to meet with a fellow-creature whom I could admire for doing a *disinterested* act of kindness.' Yet the identity of the donor remains puzzling. It is hardly conceivable that Mary would have accepted money from a stranger. Could this 'disinterested' friend be the elusive Joshua Waterhouse, who is known to have frequented the Hot-wells? But it may equally have been Mr Ogle, or some other friend of the Kingsboroughs who was well-disposed towards their most unusual governess. Mary's proud nature was innocent of false pride and she could accept the gift in the spirit in which it was offered. With some ready cash in her pocket, she at once began planning for the future. The money would not, of course, be spent on herself; but it would free her from the burden of debt, enable her to visit her sisters and provide the means for them to spend the winter school-vacation together: 'the only alleviation I can devise to render your confinement tolerable'.

Mary also disclosed in this letter that, between more trivial occupations, she was at work on another book:

In a trifling way I net purses, and intend having two smart ones to present to you and Everina—and when I have more strength I read Philosophy—and write (I *hope* you have not forgot that I am an Author) yet many are the hours that are loaded with cares. I shake my head but it remains heavy—and I *ruminate* without digesting.

Mary's rumination was more effective than she supposed. The result was to emerge—no doubt with some help from Rousseau—in the form of a novel; or rather, a thinly-disguised exercise in autobiography. *Mary: a Fiction*, as she called it, could have deceived nobody who was acquainted with the circumstances of the author's life. The work was completed by the time the Kingsboroughs travelled up to London in August as the next stage on the journey to Europe. Mary's persuasion had succeeded so far, but now a sudden hitch occurred.

Before leaving England she wished to take a short holiday in order to visit Eliza at Market Harborough and Everina at Henley-on-Thames, where the youngest sister had now taken a post in a school run by a Miss Rowden. But the prospect of being parted from her governess precipitated such a scene with Margaret King, the eldest daughter, that in a fit of jealousy Lady Kingsborough peremptorily dismissed her. The trip to the Continent was abandoned, the Kingsboroughs returned to Ireland—and Mary was alone again. This, at least, is Godwin's version of the incident, but it does not altogether ring true. With her second book completed, Mary may have decided herself that the time had come to make a break. Or the clash with the Kingsboroughs may have arisen from some more serious difference than a mere fit of pique. Margaret was a girl of some spirit, as her later history shows, and Mary would certainly have encouraged this budding independence[10].

Mary must have regretted leaving her young charges to the uncertain mercies of their mother, but for herself she felt nothing but relief. The change of plan may have come more abruptly than she had anticipated, but she was not unprepared for it. She was quite clear in her own mind what she wanted to do; and equally determined that she was now going to do it. She wrote to Joseph Johnson from Henley on 13th September[11]:

> I often think of my new plan of life; and, lest my sister should try to prevail on me to alter it, I have avoided mentioning it to her. I am determined!—Your sex generally laugh at female determinations; but let me tell you, I never yet resolved to do anything of consequence, that I did not adhere resolutely to it, till I had accomplished my purpose, improbable as it might have appeared to a more timid mind.

There is something a little frightening in Mary's single-minded application to her goal. One can almost hear the voice of Lady Macbeth: 'Infirm of purpose! Give me the daggers.' It was the same ruthless spirit that had—literally—driven a coach and horses through Eliza's marriage. Now, for once, she was acting on her own behalf; and she would need all her ruthlessness to carry her through. For the moment, 'nerves' were banished and ailments forgotten. Mary had found a new focus for her energies, and one that promised to be more creatively rewarding than anything she had hitherto attempted.

Johnson at any rate took her seriously. He had published her first book, on the recommendation of Hewlett, and now had the manuscript of a second. While Mary was visiting her sisters and worrying about their future, he was coming to a decision about hers. Not only would he accept her manuscript: he would offer her regular employment at his publishing firm and the shelter of his home until suitable lodgings could be found for her. One is tempted to surmise at this point that Johnson may even have been Mary's anonymous benefactor. 'I left Bristol to visit my friend,' she wrote to Henry Gabell from Henley on the same day that she was writing to Johnson. She certainly came to London from Bristol. She had other friends, of course, all of whom were generously disposed towards her. But from now on she enjoyed a unique relationship with Joseph Johnson that was to endure for the rest of her life. Mary had found a new champion, as well as a new career.

CHAPTER FIVE
Report in Triplicate

By Michaelmas 1787 Mary Wollstonecraft was established in her own quarters at No. 49 George Street, Blackfriars (now Dolben Street, and largely demolished), with the prospect of regular and congenial employment in Joseph Johnson's publishing business at No. 72 St Paul's Church-yard. Now at last her longed-for independence seemed certain of achievement. She wrote to Everina[1]:

> Mr Johnson has now settled me in a little house in a street near Blackfriars Bridge. He assures me I can earn a comfortable maintenance if I exert myself. I have given him *Mary* and before your vacation I shall finish another book for young people which I think has some merit . . .

Joseph Johnson's generosity was legendary, and never was it displayed more handsomely than in his dealings with Mary. She had evidently made a considerable impression, which must have owed as much to her personal qualities as to her literary abilities. Johnson's own character was exceptional and he seems to have been motivated by a spirit of pure benevolence. The son of a Baptist farmer, he was born at Everton near Liverpool in 1738 and had come to London as a young man to learn his trade as a bookseller. He was by now a respected figure, on terms of intimacy with the leaders of progressive thought, and in the shadow of St Paul's his home had become a centre for radical dissent. Yet, in all this dazzling company, he had selected Mary as his chief *amanuensis* and opened the hospitality of his home not only to herself but to her family. 'Johnson has offered you both a bed in his house.' Mary told Everina, 'but that would not be pleasant. I believe I must try to purchase a bed, which I shall reserve for my poor girls while I have a house'.

Her sisters were still causing her anxiety. Neither was happily settled and it was not easy to place them in more suitable situations. As she wrote to George Blood[2] from Henley on 11th September: 'Eliza wants activity; and Everina's vivacity would, by the injudicious, be termed giddiness'. Two days later she was appealing to Henry Gabell[3] for help, at the same time disclosing a little more of the family history:

> The extravagance of a Father, and his second marriage, has left my sisters friendless; I would fain be their mother and protector; but I am not formed to obtain the good things of this world—on their account they would be valuable.

Everina—'a fine girl', she informed Mr Gabell—was teaching in a 'vulgar school' and she wished to place her 'in a Gentleman's family'. Gabell was then staying in Ireland with the Member of Parliament for Antrim, John O'Neill, and Mary enquired somewhat diffidently—'If you do not think there would be a *great* impropriety in it'—whether he might not put in a word for Everina with Mrs O'Neill. But nothing came of this request. No doubt Gabell had other things on his mind and was less concerned about Mary than she supposed. Although she addressed him as 'mon cher ami' she knew that he was engaged to be married, and she could not resist a slightly derogatory reference to this young lady:

> I suppose your *own Ann* has informed you that I wrote to her. I intended visiting her; but it was not convenient.

Mary saw herself now as a woman with a profession and believed that henceforth this was to be her destiny. 'I have *done* with the delusions of fancy,' she informed Everina—who had already heard the same story from Eliza and, being young and frivolous, could hardly have appreciated its significance. 'I only live to be useful—,' Mary continued, 'benevolence must fill every void in my heart.' This was no more than a pious hope. 'Benevolence' might serve as an extension of personal love—Mary believed that it should—but it could never be an adequate substitute. She, above all women, was aware of the primacy of the one over the many: as she had already attempted to demonstrate in a second, fragmentary novel which she never completed. *The Cave of Fancy* has received little critical appreciation, yet it was a crucial signpost on Mary's road to maturity. Together with *Thoughts on the Education of Daughters* and *Mary: a Fiction* it sums up the first phase of her adult life in three dimensions: the intellectual, the emotional and the imaginative. This does not mean that *Thoughts on the Education of Daughters* is devoid of feeling; that *Mary: a Fiction* is devoid of thought; or that *The Cave of Fancy* is not largely an amalgam of both. On the contrary, it is the continuous interaction of thought, emotion and imagination that stamps these minor works with the imprint of originality. They have the added interest of being the most directly concerned of all Mary's writings with her own private experience.

Thoughts on the Education of Daughters: with reflections on female conduct, in the more important duties of life sounds suspiciously like one of those tracts for self-improvement so dear to the late eighteenth century and immortalised in Thomas Day's *Sandford and Merton* (published in three volumes from 1783 to 1789). But Mary's *Thoughts* were uniquely her own, even though she attempted to confine them within the prescribed framework of moral uplift. Forged out of the purgatory of her own faulty upbringing, her precepts anticipate modern theories of child psychology by nearly two hundred years. She starts, logically enough, in 'The Nursery'—and at once sees that all is not well:

> Indolence, and a thoughtless disregard of every thing, except the present indulgence, make many mothers, who may have momentary starts of tenderness, neglect their children.

This is a serious charge, and she goes on to substantiate it. First and foremost, Mary believed, mothers should suckle their babies. This was not only good for the baby, but also helped to stimulate maternal tenderness—which, she observes, 'arises quite as much from habit as instinct'. This is followed by another perceptive insight: that infants should be guarded against bodily pain, because 'their minds can afford them no amusement to alleviate it'. The next precept is the need for 'consistency' in making rules for children; which is immediately followed by a plea for flexibility and the avoidance of needless restraint. Mary disliked the habit of speaking to young children in 'nursery prattle', which some girls seemed unable or unwilling to outgrow: 'and do not forget to lisp, when they have learnt to languish' (another aspect of female behaviour which she deplored). A more serious criticism was that children were taught to take revenge and 'return the injury' if they were hurt; worst still, perhaps, was the adult habit of threatening punishment to a pet animal if a child misbehaved.

The drift of Mary's thinking is already clear in this first chapter: that children should be treated with respect and accorded the same justice that adults would expect from each other. But were the adult standards themselves above criticism? She did not think so. Moving to a section on 'Moral Discipline', she had some sharp reproofs for parents who imagined that they were fit to train children when they had not subdued their own passions. 'The marriage state,' she observed, 'is too often a state of discord.' There were dangers, too, from over-indulgence; and all too often, having thoroughly spoilt a child, the parent would hand him over to a servant who would then complete the corruption by teaching him cunning and deceit. Above all, Mary urged that children should be taught 'to combine their ideas'; in other words, 'to think'. But she added a caution: 'Not that I would have them make long reflections; for when they do not arise from experience, they are mostly absurd'. It is doubtful if many of her readers appreciated the revolutionary nature of this remark, or even if she appreciated it herself. It was so obvious to Mary that 'experience' was the best teacher that it never occurred to her to live by any other rule. She did not then understand how thoroughly the conventional rule-book was designed to obviate just this.

She made short shrift of 'manners' and 'accomplishments'. The touchstone for all behaviour, in Mary's view, was 'sincerity'. Yet all too often social judgments were made on the basis of exterior appearance alone. This meant that dress and adornment were given an exaggerated place in a girl's life. 'The beauty of dress,' she observed, '(I shall raise astonishment by saying so) is its not being conspicuous one way or the other.' There was the further moral to be drawn that money squandered on dress might better be saved to 'alleviate the distress of many poor families'. From the cultivation of the person she passed to the cultivation of the mind: and noted that this too could be overdone. Too much reading might give a false view of life. Dealing with the education of girls in particular, she touched only briefly on the theme to which she later returned much more forcibly; namely, that for a woman to employ her mind was not incompatible with her domestic duties:

'A woman may fit herself to be the companion and friend of a man of sense, and yet know how to take care of his family'. Mary's view of the woman's role was far from revolutionary at this stage. She regretted the time spent in girls' schools on dress and social accomplishments, because she felt the pupils should be given a better preparation than this 'to fulfil the important duties of a wife and mother'.

Mary turned then to the 'Unfortunate Situation of Females, fashionably educated, and left without a Fortune'. She spoke here from the heart. How well she knew the humiliations of the poverty-stricken 'companion':

> Above the servants, yet considered by them as a spy, and ever reminded of her inferiority when in conversation with superiors. If she cannot condescend to mean flattery, she has not a chance of being a favorite; and should any of the visitors take notice of her, and she for a moment forget her subordinate state, she is sure to be reminded of it.

Here, we may be sure, Mary was re-living her experiences with Mrs Dawson. The next paragraph, too, echoes her letters to her sisters:

> She is alone, shut out from equality and confidence, and the concealed anxiety impairs her constitution; for she must wear a cheerful face, or be dismissed. The being dependent on the caprice of a fellow-creature, though certainly very necessary in this state of discipline, is yet a very bitter corrective, which we would fain shrink from.

The situation of the school-teacher was little better: 'only a kind of upper servant, who has more work than the menial ones'. To be a governess, as she also knew, was 'equally disagreeable':

> It is ten to one if they meet with a reasonable mother; and if she is not so, she will be continually finding fault to prove she is not ignorant, and be displeased if her pupils do not improve, but angry if the proper methods are taken to make them do so.

She also spoke on behalf of the girl who—like herself and her sisters—has come down in the world:

> How cutting is the contempt she meets with!—a young mind looks round for love and friendship; but love and friendship fly from poverty: expect them not if you are poor! The mind must then sink into meanness, and accommodate itself to its new state, or dare to be unhappy.

Above all, Mary knew that the girl of slender means must be wary of her own heart:

> Few men seriously think of marrying an inferior; and if they have honor enough not to take advantage of the artless tenderness of a woman who loves, and thinks not of the difference of rank, they do not undeceive her until she has anticipated happiness, which, contrasted with her dependant situation, appears delightful. The disappointment is severe; and the heart receives a wound which does not easily admit of a compleat cure, as the good that is missed is not valued according to its real worth: for fancy drew the picture, and grief delights to create food to feed on.

There is an obvious link in this passage with Mary's own condition during that dreary winter in Ireland, even to the acknowledgement that sometimes it is a girl's imagination, or 'fancy', that is to blame for her disappointment. It offers another tenuous clue to the mystery of an early love affair from which she seems never to have fully recovered. More light is shed on this in her subsequent chapter on the theme of 'Love'. The expression of her feelings is so clearly the voice of experience that one can only regret that she did not abandon the fictitious pretence altogether and supply a few hard facts:

> A variety of causes will occasion an attachment; an endeavour to supplant another, or being by some accident confined to the society of one person. Many have found themselves entangled in an affair of honor, who only meant to fill up the heavy hours in an amusing way, or raise jealousy in some other bosom.

Mary knew well during the 'heavy hours' of boredom in Bath or Dublin how trivialities could be inflated into high emotional drama and how easily she could have been compromised by her own 'artless tenderness'. The situation was far worse, however, when in spite of herself a young woman's feelings became genuinely engaged:

> People of sense and reflection are most apt to have violent and constant passions, and to be preyed on by them. Neither can they, for the sake of present pleasure, bear to act in such a manner, as that the retrospect should fill them with confusion and regret. Perhaps a delicate mind is not susceptible of a greater degree of misery, putting guilt out of the question, than what must arise from the consciousness of loving a person

whom their reason does not approve.

Here the cat is right out of the bag. The problem of 'loving a person whom their reason does not approve' is not a common one, at any rate for the female sex which has the faculty of adapting 'reason' to the prior demands of nature. But Mary was not an average woman, and this problem was acutely her own. She strove valiantly to overcome it: 'I am very far from thinking love irresistible, and not to be conquered,' she wrote hopefully, and went on to give an example:

> I knew a woman very early in life warmly attached to an agreeable man, yet she saw his faults; his principles were unfixed, and his prodigal turn would have obliged her to have restrained every benevolent emotion of her heart. She exerted her influence to improve him, but in vain did she for years try to do it. Convinced of the impossibility, she determined not to marry him, though she was forced to encounter poverty and its attendants.

Not only does this passage reflect Mary's past experience—her description of the 'agreeable man' could fit the character of Joshua Waterhouse or George Blood, for instance—but like so much of her writing it presages the future. She was to taste this bitter cup to the full. Again, in next discussing 'platonic love', she displayed an uncanny prescience:

> Nothing can more tend to destroy peace of mind, than platonic attachments. They are begun in false refinements, and frequently end in sorrow, if not guilt... Not that I mean to insinuate that there is no such thing as friendship between persons of different sexes; I am convinced of the contrary. I only mean to observe, that if a woman's heart is disengaged, she should not give way to a pleasing delusion, and imagine she will be satisfied with the friendship of a man she admires, and prefers to the rest of the world. The heart is very treacherous, and if we do not guard its first emotions, we shall not afterwards be able to prevent its sighing for impossibilities.

How did Mary gain these insights, if not from experience? Partly from observation, no doubt, and partly from an intuitive knowledge of her own nature, whereby she could rehearse the future without actually playing the role. To be forewarned, however, was not necessarily to be forearmed.

On the subject of 'Matrimony' Mary was on less certain

ground. She quite honestly did not know her own mind about this. She had not yet evolved the philosophy of marriage which she was to express in *The Rights of Woman*, although she was groping towards it. So she confined herself to a fairly conventional exposition of the virtues of modesty, dignity and self-restraint. Her only original contribution is the stress she placed on the need for a woman to have a 'cultivated mind' if only to enable her the better to endure an unsatisfactory marriage:

> A sensible, delicate woman, who by some strange accident, or mistake, is joined to a fool or a brute, must be wretched beyond all names of wretchedness, if her views are confined to the present scene. Of what importance, then, is intellectual improvement, when our comfort here, and happiness hereafter, depends upon it.

Mary had already discovered the solace of 'intellectual improvement' in her own different state of wretchedness; although she had also discovered that it was not a complete cure. She passed on this knowledge, too, in a later section of 'Desultory Thoughts' on various aspects of social behaviour—from card-playing to Sunday observance—which is mainly interesting for the sparkling aphorisms which are tossed out almost as asides. On 'Reason' she observed:

> Reason is indeed the heaven-lighted lamp in man, and may safely be trusted when not entirely depended on; but when it pretends to discover what is beyond its ken, it certainly stretches the line too far, and runs into absurdity.

Mary must have encountered the 'absurdity' of pure reason as applied to human affairs in the high-flown discussions at Newington Green. How could reason encompass religion, for instance? 'Did our feelings and reason always coincide', she observed, '... faith would no longer be a virtue'. 'It is our preferring the things that are not seen, to those which are, that proves us to be the heirs of promise.' To the rationalist, of course, 'the things that are not seen' are unreal. But what of the emotions? Mary knew that emotional states could have a profound effect on the mind: 'for if the mind is not kept in motion by either hope or fear, it sinks into the dreadful state before-mentioned (apathy)'. This may be explained as a flight from both the past and the present into the ever-hopeful promise of the future. But how could one ever catch up with the future? Mary was too fundamentally realistic to be content with a promise that never materialised. Yet all too often, the promise only turned to ashes in the mouth: 'I have often thought it might be set down as a maxim,' she remarked, 'that the greatest disappointment we can meet with is the gratification of our fondest wishes'. She knew this too. Her greatest wish had been to become independent; and independence, so far, had been the greatest disappointment of her life. The real root of her dissatisfaction, perhaps, lay in the imbalance between reason and emotion which she saw not only in herself but in the world around her. Neither personal love nor abstract thinking was sufficient in itself; they must somehow be reconciled in the interests of a greater good. 'Women too often confine their love and charity to their own families,' she noted:

> Goodwill to all the human race should dwell in our bosoms, nor should love to individuals induce us to violate this first of all duties, or make us sacrifice the interest of any fellow-creature, to promote that of another, whom we happen to be more partial to.

If one area of conflict was between passion and reason, another was between the individual and society. These were the two major themes that were now emerging as the driving force of Mary's future life and works.

Thoughts on the Education of Daughters marked out a sketch-map for futher exploration. In her second book, *Mary: a Fiction*, the author looked back and retraced a course already trodden and memorised. The story is banal, and the telling of it conventional. But the 'fiction' is the least of it; the 'sentiment' is all. To Godwin, at any rate, this was enough. If Mary had written nothing else, he said, this book would serve 'to establish the eminence of her genius'[4]:

> He that looks into the book only for incident, will probably lay it down with disgust. But the feelings are of the truest and most exquisite class; every circumstance is adorned with that species of imagination, which enlists itself under the banners of delicacy and sentiment. A work of sentiment, as it is called, is too often another name for a work of affectation. He that should imagine that the sentiments of this book are affected, would indeed be entitled to our profoundest commiseration.

To the modern reader, the eighteenth-century adulation of 'delicacy' and 'sentiment' is less than riveting. The main interest of the book lies in its parallels with the real Mary's experience and in the observations of the heroine which are so clearly her own. As a work of fiction, it can only be judged against the standards of its time. The English novel was still largely unformed. *Mary* was published in 1788, ten years after Fanny Burney's *Evelina*. Apart from Defoe and Swift, who were pamphleteers rather than novelists, only Richardson, Fielding, Smollett and Sterne had gone before. The contemporary ideal of the heroine was the product of the masculine imagination and her chief virtue was faithfulness in the face of man's infidelity; she was exemplified in the characters of Sophia in *Tom Jones*, Emilia in *Peregrine Pickle* and Richardson's *Pamela*[5]. Fanny Burney satirised this image so gently that she scarcely dented it; she was concerned with manners rather than morals. Mary Wollstonecraft, who was passionately concerned with morals and scarcely at all with manners, attacked it head-on, though with little more success. She was still too inexperienced a writer to match her technique to her argument.

She spelt out her intention in the preface to *Mary*: 'In an artless tale, without episodes, the mind of a woman, who has thinking powers is displayed'. This was a new development indeed. If Mary had pursued her stated intention with the necessary refinements of art she might have precipitated the trend that led on to Jane Austen and George Eliot; but she scarcely attempted this. She had little interest in 'the novel' as an art form and was always in too much of a hurry to give her books a proper shape. She utilised the existing channels of communication as a medium for expressing her most urgent thoughts and feelings, and if the result was a work of art this was an almost accidental bonus. She expressed her present purpose, in slightly different terms, in a postscript to her letter to Henry Gabell of 13th September 1787:

I have lately written a fiction which I intend to give to the world; it is a tale, to illustrate an opinion of mine, that a genius will educate itself. I have drawn from Nature.

By 'Nature' she undoubtedly meant her own experience. By 'genius' she almost certainly meant to express the more general, eighteenth-century definition of a 'natural character' or 'inherent tendency', rather than the later connotation of 'a genius' as a uniquely-gifted being.

The 'tale', as such, may be disposed of in a paragraph. It is no more than a peg for the author's own reflections, so thinly disguised as 'fiction' that not even the heroine's name is changed. The main plot, according to Godwin, was based on her friendship with Fanny Blood, but the minor incidents were invented. The *Mary* of the story has a bosom friend called *Ann* who like her prototype (Fanny) develops a dangerous fever and is sent to Lisbon for her health. *Mary* goes with her, having recently inherited a considerable estate; and having also contracted a marriage of convenience with a juvenile cousin, who conveniently left her at the church door in order to take the obligatory 'grand tour' of Europe with his tutor. In Portugal *Ann* (predictably) dies, while *Mary* (unpredictably) falls in love with an English visitor, *Henry*. After some soulful exchanges, *Mary* returns to England in despair. *Henry*, who is a musician and also delicate, declines in health and finally follows her to England where he expires in her arms, chaperoned by his mother. *Mary* had resolved never to live with her lawful husband, but after *Henry's* death she agrees to do so on condition that she first spends a year travelling abroad without him. Such is the plot, no more and no less ludicrous than any other of its genre. Which incidents are fact and which fiction hardly matters, so imbued is the whole book with the spirit of its author.

There are many revealing touches; for instance, in the character of *Mary's* mother. This woman is fond of her son, but when *Mary*, 'the little blushing girl', approached her, she 'would send the awkward thing away'. Here perhaps lay the root of the real Mary's unquenched—and unquenchable—need for affection. Similarly when the mother in the story falls sick, *Mary* 'exercised her compassion so continually, that it became more than a match for self-love'. Starved of human affection, the youthful *Mary* turns to religion: 'Could she have loved her father or mother, had they returned her affection, she would not so soon, perhaps, have sought out a new world.' But this enlargement of vision only sharpens her apprehensions and increases her pain:

> She was miserable when beggars were driven from the gate without being relieved; if she could do it unperceived, she would give them her own breakfast, and feel gratified when, in consequence of it, she was pinched by hunger.

Faced with a mother's indifference and a father's vices, this sensitive child is driven into herself. Mary knew exactly how she

feels:
> She had once, or twice, told her little secrets to her mother; they were laughed at, and she determined never to do it again. In this manner was she left to reflect on her own feelings; and so strengthened were they by being meditated on, that her character early became singular and permanent. Her understanding was strong and clear, when not too clouded by her feelings; but she was too much the creature of impulse, and the slave of compassion.

How well she knew herself! How well she knew, too, the inexorable grinding of cause and effect, from the cradle to the grave. At the age of twenty-eight Mary had virtually written her own epitaph.

As in real life, the fictitious *Mary* is rescued from despair by her friendship with *Ann* (Fanny). But with hindsight even this is not quite so idyllic as it at first appeared. In setting down her recollections on paper, Mary could see both her own motives and her friend's character in a clearer light:
> She felt less pain on account of her mother's partiality to her brother, as she hoped now to experience the pleasure of being beloved; but this hope led her into new sorrows, and, as usual, paved the way for disappointment, Ann felt only gratitude; her heart was entirely engrossed by one object, and friendship could not serve as a substitute.

To *Mary*, with no other being to love, her friend was 'all the world' to her. Not so with *Ann*; like Fanny she was dreaming of romantic love, and her girl-friend was 'not as necessary to her happiness'. To compensate, *Mary* would imagine that *Ann* looked sick or unhappy: 'and then all her tenderness would return like a torrent, and bear away all reflection'. But was *Ann* (or Fanny) really worthy of this devotion? The mature Mary must have seen that she was not. She described her friend in the story as 'timid and irresolute, and rather fond of dissipation; grief only had power to make her reflect.' *Ann*, in fact, is shown up in every way as very much the inferior of *Mary:*
> In every thing it was not the great, but the beautiful, or the pretty, that caught her attention. And in composition, the polish of style, and the harmony of numbers, interested her much more than the flights of genius, or abstracted speculations.

The bond between the two girls was forged by circumstances

rather than any real affinity. *Mary* concludes sadly:
> She had not yet found the companion she looked for. Ann and she were not congenial minds, nor did she contribute to her comfort in the degree she expected.

This confession of disenchantment marked the end of a phase for Mary Wollstonecraft. After Fanny Blood's death she never again looked to her own sex for the satisfaction of her emotional or intellectual needs.

Another aspect of Mary's development which is retraced in this book is the religious awakening she experienced in adolescence:
> Many nights she sat up, if I may be allowed the expression, *conversing* with the Author of Nature, making verses, and singing hymns of her own composing. She considered also, and tried to discern what end her various faculties were destined to pursue; and had a glimpse of a truth, which afterwards more fully unfolded itself.

This 'truth' is then revealed, in terms which may more accurately be described as 'mystical' than religious. Mary was at her least convincing when she aspired to other worlds than this earth in which she was so deeply rooted:
> She thought that only an infinite being could fill the human soul, and that when other objects were followed as a means of happiness, the delusion led to misery, the consequence of disappointment. Under the influence of ardent affections, how often has she forgot this conviction, and as often returned to it again, when it struck her with redoubled force. Often did she taste unmixed delight; her joys, her ecstacies arose from genius.

The *Mary* of the story was fifteen when she made this discovery; so, no doubt, was the real Mary. Somewhere along the road she had already become aware that the 'infinite' was a manifestation of her own 'genius'. However, the fictitious *Mary* persisted with her religious studies, read Butler's *Analogy*, and came to the conclusion that she was 'a Christian from conviction'. In Lisbon, like the real Mary, she was shocked by the superstitions which clouded the Roman Catholic faith and which forced the Protestant burial of her friend to be carried out secretly: 'The body was stolen out of the house the second night'. On the state of Portugal in general Mary made some scathing comments:
> The Portuguese are certainly the most uncivilised nation in

Europe. Dr. Johnson would have said, "They have the least mind"... Taste is unknown; Gothic finery, and unnatural decorations, which they term ornaments are conspicuous in their churches and dress. Reverence for mental excellence is only to be found in a polished nation.

As she had visited no other country in Europe with which to compare Portugal, Mary's account may be regarded as somewhat prejudiced by her depressing memories of it.

In the hero of this story, *Henry*, Mary conjured up her vision of the perfect man. He has no obvious parallel in real life, being an amalgam of the most attractive characteristics of her masculine acquaintances from Joshua Waterhouse to Henry Gabell. His face was 'rather ugly', with 'strong lines of genius' (George Ogle, perhaps); his manners were 'awkward' (George Blood); he was 'a thinker' and had 'rational religious sentiments' (Richard Price); he was 'gentle, and easily to be intreated' (Joseph Johnson). But the conventions of the novel raised barriers to the union of *Henry* and *Mary*: each was already married to an uncongenial spouse. Inevitably they must part and *Mary* sails back to England alone. On the voyage she prays for strength to bring her composure of spirit—as was only right and proper for a heroine in such circumstances. But Mary Wollstonecraft was not a whole-hearted novelist, and truth keeps breaking through the façade of convential fiction. *Mary* cannot help adding a postscript to her prayer, which must effectively have nullified it: 'Do I indeed wish it [her spirit] to be composed—to forget my Henry?'

Mary knew that she did not. She could not relinquish her affections, any more than she could abandon her intelligence, for the sake of some abstract 'virtue' or 'truth'. A passage in her heroine's diary, which she may or may not have written on her own dark journey from Lisbon, conveys the essence of her spiritual conflict more starkly than anything she had so far expressed:

> I try to pierce the gloom, and find a resting-place, where my thirst of knowledge will be gratified, and my ardent affections find an object to fix them. Every thing material must change; happiness and this fluctuating principle is not compatible. Eternity, immateriality, and happiness,—where are ye? How shall I grasp the mighty and fleeting conceptions ye create?

In 1788, Mary was not able to answer these questions; she was still caught helplessly in the flux of being. She could only continue her journey by returning to a more mundane level. The fictitious *Mary* arrives back in London, and the real Mary steps in to make her comment:

> She knew none of the inhabitants of the vast city to which she was going; the mass of buildings appeared to her a huge body without an informing soul...
>
> She saw vulgarity, dirt, and vice—her soul sickened; this was the first time such complicated misery obtruded itself on her sight. Forgetting her own griefs, she gave the world a much indebted tear; mourned for a world in ruins.

This was a different view of Georgian London, but one that had evidently struck Mary forcibly as she contrasted it with the rural charms of Beverley or the elegance of Bath. The 'vast city' had still a population of less than a million and the condition of the people had greatly improved since the days of Hogarth's 'Gin Lane'. (What would she have made of the modern megalopolis?) It may be said that personal melancholy clouded her vision and that ugliness was in the eye of the beholder; but Mary did not invent the 'complicated misery' that afflicted the lives of the urban poor. The rise of the English radical movement was independent witness to that.

The story of *Mary* ends on a note of resignation. The heroine finally accepts the reality of her marriage, but this is a far cry from the conventional happy ending:

> Her delicate state of health did not promise long life. In moments of solitary sadness, a gleam of joy would dart across her mind. She thought she was hastening to that world *where there is neither marrying* nor giving in marriage.

An unkind critic might scent a whiff of sour grapes about that closing statement, italicised by the author. But there is little doubt that Mary's repudiation of marriage was genuine, springing as it did from her inability to reconcile its demands with those of her own complex nature. She had yet neither the philosophy nor the partner to enable her to resolve this conflict.

Instead, she sought relief from the *impasse* in the realm of fantasy. The excursion was a brief one and her record of the flight, *The Cave of Fancy,* is no more than a fragment. For this reason, perhaps, it has usually been dismissed as a whimsical digression on the part of an otherwise rational thinker. This may even have been Mary's first intention—to relieve the burden of thought by writing a fairy tale—but the work soon developed its own creative momentum. Imperfect and incomplete as it is, *The Cave of Fancy* enshrines one of its author's most profound insights. The style is artificial and the story unconvincing, but this scarcely matters. The form is only a means for the imaginative process to work through; and in this fragment it works to greater effect than in anything Mary Wollstonecraft ever wrote. It was as if, in *The Cave of Fancy*, she reached the outermost limit of her vision. Everything that came after was an elaboration of this insight, an attempt to clarify it and ultimately to live by it.

At the narrative level, the 'cave of fancy' of the title is the abode of a wise man *Sagestus* who lives on a solitary sea-shore in communion with the spirits of nature. One day a ship is wrecked on the shore and all lives are lost save for one young girl, whom *Sagestus* adopts and christens *Sagesta*. The rest of the story is hers, unfolding the familiar pattern of unhappy love and culminating in a loveless marriage entered upon for financial reasons. If there are autobiographical echoes here, they are much fainter than in *Mary*. In *The Cave of Fancy* the original impulses behind the story are far more successfully 'sublimated' in an art form. This dimension is reflected in Mary's definition of 'sensibility'. Previously, in *Mary*, she had utilised the vocabulary of the sentimental novel:

> Sensibility is indeed the foundation of all our happiness; but these raptures are unknown to the depraved sensualist, who is only moved by what strikes his gross senses; the delicate embellishments of nature escape his notice; as do the gentle and interesting affections.—But it is only to be felt; it escapes discussion.

Such a passive acceptance had little place in the real world of Mary Wollstonecraft: 'it is only to be felt; it escapes discussion' could never have satisfied her own enquiring mind. As she cogitated more deeply a very different aspect of 'sensibility' emerged through the mouth of *Sagestus*:

> To give the shortest definition of sensibility, replied the sage I should say that it is the result of acute senses, finely fashioned nerves, which vibrate at the slightest touch, and convey such clear intelligence to the brain, that it does not require to be arranged by the judgment.

This triple interaction of senses, nerves and brain, Mary now realised, was the key to her own transports of feeling; and to be thus endowed with 'sensibility' was not an unmixed blessing:

> Such persons instantly enter into the character of others, and instinctively discern what will give pain to every human being... Exquisite pain and pleasure is their portion; nature wears for them a different aspect than is displayed to common mortals. One moment it is a paradise; all is beautiful; a cloud arises, an emotion receives a sudden damp; darkness invades the sky, and the world is an unweeded garden.

An emotion 'receives a sudden damp'—how revealing that is! The little girl rebuffed by her mother (who would 'send the awkward thing away') rose again in the adolescent (seeking 'the pleasure of being beloved') and even in the adult, as Mary struggled to establish a mature relationship on equal terms. But at least she had the clue now to her own nature and could recognise the validity of her seemingly irrational impulses.

The ultimate revelation of *The Cave of Fancy*, beyond which Mary could progress no further, is expressed through the medium of a spirit summoned by *Sagestus* to tell her story. On hearing this tale *Sagesta* receives a flash of illumination of a blinding intensity. She has discovered the power of love:

> ... a strange association was made in my imagination; I thought of Galileo, who when he left the inquisition, looked upwards, and cried out, "*Yet it moves*". A shower of tears, like the refreshing drops of heaven, relieved my parched sockets; they fell disregarded on the table; and, stamping my foot, in an agony I exclaimed: "*Yet I love*".

Here was Mary's own declaration of faith, the banner nailed to her masthead: 'Yet I love'. As Galileo was ready to die for the love of truth, so Mary was ready to die (and very nearly did) for the truth of love. It was her vindication of the feminine principle in human nature as being of equal importance with the masculine—in the highest sense of both. If the (largely masculine) search for 'truth' had hitherto held priority, this was because the very nature of the exercise led to its articulate exposition. While men spun theories, in the dawn of civilisation, women conserved the species. Now, Mary was asserting, it was time for the male to temper his truth with compassion; and for the female to give backbone to her sensibility by its positive avowal.

Of course, saints of both sexes had been aware of this duality since the beginning of history; but their vision of perfection had usually been projected into 'heaven'. Christ taught that 'the kingdom of heaven is within you'. Mary Wollstonecraft looked neither heavenwards nor exclusively into her own soul for salvation. The vision she apprehended—and personified in her own life—was a social application of love. It was towards this end that all her efforts were henceforth directed, in her failures no less than in her triumphs. To judge her behaviour by any other moral criterion is irrelevant and misleading.

The Cave of Fancy was abandoned unfinished, and Mary never returned to its theme. It was as if, having discovered her first principle, she put it behind her in order to get on with the business of living in accordance with its dictates. Already, at the point where the fragment ends, she had applied the first lesson from her thesis: she found that the 'truth' of love could be a lie. *Sagesta*, separated from her chosen lover as *Mary* had been in the earlier story, reaches a more realistic conclusion:

> Remorse has not reached me, because I firmly adhered to my principles, and I have also discovered that I saw through a false medium. Worthy as the mortal was I adored, I should not long have loved him with the ardour I did, had fate united us, and broken the delusion the imagination so artfully wove.

With this firm repudiation of the romantic imagination Mary may have convinced herself that she had conquered her own heart, outgrown the vacillations of fancy, and separated the wheat of disinterested love from the chaff of passion. How little did she realise that she had come no further than the prologue, and the real drama of the heart's affections was only just beginning.

PART TWO: THE SOCIAL CHALLENGE

CHAPTER SIX

A Journalist in London: 1788–1790

True to her intention of abjuring 'the delusions of fancy' and henceforth living only 'to be useful', Mary threw herself wholeheartedly into her new work. Her knowledge of French, painfully acquired to equip her for the duties of a governess, now bore dividends as Johnson began to entrust her with some important works of translation. She also began to teach herself German, so that she might accept commissions in that language; and a little later she extended her studies to Italian for the same purpose. In May 1788 Johnson, together with a Scottish Unitarian banker, Thomas Christie, founded the *Analytical Review*, a monthly journal of criticism and comment. Mary served as editorial assistant for the magazine and was herself a regular contributor.

All this was a far cry from *The Cave of Fancy*. London in 1788 was a place for the critic rather than the creator. Samuel Johnson was dead, but his influence still prevailed. Joseph Johnson's *Analytical Review* speaks for itself, and one may surmise that Mary's brief flight of 'fancy' would not have been sympathetically received at his rationalist dinner parties. She may even have consigned it herself to the same category as her sister Eliza's irrational 'flights'. It is significant that she never tried to finish *The Cave of Fancy* after she came to London, nor thought of publishing it during her lifetime. This was left to Godwin in his collection of her *Posthumous Works*, and even then he may have had some misgivings about its value. In his *Memoirs* he referred to it simply as 'a sort of oriental tale' and stated that Mary 'thought proper' to lay it aside unfinished. So it is only by the merest chance that this vital key to her character survives at all.

She was certainly trying at this time to succeed in her new role. Mary Wollstonecraft, romantic visionary, was bolted and barred from Mary Wollstonecraft, journalist. She developed a 'vehement aversion', says Godwin, to being regarded 'in the character of an author'. The frank outpouring of feeling she had expressed in *Mary: a Fiction* had now become something of an embarrassment to her and she preferred not to call attention to it. 'I am going to be first of a new genus...', she wrote to Everina on 7th November 1787[1], on the crest of the wave. 'This project has long floated on my mind. You know I am not born to tread the beaten track—the peculiar bent of my nature pushes me on.' This was true, but Mary did not then realise how far her 'peculiar bent' was to drive her, even against her stated intentions. The new woman she envisaged was to prove scarcely a match for the old.

Meanwhile, one outstanding commitment remained to be fulfilled. Soon after coming to London Mary had mentioned to Everina that she would shortly be completing another book 'for young people'. *Original Stories from Real Life*, published early in 1788, was her only attempt at imaginative writing during her period of employment with Johnson. Godwin noted that her literary output during this period was useful rather than inspired. Her labours, he wrote in his *Memoirs*, though prolific were 'of little eclat'. *Original Stories*, though it was to prove the most popular of all Mary's books and quickly ran through five editions[2], may be included in this category. The didactic tone is set in the opening sentence of the preface: 'These conversations and tales are accommodated to the present state of society; which obliges the author to attempt to cure those faults by reason, which ought never to have taken root in the infant mind'. This is a forbidding start, but the severity soon melts as a warm human relationship is developed between the narrator (Mrs Mason) and the two little girls to whom the stories are addressed. Though there is much less autobiography in these tales than in *Mary: a Fiction*, some parallels can be seen with Mary's own experiences as governess to the daughters of Lady Kingsborough. These children, too, are the daughters of wealthy parents and have been spoilt by being left too much in the care of servants: 'They were shamefully ignorant, considering that Mary had been fourteen, and Caroline twelve years in the world'. How could the damage caused by a faulty upbringing best be put right? It was not an easy task, as the author's preface again indicated:

> The way to render instruction most useful cannot always be adopted; knowledge should be gradually imparted, and flow more from example than teaching; example directly addresses the senses, the first inlets to the heart; and the improvement of those instruments of the understanding is the object education should have constantly in view, and over which we have most power. But to wish that parents would, themselves, mould the ductile passions, is a chimerical wish, for the present generation have their own passions to combat with, and fastidious pleasures to pursue, neglecting those pointed out by nature: we must therefore pour premature knowledge into the succeeding one; and, teaching virtue, explain the nature of vice. Cruel necessity!

In her belief that primary education should be grounded on sensory perception rather than instruction, Mary was years ahead of her time. Johnson, however, objected to this preface because he feared it would upset some of the parents to whom it was addressed. But Mary refused to alter it, writing to him in an undated letter[3]:

> Though your remarks are generally judicious—I cannot *now* concur with you, I mean with respect to the preface, and have not altered it. I hate the usual smooth way of exhibiting proud humility. A general rule *only* extends to the majority—and, believe me, the few judicious parents who may peruse my book, will not feel themselves hurt—and the weak are too vain to mind what is said in a book intended for children.

Original Stories consists of a series of episodes each of which is designed to illustrate a fairly obvious moral precept, which the impeccable Mrs Mason is not slow to point out. The moral in most instances has a practical rather than a sentimental connotation, and it is certainly not to be despised, even by twentieth-century criteria. Indeed, although we have moved away from this kind of explicit moralising, the sentiments expressed in some of the stories are possibly closer in spirit to the twentieth century than to the eighteenth. This is particularly noticeable in Mary's attitude towards the natural creation. Whilst her contemporaries were thinking in terms of categories and species, Mary applied the methods of psychological analysis to the animal kingdom. In chapter two, on the treatment of animals, she wrote:

> Animals have not the affections which arise from reason, nor can they do good, or acquire virtue. Every affection, and impulse, which I have observed in them, are like our inferior emotions, which do not depend entirely on our will, but are involuntary; they seem to have been implanted to preserve the species, and make the individual grateful for actual kindness.

There was nothing unique in this plea for kindness to animals; many children's stories were being written on that theme. But Mary based her attitude on the natural rights of animals rather than on sentiment. She did not, like so many of her contemporaries, falsely endow them with human characteristics, as her next sentence shows:

> If you caress and feed them, they will love you, as children do, without knowing why; but we neither see imagination nor wisdom in them; and, what principally exalts man, friendship and devotion, they seem incapable of forming the least idea of.

This was a very different view from that put forward by Mrs Sarah Trimmer, for instance, in her charming tale about a family of robins which displayed remarkable moral qualities (*Fabulous Histories*, 1783). Mary believed that by showing kindness to animals man could best demonstrate his own moral superiority; this was particularly necessary in the case of children: 'It is only to animals that children *can* do good; men are their superiors'. The children, too, would benefit from this exercise, as Mrs Mason explains to Mary and Caroline (and here the author, too, is speaking). In her own childhood, she said, she delighted to feed the 'dumb family' that surrounded the house:

> This employment ... humanised my heart, while, like wax, it took every impression ... I, who never wantonly trod on an insect, or disregarded the plaint of the speechless beast, can now give bread to the hungry, physic to the sick, comfort to the afflicted ...

In the story of 'Crazy Robin' (chapter three), in which a poor, witless creature was sent to jail for debt while his wife and children starved to death, Mary Wollstonecraft put on record for the first time her new consciousness of events in the wider world:

> I told you, that Robin was confined in a jail. In France they

have a dreadful one, called the Bastille. The poor wretches who are confined in it live entirely alone; who have not the pleasures of seeing men or animals; nor are they allowed books. They live in comfortless solitude. Some have amused themselves by making figures on the wall; and others have laid straws in rows. One miserable captive found a spider; he nourished it for two or three years; it grew tame, and partook of his lonely meal.

Then, she continued, on the orders of a superior officer the jailor crushed the spider, and 'the unhappy wretch felt more pain when he heard the crush, than he had ever experienced during his long confinement.' This little episode encompasses the whole range of Mary's sensibility, which could be moved no less by the oppressiveness of a state, the misery of a single human being, or the stamping out of one harmless insect's life.

In other chapters *Original Stories* reinforces the lessons of *Thoughts on the Education of Daughters* on the virtues of truth, sincerity and simplicity. But Mary had a marvellous knack of adapting her material to the level of her readers. When addressing children she never talked down to them, but practised her own precept that the best kind of teaching is by personal example. If Mrs Mason's impregnable nobility becomes a little cloying within the confines of a story, it faithfully represented the author's own model of behaviour. It is this rendering of moral precept in terms of personal experience that distinguishes *Original Stories* from the didacticism of Thomas Day's *Sandford and Merton*. Mary did not fall into the error of that humane (and wealthy) liberal who saw something ennobling in the state of poverty. She knew at first hand that poverty was far more likely to degrade and brutalise than to ennoble; and she was beginning to realise that charity alone was not enough to absolve the conscience of the rich.

Another story in the volume is of interest in prefiguring Mary Wollstonecraft's later themes. In this episode a young girl seeks an escape from poverty and grief for a lost lover by marrying an elderly rake: 'He was ill-humoured, and his vicious habits rendered him a most dreadful companion.' Why then, asks little Mary with the logic of childhood, did she marry him? 'Because she was timid,' replies Mrs Mason—'but I have not told you all; the grief that did not break her heart, disturbed her reason; and her husband confined her in a mad-house.' The heroine of Mary's last book *The Wrongs of Woman* was also thus incarcerated. The moral here seems to be that girls should be taught to be independent, both financially and emotionally; and this plea was to become the main burden of *The Rights of Woman*. But there was also a more subtle implication, going beyond the lessons of childhood: that if natural emotion is denied a satisfactory outlet, not only the heart but the mind will be affected. Mary Wollstonecraft had learned this lesson, too, from her own experience. The nervous disorders that had afflicted her in Ireland, she wrote to George Blood in December 1786, 'are particularly distressing and they seem entirely to arise from the mind'.

By the end of the book Mary gave the impression of running out of steam. Mrs Mason's farewell advice to her charges would not have disgraced Thomas Day or Mrs Trimmer:

> Avoid anger; exercise compassion; and love truth. Recollect, that from religion your chief comfort must spring, and never neglect the duty of prayers. Learn from experience the comfort that arises from making known your wants and sorrows to the wisest and best of Beings, in whose hands are the issues, not only of this life, but of that which is to come.

Mary was at her least convincing when she tried to generalise her insights. Generalisations had little meaning for her, except as deductions from a concrete situation; and though she sometimes felt obliged, as here, to throw in a platitude for the general reading public, she could never give it any real conviction.

Mary Wollstonecraft made no further attempt to express her ideas in fiction until the last year of her life; by then, all her revolutions were behind her. Now, in London in 1788, they were just beginning. Dr Price and his Newington Green circle had already sown the seeds of dissent in her mind, but in those days Mary was too preoccupied with financial and personal difficulties to become actively involved in the political and social upheavals that were shaking Europe and the New World. The American struggle for independence came to a victorious conclusion in 1783. English radicals had played no mean part in it and Tom Paine had influenced the Declaration of Independence with his pamphlet *Common Sense*, published in Pennsylvania in 1776, and the same year Dr Price issued his *Observations on Civil Liberty* in which he linked the republican cause with the nonconformist conscience:

From one end of North America to the other they are fasting and praying. But what are we doing?—shocking thought—We are running wild after pleasure and forgetting everything serious and decent in Masquerades.—We are gambling in gaming houses; trafficking in boroughs; perjuring ourselves at elections; and selling ourselves for places—which side is Providence likely to favour?

The answer was soon clear: Providence was on the side of the rebels. But the revolution had a three-way effect. France, having encouraged the Americans for her own purposes was now hoist with her own petard. America was backing another revolution, and there was little the bankrupt French government could do to stop it. Britain meanwhile, despite Providence and Dr Price, went on quietly booming: consolidating her grip on Canada and India and getting a first toe-hold, through the person of Captain Cook, on the distant lands of Australia and New Zealand. As one empire collapsed, another was beginning to be born.

One consequence of the French bankruptcy was the sacking of the finance minister, Jacques Necker, who made a virtue out of necessity in his enforced retirement by writing a book *De l'Importance des Opinions Religieuses*. This work, in due course, arrived on Mary's desk for translation. It was a fortunate coincidence that Everina was then in Paris[5], and Mary immediately sent an urgent request to her sister for some first-hand information about the book and its author. 'It pleases me,' she wrote on 22nd March 1788, 'and I want to know the character of the man in domestic life and public estimation etc. and the opinion the French have of his literary abilities'. How typical it was of Mary that she was unwilling to consider a man's religious opinions until she knew what relation they bore to the way he actually lived.

The author was at least frank in his introduction, in explaining how he came to write the book: 'being no longer obliged to fix any attention on those particular arrangements of the public interest, which are necessarily connected with the operations of government, I found myself abandoned, as it were, by all the important concerns of life'. Mary evidently rated it more highly, for she wrote to George Blod on 16th May that she had 'lately been very busy translating a work of importance, and have made a very advantageous contract for another'.

Necker represented a straightforward job of translation. Mary put little of herself into it. Despite her obeisance to piety, the subject was not one to fire her imagination. Her sense of morality went deeper than the mere expression of 'religious opinions'. The other 'work of importance' to which she referred, however, was much more after her own mode of thinking, as the title itself suggests: *Elements of Mortality* (on which she must already have been working, although the first of its three volumes in English was not published until October 1790) was a translation from the German of Rev. C. G. Saltzmann's *Moralisches Elementarbuch*. The book was devised for the instruction of children and had similarities to Mary's *Original Stories*. She drew a parallel herself in her preface to Saltzmann: 'All the pictures were drawn from real life, and that I highly approve of this method, my having written a book on the same plan is the strongest proof.' She explained that she started the translation merely as an exercise in German, only to discover that 'chance had thrown in my way a very rational book, and that the writer coincided with me in opinion respecting the method which ought to be pursued to form the heart and temper, or, in other words, to inculcate the first principles of morality'.

The preface also reveals something of Mary's developing attitudes as her knowledge of the world extended beyond the British horizon. She had already acquired an antipathy to the French way of life as exemplified in the *ancien régime*: 'If it had been a French work I should, probably, have had to curtail many smooth compliments, that I might not have led my little readers to the very verge of falsehood'. Looking further afield, she explained why she had seen fit to add to Saltzmann's stories an episode of her own: 'I have here inserted a little tale, to lead children to consider the Indians as their brothers, because the omission of this subject appeared to be a chasm in a well-digested system'.

The Indians—in this case the Red Indians of North America—were no doubt closer to the British consciousness, and conscience, than to the German at this moment of conquest and revolution in the New World, as the black men of Africa were to be a century later. Mary's story describes a soldier in America who, fleeing from a body of 'copper coloured men', falls from his horse and breaks his leg. He is found by an Indian, 'one of those men, whom we Europeans with white complexions call savages'. The man carries the soldier to his cabin and cares for him until he

is strong enough to return to his comrades:
> Every day did he hunt for food, and dress it for his enemy, and when he could limp along carried him within sight of his camp, and pressing his sick brother's hand against his forehead, he prayed the Great Spirit to take care of him, and conduct him safe to his own country.

If Mary's internationalising of Saltzmann's morality was her own invention, the author was himself an innovator in another sphere. His 'Introductory Address for Parents' is outspoken on the need for what we would now call sex education. The best way of upholding chastity, he believed, would be 'to speak to children of the organs of generation as freely as we speak of the other parts of the body and explain to them the noble use which they are designed for'. This passage may have influenced Mary when she came to deal with the subject herself in *The Rights of Woman*. But there was another good reason for expounding the mechanics of procreation: to illustrate the sheer miracle of any work of nature. In one of the stories a small boy is reproved for wishing to cut off the ears and tail of a mouse. How much is Saltzmann, and how much is Mary, in this enchanting description of the tiny creature's structure?—

> Look at this little ear through which it hears all that passes round it: through this organ it was warned when your pursued it: and these pretty eyes, in which the forms of all the objects before it are painted: and these sharp teeth, with which it can gnaw the hardest grain: and these neatly turned paws: this skin as soft as velvet. But you would be still more astonished if you could see its inside; if you could observe how every thing passes there to preserve life; how the little stomach dissolves the food; how it separates the best juices, and carries them by very fine channels, still further; how flesh, blood, and bones, are formed of them; and how the excrements pass through the guts and intestines. Put your hand on its breast, and feel how its heart beats, to push the blood through the little veins.

The marvels of nature were, of course, just beginning to be systematised; and in this very year, 1788, the Linnean Society had been founded for the study of natural history. A whole world of science was in creation: not only in natural history but in chemistry, physics, astronomy, engineering and medicine. A new generation was eager to absorb new knowledge and never was informed instruction more necessary, as science struggled to break free from its enveloping chrysalis of theology. Mary, however, was no scientist; neither was the Rev. Saltzmann. Their new worlds were still entwined with the old—as their joint projection into the realms of outer space indicates. Undoubtedly, says the clergyman in this episode, there are people in the stars:

> Cut a tree in two, and you will see that it contains a little city, in which there is a multitude of inhabitants. How many thousands of insects live in a single cheese! If God thus fills every little corner of the earth, do you think that he would leave those great globes like a desart? Would he have gathered together all the living creatures upon such a small point as our earth?

The new science of astronomy is harnessed to the omnipotence of God, as he continues:

> The stars which we see are only a small part of the universe. Look at that broad white strip which crosses the sky, it is all composed of stars, which men discovered through good telescopes, and who knows how many thousand are still above them! God has made all these, they belong to God—*Oh God, how great art thou!*

The power of God is illustrated not only in the majesty of the universe, but in the smallest atom of which it is composed:

> With the smallest things He can produce the greatest effects. What, in comparison with man, is a caterpillar? nevertheless, when He causes these insects to multiply abundantly, He can, by their means, destroy the trees of a whole country. What is smaller than a drop of blood? yet, when it does not circulate through my body, but becomes corrupt, it will soon kill me. A single spark of fire, if it fell into combustible matter, in a few hours might burn our whole city to ashes.

This kind of natural theology was very much to the taste of mid-eighteenth century attitudes, and Mary Wollstonecraft never seriously questioned it. She was always concerned with the social applications of morality rather than with its natural, or supernatural, origins.

It must have seemed to Mary at this time that she was becoming type-cast as an expert in moral instruction for the young. During 1789 she undertook the preparation of two more works in the same *genre*. The first was an anthology with the grandiose title *The Female Reader; or Miscellaneous Pieces, in Prose and Verse; Selected from the Best Writers, and Disposed under Proper Heads; for the Improvement of Young Women.* Mercifully perhaps, no surviving copy of this formidable work has been traced[6]. The second book, *Young Grandison*, consisted of a series of didactory letters compiled by a Dutch author, Madame de Cambon, which had first been translated into English by Rev. John Hall, a Scottish minister resident in Rotterdam. Mary's extensively revised version was published by Johnson, without attribution, in 1790; again, no copy appears to have survived.

If this had been her only occupation, one can imagine Mary getting somewhat restive under the yoke of repetitive hack-work. But during the same period she was also busily engaged as a contributor to the *Analytical Review*. It has been calculated that she was responsible for nineteen review articles from July to December 1788, the first few months of the journal's existence. But in 1789 she supplied the astonishing total of 153 articles; while in 1790 her score reached 99[7]. There is, however, an element of speculation in these estimated figures since many of the articles appeared unsigned. One review certainly written by Mary was the notice of *A Sermon written by the late Samuel Johnson, LL. D., for the Funeral of his Wife*, which was published in the *Analytical Review* in August 1788 and was thus one of her earliest contributions. She had written to Joseph Johnson the previous month: 'I was quite glad, last night, to feel myself affected by some passages in Dr J——'s sermon on the death of his wife.—I seemed (suddenly) to *find my soul again.*—It has been for some time I cannot tell where.' She added a somewhat defensive postscript:

> If you do not like the manner in which I reviewed Dr J——'s s— on his wife, be it known unto you—I *will not* do it in any other way.—I felt some pleasure in paying a just tribute of respect to the memory of a man—who, in spite of his faults, I have an affection for—I say *have*, for I believe he is somewhere—*where* my soul has been gadding perhaps; but *you* do not live by conjectures.

Mary seems to be smarting a little from the impact of her radical friends. Not only her own emotional temperament, but her equivocal position as an 'independent' woman made her doubly susceptible to criticism. Mary Wollstonecraft's consciousness of the inferior status accorded to women by society was already finding expression in the pages of the *Analytical Review*. Through this medium she launched an attack on her erstwhile hero Rousseau and extolled the good sense of Mrs Catherine Macaulay's *Letters on Education;* she was to expand on both themes later in the *Rights of Woman*.

Nevertheless, despite these natural handicaps it is clear that by the autumn of 1790 Mary had won recognition in London's intelligentsia. Thanks to Johnson's publishing acumen and humane sympathies she was at home with some of the most distinguished names in literature, the arts and science. His authors included William Cowper, William Blake, Joseph Priestley, Erasmus Darwin, Tom Paine and Horne Tooke[8]. Amongst habitual guests at his dinner-table—Johnson's hospitality was legendary—were to be found, according to Godwin: the mathematician, John Bonnycastle; George Anderson, 'accountant to the board of control'; Dr George Fordyce, physician and a nephew of the famous preacher; and the painter, Henry Fuseli. Godwin himself also joined the company on occasion, as did Tom Paine whenever he was in England. Nor was it an exclusively masculine club. Mary's presence was assured by virtue of her position with Johnson and she may have been surprised at first to find other intellectual women in his circle. Two of the most notable were Anna Laetitia Barbauld, daughter of the renowned Dr Aiken and herself a respected writer on education; and Elizabeth Inchbald, a former actress widowed at the age of twenty-six who struggled to maintain herself and her child by writing novels and plays. These women, like Mary Wollstonecraft, had little in common with 'blue-stockings' in the genre of Mrs Montagu, Mrs Vesey and Mrs Chapone who had established their influence a decade earlier on the model of the *bas bleus* of the French salons; for them, learning was cultivated as a status symbol rather than as a means to social improvement and in their heyday they had counted Dr Johnson and Edmund Burke amongst their most prized 'lions'. The real dividing line, then as always, was not the artificial barrier of sex-discrimination but inherent attitudes to life.

Mary was on the side of change and eagerly sharpening her tools the better to effect it. Her struggle for independence was only a first step in the quest for a better life, not only for herself but for her sister-women and fellow-men. But independence was a fragile plant and must be tended without remission, so that the new 'professional' woman had literally no time for sentiment. Whatever the state of her emotional temper—and it was always in some sort of state—Mary had no option but to apply herself rigorously to her chosen career. From 1788 to 1790, work came first. Johnson later described this time as 'the most active in her life'[9]. Three immediate objects dominated her labours: to achieve financial stability; to be a useful member of society; and to settle her younger sisters and brothers in respectable situations. Though Mary was never to be quite solvent, her employment by Johnson as reader, editorial assistant and book-reviewer brought her a regular income as well as a more worthy status. This remuneration, together with the provison of a lodging in George Street, secured her the necessities of life. Anything left over went towards the support of her family, on whom (Johnson told Godwin) she spent at least two hundred pounds in this period. Mary was by nature abstemious, caring little for her own comfort; while her indifference to personal adornment approached self-neglect. She has been described at this time of her life as 'a philosophical sloven: her usual dress being a habit of coarse cloth, such as is now worn by milk-women, black worsted stockings, and a beaver hat, with her hair hanging lank about her shoulders'[10]. This unsympathetic view ignores the many natural charms to which others have borne witness: a well-proportioned figure, expressive features, light brown eyes and a mass of auburn hair. If these attractions were not immediately obvious this was due to her mode of life. All work and no play never made Mary Wollstonecraft dull, but it took its toll in mental depression and physical debility.

In January 1788 Mary had both her sisters at George Street. Eliza was unhappy in Leicestershire and did not wish to return to Market Harborough after the Christmas break, but she was finally persuaded to do so until a more congenial situation could be found. Some months later an opportunity arose in a school at Putney run by a Madame Bregantz, where for a time all seemed well. Poor Eliza! She had known little happiness or security since the break-up of her marriage. Everina too was restless and had resigned from her post at Henley. What was to be done with her now? Somehow, in February, Mary scraped together the money and sent her to stay with a family in Paris to improve her knowledge of French; she was to remain in France until the summer of 1790. This must have been a relief to Mary, who had found her youngest sister something of a trial. She was not very sympathetic when Everina wrote complaining of the difficulties she was meeting in her new situation. 'It is proper that some people should be roused,' Mary wrote to George Blood on 3rd March, 'or they would be devoted to pleasure'. As for herself, she was now alone again and, she confessed to George, 'too studious'. Her nervous complaints had returned and 'the thick blood lagging in the veins, gives melancholy power to harass the mind'. She was cheered, however, by Johnson's goodness to her: 'I often visit his hospitable mansion—where I meet some sensible men, at any rate my worthy friend—who bears with my infirmities'. The 'worthy friend' was presumably Johnson himself. Again, on 16th May, she wrote to George: 'You would love Mr. Johnson, if you knew how *very* friendly he has been to the *princess*'. Despite her attacks of melancholy Mary did not regret being alone and she confided to George that she was determined '*never* to have any of my sisters to live with me'. When Everina subsequently returned from France Mary sent her to join Eliza at Putney. Mme Bregantz was evidently sympathetic to the sisters, and she was to enter into Mary's life again.

It also fell to Mary to look after her two younger brothers' interests. James had lodged with her for a time after a spell at sea, and she then arranged for him to study mathematics under Mr Bonnycastle at Woolwich naval academy and so qualify himself as an officer. He later joined Admiral Hood's fleet as a midshipman and subsequently became a lieutenant. Charles, however, presented more serious problems. He had quarrelled with his elder brother Edward—who seems to have been a singularly unhelpful character—and left his employment. Mary then found him a clerkship with another attorney, but he was dismissed from this post—for reasons not stated—and took himself over to Ireland. Mary wrote to a Mr Cristall, father of one of her friends, in March 1789 that 'Charles is now at Cork eating the bread of idleness, and living on the kindness of relatives who do not respect him'[11]. She also wrote to George Blood on 16th April, begging him to keep an eye on Charles and to try and find him some employment. The young man had evidently been behaving very badly; for she wrote that she had been vexed and deeply wounded by his conduct. Like Everina, Charles was too frivolous for Mary's puritanical tastes: 'I know he will plunge into pleasure while he has a farthing left,' she added glumly.

As if this were not enough, Mary was also saddled with her father's chaotic affairs. Mr Wollstonecraft was still living in Wales and was sinking ever more deeply into debt, drink and squalor. For a time another relative took over the management of his affairs, apparently with little success, and inevitably the job of sorting out the muddle devolved upon Mary—assisted by the kindly Johnson, 'with no little trouble to both of us'[12]. But despite their combined efforts no way could be found of maintaining Mr Wollstonecraft in solvency, and Mary continued to give him financial support for as long as she lived.

She was at the same time constantly concerned with the affairs of her adopted family, the Bloods. When George, and then his parents, had migrated to Ireland, a younger sister Caroline was for some reason left behind in London. Without parental support she had fallen into bad company, and so desperate was her situation in January 1788 that Mary reported to George that she had been placed in the workhouse after being found by the parish officers 'in a dreadful situation'. Two weeks later she wrote again requesting Mr Blood to send ten pounds to buy clothes for the girl. She was hopeful that her old friend at Newington Green, Mrs Burgh, would take charge of Caroline; failing that, she would have to be sent to her parents in Ireland. Evidently Mrs Burgh came to the rescue, and a year later Mary was able to write that Caroline was 'very well and industrious', having been placed in a domestic situation. But it was Mary who paid off the debt to the workhouse for her board and lodging.

Mary's letters to George in this period strike a very different note from the feverish intensity of their earlier correspondence. Now she wrote to him in the guise of an elder sister, with a detachment befitting her position as an independent professional woman: she was concerned about his prospects rather than her own. Mr Blood had eventually succeeded in finding at situation in Dublin, and since Fanny's death Hugh Skeys had returned there. Mary was asking George in March 1788 whether he had decided to go into his father's office or go into partnership with Skeys. Apparently he did neither, for the following February she counselled him not to entangle himself in the affairs of a 'Mr. Home'; and in September she urged him not to be a slave to his father's selfishness. In the same letter Mary suggested that if George could take a week off from his 'business' they might meet in Wales—where presumbably she was going to visit her father. But there is no record that he came, and two months later Mary was reproaching him in something like her old style, accusing him of a long silence and then an 'unfriendly' letter. Indeed, she went so far as to say that only the fact of his being Fanny's brother preserved her affection for him: 'I do not think it probable that I shall ever be able to respect and trust you as I habitually did', she concluded. Mary still suffered intermittently from the long drawn-out battle with her own emotional needs.

That this conflict was never far from the surface, even when outwardly life flowed smoothly and busily, is revealed in Mary's correspondence with Joseph Johnson, who had replaced George as the confidant of her innermost thoughts and feelings. Soon after she settled in George Street Mary was writing that she still missed the Kingsborough children, especially the eldest daughter Margaret: 'I miss her innocent caresses—and sometimes indulge a pleasing hope, that she may be allowed to chear my childless age—if I am to live to be old'[13]. She continued:

> At any rate, I may hear of the virtues I may not contemplate—and my reason may permit me to love a female.—I now allude to —. I have received another letter from her, and her childish complaints vex me—indeed they do.

Mary seems to be saying here that if she cannot herself become a wife and mother she can at least enjoy the affection of a friend; and that it is perhaps easier to 'love a female' because there is no conflict between reason and passion. Yet in the next breath she spoke of her vexation with her unnamed female correspondent (to whom she may or may not have been referring in the previous sentence: 'I now allude to . . .' could mean a change of subject). Throughout her life Mary had devoted friends of both sexes, which is a tribute to her own breadth of sympathy; but she could never be satisfied only with the love of women.

Once Johnson had won Mary's trust she saw no reason to withhold from him any aspect of her real self. The façade of the brisk and efficient professional woman soon peeled away. She may keep meticulous accounts of her income and expenditure, study foreign languages to increase her proficiency, turn in her copy on time for the avaricious maw of the *Analytical Review*—but still the original, authentic Mary kept breaking through: unhappy, insecure, and so wretchedly frustrated as to undermine her health. The catalogue of miseries, so precisely recorded, has even its comic side. At one moment, as the result of a fancied injury she had caused to an acquaintance, she was plunged into a hell of self-despisal. She described the result to Johnson: 'My stomach has been so suddenly and violently affected, I am unable to lean over the desk'[14]. A little later, she revealed her hyper-sensitive response to some critical remark from him, made worse by her fear that the criticism was justified[15]:

> You made me very low-spirited last night, by your manner of talking. You are my only friend—the only person I am *intimate* with. —I never had a father, or a brother—you have been both to me, ever since I knew you—yet I have sometimes been very petulant.—I have been thinking of those instances of ill-humour and quickness, and they appear to me like crimes.

To be so deeply hurt by a casual remark was a sign of nervous debility. Mary was evidently descending to one of her periodic nadirs, and in the next letter she seems to have reached it. This has often been quoted, by both defence and prosecution, in the trial of Mary's good name. Surely no other chief witness ever provided so much evidence both for and against herself! She had been very ill, she said, and it was 'more than fancy'. In this low state she took stock of herself and not surprisingly reached some gloomy conclusions[16]:

> I am a mere animal, and instinctive emotions too often silence the suggestions of reason ... I acknowledge that life is but a jest—and often a frightful dream—yet catch myself every day searching for something serious—and feel real misery from the disappointment. I am a strange compound of weakness and resolution! However, if I must suffer, I will endeavour to suffer in silence. There is certainly a great defect in my mind—my wayward heart creates its own misery.—Why I am made thus I cannot tell; and, till I can form some idea of the whole of my existence, I must be content to weep and dance like a child—long for a toy, and be tired of it as soon as I get it.
>
> We must each of us wear a cap and bells; but mine, alas! has lost its bells, and is grown so heavy, I find it intolerably troublesome.—Goodnight! I have been pursuing a number of

strange thoughts since I began to write, and have actually wept and laughed immoderately.—Surely I am a fool—.

Mary was always harder on herself than on others, and this analysis is no exception. She could be as foolish as the next woman, often more so, and well she knew it—'my wayward heart creates its own misery'. But she was not, and could never be, 'a fool'.

She knew that too, with her mind if not her heart; which was why, once purged of this crisis, she was able to take up her daily life as if nothing had happened. Soon she was requesting a German grammar, and flinging herself into her studies again: 'While I live, I am persuaded, I must exert my understanding to procure an independence, and to render myself useful.' 'You perceive this is not a gloomy day,' she added, and expressed her gratitude to Johnson for his 'humane and *delicate* assistance': 'too often should I have been out of patience with my fellow creatures, whom I wish to love!—Allow me to love you, my dear sir, and call friend a being I respect'.

As ever with Mary, the relationship continued to have its ups and downs. If on some occasions she was cast down by the least murmur of criticism, at other times she replied with spirit. Here Mary took a much more positive view of herself[17]:

I thought you *very* unkind, nay, very unfeeling, last night. My cares and vexations—I will say what I allow myself to think—do me honour, as they arise from my disinterestedness and *unbending* principles; nor can that mode of conduct be a reflection on my understanding, which enables me to bear misery, rather than selfishly live for myself alone. I am not the only character deserving of respect, that has had to struggle with various sorrows—while inferior minds have enjoyed local fame and present comfort.—Dr. Johnson's cares almost drove him mad—but, I suppose, you would quietly have told him, he was a fool for not being calm, and that wise men striving against the stream, can yet be in good humour.

Johnson had evidently, for once, lost patience with Mary's tale of woes; or of her family's woes, with which he was reluctantly involved. Perhaps he had been tactless enough to advise her to tone down those 'unbending principles' when expressing her opinions in the *Analytical Review*.

But Mary's real wrath was saved for the unfortunate

gentleman (not named) who had the temerity to propose to her—she suspected, at Johnson's prompting:

Mr. — called on me just now.—pray did you know his motive for calling?—I think him impertinently officious.—He had left the house before it occurred to me in the strong light it does now, or I should have told him so —my poverty makes me proud—I will not be insulted by a superficial puppy ...

In two further letters, addressed to the 'superficial puppy' himself[18], Mary's indignation knows no bounds; indeed, it goes beyond the bounds of reason. In a calmer mood, she might just as easily have refused her suitor with courtesy, dignity and compassion. Here, one cannot help feeling, 'the lady doth protest too much':

... let me first tell you, that in my *unprotected* situation, I make a point of never forgiving a *deliberate insult*—and in that light I consider your late officious conduct. It is not according to my nature to mince matters—I will then tell you in plain terms, what I think.

The main burden of her complaint was that the man was no more than an acquaintance, that she had never considered him even as a friend let alone a prospective husband: therefore, by her reasoning, his conduct was 'rude and cruel'. A rather odd comment follows:

If my friend, Mr. Johnson, had made the proposal—I should have been severely hurt—have thought him unkind and unfeeling, but not *impertinent*.

Mary could only have meant, in this context, that the 'proposal' might have appeared less insulting if it had been conveyed to her indirectly by way of Johnson. There was no question of a romantic attachment between Mary and her employer: he was father, brother and friend, but never a prospective husband. (Johnson had no such attachment to any woman and died unmarried.) Even so, she would have felt 'sorely hurt' by his intercession. She now explained why:

I am, sir, poor and destitute.—Yet I have a spirit that will never bend, or take indirect methods, to obtain the consequence I despise; nay, if to support life was to act contrary to my principles, the struggle would soon be over. I can bear anything but my own contempt.

The struggle for independence was still not won; Mary knew that to compromise at this stage would be fatal to her larger aim. It was perhaps to strengthen her own resolve that she exaggerated the difficulties, for she was certainly not 'destitute' at this time. But even with regular employment her financial position was precarious and her commitments always exceeded her income. To think of marriage in these circumstances, she asserted, would be 'prostituting my person for a maintenance'. We may surmise, from the sternness of her tone, that this was the first time the choice had been offered and Mary was taking a firm stand against temptation. She ended her letter with a little flourish of bravado: 'I tell you, sir, I am POOR—yet can live without your benevolent exertions'.

Mary had less compunction about accepting the 'benevolent exertions' of Joseph Johnson. She could tell him, in very different tones, that she was 'head and ears in debt' but had not 'that kind of pride which makes some dislike to be obliged to those they respect'[19]. On the contrary, she continued:

> I thankfully recollect that I have received unexpected kindness from you and a few others.—So reason allows, what nature impels me to—for I cannot live without loving my fellow-creatures—nor can I love them, without discovering some virtue.

It was one of Mary's most endearing characteristics—as Johnson must have found, to his cost—always to discover some high moral purpose in her chronic indebtedness to her friends.

In the late summer of 1790 Mary went to stay for three weeks in Wiltshire as the guest of Rev. Henry Gabell, now married to his 'Ann' and recently appointed headmaster of Warminster school. The coach on which she travelled was delayed by a slight accident at Salisbury, so that the journey took two days. Inveterate traveller as she was, Mary's journeys were usually fraught with such minor disasters. She had only to step inside a carriage for it to overturn or board a sailing-ship for the winds to veer sharply in a contrary direction. However, eventually she arrived safely at her destination, as she wrote to Everina at Putney on 23rd August. Her description of her hostess here shows a felicity in characterisation that is sadly lacking in her works of fiction. Mary the novelist was always overshadowed by the propagandist and she could never rest content with a character for its own sake. Yet how clearly Mrs Gabell shines through these few haphazard

phrases:
> She has it is true light full eyes, with scarcely any eyebrows, a fair complexion and soft brown hair; yet she is rather a fine, than a pretty woman—and has an expression of bluntness instead of the gentleness I expected to see in her countenance. Her person is large and well-proportioned—she made me think of a Doric pillar, for proportion without beauty—symmetry without grace, appear in her person, and activity and ease in her gestures ... she manages her large family with a degree of cleverness that surprises me, considering how little experience she has had.

Little remains to be said about Ann Gabell—or about Mary's attitude to her. The 'large family' she referred to must have been the boys of Warminster school, since the Gabells were newly married. Perhaps Mary could not help feeling a twinge of regret that it was not she, with her eminently suitable qualifications, who was occupying this position.

At first, however, the domestic bliss of this household filled Mary with delight. 'You can scarcely imagine,' she told Everina, '*how much* happiness and innocent fondness constantly illumines the eyes of this good couple—so that I am never disgusted by the frequent *bodily* displays of it'. Nevertheless, this was not everything: 'I caught myself wishing this morning,' she continued, 'for a sight of my little room, and a ramble to St. Paul's Churchyard'. Mary the country girl was now a Londoner by adoption and needed the stimulus of the city to offset rural stagnation. By the end of two weeks she was beginning to feel something of an intruder in this garden of Eden and to be conscious of her own apartness. 'My die is cast,' she wrote to Everina, '—I could not now resign intellectual pursuits for domestic comforts—and yet I think I could form an idea of a more *elegant* felicity—where mind chasten (sic) sensation, and rational converse gave a little dignity to fondness'. Mary was reluctant to abandon her dream of a union of heart and mind; but if she had to choose between them, she would still sacrifice her feelings. What she now saw as the smugness of the 'good couple' also brought an awareness of unsuspected virtues in her own family. The occasion produced a rare compliment to her sisters: 'Will you think me saucy when I say, that you and Eliza appear to me to (sic) *very* clever, and *most* agreeable women, compared with the Goddess of this place?' By

10th September, shortly before her return to London, she was thoroughly disillusioned with her hosts, as she again confided to Everina:

> *happiness* is not a softener of the heart—and from them I should always expect little acts of kindness and grateful civilities—but never any great exertion, which might disturb, for a moment, the even tenor of their loves and lives.

Mary had evidently been reading Milton, and she wrote that his 'first pair'—like this latter-day Adam and Eve—seemed to her inferior beings because they were able to 'find happiness in a world like this'. From the comfort of a country vicarage the world might indeed seem an earthly paradise, but Mary knew better. She had come a long way in two years, from her painful dependency as a governess through authorship to professional journalism. In England, Wales and Ireland she had seen many conditions of men—most of them nearer to hell than to heaven. In London, at the centre of events, she was hearing of many more—and hearing too that such conditions were not immutable. At Johnson's dinner-table she had sipped the wine of dissent, and her thoughts were fixed on revolution.

CHAPTER SEVEN

The Radical Revolt: 1789–1790

It was Mary's old friend Dr Richard Price, the dissenting minister, who really set the cat among the pigeons and brought home to the British breakfast table the *fait accompli* of the French Revolution. Before his famous sermon of 4th November 1789, and Burke's even more famous reply, the Revolution as far as England was concerned had been little more than a hobby of the intelligentsia.

Edmund Burke, however, was expressing his disquiet about events across the channel within weeks of the fall of the Bastille. He wrote to Lord Charlemont on 9th August 1789 that England was 'gazing with astonishment at a French struggle for Liberty and not knowing whether to blame or to applaud ... The spirit it is impossible not to admire; but the old Parisian ferocity has broken out in a shocking manner'[1]. His forebodings seemed to be confirmed two months later, when on 6th October the King and Queen of France were forced out of the palace of Versailles by the Revolutionary Army and confined at the Tuileries in Paris. This, at least, was Burke's construction of the event; others saw it differently.

Dr Price, as a Christian minister, did not seem unduly alarmed. His 'Discourse on the Love of our Country', though described as a 'sermon', was in fact an address delivered at the Old Jewry meeting-house to the annual meeting of the Revolution Society. Despite its name, this was a perfectly respectable institution which had been established to commemorate the 'glorious' English Revolution of 1688. The centenary of the Society, coinciding with the birth of the French Revolution, naturally brought an added excitement to the meeting of 1789. It was almost inevitable that the opportunity should be taken to send a congratulatory message to the French National Assembly. This proposal was made by Dr Price himself and the message was conveyed by the Society's chairman, Lord Stanhope, to the President of the Assembly—not really such a shocking thing to do, bearing in mind that this office was then held by the Archbishop of Aix (later, like so many of the Revolution's founding fathers, he fled from France—but this is to be wise after the event). Dr Price's discourse, the congratulatory address and the archbishop's reply were all subsequently published by the Revolution Society, and it was after reading these papers in January 1790 that Edmund Burke started to compose his *Reflections*.

It was the activities of the English revolutionists rather than actual events in France that swung Burke into the attack[2]. As an Anglican with Roman Catholic sympathies, his natural antipathy to the religion of the Dissenters was reinforced by their political activities. Their support of Pitt against the Whigs in the election of 1784 (before his own change of party) had contributed to his fall from office. Burke's attack on Dr Price may therefore have been not entirely unbiased. Both Mary Wollstonecraft and Tom Paine, in their replies to his *Reflections,* were to accuse him of vindictiveness.

The theme of Price's discourse which gave rise to Burke's savage attack was quite simply the brotherhood of man. Love of our own country was not enough, he proclaimed: we should learn to see ourselves as 'citizens of the world'. He had even proposed, a few years earlier, that an international tribunal should be set up for the settlement of disputes. Richard Price, it has been said 'followed Leibnitz, as he anticipated Kant'[3]. This was no callow cleric, defying the establishment for the sake of notoriety. Yet Price remained true to orthodox, eighteenth-century thinking in his belief that intellectual enlightenment would solve all human problems. 'Ignorance is the parent of bigotry, intolerance, persecution and slavery,' he declared. 'Inform and instruct mankind and these evils will be excluded.' He hailed the French Revolution because he saw it as a means of ending the traditional enmity between France and England: if the two countries could be united in a free partnership, not only would they stop fighting each other but they could together act to prevent wars everywhere. He hailed the Revolution also as a blow struck for liberty:

> And now methinks I see the ardour for liberty catching and spreading, a general amendment beginning in human affairs; the dominion of kings changed for the dominion of laws, and the dominion of priests giving way to the dominion of reason and conscience.

It is easy, with hindsight, to see Dr. Price's vision of the future as partial and naive. Yet without such a vision, and visionaries to express it, even the most halting steps of progress could never be made.

This, for all his powerful rhetoric and deeper consciousness of human destiny, was Burke's blind spot: he did not want progress. He did not really want to face the future at all. He had passed his own personal climacteric of influence and power and looked only to the glories of the past. Into his *Reflections*, published on 1st November 1790, he poured a whole philosophy of politics and patriotism, of church and state, of rulers and ruled. The French Revolution was no more than the occasion. His real target was the English radical movement which, in his opinion, was threatening to break up the established social order; an order which seemed to him to encompass the sum of political wisdom—past, present and to come.

Since the text is easily available to the interested reader, it is not necessary here to spell out Burke's *Reflections* in detail. His main themes emerge in the reactions the book provoked. As Burke was a reply to Price, so Mary Wollstonecraft's *A Vindication of the Rights of Men* was a reply to Burke, to be followed in hot pursuit by Tom Paine's more famous *The Rights of Man*. Mary's *Vindication* appeared in December 1790, rushed into print by the faithful Johnson almost as it was written. The first, anonymous edition was followed in the same month by a second issued under her own name. Tom Paine published the first part of his two-volume *critique* the following March. Johnson had refused to print it, on the grounds that certain passages were treasonable, and Paine had to go to another more daring or less scrupulous publisher, Jordan of Fleet Street. Perhaps Johnson wanted to give his favourite *protegée* the first right of reply.

Mary went to her task with a will and in a mood of high indignation: after all, she was rushing to the defence not only of a principle but of a friend. Dr Price, she believed, had been grossly maligned by Burke and she was eager to clear his good name. Despite the spur of indignation, however, she is said by Godwin to have flagged half-way through the writing of her *Vindication*; only the goading of Johnson persuaded her to finish the book. Her hesitation is not really surprising. She may well have wondered whether she had not bitten off more than she could chew in taking on in public one of the country's most influential men. Who was this Mary Wollstonecraft? An unknown woman without power or wealth, having none of the right connections—not even a husband!—was hardly likely to be taken seriously. But once persuaded that her case was worth making, Mary sailed into the attack with all guns firing. Her reply to Burke is unique amongst her writings in using the weapon of personal invective as a means of furthering her cause. This untypical behaviour is itself a sign that she was uncertain of her ground. It is doubtful if she had even read Burke with the care his essay merited, and she confessed as much in her preface:

> Not having the leisure or patience to follow this desultory writer through all the devious tracks in which his fancy has started fresh game, I have confined my strictures, in a great measure, to the grand principles at which he has levelled many ingenious arguments in a very specious garb.

Had she been less hasty, and less emotionally involved in the argument, Mary might have found a good deal in Burke to agree with. In a rather condescending estimate of his character she allowed that he is 'a good, though a vain man'; and even in his vanity she found 'extenuating circumstances'. Rooted in the past as he was, Burke's record showed him to be by no means a political 'reactionary': he had upheld the American claim to independence, abhorred slavery, attacked the harshness of the penal system and caused the impeachment of Warren Hastings for alleged ill-treatment of the native people of India. His 'vanity' was perhaps a facet of his sensitivity to cruelty as well as to criticism; his nerves, it is said, 'twitched' at the sight of suffering[4].

This was akin to Mary's own temperament—but with a difference. She was suspicious of the kind of sensibility that could be blind to injustice. 'All your pretty flights,' she told Burke severely, 'arise from your pampered sensibility ... you foster every emotion till the fumes, mounting to your brain, dispel the sober suggestions of reason'. Here again is an echo of herself, and there is something faintly comic in the spectacle of this highly emotional woman accusing the worldly-wise politician of letting his feelings outrun his judgment! But there is worse to come, and a page or two later she delivered her coup: 'I perceive, from the whole tenor of your Reflections, that you have a mortal antipathy to reason'. This again may sound like David blowing a dart at Goliath, but there is little to fault in Mary's logic as she develops her attack. She can only be criticised, perhaps, for a partial selection of evidence and a one-dimensional view of her opponent. The Edmund Burke she presented is an aunt sally set up solely to be shot at. And the shooting-match is soon over. Having disposed of her victim, Mary was free to expatiate on her own philosophy of the rights of men.

Her definition of these disputed rights—what she called 'the birthright of man'—is so innocuous that Burke could almost have written it himself:

> such a degree of liberty, civil and religious, as is compatible with the liberty of every other individual with whom he is united in social compact, and the continued existence of that compact.

This was such a reasonable demand that the question had next to be asked: why had this liberty never been achieved? Here came the nub of the argument, the great divide that separated the 'haves' from the 'have-nots' and put Mary on the side of the revolutionists:

> the demon of property has ever been at hand to encroach on the sacred rights of men, and to fence round with awful pomp laws that war with justice.

On this point Mary and Burke were immediately placed at opposite poles. There was no possible reconciliation between his view that the laws of inheritance were themselves the chief bastion of a civilised society; and her conviction that the very existence of these laws prevented such a society from ever being established. Why, she asked, had the civilisation of Europe progressed so slowly and so incompletely? The answer was so simple that it could be stated in four words: 'hereditary property—hereditary honours'.

Those same four words could as well have been used to sum up

Burke's *defence* of civilisation—at least as it was symbolised in the British hierarchy of crown and commons on which he rested his whole case. In so limiting himself, he made his opponents' task almost too easy. Mary pounced like a hawk. In what did this glorious British constitution consist? How did it originate? Again the answer was plain and simple: the British social system was founded at the point of the sword, by the imposition of petty tyrants. Looking back into history, Mary saw that the king submitted to the barons only to obtain more revenue for foreign wars; while the barons with their private armies battened on a terrorised populace. Was this the example that Burke sought to uphold?—

> Are we to seek for the rights of men in the ages when a few marks were the only penalty imposed for the life of a man, and death for death when the property of the rich was touched? . . . Are these the laws that it is natural to love, and sacrilegious to invade?—Were the rights of men understood when the law authorised or tolerated murder?—or is power and right the same in your creed?

Mary's accusation that, by Burke's philosophy, 'might is right', was unanswerable. So was her further charge that his fear of change would even have led him to support the crucifixion of Christ: who 'must have been a dangerous innovator in your eyes, particularly if you had not been informed that the Carpenter's Son was of the stock and lineage of David'. This was a nasty knock at Burke's snobbery as well as his wrong-headedness. She went on to demolish his logic. If he so reverenced the past, then according to his own lights he should have upheld the system of slavery—which he had opposed—simply because it existed as an established custom. And on what grounds could he defend the principle of American independence? Poor Burke! Even when he was on the side of the angels, he had no right to be there.

Another shining example of British 'justice' was the perpetuation of iniquitous game laws:

> In this land of liberty, what is to secure the property of the poor farmer when his noble landlord chooses to plant a decoy field near his little property? Game devour the fruit of his labour; but fines and imprisonment await him if he dare to kill any—or lift up his hand to interrupt the pleasures of his lord.

Mary's own father may have suffered in this respect, during his unsuccessful farming ventures in Essex. 'You seem to consider the poor,' she cried to Burke with some feeling, 'as only the live stock of an estate, the feather of the hereditary nobility'. Had his respect for rank quite swallowed up his humanity?

Was the same kind of snobbery at the root of his attack on Dr Price, 'whose brow a mitre will never grace'? Or was it caused by jealousy of Price's popularity? Burke accused the minister of exploiting the pulpit for political ends, and Mary agreed with him that the pulpit was not the place for politics—although pointing out that the occasion in question was actually the commemoration of a political revolution rather than a religious service. But what she could not forgive was the personal abuse of Dr Price:

> In reprobating Dr. Price's opinions you might have spared the man; and if you had had but half as much reverence for the grey hairs of virtue as for the accidental distinctions of rank, you would not have treated with such indecent familiarity and supercilious contempt, a member of the community whose talents and modest virtues place him high in the scale of moral excellence.

Nevertheless, Mary found herself again agreeing to some extent with Burke's criticism of Price's revolutionary fervour:

> Granting, for a moment, that Dr. Price's political opinions are Utopian reveries, and that the world is not yet sufficiently civilised to adopt such a sublime system of morality; they could, however, only be the reveries of a benevolent mind.

Mary's own attitude to society was indeed more realistic than that of either Burke or Price: the one intent on the past and the other on the future. Mary was one who lived, and suffered, in the present. She looked at life through the eyes of living men and women; and what she saw with these eyes was injustice. To witness an injustice, in her philosophy, was to cry out for its remedy. Burke's appeal for the *status quo* had nothing to offer in this direction. It seemed to her, therefore, a mockery of the liberties he was purporting to defend and an insult to those millions of citizens for whom the existing system provided no prospect of betterment, or even of representation.

The farce of British 'parliamentary democracy' in those days was one of Tom Paine's strongest points of attack in his *Rights of Man*. He pointed out to Burke that the new French constitution laid down that 'the number of representatives for any place shall be in a ratio to the number of taxable inhabitants or electors', whereas in England:

> The county of Yorkshire, which contains nearly a million of souls, sends two county members; and so does the county of Rutland, which contains not an hundredth part of that number. The town of Old Sarum, which contains not three houses, sends two members; and the town of Manchester, which contains upwards of sixty thousand souls, is not admitted to send any.

Mary Wollstonecraft was more concerned with the morality, or immorality, of the system than with facts and figures. The corruption of Parliament was an open scandal, and she reminded Burke that he himself was part of it:

> You have been behind the curtain . . . Then you must have seen the clogged wheels of corruption continually oiled by the sweat of the laborious poor, squeezed out of them by unceasing taxation. You must have discovered that the majority in the House of Commons was often purchased by the crown, and that the people were oppressed by the influence of their own money, extorted by the venal voice of a packed representation.
>
> You must have known that a man of merit cannot rise in the church, the army, or navy, unless he has some interest in a borough; and that even a paltry exciseman's place can only be secured by electioneering interest.

Was this really the good society of Burke's romantic vision? Mary renewed her attack on the laws of inheritance: to Burke, one of the bulwarks of civilisation; to Mary, an 'everlasting rampart' of a 'barbarous feudal system'. Property, she maintained, should be 'fluctuating', and it should be shared amongst all the children of a family, not confined to the eldest son. It should even be left outside the family if the owner so wished:

> The only security of property that nature authorises and reason sanctions is, the right a man has to enjoy the acquisitions which his talents and industry have acquired; and to bequeath them to whom he chooses.

The supreme guardian of property in England was of course the monarch. Mary did not attack the monarchy as such. (This was left to Tom Paine, the avowed republican, to whom the monarchy was 'the master-fraud, which shelters all others'.) She limited herself to attacking Burke's inconsistency. If the throne of France was so sacred, what about poor George III? She reminded him of his mockery of the King in his speech on the bill for a Regency when George's sanity was in doubt in 1788:

In this state was the King, when you, with unfeeling disrespect, and indecent haste, wished to strip him of all his hereditary honours.—You were so eager to taste the sweets of power, that you could not wait till time had determined, whether a dreadful delirium would settle into a confirmed madness; but, prying into the secrets of Omnipotence, you thundered out that God had *hurled him from his throne*, and that it was the most insulting mockery to recollect that he had been a king, or to treat him with any particular respect on account of his former dignity.—And who was the monster whom Heaven had thus awfully deposed, and smitten with such an angry blow? Surely as harmless a character as Lewis XVIth; and the queen of Great Britain, though her heart may not be enlarged by generosity, who will presume to compare her character with that of the queen of France?

How could Burke square this attitude with his belief in the 'infallibility' of rulers? She suggested that it was time he learned to respect 'the sovereignty of reason'. Yet even as she was defending the supremacy of reason, Mary acknowledged how fragile are its ramparts:

I perceive that my passions pursue objects that the imagination enlarges, till they become only a sublime idea that shrinks from the enquiry of sense, and mocks the experimental philosophers who would confine this spiritual phlogiston in their material crucibles. I know that the human understanding is deluded with vain shadows, and that when we eagerly pursue any study, we only reach the boundary set to human enquiries.—Thus far shalt thou go, and no further, says some stern difficulty; and the *cause* we were pursuing melts into utter darkness.

Nevertheless, she maintained, to go exercising our understanding (with all its limitations) is our only hope. It is by the exercise of reason that we achieve the 'primary morality' which Burke called 'untaught feelings'. Mary had no such faith in the natural man. Her belief in acquired, rather than instinctive, morality underpinned her whole philosophy:

If virtue be an instinct, I renounce all hope of immortality; and with it all the sublime reveries and dignified sentiments that have smoothed the rugged path of life: it is all a cheat, a lying vision; I have disquieted myself in vain; for in my eye all feelings are false and spurious, that do not rest on justice as their foundation, and are not concentred by universal love.

This was a brave and noble statement—and more than a statement. For to Mary philosophy was not a matter of putting fine words on paper; or even of uttering resounding slogans and making gestures to revolution. Every word in her philosophy was meant to be lived; and every word was hammered from her own living experience. No wonder she saw Burke's piety without justice as a sham; as she was later to see the revolutionists' justice without love as a delusion.

The very society which Burke was defending, Mary pointed out, had been formed as much by innovation as by what he called 'the sanctions of religion and piety', and as a politician he could not fail to be aware of it: 'Factions, sir, have been the leaven, and private interest has produced public good'. As for his notion of 'consecration of the state' by the established church—how was this exemplified in the electoral system?—

Sir, let me ask you with manly plainness—are these *holy* nominations? Where is the booth of religion? Does she mix her awful mandates, or lift her persuasive voice, in those scenes of drunken riot and beastly gluttony?... Experience, I believe, will shew that sordid interest, or licentious thoughtlessness, is the spring of action at most elections.

Burke believed that because education was largely in the hands of the clergy, a continuation of respect for the religious establishment was assured. Mary begged to differ, speaking no doubt from her own experience in Ireland: 'The little respect paid, in great houses, to tutors and chaplains proves, Sir, the fallacy of your reasoning'. There was also the awkward fact that 'when *we*, the people of England, have a son whom we scarcely know what to do with—*we* make a clergyman of him'.

Here Mary launched into one of her fiercest attacks. Far from being founded on respect, she declared, the Church was based on ruthless greed:

What; but the rapacity of the only men who exercised their reason, the priests, secured such vast property to the church, when a man gave his perishable substance to save himself from the dark torments of purgatory; and found it more convenient to indulge his depraved appetites, and pay an exorbitant price for absolution, than listen to the suggestions of reason and work out his own salvation?

Mary was speaking now for the Nonconformist conscience, accusing the Church not only of institutional corruption but of exercising a corrupting influence on the souls it was charged with saving. In short, 'was not the separation of religion from morality the work of the priests'? This alone, apart from its more venial sins, was enough to condemn the Church in her eyes. It did not mean, however, that Mary Wollstonecraft had suddenly become converted to atheism, and she was at pains to make her position clear on this score by adding a footnote to the text: 'As religion is included in my idea of morality,' she observed, 'I wish to guard against misrepresentation'. Her religion, like the rest of her philosophy, was grounded in experience. Mary never offered any proof for the existence of a 'Supreme Being': she had simply found him to be a necessity. 'What can make us reverence ourselves,' she asked, 'but a reverence for that Being, of whom we are a faint image?' And in the hour of suffering and bereavement, 'there is but one cource of comfort ... the world appears to contain only the Creator and the creature, of whose happiness he is the source'.

This statement represented not so much an exercise of the 'understanding' as a semi-mystical reverie. In the non-rational side of her nature she had some affinities with Burke himself. He too had suffered his share of bereavement and failure. If they had ever met (which is improbable) they might have become friends. Even in reading him, Mary responded intuitively to the man behind the print:

> There appears to be such a mixture of real sensibility and fondly cherished romance in your composition, that the present crisis carries you out of yourself; and since you could not be one of the grand movers, the next *best* thing that dazzled your imagination was to be a conspicuous opposer. Full of yourself, you make as much noise to convince the world that you despise the revolution, as Rousseau did to persuade his contemporaries to let him live in obscurity.

This was an insight that went beyond politics. Mary's linking of Burke with Rousseau (and thereby, indirectly, with herself) was perhaps no more than an involuntary coincidence, but she had stumbled on the common thread of a romanticism that was still scarcely articulate. Now she followed it somewhat further to an

even more startling conclusion:
> Reading your Reflections warily over, it has continually and forcibly struck me, that had you been a Frenchman, you would have been, in spite of your respect for rank and antiquity, a violent revolutionist... Another observation which, by frequently occurring, has almost grown into a conviction, is simply this, that had the English in general reprobated the French revolution, you would have stood forth alone, and been the avowed Goliath of liberty.

She saw that, in different circumstances, this is where Burke's romanticism would have led him; and in this sense he was closer to the revolutionaries than she was herself. Her own 'respect' for democracy and innovation would never make her 'a violent revolutionist'.

As if Burke was not by this time squirming on the pin, Mary probed even deeper into his weaknesses. She reiterated her suspicion that his attack on Dr Price was actuated not so much by patriotism as by envy; that his expressions of contempt for the minister were the sour grapes of 'personal pique and hurt vanity'. Still on this personal note, she berated Burke's attitude to women as revealed in his earlier essay on *The Sublime and the Beautiful* (1756). His concept of beauty seemed to her far from sublime. If the essence of feminine beauty was '*littleness* and *weakness*', as he had indicated, this implied that women should not cultivate moral virtues 'that might chance to excite respect, and interfere with the pleasing sensations they were created to inspire'. But if moral virtues were to be confined to 'manly morals', Burke seemed to be trying to prove that 'one half of the human species, at least, have not souls'. Just as his attitude to the Church had separated morality from religion, so his attitude to women divorced love from respect, making them 'antagonist principles'. This was a crucial theme in Mary's succeeding dissertion on the *Rights of Women*, and Burke may well have been at the root of it. In denouncing his philosophy, she was evolving her own concept of 'the sublime and the beautiful'.

Digressions into the roots of private morality, however, were only incidental to her *Vindication of the Rights of Men*, which was primarily an exercise in social justice. But to Mary the public and the private virtues were closely intertwined, and she swung naturally from one to the other. As in her assessment of Necker she had looked for the man behind the public mask, so now she looked for an amelioration of personal deprivation in the state of society. But for this to come about there must be a change in the social order: 'Inequality of rank must ever impede the growth of virtue, by vitiating the mind that submits or domineers'.

With this thought she returned to the French National Assembly and Burke's contemptuous dismissal of it as, in her words, 'an assembly of unlettered clowns'. Burke's actual phrase was 'country clowns' and his chief objection was to the vast preponderance of lawyers in the Assembly—and obscure, provincial lawyers at that: they were 'men of theory', with no practical experience in the state. If Mary had read his text more carefully she would have found much to agree with there. However, she profoundly disagreed with his view that only the great are fitted to rule. On the contrary, she said, it is to *poor* men, or philosophers' that we must turn in order to establish liberty on firm foundations; that is, 'if a sufficient number of men, disinterested from principle, or truly wise, could be found'. She made this proviso because she had to admit that the majority of members of the National Assembly were not acting from disinterested principles: 'I am afraid that human nature is still in such a weak state, that the abolition of titles, the corner-stone of despotism, could only have been the work of men who had no titles to sacrifice'. Nevertheless, she believed that the revolution gave a 'glorious *chance*' of attaining 'more virtue and happiness than has hitherto blessed our globe'; and that some kind of revolution was necessary to loosen the grip of the Church and the nobility. Above all, it was the Church that had sinned.

Why, she asked, was Burke so bitterly opposed to the redistribution of property in France? Whom did it injure, compared with all the wrongs of the past?—

> How has posterity been injured by a distribution of the property snatched, perhaps, from innocent hands, but accumulated by the most abominable violation of every sentiment of justice and piety? Was the monument of former ignorance and iniquity to be held sacred, to enable the present possessors of enormous benefices to *dissolve* in indolent pleasures?

Mary's diatribe against what she calls the 'monkish rapacity' of the Church matches in violence Burke's invective against the Revolution. The fathers of the Church she described as

'monsters', devoted to perpetuating 'the sacred majesty of Property'. Many of the present clergy, on the other hand, were poor; therefore, she reasoned, the loss of the Church revenues would affect them little. And if the bishops in future were to be chosen 'on account of their personal merit', so much the better for religion. Far from upholding morality, she argued, Burke's veneration for the past was maintaining a monstrous injustice:
> Can there be an opinion more subversive of morality, than that time sanctions crimes, and silences the blood that calls out for retribution, if not for vengeance?

But in the name of the Revolution (over-optimistically, as it turned out), she repudiated any thought of 'vengeance'. It was not, she maintained, so as to 'punish' the clergy that the Church revenues were being confiscated, but in order to right a wrong. Here again Mary made a comparison with the slave-trade, which Burke to his credit had opposed and yet which according to his political philosophy he ought to have defended:
> There is not one argument, one invective, levelled by you at the confiscators of the church revenue, which could not, with the strictest propriety, be applied by the planters and negro-drivers to our Parliament, if it gloriously dared to shew the world that British senators were men.

The same argument could be applied to every vice and oppression that society was capable of.

The only people to benefit from Burke's attitude, she observed, were the rich and the weak, who would rather justify oppression than think how to correct the abuse:
> *The rights of men* are grating sounds that set their teeth on edge; the impertinent enquiry of philosophic meddling innovation.

Even when the intentions of the rich were benevolent, they expected 'gratitude' from the poor, making a favour of what ought to be a right. No wonder that the poor in their turn regarded the rich as their 'lawful prey'. Here Mary conceded that the existence of evil seemed to be part of the Divine Plan; but it was the business of the good man 'to separate light from darkness; to diffuse happiness, whilst he submits to unavoidable misery'. Mary's passing salute to 'happiness' was a perfunctory one. She did not share the optimistic belief of the utilitarian philosophers that the greatest good lay in the happiness of the greatest number. To sacrifice the

The Radical Revolt: 1789–90

happiness of one individual in order to promote the welfare of ten, or ten thousand, seemed to her 'impious'. She put forward a precisely opposite view:

> The happiness of the whole must arise from the happiness of the constituent parts, or the essence of justice is sacrificed to a supposed grand arrangement.

By this argument, whether consciously or not, she was refuting not only Burke but all other theorists who tried to make bricks without straw and build systems on no better basis than what she called 'the vague declamation of sensibility'.

It is, however, Burke's attitude to the poor that calls forth Mary's greatest indignation. She flung back at him his own much-quoted passage on 'the principles of natural subordination', with italics added for good measure:

> They *must* respect that property of which they *cannot* partake. *They must labour to obtain what by labour can be obtained; and when they find, as they commonly do, the success disproportioned to the endeavour, they must be taught their consolation in the final proportions of eternal justice.*

Such an attitude, in Mary's view, was an insult to both man and God:

> This is contemptible, hard-hearted sophistry, in the specious form of humility, and submission to the will of Heaven.—It is, Sir, *possible* to render the poor happier in this world, without depriving them of the consolation which you gratuitiously grant them in the next. They have a right to more comfort than they at present enjoy; and more comfort might be afforded them, without encroaching on the pleasures of the rich; not now waiting to enquire whether the rich have any right to exclusive pleasures.

In the rush of indignation her thoughts outstrip her pen:

> What do I say?—encroaching! No; if an intercourse were established between them, it would impart the only true pleasure that can be snatched in this land of shadows, this hard school of moral discipline.

At this point Mary seems to have stumbled upon a truth that belongs more to the nineteenth-century ideal of 'co-operation' than eighteenth-century principles of 'order', and she halted in midstream as she considered its implications. Her thoughts turned again to the wealthy landowner, building his mansion and laying out the grounds as a pleasure-garden:

> Every thing on the estate is cherished but man;—yet, to contribute to the happiness of man, is the most sublime of all enjoyments. But if, instead of sweeping pleasure-grounds, obelisks, temples, and elegant cottages, as *objects* for the eye, the heart was allowed to beat true to nature, decent farms would be scattered over the estate, and plenty smile around.

And now, letting her own heart 'beat true to nature' and abandoning the ill-fitting straitjacket of rationalism, her fancy took wing and soared over her vision of an earthly paradise in which men are bound by love rather than authority:

> A garden more inviting than Eden would then meet the eye, and springs of joy murmur on every side. The clergyman would superintend his own flock, the shepherd would then love the sheep he daily tended; the school might rear its decent head, and the buzzing tribe, let loose to play, impart a portion of their vivacious spirits to the heart that longed to open their minds, and lead them to taste the pleasures of men. Domestic comfort, the civilizing relations of husband, brother, and father, would soften labour, and render life contented.

This was an idyllic vision, a dream of the might-have-been rather than a representation of what was. It bore little relation to Mary's own experience of the 'simple life', and she soon returned to practical considerations. Why should not the large estates be divided up into small farms? Why should vast areas of land be covered by forest and heath when men needed work? Speaking no doubt from memories of her childhood in Essex, she commented bitterly: 'But commons cannot be enclosed without *acts of parliament* to increase the property of the rich!'

All these evils, she saw, sprang from the domination of man by man. Their effect was even more apparent in the town than in the country:

> In this great city, that proudly rears its head, and boasts of its population and commerce, how much misery lurks in pestilential corners, whilst idle mendicants assail, on every side, the man who hates to encourage imposters, or repress, with angry frowns, the plaints of the poor!

Were not these miseries of poverty and oppression worse evils than those 'infringements of property' which Burke so piously deprecated? In coming to her peroration, Mary looked back to the 6th October 1789, the occasion for Burke's impassioned outburst against the French Revolution:

> What were the outrages of a day to these continual miseries? Let those sorrows hide their diminished head before the tremendous mountain of woe that thus defaces our globe! Man preys on man; and you mourn for the idle tapestry that decorated a gothic pile, and the dronish bell that summoned the fat priest to prayer. You mourn for the empty pageant of a name, when slavery flaps her wings, and the sick heart retires to die in lonely wilds, far from the abodes of men.

Here Mary reaches the climax of her *Vindication*. She could use rhetoric herself, when the cause demanded it. And her imagery is at least as powerful as the often-quoted metaphor of Tom Paine: 'He pities the plumage, but forgets the dying bird'.

As she neared the end of her treatise Mary returns to the personal attributes of her protagonist—this time, more kindly. His blind devotion to the English constitution she likens to the kind of family affection that refuses to see any faults in its members, whereas a more rational affection might have helped to correct them. In the same way, the state would benefit from criticism:

> Is it absolute blasphemy to doubt the omnipotence of the law, or to suppose that religion might be more pure if there were fewer baits for hypocrites in the church?

Again she taxes Burke with inconsistency. For all his patriotism, he acknowledged that the English social system owed much to the French model. Now it was Mary's turn to play the patriot. If we were so dependent on France, she said, it was time we broke loose—'Time that Englishmen drew water from their own springs'. If only we would learn to cultivate our 'reason', we should have no need of an 'arbitrary model'. But of course, she added with heavy irony, under Burke's system nature and reason must give place to 'authority'; or, as Shakespeare expressed it, the gods 'seem to kill us for their sport, as men do flies'.

Again, using a weapon against her opponent seems to touch a secret spring of sympathy in Mary. Perhaps she found Shakespeare's analogy uncomfortably true to her own observations and experience, and only a thin veil of piety screened her from wholly accepting it. She ended the book, as she began it, in some agreement with Burke. She recognised that, misguided or not, he is a man of principle—and she has a horrid suspicion that many of the friends of the Revolution were a long way from that:

> Before I conclude my cursory remarks, it is just to acknowledge that I coincide with you in your opinion respecting the *sincerity* of modern philosophers. Your consistency in avowing a veneration for rank and riches deserves praise; but I must own I have often indignantly observed that some of the *enlightened* philosophers, who talk most vehemently of the native rights of men, borrow many noble sentiments to adorn their conversation, which have no influence on their conduct.

For all their talk, she has noted, many so-called radicals continued to bow down to rank and were careful to secure property for themselves. Nor were they very quick to discern merit in a man without fortune. No doubt, as a woman of no property, she had felt the sting herself. But Mary, like Burke in his way, remained true to her ideal principles regardless of human imperfections:

> neither open enmity nor hollow homage destroys the intrinsic value of those principles which rest on an eternal foundation, and revert for a standard to the immutable attributes of God.

So ends Mary Wollstonecraft's *Vindication of the Rights of Men*: a strange conclusion for a 'revolutionary' thinker, in close harmony with that 'arch-reactionary' Edmund Burke whose *Reflections on the French Revolution* she had set out to attack. Nevertheless, Mary remained a revolutionary; and a more fundamental one than the avowed revolutionists who sought to replace one kind of despotism by another. Although she never overlooked the reform of institutions, she was already becoming aware that the greatest revolutions took place within persons rather than states.

CHAPTER EIGHT
Women's Liberation: 1792

The *Rights of Men* represented Mary Wollstonecraft's only foray into the world of politics as such. She was too broad a humanist to be content with a 'party line', too conscious of the conditioning of a man's politics by his temperament and circumstances to commit herself to wholesale blame or praise. Her reservations on Burke and the revolutionists worked both ways, even though her personal sympathies were so strongly on the side of the radicals.

Nevertheless, her incursion into politics had opened her eyes in other directions. From the general injustice of a property-owning aristocracy it was a natural progression to consider the specific injustices bearing on the female half of society; nor were the two states unconnected, as she was to argue powerfully in her next polemic, *A Vindication of the Rights of Woman*. Mary had been moving up to this theme over a number of years; in the light of her own precarious situation she could scarcely avoid it. But she had learnt from painful experience the futility of arguing from a position of weakness. Now, with the *Rights of Men* behind her, she might justifiably expect that anything written by Mary Wollstonecraft would at least be taken seriously and considered on its merits.

Mary's own deprivations in her early years had, of course, a good deal to do with the sharpening of her apprehensions in this direction. But how untypical were her experiences? Did they not fairly reflect the general condition of women in society in the mid-eighteenth century? The only untypical thing about Mary

Wollstonecraft was the strength of her passion for justice and the active determination with which she pursued it. In her introduction to the *Rights of Woman* she quoted an unnamed writer who asked 'what business women turned of forty have to do in the world?' Fanny Burney had punched home the message even more strongly in *Evelina* (1778):

> Prithee, whispered his Lordship, is that queer woman your mother?
> Good Heavens, Sir, what words for such a question! No, my Lord.
> Your maiden aunt then?
> No.
> Whoever she is, I wish she would mind her own affairs: I don't know what the devil a woman lives for after thirty: she is only in other folks way. Shall you be at the assembly?
> I believe not, my Lord.
> No!—why then how in the world can you contrive to pass your time?
> In a manner which your Lordship will think very extraordinary, cried Mrs Selwyn, for the young lady *reads*.
> Ha, ha, ha! Egad, my Lord, cried the facetious companion, you are got into bad hands.

Fanny was born and reared in happier circumstances than Mary and could afford to take a lighter tone; but the barb, though dipped in honey, is still a sharp one. Her description of Captain Mirvan in the same novel could almost pass for Mr Wollstonecraft:

> Captain Mirvan is arrived. I have not spirits to give an account of his introduction, for he has really shocked me. I do not like him. He seems to be surly, vulgar, and disagreeable.
> Almost the same moment that Maria [his daughter] was presented to him, he began some rude jests upon the bad shape of her nose, and called her a tall, ill-formed thing. She bore it with the utmost good humour; but that kind and sweet-tempered woman, Mrs Mirvan, deserved a better lot. I am amazed she would marry him . . .

The uncouth, overbearing father was evidently a commonplace character and he crops up in much of the literature of the day; sometimes, as in Fanny Burney, satirically, but more often simply as a normal person to be accepted for what he was.

Mary was never willing to accept the grosser imperfections of character as 'normal'. A true child of the Enlightenment in this respect, she believed in the perfectibility, or at least amelioration, of human nature by the exercise of reason; this had been the substance of her case against Burke. She chose the same grounds to fight her battle for the rights of women. If she could prove her case by reason, how—in the age of reason— could it be refuted? The answer, as she freely admitted, was that it could be very easily refuted by those other elements in human nature, passion and prejudice; by Burke's 'inbred sentiments'. But she had already tried to demonstrate as a teacher that inbred errors could be eradicated by the right kind of education. Education, therefore, was the keystone round which the rights of women must be constructed.

Mary Wollstonecraft was by no means the first woman in history to have had this thought. There had been learned women in antiquity such as the Roman Cornelia, who gave public lectures in philosophy, and the poetess Sappho. The rise of Christianity offered the seclusion of the cloister to the woman of intellectual or spiritual aspiration as an alternative to matrimony while the medieval cult of chivalry induced respect for all women. During the reign of Elizabeth I and her two successors, the status of women in England rose steadily, but it drastically declined in both the Commonwealth and the Restoration periods: it has been noted that the extremes of licentiousness and puritanism are alike degrading to women[1]. The Augustan age brought a refinement of sentiment, but this was no more than a veneer on an underlying coarseness. By and large, there had been little progress in the achievements of women to match the outstanding leap forward in eighteenth-century science and philosophy. This was partly due to the general passivity of women in accepting and submitting to the view of themselves so ably propounded by men—and even, in their own limited interests, turning it to good account. But there had always been exceptions, like Mary herself, who sought a more dignified role for their sex.

Amongst her European predecessors may be mentioned Anna Maria Schurman, born at Cologne in 1607 and educated in Holland: 'perfect in ten languages, poet and philosopher, scientist, artist and musician—all before she was thirty'[2]. She joined Jean Labadie in a Mennonite sanctuary at Altona and lived with him as his wife, publishing a defence of her conduct in 1673. Nearly half a century later came Anne le Febre, born in 1651 at Saumur where her father was a professor. Even as a young girl she was a brilliant classical scholar and, as Madame Dacier, after her marriage to one of her father's former students, she became renowned in Paris for her translations of Greek and Latin authors. As the eighteenth century dawned a new star rose in Italy in the shape of Maria Gaetana Agnesi (1718–1799), daughter of a Milan professor. A precocious child, she mastered Latin, Greek, Hebrew and other languages, became a noted mathematician and philosopher, and was made an honorary lecturer at the University of Bologna by Pope Benedict XIV in 1749.

Amongst the first Englishwomen in the feminist chronology is Mary Astell (1668–1731). Born at Newcastle-upon-Tyne, she was educated by a clergyman uncle and at the age of twenty settled in London. Her claim to fame rests on *A Serious Proposal to the Ladies for the Advancement of their True and Greatest Interest* by 'a Lover of her Sex', which was published in two parts in 1696 and 1697. The book was dedicated to Princess Anne of Denmark (the future Queen Anne) and the 'serious proposal' was a very serious one: a call to women to cast off their absorption in trivialities and earn a more permanent form of beauty 'by transferring it from a corruptible body to an immortal mind'. She proposed the establishment of a 'monastery, or religious retirement' where women could retreat from the dangers and temptations of wordly society—though without taking the vows of a religious order—and submit themselves to the discipline of study. The object of the study was not to be learning for its own sake, but 'the pursuit of truth'; and 'truth' to Mary Astell was the Christian doctrine of the Church of England. Her aim, therefore, though worthy and enlightened for its day, was a limited one; and she hastened to assure her readers that she was not suggesting women should 'teach in the Church, or usurp authority where it is not allow'd them'. For this reason, ironically, her proposal came to nothing. 'Authority' in the shape of Bishop Burnet frowned on the project and persuaded her to abandon it, even though a sum of £10,000 had been offered for the foundation of the college by a wealthy patron who was rumoured to have been either Lady Hastings or Princess Anne herself.

A more interesting document of the same period is *An Essay in*

Defence of the Female Sex (1696), bound in the same volume with the *Serious Proposal* by the publisher Richard Wilkin and written anonymously by 'a Lady'. It has been attributed to Judith Drake, presumably the wife of the political pamphleteer James Drake (1667–1707) who contributed a foreword together with an adulatory poem addressed to 'the most ingenious Mrs — on her admirable Defence of her Sex'. This essay too was dedicated to Princess Anne (had she a reputation as a 'progressive'?—poor Queen Anne with her seventeen dead babies hardly gives that impression!). The *Defence* has a much more radical tone than the *Serious Proposal*—'radical' not in its political meaning but in the sense of going to the root of the argument. There is no distinction of sex in 'souls', the author asserted; neither is there any natural impediment in the structure of women's bodies. She drew an analogy from the animal kingdom: 'In Brutes and other animals, there is no Difference betwixt Male and Female in point of Sagacity, notwithstanding there is the same Distinction of Sexes that is between Men and Women'. This is a telling point, which strangely enough was not followed up by later writers, not even by Mary Wollstonecraft herself. Judith Drake was also bolder than Mary Astell in placing the blame for the inequalities between the sexes squarely upon the men: women had been kept deliberately in a state of ignorance, she declared, and were little better than slaves.

But by far the best of the feminist tracts, before that of Mary Wollstonecraft, was *Woman not Inferior to Man*: 'or, a Short and modest Vindication of the Natural Right of the *Fair-Sex* to a perfect Equality of Power, Dignity, and Esteem, with the Men', published pseudonymously in 1739 by 'Sophia, A Person of Quality'. Sophia has never been positively identified, although the most likely candidate has usually been regarded as Lady Mary Wortley Montagu[3]. Whatever her true identity, there is no doubt about her ability.

On what was the alleged superiority of man over woman based, Sophia asked? On his 'reason'? Were women without reason? Or, for that matter, were men so well endowed with it that their lives were rationally conducted? On the contrary—'we see those very men, whose ambition of ascendancy over us nothing less than absolute dominion can satiate, court the most abject slavery, by prostituting reason to their groveling passions, suffering sense to be led away captive by prejudice, and sacrificing justice, truth and honour to inconsiderate custom'. Sophia's logic was indeed merciless, and was itself sufficient answer to the detractors of her sex. She proceeded, step by step, to assault and demolish the bastions of masculine privilege. So women were 'fit only to breed and nurse children'?—*only*, forsooth! What a useful occupation this was, compared with that of many men in positions of authority!—Ah, came the answer, but women were not capable of taking these offices themselves. Oh no, declared Sophia, it was not want of capacity, but want of 'an equal spirit of violence, shameless injustice, and lawless oppression'. For the same reason, women were not seen marching at the head of armies because they preferred 'honourable peace to unjust war' (there was also the point here that since men were less useful they could more easily be sacrificed). But it was in disputing the assertion that women did not need to be educated because they did not take part in public life that Sophia coined her most famous aphorism:

> Why is *learning* useless to us? Because we have no share in public offices. And why have we no share in public offices? Because we have no *learning*.

Despite her own obvious learning, and her skill in argument, Sophia presented her case with modesty and moderation. She did not wish to cause trouble, she assured her readers, or 'to invert the perfect order of things with regard to *government* and *authority*'. Like Mary Astell before her, she was a reformer rather than a revolutionary. She was content to state her case and leave it to the common sense and fair judgment of the reader to see that it was a good one. In consequence, her arguments had little effect and brought no changes in the law. The immediate result of the tract, indeed, was to evoke a virulent reply from an anonymous 'Gentleman' entitled *Man Superior to Woman*[4].

This 'Gentleman' represented the prevailing masculine attitude at its most extreme. But amongst men no less than women there had always been honourable exceptions who questioned traditional prejudices. In English literature one of the earliest of these was Daniel Defoe. Perhaps 'all the world are mistaken in their practice about women,' he wrote in his *Essay on Projects* (1697):

> For I cannot think that God Almighty ever made them so delicate, so glorious creatures, and furnished them with such charms, so agreeable and delightful to mankind; with souls capable of the same accomplishments with men; and all to be

only stewards of our Houses, Cooks and Slaves.

Not that I am for exalting the female government in the least, but, in short, I WOULD HAVE MEN TAKE WOMEN FOR COMPANIONS, AND EDUCATE THEM TO BE FIT FOR IT.

This was a generous statement which went at least half-way towards redressing an injustice, though not to the point of doing anything about it. Defoe did, however, propose in the same essay the establishment of an academy for women, curiously enough just as the same idea was being formulated by Mary Astell (they may even have influenced each other). A little later, the feminist cause was taken up by Addison and Steele in *The Spectator* and *The Tatler*; and the great Dean Swift himself, despite his alleged misogyny, added his mite in his 'Letter to a Very Young Lady on her Marriage' (1727). 'I am ignorant of any one quality that is amiable in a man,' he wrote, 'which is not equally so in a woman ... the same virtues equally become both sexes'. That he also described women as 'a sort of Species hardly a degree above a Monkey' need not be taken too seriously; he probably thought much the same about men. In Mary Wollstonecraft's own day, Baron d'Holbach included a defence of women's rights in his *Système Social* (1773). Condorcet put forward proposals for the education of girls as well as boys in his first 'memoir on public instruction' in 1790, but on the whole the men of the French Revolution ignored the rights of female citizens. It was left to a women, Olympe de Gouges, to challenge the new régime with her 'declaration des droits de la Femme et de la citoyenne' in 1791—and she ended on the scaffold[5].

Hanoverian England, however, was a far cry from revolutionary France. What Mary had to contend with was the dead hand of tradition as exemplified by Burke and Lord Chesterfield; the sentimental piety of Dr Gregory and Dr Fordyce; and, in her own sex, the timid conservatism of Mrs Chapone and Hannah More. All these influences she sought to counteract in her *Vindication of the Rights of Woman*. Her admiration was reserved for Mrs Catherine Macaulay, a character only a little less original than herself. The widow of a respected physician, Mrs Macaulay was living in Bath at the time when Mary went there as companion to Mrs Dawson, but moved to Leicestershire after the scandal of her second marriage in 1788 to a twenty-one-year-old surgeon's mate, William Graham, the younger brother of a notorious 'quack' doctor. Her reputation was already made, however, by her *History of England*, the first volume of which had appeared in 1763, and when she travelled to North America in 1784 she was received as a guest in the home of George Washington. Mrs Macaulay, like Mary, had republican sympathies and had published her own observations on Burke's *Reflections*. But it was her *Letters on Education* (1790) that most directly influenced Mary in the composition of the *Rights of Woman*. She had reviewed the book at length in the *Analytical Review* for November 1790, and her contemporary Mary Hays is said to have observed that the principles expounded in the *Rights of Woman* were to be found in Mrs Macaulay[6].

It would perhaps be more accurate to say that some of Mrs Macaulay's precepts were to be found in the *Rights of Woman*, together with a great many other things which did not appear in the earlier book. Mrs Macaulay was intelligent, enlightened and far-sighted; yet her book is a dull one, and little read. She lacked the emotional fervour that has kept the *Rights of Woman* burning like a beacon for two hundred years. It has been called 'the first passionate protest against subjection which ever sprang from the pen of an Englishwoman'[7]; and 'perhaps the most original book of its century'[8]. Neither of these statements is strictly true. There were earlier pioneers, as has been indicated, and the *Rights of Woman* has acquired a reputation for originality which is not entirely justified. Its value is less as an original book, or even as a contribution to women's emancipation, than as the expression of an original life. It was published in January 1792, just one year after the *Rights of Men*. It had been written equally quickly—or some would say, hastily—in the space of six weeks[9]. Had Mrs Macaulay not died six months previously it is probable that the book would have been dedicated to her, for Mary spoke of having anticipated her 'approbation' and described her as 'The woman of the greatest abilities, undoubtedly, that this country has ever produced'. Instead, the dedication went to 'M. Talleyrand-Perigord, late Bishop of Autun', with the avowed object of convincing him that his *Report on Public Instruction* to the French National Assembly was inadequate in its treatment of female education. (Talleyrand's proposals recommended state education of girls, together with boys, only up to age of eight.) Mary's concern, she assured him, was quite disinterested: 'I plead for my sex, not for myself'; but she could not resist mentioning her own passion for independence as 'the grand blessing of life'.

She did not, however, delude herself that this passion was common to all her sex. She was aware not only that women suffered wrongs, but that very often these wrongs were perpetuated by their own weaknesses. She therefore made it clear at the start that she was concerning herself not solely with rights, but with the 'rights and duties' of woman; and that these rights and duties were important not only as they affected her own sex but in their bearing on society as a whole. Unless woman was educated 'to become the companion of man' she wrote to Talleyrand (echoing Defoe's sentiment nearly a hundred years earlier), the general progress of mankind would be halted: 'for truth must be common to all, or it will be inefficacious with respect to its influence on general practice'. To this end the education of women was crucial, since women usually inculcated the first principles of morality in young children. For example:

> If children are to be educated to understand the true principle of patriotism, their mother must be a patriot; and the love of mankind, from which an orderly train of virtues spring, can only be produced by considering the moral and civil interest of mankind; but the education and situation of woman at present shuts her out from such investigations.

It was quite impossible, she maintained, to confine women to domestic concerns 'by force'; and the attempt to keep them in a state of ignorance spread ill effects through the whole of society. On the other hand, if there were no coercion the sexes would 'fall into their proper places'. The delineation of these 'proper places'—for men no less than for women—forms the real burden of the somewhat inaptly titled *Vindication of the Rights of Woman.*

This is undoubtedly the most important of Mary Wollstonecraft's works, though superficially not the most attractive. It is a compelling and difficult book, the concentrated essence of a philosophy that yields up its message only after a considerable study. It was obviously written under emotional stress as well as from intellectual conviction, and the two strands are not always perfectly intertwined. Godwin himself called it 'a very unequal performance... deficient in method and arrangement', in temper 'rigid, and somewhat amazonian'; yet at the same time displaying 'a luxuriance of imagination, and a trembling delicacy of sentiment'. This was the mark of Mary's genius, that could encompass so many moods within a single theme and never lose sight of the predetermined end. Between her introductory comment that the minds of women were 'not in a healthy state' and the her concluding plea to 'Let woman share the rights, and she will emulate the virtues of man', there is a whole new world in the making. The reader is advised to explore it for himself (the generic 'he' is used in this case advisedly); at least not to dismiss the book unread; and to remember that those who derided the 'rights of woman' were by and large the same as those who derided the 'rights of man'.

The challenge of the book is immediately obvious in its style, or rather its lack of a conscious 'style'. Mary made clear in her introduction that this apparent clumsiness was deliberate; the style of writing was dictated by the subject and object of the book. Against the whole spirit of her age, she put matter before manner, aiming only to achieve usefulness and sincerity:

> I shall not waste my time in rounding periods, or in fabricating the turgid bombast of artificial feelings, which, coming from the head, never reach the heart. I shall be employed about things, not words!

There was a new spirit of confidence in this declaration. By 1792 Mary had conquered the deficiencies in her education and was in every sense a 'cultivated' woman. Her work for the *Analytical Review* had given her access to the best of eighteenth-century thought. She was well-read in the literature of her time, well-versed in its mores, and qualified to form her own judgment of its values and limitations. If the Age of Reason was deductive rather than inspirational in its thinking, Mary Wollstonecraft's aggressive creativity was all the more remarkable.

By what criteria, then, should the *Rights of Woman* be assessed? Mary staked out the battlefield herself, and named her adversaries, thus presenting us with the evidence on both sides of the argument. She took issue with two of the most popular books of her day, Dr Fordyce's *Sermons* and Dr Gregory's *Legacy*. *Sermons to Young Women* was first published in 1765 and became a best-seller. Its author, James Fordyce, was a Presbyterian minister and uncle of the George Fordyce who was a member of Joseph Johnson's circle. He may, therefore, be presumed to have been, by Mary's own standards, a reasonably enlightened character. It was perhaps his stress on 'female virtue', rather than virtue as such, that pricked her sensibilities; together with his extremely limited concept of what female virtue should be. She also deplored his affectation and sentimentality. To Dr Fordyce all young women were 'smiling innocents', timid and defenceless; to which the masculine counterpart was the barbarian who would despoil that innocence. Mary rejected both these concepts, well aware that an excessive exaltation of women was only the other side of the sensualist's coin. Dr Fordyce admitted as much, with his diatribe against the 'destructive syrens' who had 'forgotten to blush'. It was obviously his own fear of the power of unscrupulous women that was at the root of his attack. Mary, oddly enough, seems to have missed this interpretation of his attitude; she was no more in favour of 'destructive syrens' than he was. Nor could she have disapproved of his conclusion that the fashion of what he called 'a distracted and degenerate age' shunned women of accomplishment and modesty. She had suffered from these standards herself, and to change them was the theme-song of her own book.

A Father's Legacy to his Daughters by Dr John Gregory, professor of medicine at Edinburgh University, was published posthumously in 1784 and proved equally popular. It took the form of a series of letters to his daughters, written after the death of his wife and expressing such 'paternal solicitude', Mary confessed, that she criticised it 'with affectionate respect'. Yet criticise she must, believing as she did that the opinions expressed had had 'the most baneful effect on the morals and manners of the female world'. Though she disliked the doctor's conventional views on dress and 'delicacy', manners were a comparatively minor issue. It was his morality that really shocked her, with his advocacy of the art of 'dissimulation'. The unforgivable sin, in his spectrum, was for a girl to show her feelings. She should not even dance with too much spirit, lest this should be misunderstood. 'In the name of truth and commonsense,' cried Mary, 'why should not one woman acknowledge that she can take more exercise than another?' Because, the good doctor might have replied, one thing may lead to another—for instance, to falling in love. And in that event, he advised his daughters, never let the young man know 'the full extent of your love; no, not although you marry him.' Why ever not, asked Mary? A good wife had nothing to hide, and a strong mutual affection was the best guarantee that love would be succeeded by friendship rather than indifference. But Dr Gregory went further. Women should not only conceal their real feelings; they should also conceal their abilities. 'If you happen to have any learning,' he wrote, 'keep it a profound secret, especially from the men; who generally look with a jealous and malignant eye on a woman of great parts, and a cultivated understanding'. This was morality stood on its head with a vengeance! So 'the behaviour of the whole sex should be modulated to please fools!' snorted Mary, and turned to Hamlet for support: 'Seems! I know not seems! Have that within that passeth show!'

A feminine parallel with Dr Fordyce and Dr Gregory was to be found in Mrs Barbauld and Mrs Chapone, who may be taken as fair examples of the educated women of their day. Mrs Barbauld (née Anna Laetitia Aiken) had married a dissenting minister and helped him to run a boys' school at Palgrave in Suffolk, where she was said to have been a successful and popular teacher. Earlier, she had turned down a suggestion by the blue-stocking Mrs Montagu that she should open a college for young ladies. Her reasons for doing so show the great gulf that existed between Mary Wollstonecraft and even her most 'enlightened' contemporaries. Young ladies, Mrs Barbauld believed, should have only 'such a general tincture of knowledge as to make them agreeable companions to a man of sense' and, echoing Dr Gregory, she continued[10]:

> The thefts of knowledge in our sex are only connived at while carefully concealed, and if displayed, punished with disgrace. The best way for women to acquire knowledge is from conversation with a father, a brother, or a friend, in the way of family intercourse and easy conversation, and by such a course of reading as they may recommend.

Nevertheless, belying her own false modesty, Mrs Barbauld was an author of acknowledged repute who contributed prefaces to Akenside's *Pleasures of the Imagination* and Collins' *Odes*, and her *Miscellaneous Pieces in Prose* was one of the few works singled out for praise by Mary in her *Rights of Woman*. She also paid respect to the 'good sense and unaffected humility' of Mrs Chapone's *Letters on the Improvement of the Mind* (1773), even while not always agreeing with her. This book has been described as a standard work on female education which 'has never been surpassed'[11]. It certainly displays a humane good sense, particularly in its treatment of history ('little else than a shocking account of the wickedness and folly of the ambitious'); but Mrs Chapone was strictly conventional in her attitude to 'virtue' and religion, and circumspect on the place of the emotions.

Another female educationist then much in vogue was the French Madame de Genlis. Mary was not, however, impressed with her *Letters on Education* (1782), finding her views narrow and prejudiced and particularly objecting to the author's advocacy of '*blind* submission' both to parents and to the opinions of the world. 'Submission' was a word second only to 'weakness' in raising all Mary's feminist and radical hackles, and in this instance it provoked a typical footnote: 'Let people but watch their own hearts, and act rightly, as far as they can judge, and they may patiently wait till the opinion of the world comes round.' This, of course, was to foreshadow her own future. She had little patience either with the attitude of Mrs Piozzi (formerly Mrs Thrale) and her slavish imitation of the style and sentiments of Dr Johnson, as in this passage which she quoted:

> that a woman will pardon an affront to her understanding much sooner than one to her person is well known; nor will any of us contradict the assertion. All our attainments, all our arts, are employed to gain and keep the heart of man; and what mortification can exceed the disappointment, if the end be not obtained?

'All our *arts*,' echoed Mary scornfully—'Noble morality!' She equally condemned Madame de Stael's adulation of Rousseau, which she quoted with italics added: 'though he be full of indignation against them when they endeavour to resemble men, yet when they come before him with all the *charms, weaknesses, virtues*, and *errors* of their sex, his respect for their *persons* amounts almost to adoration'. True, commented Mary: 'For never was there a sensualist who paid more fervent adoration at the shrine of beauty'. Mary's sensitivity to the charm of the senses had complex causes. But before considering the emotional roots of the *Rights of Woman* it would be as well to look at Mary's assessment of the general status of women in society.

As already noted, her concern for the rights of women was a natural progression from a study of the rights of men. To obtain civil liberties and democratic rights, she had seen, men must throw off their shackles of servitude. But she had also discovered that even when civil rights were granted to the common man, certain sections of society seemed automatically to be excluded. It was this exclusion that focused her attention on the position of women, which she linked rather unusually with that of the soldier. Both women and soldiers lived in their own self-self-contained communities; both, in a sense, had power without responsibility; both were frequently admired for the wrong reasons. There were, of course, important differences. She maintained that the existence of a standing army was incompatible with freedom, because military discipline was based on despotism; the army was also a hotbed of vice and corruption for the idle young men in its service in peacetime. She hastened to add, too, that in comparing women with soldiers she was not advising them to change their distaff for a musket, though 'I sincerely wish to see the bayonet converted into a pruning hook'. In short, what she wanted was a society in which every man fulfilled the duties of a citizen (which a soldier did not); that his wife should share those duties (which most did not) and that she should at the same time 'be equally intent to manage her family, educate her children, and assist her neighbours'. This was a harmless enough recipe from an allegedly fire-eating feminist!

Mary stepped further from the path of convention when she considered the kind of education that would produce this end. The aim of education, in this context, should be 'to form citizens' rather than to produce a few brilliant scholars 'at the expense of the multitude'. Children should be taught with other children, not privately at home; girls and boys should go to the same schools; and these should be day schools, properly organised on a national basis. Mary expressed a horror of the boarding-school system that could not have arisen solely from her brief experience of Eton in 1786. She was equally vehement against female boarding-schools and was not too squeamish to point out that girls no less than boys could be made vicious by too close confinement with their own sex. What she proposed, briefly, was the provision of free, universal education for all children from the age of five to nine, with no distinctions of class or sex; after nine, children would proceed to different types of school according to their abilities and future prospects, concentrating on either practical instruction or academic studies. 'Boys and girls still together?' Mary at this point interposed. She answered with a firm 'yes'. She granted that this continued co-education might lead to some early attachments, and earlier than average marriages, but she was not averse to that; it would not hurt the children, she thought, to be allowed to choose their own 'companions for life'. Indeed, her main reason for wishing to see the sexes educated together was 'to perfect both'. But this improvement would not come about until girls were offered the same range of studies as boys, thus leading to the emancipation of the whole sex and avoiding the isolation of a few learned women as a species apart: 'men of genius and talent have started out of a class,' she commented, 'in which women have never yet been placed'. In this wider curriculum girls would be taught anatomy and medicine, as well as 'the anatomy of the mind'; they should pursue the arts and sciences, and study morality and political history. Mary would also do away with the 'ridiculous falsities' which were told to children about the facts of reproduction. Children were accustomed to seeing cats with their kittens and birds with their young, she noted: 'Why then are they not to be told that their mothers carry and nourish them in the same way? As there would then be no appearance of mystery, they would never think of the subject more.' Children were not hurt by being told the truth, she added: 'it is the modesty of affected modesty that does all the mischief'. True modesty was a different matter, and Mary never diverged from this. She described her own experience in discussing anatomical subjects with medical men and the proportions of the human body with artists: 'yet such modesty did I meet with, that I was never reminded by word or look of my sex'.

Mary Wollstonecraft's purpose in promoting women's education was characteristically her own and differed considerably from the aims of the blue-stockings. She was not concerned with the acquisition of learning for its own sake, nor for the improved status that learning would bring. If she had concentrated on *female* education, she explained, rather than education in general, this was because she regarded the female world as oppressed; and because the vices engendered by oppression were not confined to the oppressed sector but pervaded society as a whole. To educate women, therefore, was for the good of society and not just for the benefit of women. Nor were women to be educated simply in order to make them intellectuals—far from it. 'Make women rational creatures and free citizens,' Mary observed at the end of her chapter on education, 'and they will quickly become good wives and mothers'.

There was little in this text to presage Mary Wollstonecraft's later reputation as a dangerous liberationist, a subverter of home and family. Her glorification of motherhood even included a revival of the custom that mothers should suckle their own babies. In her conception of the fundamental role of woman Mary was indeed a dyed-in-the-wool traditionalist. In her conception of the status of woman in society she made little advance on her predecessor 'Sophia', in advocating that women should be trained as physicians no less than nurses; should study politics as well as history, and thereby change the course of history; and should support themselves by conducting their own business. But she did not stop there. She linked the struggle for women's rights with the wider struggle for a just society and saw that neither could be achieved in a vacuum. Women, therefore, should be not only good mothers but good citizens, and *vice versa*; the two things were inseparable in her mind. The domestic roots of society spread out into all its reamifications—'Public spirit must be nurtured by private virtue,' she observed; and conversely, a repressive social order distorted the basis of personal relationships.

In her chapter on 'The Pernicious Effects which Arise from the Unnatural Distinctions established in Society' she returned to her attack on the respect paid to property as the 'poisoned fountain' from which most evils and vices flowed. The rich no less than the poor suffered from this system, since she regarded idleness as the greatest threat to virtue. There could, therefore, be no advance in virtue without an advance in equality, whether between classes or sexes. Whilst women were totally dependent on their husbands, she observed, they would be 'cunning, mean and selfish'. The same effects might be seen in any sector of society which was exempted from the full duties of citizenship—and here Mary became surely one of the first advocates of a 'meritocracy':

> I mean therefore to infer that the society is not properly organised which does not compel men and women to discharge their respective duties by making it the only way to acquire that countenance from their fellow-creatures, which every human being wishes some way to attain.

She drew an idyllic picture of a man and wife, 'equally necessary and independent of each other' and enjoying the respect of their fellows:

Raised sufficiently above abject poverty not to be obliged to weight the consequence of every farthing they spend, and having sufficient to prevent their attending to a frigid system of economy which narrows both heart and mind... I know not what is wanted to render this the happiest as well as the most respectable situation in the world, but a taste for literature, to throw a little variety and interest into social converse, and some superfluous money to give the needy and to buy books.

Such an ideal state has the simplicity not of naivety but of wisdom. Mary knew it would not easily be won; in fact could not be won without a revolution in manners, morals and social priorities. For instance, 'when poverty is more disgraceful than even vice, is not morality cut to the quick?' Mary wanted to abolish both poverty and vice, by making society more just and personal relations more honest. In this task she appealed to men, in their own interests, to support the cause of women's liberation:

Would men but generously snap our chains, and be content with rational fellowship instead of slavish obedience, they would find us more observant daughters, more affectionate sisters, more faithful wives, more reasonable mothers—in a word, better citizens.

It was above all in her conception of the relation of the sexes, both to each other as individuals and to society as essential components in its structure, that Mary showed herself a true revolutionary. 'The two sexes mutually corrupt and improve each other,' she wrote. 'This I believe to be an indisputable truth, extending it to every virtue.'

The first essential for this mutual improvement must be the imposition of a common standard of morality. The greatest single cause for the weaknesses of women, Mary maintained, was want of chastity in men. But she was sufficient of a realist to recognise that the common standard must be an attainable one for the average human being. This brought her to the thought that if chastity had hitherto been under-rated in men, it was perhaps over-rated in women: 'If the honour of a woman, as it is absurdly called, be safe, she may neglect every social duty'. She quoted Mrs Macaulay in support of this view: it was 'trite and foolish', the latter had written, to suppose that one lapse from chastity in a woman had the power to deprave her character; the human mind was not so easily corrupted, and if some women were driven to subsequent 'abandonment' this was usually due to 'the venomous rancour of their own sex'. Mary added here an original thought of her own. In proportion as chastity was prized by women, she observed, it was despised by men: and 'the two extremes are equally destructive of morality'. This is perhaps the first clue to Mary Wollstonecraft's theory of a new morality between the sexes; a morality based on other values than those of the laws of property. These values she summed up as: 'Chastity, modesty, public spirit, and all the noble train of virtues, on which social virtue and happiness are built'.

Mary saw little of this 'social virtue' in the structure of British society in 1792. It seemed to her unjust, repressive and corrupt; and the root of its corruption, she was convinced, lay in the laws of property. Since the institution of marriage was closely bound up with those laws, this too seemed to her corrupt—and she would have no part in it. This was the real reason, whether consciously or not, that Mary had remained unmarried so far. ('Sir, I am POOR,' she had cried to her suitor the previous year.) But the corruption of an institution did not diminish the functions of a good wife and mother. A wife, in her view, was a person not a commodity; and the better the person, the better the wife. The same standard applied to the husband; he too was a person before he was a breadwinner and should be judged as such. The basis of any true relationship, in short—whether of husband, lover or friend—must be mutual esteem rather than material gain. What Mary advocated, therefore, was not an equality of women with men—which assumes the superiority of the masculine standard—but an equality of men and women *with each other*. This was an infinitely more revolutionary doctrine than mere feminism; a searching towards a supra-feminine and supra-masculine humanism, in which the self-interest of each was subordinated to a whole that was greater than either. But where was the man who could subscribe to so exacting a doctrine? Mary had not found him yet.

Instead, she was presented with the worldly cynicism of a Chesterfield and the ultra-romanticism of a Rousseau. Though poles apart politically, the two men shared certain attitudes towards women that caused Mary to cast them together in the same camp. These sentiments were crystallised in two books, Lord Chesterfield's *Letters to his Son* (1774) and Rousseau's *Emile*

(1762); and the complex ramifications of the authors' characters may be traced to a common root. The fact that the famous son of the Chesterfield letters, Philip Stanhope, was illegitimate may be balanced against Rousseau's five bastard children by the serving-maid Thérèse le Vasseur with whom he maintained a stable relationship for over thirty years. As he wrote in his *Confessions*: 'I declared to her beforehand that I would never forsake her, but that I would never marry her'; and this 'social contract' he fulfilled to the letter. At the same time, he formed a series of sentimental attachments to ladies of rank as a sort of fantasy compensation for the sordid reality of his 'marriage'.

Lord Chesterfield's *liaison* was formed during his term as British ambassador at The Hague, and he provided generously for both mother and child after the birth of his son in 1732. This he could well afford, having contracted a marriage of convenience the following year with the wealthy Countess of Walsingham (a natural daughter of George I). Chesterfield's devotion to Philip Stanhope, to whom he offered all the advantages due to a legitimate heir, was a mitigating factor in the affair. Thus neither man was in the conventional sense a 'scoundrel' or callous seducer of women. By the standards of their time, indeed, they behaved extremely well and their degradation of the status of women was unconscious and instinctive rather than a deliberate policy. They were blinded to the human qualities of their unofficial partners by the exigencies of snobbery and place-seeking, an attitude as natural as the air they breathed (if the air of a hot-house society is natural at all). Rousseau repudiated his bastard children, who were despatched to a foundling hospital after each birth since he was unable to support them himself. Chesterfield, to his credit, was eager to acknowledge his son—what was one bastard more or less among gentlemen? He erred in wishing to remake him in his own image, by his own social values, ignoring the boy's natural claims as a human being; in consequence of which, the son in his turn contracted a secret marriage with a 'worthy but undistinguished' wife which was only discovered by his father after Philip's early death at the age of thirty-six.

Thus both Rousseau and Chesterfield linked the 'inferior' status of women with the 'inferior' side of their own nature. A woman, it seemed, could only be regarded as man's equal in an open and acknowledged way if she made up for her natural deficiencies by the possession of wealth and influence. Mary Wollstonecraft, always conscious of her own early poverty, was quick to sense this underlying arrogance. But there was another factor involved. If the attitude of Rousseau and Chesterfield displayed a contemptible snobbery it also revealed a conflict between mind and body, spirit and sense, which was itself the cause of their predicament. If no such conflict had existed, they would never have been in the situation of taking a mistress who by any rational standards must have been judged 'inferior': not by virtue of her sex but because of her more limited human faculties. Rousseau's genius found no answering spark in his chosen partner; nor presumably did Lord Chesterfield's more superficial brand of sophistication, if the painful gaucheries of his son are anything to go by. Mary was aware of this conflict because she had experienced it herself. Unlike her male protagonists, however, she did not accept such a dichotomy as the natural order of things. Man, in her view, was neither an upgraded animal nor a fallen angel, but a being in his own right; since women belonged equally in the human order, and nowhere else, so was woman. 'I wish to see women neither heroines nor brutes,' she wrote, 'but reasonable creatures'.

But she had not yet reached that stage of integration in her own development, and in refuting what she regarded as the pernicious doctrines of Rousseau and Chesterfield her own emotions were obviously engaged. Lord Chesterfield's concept of a social structure based on worldly wisdom and what he called 'the Graces' was anathema to her. She was not alone in this. Dr Johnson remarked that the *Letters* 'teach the morals of a whore and the manners of a dancing-master'. Cowper, in his *Progress of Error* (1780), described Chesterfield as 'Graybeard corrupter of our listening youth'. In his advocacy of the art of dissimulation Lord Chesterfield anticipated Dr Gregory, though on a grander scale: the whole purpose of life, it would appear from his letters, was to gain advancement by the most barefaced flattery and sycophancy. Inevitably, in this system of values, women were objects to be exploited; though it was also true that the women who upheld and connived at the same system were adepts at exploitation themselves. The two sexes, as Mary had observed, corrupt each other. If Chesterfield described women as 'only children of a larger growth', Dryden had already said the same of men ('Men are but children of a larger growth'—*All for love*, iv, 1), though Mary seemed unaware of this when she rose to Chesterfield's taunt. So, perhaps, was he. 'A man of sense', he continued, 'only trifles with them, plays with them, humours and flatters them, as he does with a sprightly, forward child . . . No flattery is either too high or too low for them'.

Chesterfield was judging women by his own corrupt standards, without even being conscious that they were corrupt. Was it worth taking seriously a man who could write to his son, 'your dancing-master is at this time the man in all Europe of the greatest importance to you'; that 'air, manners, graces, style, elegancy, and all those ornaments, must now be the only objects of your attention'; that 'your sole business now is to shine . . . you had better talk trifles elegantly, to the most trifling woman, than coarse inelegant sense to the most solid man'? It is a wonder that Mary thought it necessary to spend ten pages refuting this nonsense. She would hardly have done so if the nonsense had not been generally accepted by society as good sense; and if she had not, like the poet Cowper, feared for its influence on impressionable youth. She condemned what she called the 'shuffling worldly wisdom' of trying to serve both God and mammon: 'If you wish to make your son rich, pursue one course—if you are only anxious to make him virtuous, you must take another; but do not imagine that you can bound from one road to the other without losing your way'.

This, perhaps, was what Rousseau had done, and where Mary parted company from him. For it must not be forgotten how much they had in common and how Mary had thrilled to the shock of recognition when she first read *Emile* in Dublin in 1784. There were still many general issues on which his thinking harmonised with her own, particularly on the care and education of young children. Like Mary, Rousseau advocated suckling by the mother; freedom from unnecessary restraints such as swaddling; fresh air and exercise; learning from sensory experience rather than verbal lessons; and relationships with adults based on affection. But with adolescence this harmony of thinking came to an abrupt halt. From then on, Rousseau was concerned with an education for boys that would fit them to take their place in the world of men; a world in which the girl's place was limited to a biological role. 'It is perhaps one of the greatest of marvels,' he wrote, 'how nature has contrived to make two beings so like and yet so different'. Mary would not have disagreed with this. She did not want women to be imitation men; but neither did she want them to be imitation human beings, as it seemed to her that Rousseau did. Women's opinions might be consulted on bodily matters, he advised, but in matters of morality and 'all that concerns the understanding' one should turn to men. Even at the biological level, however, women were not granted equality: man was the active partner, woman the passive; hence men must be strong and women weak—though this weakness itself could be used as a weapon to ensnare the strong (a recipe for 'cunning and lasciviousness', in Mary's view). Rousseau conceded that women and men were 'made for each other' but did not concede an equality of need. They need us more than we need them, he argued (ignoring the individual idiosyncracies that make every relationship different in degree if not in kind); therefore, the education of women should be relative to that of men and geared to the maintenance of nature's grand design:

> To please, to be useful to us, to make us love and esteem them, to educate us when young, and take care of us when grown up, to advise, to console us, to render our lives easy and agreeable—these are the duties of women at all times, and what they should be taught in their infancy.

Faced with this monumental smugness, Mary could only appeal to the deity. 'Gracious Creator of the whole human race!' she cried, 'hast Thous created such a being as woman . . . for no better purpose? Can she believe that she was only made to submit to man, her equal—a being who, like her, was sent into the world to acquire virtue?' Granted this basis, which Rousseau did not, the corollary was obvious: 'And can she rest supinely dependent on man for reason, when she ought to mount with him the arduous steeps of knowledge?'

But Rousseau was more interested in self-justification than in the sharing of knowledge or virtue. Women were mistaken, he continued, in complaining about 'the inequality of man-made laws' because the inequality was not of man's making! He qualified the absurdity of this statement by adding hastily—'or at any rate it is not the result of mere prejudice, but of reason'. Even Edmund Burke had not claimed that; he had simply sought to justify prejudice. On what grounds could such an attitude be countered? Mary set out her terms in the third chapter of her

Vindication:
> I here throw down my gauntlet, and deny the existence of sexual virtues, not excepting modesty. For man and woman, truth, if I understand the meaning of the word, must be the same... Women, I allow, may have different duties to fulfil; but they are *human* duties, and the principles that should regulate the discharge of them I sturdily maintain, must be the same.

Rousseau, however, seemed unable to grasp the distinction between duties and principles. 'Educate women like men,' he said, 'and the more they resemble our sex the less power will they have over us'. This statement was both untrue and offensive to Mary. To educate women, she reiterated time and again, would result in better *women*; and better women would not wish to exploit their power over men: 'This is the very point I aim at. I do not wish them to have power over men; but over themselves.' What a world of separation between Mary Wollstonecraft and Rousseau this one sentence reveals! And what nonsense it makes of his unreasoned claim to a *de facto* masculine superiority! Mary was indeed far more modest in her own claims. She did not even go as far as Judith Drake and 'Sophia' in asserting women's equality with men (far less their 'superiority') as a right. She only asked that women's capacities should be put to the test on equal terms, and judged accordingly: 'for she must grow more perfect when emancipated, or justify the authority that chains such a weak being to her duty'.

It hardly seems necessary to pursue the argument any further, but in all fairness to Rousseau it should be pointed out that his attitude was not quite so purblind as the extracts chosen by Mary for attack would indicate. Perhaps, in her indignation, she did not read *Emile* any more carefully than she had perused Edmund Burke. In delineating the character of 'Sophy' as the perfect mate for Emile he made a more generous assessment of the influence of women, in the state as well as in the home. That 'every virtuous nation has shown respect to women' was little more than a pious platitude, but he went further in declaring: 'Every great revolution began with the women', citing the example of Rome where women were responsible for overthrowing a tyranny and saving the city when it was beseiged by Coriolanus.

But Rousseau contradicted his own thesis when he admitted

that Sophy was really quite an ordinary girl: 'her education is responsible for everything in which she excels other women'. His concept of 'education' was perhaps rather different from Mary Wollstonecraft's, but he showed an even more startling reversal of his previously stated attitude when he now declared: 'In both sexes alike I am only aware of two really distinct classes, those who think and those who do not; and this difference is almost entirely one of education'. And how could Mary have overlooked this confirmation by Rousseau of her own most steadfast principle?—'A man who thinks should not ally himself with a woman who does not think, for he loses the chief delight of social life if he has a wife who cannot share his thoughts'. No doubt he spoke here from experience. But it was in exploring the heart of Sophy that he came closest to Mary's own being:

> All these dashing young men were only her equals in age, in everything else they were found lacking; their empty wit, their vanity, their affectations of speech, their ill-regulated conduct, their frivolous imitations alike disgusted her. She sought a man and she found monkeys; she sought a soul and there was none to be found.

Sophy's search was also Mary's, and she too had tasted its bitter fruits:

> She would rather consume herself in ceaseless conflicts, she would rather die free and wretched, than driven desperate by the company of a man she did not love.

This, Mary believed, was to be her own fate; and in vindicating the economic and intellectual independence of women she was conditioning herself to accept it. She had, she believed, put away the 'delusions of fancy', but fate itself decreed otherwise. And reading between the lines of the *Vindication* the actual fate of Mary Wollstonecraft can also be discerned with prophetic irony.

'Highly as I respect marriage,' she wrote, in discussing the virtues of monogamy, 'I cannot avoid feeling the most lively compassion for those unfortunate females who are broken off from society, and by one error torn from all those affections and relationships that improve the heart and mind'. Was she aware, as she wrote, that within herself were the seeds of that 'error'? Her description of the fate of the 'fallen woman' is so vivid that it seems already to belong to the past rather than the future:

> In a dream of passion thou consented to wander through

flowery lawns, and heedlessly stepping over the precipice to which thy guide, instead of guarding, lured thee; thou startest from thy dream only to face a sneering, frowning world, and to find thyself alone in a waste, for he that triumphed in thy weakness is now pursuing new conquests.

As if to strengthen her own defences, she attempted to scale down the importance of 'love' in favour of 'friendship'—'the most sublime of all affections, because it is founded on principle, and cemented by time. The very reverse may be said of love.' Mary, of course, had been disappointed in all her love-relationships so far and would be disappointed again. She was, therefore, driven to conclude that perhaps marriage was better founded on 'esteem', at least on one side: this too was to be her own lot. Yet she knew that love could not be driven out completely, not even by the most rational of women—and she was far from being that! Let women be contented 'to love but once', therefore, 'and after marriage calmly let passion subside into friendship—into that tender intimacy, which is the best refuge from care'. Again, Mary was presaging her own future, although her deductions were still based on theory and observation rather than practice. Would she have spoken so confidently if she had known at what cost the 'tender intimacy' was to be won?

In conclusion, then, Mary Wollstonecraft's *Vindication of the Rights of Woman* is not really about women's rights at all. It is about the desirability of an equal participation by all men and all women in common rights and common duties: 'Let woman share the rights', Mary had written, 'and she will emulate the virtues of man'. This presupposes a degree of morality that did not generally exist in either, but because she was addressing herself to women Mary was harder on her own sex. If woman did not 'grow more perfect when emancipated', then her chains were justified (the same, of course, might be said of men). Both sexes, indeed, must justify their existence at the bar of reason: 'the divine, indefeasible earthly sovereignty breathed into man by the Master of the universe'. It should not be forgotten, in the rush of revolutionary fervour that carries the book along, that Mary Wollstonecraft's morality—whether old or new—was still firmly based on the principles of natural religion; and that the Supreme Being was a far more important character in her cast than Rousseau, Lord Chesterfield, Mrs Macaulay, and the whole armies of feminists and anti-feminists put together.

Mary had planned a second volume of the *Rights of Woman* to elaborate her thesis that the 'improvement of female manners' would lead towards a 'general reformation of society'; but this was never written. With the completion of the *Vindication* Mary had reached her peak of intellectual exploration. She never climbed higher; and in the valley beyond, life was beckoning again.

CHAPTER NINE

Life and Art: 1791–1792

The publication of her *Vindication of the Rights of Men* at the end of 1790 had made no obvious difference to Mary's way of life. It must have enhanced her reputation in circles where she was already known, but the book was soon overshadowed by Tom Paine's best-selling *Rights of Man*. A more solid success was achieved by her translation of Saltzmann, the second and third volumes of which appeared in January and March 1791, with illustrations by William Blake. Subsequent editions were printed in 1792 and 1793, and the book was also published in America. (In 1793 Saltzmann demonstrated his approval of Mary's work by translating her *Rights of Woman* into German.)

For the time being Mary remained at her modest lodging in George Street, still plagued by family problems. Everina's sojourn in France seemed to have done little to improve her prospects, and she was back with her sister early in 1791. In April Eliza left Mrs Bregantz' school at Putney and travelled to Wales, where she visited her father at Laugharne before going on to a new situation at Upton Castle in Pembrokeshire. On 4th February Mary had written to her old friend George Blood[1], stamping on any hopes he may have had of uniting himself with one or other of the sisters: 'I ought to have done so sooner,' she observed, 'but there was an awkwardness in the business that made me shrink back.' George evidently still believed that there was some understanding between himself and Everina, and Mary hastened to disabuse him:

We have all, my good friend, a sisterly affection for you—and this very morning Everina declared to me that she had more affection for you than for either of her brothers . . . accustomed to view you in that light, she cannot view you in any other—

Why, at the age of twenty-five, Everina was unable to speak for herself only Mary, presumably, knew. At least, in this case, she could not be accused of jealousy of her younger sister, and she proceeded to give George some sensible advice:

Let us, then, be on the old footing—Love us as we love you—but give your heart to some worthy girl, and do not cherish an affection which may interfere with your prospects when there is no reason to suppose that it will ever be returned.

And that, it seemed, was that. Only two further letters from Mary to George have been recorded, and neither refers to the matter again.

In this same letter Mary observed that 'Everina does not seem to think of marriage, she has no particular attachment'. This hunch proved to be true, for despite her reputation as the most pleasure-loving of the three sisters Everina remained a spinster and became a school-mistress. Eliza, although married in name, was virtually in the same position and continued to seek a livelihood in a succession of unsatisfactory situations. She described her tribulations in a series of letters to Everina written between April and June 1791[2]. In the first of these, whilst still at Putney, she speaks of 'past pains and pleasures that are forever gon (sic)'. She also described with unusual frankness her distress at parting from her younger brother James, then completing his training as a naval officer at Woolwich: 'I felt more at parting with poor James than I could well *analyze* on recollection, *without blushing*. Well, what will not bear to be analyzed is well not talked of.' The Wollstonecrafts resembled that other literary family, the Brontës, in their emotional interdependence. Both families had suffered as children from an ill-tempered and domineering father and were driven for protection into clandestine alliance. Even the independent Mary, however far she travelled from them in spirit, could never break these family ties.

The following month found Eliza at Laugharne, after a brief stay with friends at Bradford-on-Avon where she evidently had some unpleasant experiences and left in a state of dudgeon. Her time spent at Bradford, she wrote to Everina, 'will shock and surprise you'. She did not specify in what way, beyond saying that she was obliged to speak frankly to the master of the house about his 'selfish behaviour' towards her. Eliza, like Mary, was liable to imagine slights or insults where none were intended. There was nothing imaginary, however, in the shock she received when she sailed down the river Severn to Laugharne and encountered her father: 'I thought I should have sank into the ground when I beheld his ghastly visage,' she wrote. Mr Wollstonecraft had been gravely ill, was in his habitual state of debt, and in addition had quarrelled with his youngest son Charles who was still living with him. The boy was obviously grossly neglected: 'I soon after met Charles,' Eliza continued, 'almost naked and the sight of him chilled my very soul'. She tried to remonstrate with her father to mend his ways by telling him how 'distressed' Mary had been about him, but he only flew into a passion. 'He is mad to be in London,' Eliza observed. No doubt Mr Wollstonecraft was envious of Mary's independent life and resented her efforts to help him.

From Laugharne Eliza travelled to Milford Haven to take up her post at Upton Castle, a historic seat which had passed into the hands of a Captain Tasker who had made his fortune in India. Mr Tasker was a bachelor and Eliza was presumably engaged as governess to his three nieces, to whom he subsequently bequeathed the estate[3]. She did not care for the family, but she found one friend in the district in the shape of a clergyman named Woods, whom she described in her letters a little disparagingly as 'this good *Welch parson*'. She hoped he would intercede with her father on behalf of the wretched Charles, but Mr Woods seemed to be more interested in Eliza herself: he was 'very attentive', she wrote to Everina. She was evidently not very impressed, however, for in the same letter she remarked: 'The only thing here that resembles man, is a noble Newfoundland dog; and a fine Greyhound'. These two dogs, said Eliza, were her *friends*. The greyhound was called Shank and the Newfoundland—Neptune! Was this just a coincidence, or had Eliza so christened the dog as a jibe at Mary and her *amours*? The two younger sisters could be both envious and sarcastic at her expense. In this letter, dated 17th June, Eliza let slip a revealing remark: 'I regret your last disappointment my dearest Everina more than any I ever met with, how different from *mine the one she has madly* thrown away!' The emphasis is erratic, but this would seem to suggest either that Mary had herself turned down a good offer of marriage or that she was now interfering with Everina's prospects as she had intervened in Eliza's case and destroyed her marriage. That Mary had refused a proposal of marriage we know from her angry correspondence with Joseph Johnson, and this is the more likely explanation. Everina may well have hoped that such a marriage, which she knew Mary to be capable of securing, would have solved the economic problem for all the sisters. But this was not Mary's way, and well they knew it; though they chafed at her unbending principles, they respected her intellect. Eliza at the same time requested that Mary should send 'some of the best sermons she can get' for Mr Woods and told Everina not to send the 'writing box' until she was sure 'what Mary thinks will be useful to him'. She also requested a copy of *'Burke's Pamphlet'*.

The 'pamphlet' was of course Burke's *Reflections* on the French Revolution to which Mary had published her reply in December 1790. Mr Woods evidently wished to read both sides of the case for himself. The publication of part one of Tom Paine's *Rights of Man* early in 1791 added fuel to a controversy that was spreading across the country and sending a flutter of fear through the English dovecotes. On the surface at least, Britain was prosperous and at peace. But under-currents of discontent were stirring with increasing menace. The threat to the traditional values on which the nation's prosperity was founded brought an inevitable reaction against the forces of dissent. On 14th July, the second anniversary of the storming of the Bastille, a mob broke into the home of Dr Priestley in Birmingham, ransacked his library, destroyed his scientific apparatus, then burned down the house and the nearby chapel where he preached—all in the name of Church and King. That same month, Tom Paine returned to England from Paris and started work on the second part of his inflammatory book. It was dedicated to the hero of the American and French revolutions, General Lafayette, and addressed to 'the people of England'. The message was obvious: it was time for England to rise too and throw off her shackles.

What shackles, it might be asked? There was no obvious repression, as in the case of colonial America or decadent France. In the view of one historian the average Englishman 'felt not the slightest wish' to despatch to the guillotine (or the gallows) the 'liberal-minded, open-hearted aristocrats'. Trevelyan's estimation of the late eighteenth century as a golden age of toleration, good manners and good taste may, however, be over-generous: 'the intellectual life of the country was never more brilliant, and the proportion of men of genius per head of population ... immensely greater than in our own day'[4]. This was an assessment of an élite, not of an age. But sufficient evidence of the good life in Georgian England has been handed down in its art and literature, and in the work of its craftsmen, to explain the absence of revolutionary fervour amongst the common people. Constable's idyllic landscapes do not portray a downtrodden rural populace, and the vices of the city had been much reduced since Hogarth's day. If only briefly, urbanity triumphed over squalor. Literacy, though not universal, was spreading rapidly thanks to the charity schools and Sunday schools; and literacy still bore some relation to literature. Trevelyan quotes the comment of the German pastor Karl Philip Moritz who visited England in 1782:

> My landlady, who is only a taylor's widow, reads her Milton; and tells me that her late husband first fell in love with her on this very account: because she read Milton with such proper emphasis.

There was, of course, a darker side of the picture. Gross poverty existed cheek by jowl with gross living; gross injustice was buttressed with gross corruption. England was poised between the old 'domestic' order and the new age of mass-production accompanied by mass-misery; and the coming disaster of the industrial revolution was not averted. For all its civilised veneer, something was rotten in the state of England. It was not the tyranny of the ruling-classes that Tom Paine and Mary Wollstonecraft were driven to attack, so much as their corruption: too often, liberal-mindedness was a cover for indifference and open-heartedness a cloak for licence. In the event, the guillotine was not necessary; the aristocrats laid their own heads on the block of mammon. What came after, however, was not the brave new world of the revolutionaries but the grasping materialism of the rising *bourgoisie*. This development, mercifully, was veiled from the reformers of the 1790s.

Mary Wollstonecraft had openly committed herself in the *Rights of Men* and the *Rights of Woman* to the radical cause. Her opinions must have been listened to with greater respect at Joseph

Johnson's dinner-table than in the days when she had almost to apologise for breathing the word 'soul' in that enlightened company; 'rights' were much more fashionable. Publicly, Mary had 'arrived'; from now on any pronouncement she made would demand attention, even from her opponents. Yet this success did little to ease her personal predicament. She had found a niche, of sorts, but only the uncomfortable one of the 'controversial' woman. This in itself put a strain on her already anguished nerves and pushed her prospects of personal happiness even further away. The 'hyena in petticoats' of the public image[5], however far from the truth, would not seem to most people a suitable creature to keep as a domestic pet.

In April 1791 Mary passed her thirty-second birthday: a great age for a woman to be still unmarried at a time when girls were commonly betrothed at seventeen and the average life expectancy was something under fifty years. Though her own sister Eliza was married at nineteen, she had eschewed an early marriage for herself because she knew it could only have been contracted on adverse terms. Nor did she relish the prospect, as she had confided to Jane Arden, of 'half a hundred children' by the time she was thirty. This did not mean, however, that she wished to eschew marriage and children altogether; her history so far had made that very plain. It did not seem impossible that ultimately both kinds of destiny could be achieved. Jane Arden had made an eminently suitable marriage in 1787 and as Mrs Gardiner was continuing her career of schoolmistress at Elsham Hall in Lincolnshire. But the chances for Mary to find a similar fulfilment were beginning to look rather thin. She had learnt to some extent to discipline her emotions, as she had disciplined her mind in the framework of the *Analytical Review*, and for the past two years there had been no visible sign of her former oscillations between ecstasy and despair. But the instincts are less amenable to regimentation. The natural longing of a healthy woman for a mate and a child was no less real for being suppressed and could not indefinitely be appeased by the substitute of professional recognition. Mary was only too well aware that 'the heart has its reasons', no less than the mind.

So what was she to do? The greater her achievements as an emancipated woman, the more exacting were her standards and the fewer the men who came up to them; and fewer still, those who were willing to try. By creating an unfamiliar image of what a woman should be, she had effectively isolated herself from the opportunity to put her theories into practice. Mary could only put a brave face on her predicament and extract what benefit she could from it. In September 1791 she moved from George Street to more spacious accommodation in Store Street, just north of Bedford Square. That same month Johnson published the second edi- of her *Original Stories*, with Blake's illustrations. Everina was with her at this time, but she left the following month to take a post as governess at Waterford in Ireland. Her brother James also spent some time with her. But Mary must still have felt lonely. For her family she was only a staging-post on the road to their own advancement; this was no substitute for permanent relationships of her own. She made the decision, therefore, at about this time, to 'adopt' a child. The young girl whose guardianship she assumed, known only as 'Ann', was said by Godwin to be a niece of 'the present Mrs Skeys'; she was about seven years old and her mother, a friend of Mary's, had recently died. If this was the same Hugh Skeys, it was strange that Mary should again be linked to him through the death of a friend. But the facts are in some doubt. Another story circulated by an American, Mrs Mark Leavenworth, who had known Mary in London at that time, was that the child was 'an orphan Girl, which the dying mother of the Child an East Indian gave her to bring up, and which she is educating she says a child of nature, aet.11'[6]. This more exotic explanation has a bizarre authenticity which is in keeping with Mary's impulsive generosity, as well as her theories of education. But however arrived at, the arrangement was not an unmixed blessing for either party and the experiment proved short-lived.

On 6th October Mary was writing to George Blood that after Everina went to Ireland she had found 'little Ann' very troublesome; and, although she was learning to manage her better, the child's 'great spirits' sometimes oppressed her. Since she believed in giving children freedom of expression, however, Mary would have been reluctant to damp these spirits, and it also pleased her to find that Ann was 'an affectionate, artless child'. Nevertheless, the effort to accommodate herself to her young ward was a constant strain on her nerves, and doubtless an interruption to the work on which their support depended. There was, moreover, another reason why the child's presence soon became somewhat irksome. Eliza let this cat out of the bag in a letter to Everina on 4th October, passing on news from Mary about the child's progress and about their brother James who had just returned to sea:

> She is heartily tired of her *daughter* Ann and brimful of her friend Fuseli, and a visible pleasure at her brother's departure is expressed.

Here is the first mention in the family correspondence of an influence that had been building up in Mary's life over the past two years and was now becoming dominant. Her relationship with the painter Henry Fuseli was obliquely referred to in a number of contemporary records but has never been clearly explained; perhaps, with the scanty evidence available, it never can be. But whether accounts of her feeling for him have been exaggerated or played down, the attraction was evidently a powerful one and is interesting if only for its incongruity. Though there were certain parallels in their temperaments and early experiences, in character and convictions Mary and Fuseli were totally opposite. Their common meeting-ground was with their intermediary, Joseph Johnson.

Fuseli's connection with Johnson went back much further than Mary's. When he first came to England from Switzerland at the age of twenty-three in search of a literary career he lodged in Johnson's house and the friendship was maintained through many vicissitudes. His early life is worth recounting for the light it sheds on his character and later development, and on the sources of his fascination for Mary Wollstonecraft. Henry Füssli, to give him his patrial name, was born at Zürich in 1741 into a family with an ancestry of painters. Henry inherited this bent and as a small child was passionately fond of drawing. Unfortunately, his father decided that this son should be trained as a 'scholar' and that his brother should be the painter. 'Letters were beat into him,' Joseph Farington observed in his diary[7]; and Fuseli later recalled that he spent his early days in 'floods of tears' at being forced to read instead of draw. Nevertheless he was made to persist in his studies, and and at the age of twenty he was ordained as a Zwinglian minister in the reformed church.

Fuseli's formative years were thus marked by conflict and repression. As a student he fell under the influence of Bodmer, professor of Helvetian history at Zürich and father of the *Stürm und Drang* movement that briefly dominated the intellectual life of Europe and came to be personified in Goethe and Schiller. Bodmer was a passionate admirer of the English literary tradition, as opposed to French classicism, and had translated *Paradise Lost* into German in 1732. These influences were deeply absorbed and never dislodged from Fuseli's consciousness, although temporarily buried beneath a superstructure of theology. But his vocation as a minister was short-lived and was terminated for reason which Mary would certainly have approved. In 1763, together with his friend Johann Kaspar Lavater and a fellow-student called Felix Hess, Fuseli was involved in the publication of a pamphlet exposing the corruption of a local magistrate; owing to this man's influential connections the three were advised to leave the country. Switzerland in the eighteenth century was not the tolerant haven for the exile that it became in the twentieth; only two years later Rousseau was expelled from his native Geneva, as he had previously been driven from France, because of the 'heresies' expressed in *gemile*. Fuseli and his friends fled to Prussia and here at last he was able to develop his talent for drawing. His first professional work may have been his illustrations for Bodmer's *Noachide*, published in 1765. Also, curiously enough, Fuseli undertook a German translation of Lady Mary Wortley Montague's letters. This must have been hack-work—he had little sympathy with feminism—but it may well have led to his acquaintance with the British ambassador in Berlin, Sir Andrew Mitchell, who invited this promising young man to accompany him to England in 1764. Since Lavater and Hess were then returning to Zürich, which Fuseli was reluctant to do because of family opposition, he accepted the invitation despite the terrible wrench of parting from Lavater. 'My God, my God!' he wrote to his friend, 'when shall I see you again, when shall I once more lay my hand in your hand, my breast against your breast, against that truest of all hearts, and be in bliss—?'[8] Other letters expressed equally strong emotion; this was evidently a young man's passionate friendship. They did not meet again for sixteen years; and then Fuseli's affections found another focus. His youthful attachment to Lavater, however, has some parallels with Mary's devotion to Fanny Blood. Thanks to Bodmer's influence, in coming to England the young Fuseli was culturally at home. His admiration for Shakespeare and Milton was akin to worship, and he is said also to have been profoundly influenced by Edward Young's poem cycle, *Night Thoughts*. His linguistic ability soon brought him translating work and in this, like Mary, his benefactor was Joseph Johnson. Also like Mary, Fuseli had a spell as tutor in a noble family, being employed in 1765 by the Earl of Waldegrave. Unlike Mary, however, he did not despise the aristocracy but wished to be regarded as their equal: but he went too far in boxing the ears of his young master, Lord Chewton, during a tour of France, and was dismissed from his post. Fuseli was no more fitted by temperament than Mary to remain in a subservient position. 'The noble family of Waldegrave took me for a bear-leader,' he commented later, 'but they found me the bear'. He did, indeed, have a reputation for 'bearishness'. His manner and physique were unprepossessing—Hazlitt described him as 'uncouth and dwarfish'—but he impressed by the power of his intellect and the force of his convictions.

Another link with Mary, perhaps, was Fuseli's admiration for Rousseau. Whilst in Paris with Lord Chewton in 1766 he actually met his hero in the company of David Hume, shortly before the famous quarrel between the two philosophers. The next year he published an essay in defence of Rousseau and attacking Hume. But Fuseli's real passion was still drawing, rather than poetry and philosophy, and in pursuing this ambition he had the encouragement of the first president of the Royal Academy, Sir Joshua Reynolds. He also became acquainted with that remarkable woman painter Angelica Kauffmann; and according to her biographer Adeline Hartcup he was 'as in love with Angelica as her friend Mary Moser was with him'[9]—but this may be mere romanticising. There is no evidence of anything more than a passing flirtation; nor that Fuseli was seriously interested in any woman at this stage of his life. This was possibly because in his own eyes he was still an incomplete man: he had not yet become an artist. To this end, therefore, in 1770 he resolved to burn his boats (in fact they were burnt for him by a fire at Johnson's house which destroyed most of his possessions) and take up the full-time study of art in Rome.

Fuseli stayed in Italy eight years, working with a fanatical intensity as he sought to emulate the perfection of his new hero Michelangelo, for whom he conceived an admiration little short of idolatry. Whilst in Rome he is said to have suffered from a fever which left him, though still comparatively a young man, with 'white hair and trembling hands'[10]. In 1778 Fuseli returned to

Zürich and visited Lavater; he also met Lavater's niece Anna Landolt, and his ardent feelings were now transferred to her. But the courtship did not prosper, and Fuseli's hopes of marriage were discouraged both by the girl herself and by her family. Their objections were mainly on account of his precarious financial situation, and soon after his departure Anna married a wealthy cousin. This snub may have confirmed Fuseli in his personal eccentricities, which became more marked as he grew older, and contributed to his generally debased view of women. Once again he fled from his native city, this time never to return.

He settled instead in London and applied himself ferociously to his new profession: he would succeed as a painter, if in no other way. The impact of Rome had been enormous and the style he had acquired from Michelangelo, and from the influence of the Italian Mannerists, was fixed for life. Fuseli's style was acquired, but his vision was entirely his own. He expressed it in a variety of themes ranging from classical mythology to biblical illustration—avoiding only those twin English pillars, the landscape and the portrait—but its essence was best conveyed in his first major picture, *The Nightmare*, which was exhibited in 1782. Much of Fuseli's work had a 'nightmare' quality, evoked from his own subconscious terrors which may have had their roots in his repressed childhood. It is perhaps significant that only in his paintings and drawings did he reveal this side of his nature. For Fuseli continued to be a writer of some distinction—being both poet and critic—and in literature he was as rational as the next man. In 1786 he collaborated with William Cowper in a translation of Homer, and he was a regular contributor to the *Analytical Review* from its foundation. He also translated his friend Lavater's *Aphorisms on Man* in 1788 and edited an English version of the same author's *Essays on Physiognomie* in 1792, a book he had already illustrated in the French version. By a strange coincidence, Mary Wollstonecraft had embarked on a translation of the *Physiognomie* for Johnson in 1789, but the project was abandoned when a translation by Thomas Holcroft was published the same year. Lavater had dedicated the original edition to his old friend, and it is possible that Mary's interest in Fuseli was first roused by this association.

As far as we know, her personal acquaintance with him dates from 1788 when she became an *habituée* of Johnson's circle. According to Cunningham's account of the affair[11], she 'conferred upon him the honour of her love' at their first interview; but this supposition seems highly unlikely. Mary was then in a period of intense literary activity, and it was not until the latter part of 1791 that her energies noticeably declined under the burden of her hopeless passion. There is evidence, however, that she was on terms of personal friendship with Fuseli as early as 1789, if his biographer John Knowles is correct in stating that during that year he attended 'a masquerade at the Opera House with Lavater's son and Mary Wollstonecraft'. That the relationship could be no more than friendship Mary must have known from the start, since in June 1788 Fuseli had married Sophia Rawlins, a young woman of unsullied reputation who was said to have sat for him as his model. This barrier, however, did not deter Mary from seeking his company. Ignoring her own warning in *Thoughts on the Education of Daughters* ('Nothing can more tend to destroy peace of mind, than platonic attachments') she was confident that the strength of her moral principles would carry her through. But nature determined otherwise.

Godwin described her dilemma thus:

She saw Mr Fuseli frequently; he amused, delighted and instructed her. As a painter, it was impossible she should not wish to see his works, and consequently to frequent his house. She visited him; her visits were returned. Notwithstanding the inequality of their years, Mary was not of a temper to live upon terms of so much intimacy with a man of merit and genius without loving him. The delight she enjoyed in his society, she transferred by association to his person. What she experienced in this respect, was no doubt heightened, by the state of celibacy and restraint in which she had hitherto lived, and to which the rules of polished society condemn an unmarried woman. She conceived a personal and ardent affection for him.

The awkward problem of Mrs Fuseli did not at first seem any problem at all. Mary had no intention of breaking up the marriage. She set great store on the sanctity of marriage; but she also, as Godwin put it, 'set a great value on a mutual affection between persons of an opposite sex'. Trouble arose when the two principles collided. Experiencing this mutual affection, based on an affinity of ideals—although it was perhaps a little less mutual, and less ideal, than she supposed—what was she to do? In

Godwin's view there was no reason to doubt that 'if Mr Fuseli had been disengaged at the period of their acquaintance, he would have been the man of her choice'.

Mr Fuseli, unfortunately, was not disengaged. Nor, if he had been, is there any certainty that Mary would have been the woman of his choice. From all that is known of his character it is highly unlikely; and it was perhaps a mercy that she did not have to put his affections to the ultimate test. Instead she attempted a compromise; and compromise was something so alien to Mary's nature that the attempt was bound to fail. Knowles, writing less sympathetically than Godwin, put the matter quite bluntly:

> She falsely reasoned with herself... that although Mrs Fuseli had a right to the person of her husband, she, Mrs Wollstonecraft, might claim, and, for congeniality of sentiments and talents, hold a place in his heart; for 'she hoped,' she said, 'to unite herself to his mind'. It was not to be supposed that this delusion could last long.

Knowles was right in his supposition, and Mary must have known it too. For in suggesting that Fuseli could somehow be sliced in two and nicely apportioned as between body and soul she was contradicting her own convictions. She did not believe in the separation of mind from matter any more than in the separation of religion from morality (as she had cogently argued to Burke). Fuseli might have been able to accept this arrangement, since his own nature was deeply divided; for Mary it was an impossibility.

Mary's delusion about her own feelings also extended to her conception of Fuseli's character. His acceptance of her devotion, with no regard to the havoc it was wreaking, was either grossly insensitive or grossly cynical. Cunningham in his life of the painter described how, instead of repelling Mary's 'ridiculous advances', Fuseli assumed a pose of platonic love and displayed 'artificial raptures' though he never had the slightest intention of abandoning his wife. He commented: 'The coquetting of a married man of fifty with a tender female philosopher of thirty-one can never be an agreeable subject of contemplation'. The besetting weakness of Fuseli—apart from his psychological quirks—was generally acknowledged to be his vanity. Mary's flattering attentions must have been too pleasing to resist, until they became a nuisance to him. Joseph Johnson is said to have remarked, when introducing him to Bonnycastle in 1779[12]:

I will now introduce you to a most ingenious foreigner, whom I think you will like; but if you wish to enjoy his conversation, you will not attempt to stop the torrent of his words by contradicting him.

This intellectual waterspout was one of his fascinations for Mary. 'I always catch something from the rich torrent of his conversation,' she observed. But she was not totally blinded by her infatuation; and once she began to see through him, her usefulness to Fuseli was at an end. On one occasion she burst out: 'I hate to see that reptile Vanity sliming over the noble qualities of your heart'[13]. Nor was 'vanity' the only viper in Fuseli's breast.

Fuseli's drawings have often been likened to those of Blake—the same flying figures, with elongated limbs, suspended in some private limbo between heaven and hell—with the assumption that Fuseli was merely a copyist. But Mason[14] has shown convincingly that his was the prior influence, and his contemporaries certainly regarded him as the greater artist of the two. His pictures still have a startling modernity; Blake is reported to have said that he was two centuries ahead of his times. But in creative imagination he is not of the same order as Blake, possibly the one man who soared above the limitations of his age. The 'imagination' of Fuseli was little more than a ragbag of fantasy, distortion and even perversion. Hazlitt, looking at the paintings rather than the man, considered that Fuseli's 'distortions and vagaries are German, and not English; they lie like a nightmare on the breast of our native art'[15]. Perhaps Hazlitt was thinking literally of Fuseli's 'nightmare' themes. Yet it was not in the overt expression of Gothic terror—a commonplace of his times—that his distorted vision was most clearly displayed, but in his so-called 'domestic' drawings and, above all, in those designed to illustrate Cowper's poems. Anything more incongruous with Cowper's quiet dreams of hearth and home than the grotesque female figures of Fuseli's portrayals would be hard to imagine. In Benjamin Haydon's view, 'his women were all strumpets'—of which 'The Debutante' is a good enough example. Nor was this the worst he could do. For after his death in 1805 a large collection of unpublished drawings was found in Fuseli's album which were described by contemporary witnesses as erotic and even obscene. Many of the drawings, not surprisingly, were believed to have been burnt by his widow; but some have since been traced.

They have been analysed by Ruthven Todd, who found some of them 'among the finest of Fuseli's works'[16]. To Sacheverell Sitwell, on the other hand, they were 'the only really evil drawings ever done' and represented 'the most extraordinary document of abnormality there has ever been'[17]. Not for nothing, it seems, was Fuseli nicknamed 'painter in ordinary to the Devil'. 'Aye!' Cunningham reported him to have said, 'he has sat to me many times'.

This was the man who so enslaved the author of the *Rights of Men* and the *Rights of Woman* that her faculties were virtually paralysed. As Johnson recalled, 'her exertions seem to have been palsied—you know the cause'[18]. The attraction must have been an affinity of opposites. Mary's humane, open-eyed vision was the antithesis of Fuseli's nightmare fantasies. Yet was there not also something a little alien and un-English in her own highly-charged emotionalism and her inability to compromise? These may have been the common attributes of a certain kind of genius, overriding nationality and morality alike. The causes of Mary's obsession are obscure, but its effects were cataclysmic. Godwin noted that 'during her residence in Store-street, which lasted more than twelve months, she produced nothing, except a few articles in the Analytical Review'. This is not quite correct. She produced her greatest work, the *Rights of Woman*, towards the end of 1791 after she had moved to Store Street, which suggests that her relationship with Fuseli had not yet reached a crisis point. Subsequently she was supposed to have been preparing a sequel to the book, and it was then, during 1792, that the rot really set in. Godwin reported that she 'scarcely left behind her a single paper' as evidence of this work. Once again—as had happened at Newington Green—it seemed that at the time of greatest opportunity Mary was unable or unwilling to profit from it.

Yet her character had changed a good deal since those early days as a school mistress; it seemed to many of her acquaintances that the change was not for the better. Whether this was due to to the bad influence of Fuseli or—as her sisters believed—a rush of fame to the head, it was noticeable that with her improved status Mary became much more conscious of herself as a woman of some importance. Godwin noted that, in contrast to her former spartan habits, she now acquired 'a certain degree of elegance' in her mode of living. Even her family noticed the difference. 'Mrs Wolstonecraft (sic) is grown quite handsome,' Charles observed to Eliza, in some surprise; adding rather spitefully, 'being conscious that she is on the wrong side of Thirty she now endeavours to set off those charms (she *once* despised) to the best advantage'. Nevertheless, Eliza reported to Everina on 3rd July 1792, Charles was 'delighted with her kindness and affection to him'. The author of the *Rights of Woman* was not so swollen-headed that she overlooked the claims of her family. Charles stayed with her for some weeks during the early part of 1792, while she made strenuous efforts to launch him on a career. Charles had by this time attained his majority, but little else, and was proving as intractable a problem to Mary as either of her sisters. She described him to Fuseli's friend William Roscoe, who she hoped might find an opening for him through his banking interests in Liverpool, as 'a thoughtless youth with common abilities, a tolerable person, some warmth of heart and a turn for humour'[19]. This was hardly a glowing testimonial, though perhaps he reminded her of that other warm-hearted young rascal, George Blood. He evidently made a favourable impression on a childless American couple, Joel and Ruth Barlow, who had come to London from Paris the previous year and soon became intimates of Mary through Barlow's association with Joseph Johnson and Tom Paine. The Barlows took a great interest in Charles, even to the point of threatening to adopt him, and finally assisted his emigration to America in November 1792. In preparation for this, Mary placed him earlier in the year on a farm near Leatherhead in order to give him some training in agriculture.

Writing to Everina in November 1791, Eliza had speculated on Mary's relationship to Fuseli: 'I will make no comment on the motives that influence her conduct. I shall be happy to hear from you what she is now absorbed into. A *Love*? or Study?' Eliza was smarting under the humiliation of her own situation as a governess. The following January she observed that 'a Venus de Medicis (sic) would not be noticed in a dependent situation. No, not even Mary's Sappho—even Fueslie (sic) was full of these human distinctions, in fact it is one of the accomplishments of high life'. Eliza had evidently been visiting Mary, perhaps for Christmas, and felt herself snubbed. Later in the same letter she commented: 'I never think of our sister but in the light of a *friend* who has been dead some years'. She also referred to 'this sudden change' in such a character and to the corrupting power of 'the

Life and Art: 1791–2

Love of Fame'. Yet two months later she was longing to see Mary again. 'Oh that M. and Johnson would spend a month at Tenby and we add our mite,' she wrote to Everina, 'for never did poor wretch sigh more for society than I.' Nor could she avoid feeling a little proud of Mary's achievements. 'Have you nought to say of your sister's Rights of Women?' she added in a postcript.

Mary revealed something of her state of mind in her own letter to Everina dated 23rd February 1792. Speaking of Charles and his prospects in America she remarked: 'Did I tell you that Fuseli insisted on making Charles a present of ten pounds, because he liked the scheme?' If there was a hint of bribery in Fuseli's evident wish to get rid of the boy, Mary was blissfully unaware of it. She saw the gesture only as proof of her hero's generous nature (though he was notoriously mean). Again, Mary's self-deception is illustrated in her changing attitude to her 'daughter'. No longer was the child a source of delight. She complained to Everina that she had caught Ann stealing the sugar—hardly an indictable offence! It was not like Mary to be harsh with a child, but now she had to admit:

> I have long been convinced that she will never be the kind of child I should love with all my heart. She has great *animal* spirits and quick feelings, but I shall be much mistaken if she has any considerable portion of sensibility when she grows up.

Poor Ann! Mary had fallen into the error, against which she had herself warned parents, of judging a child by her own standards. This in itself was a sign that her attention was fixed elsewhere. Not long afterwards, Ann was despatched to Ireland in the care of Everina and the brief experiment in character-moulding came to an end.

Mary was no longer giving her mind to the training of children, since she had discovered that adult society could offer greater rewards. In pursuit of her new role she even descended to a little name-dropping. 'Mr Opie,' she informed Everina, 'frequently calls upon me'. The young Cornish painter, himself rising to fame, shared Mary's dislike of fashionable society and perhaps found her company more congenial than that of his wife, whom Mary dismissed as 'too much of a flirt to be a proper companion to him'. This was a shrewd judgment, for Mrs Opie later left her husband for another man. But Mary was absorbed in Fuseli, and as her passion developed her own unmarried state must have become increasingly painful. She could not refrain from assuring Everina, however, that this condition was from her own choice:

> And, be it known with you, that my book &c &c has afforded me an opportunity of settling *very* advantageous in the matrimonial line, with a new acquaintance, but *entre nous*—a handsome house and a proper man did not tempt me; yet I may as well appear before you with the feather stuck in my cap.

Two years earlier Mary had regarded a proposal of marriage from an 'acquaintance' as an insult. Now she was playing the oldest ace in a woman's hand to win a cheap trick and boasting that she was quite capable of landing a good catch if she were so disposed. This was doubtless true. But Mary knew that she had no hope of ever marrying Fuseli, and her boast was only a gesture of bravado.

Perhaps this is what Godwin had in mind when he said that Mary 'came something more a cynic out of the school of Mr Fuseli than she went into it'. Mary was never a 'cynic', but her independent life in London had no doubt taught her some degree of the worldly wisdom she so conspicuously lacked before; and this may have been the more noticeable for being acquired so late. It was during this stage in her development that Godwin became acquainted with the woman who so dramatically influenced his later life; his impression at that time was not very favourable. He recalled that he first met Mary in November 1791 at a dinner-party in the house of a mutual friend. The invitation was of his own seeking, with the object of meeting not Mary Wollstonecraft but Tom Paine, since he knew that the author of the *Rights of Man* would be among the guests. To his annoyance, however, he was obliged to listen for most of the evening to Mary, who proved more than a match for Paine as a conversationalist. What he heard was not at all to his liking, for Mary had a habit of looking on the gloomy side of things 'and bestowing censure with a plentiful hand'. Godwin, on the contrary, was an optimist and 'had a strong propensity to favourable construction'. As an avowed atheist he also disliked her conventional respect for religion. They parted, he noted, 'mutually displeased with each other'. They met again on several occasions during the next year but made very little progress towards 'a cordial acquaintance'. Mary's interest in Godwin was equally cool. His sober, rather pedantic mien had none of the exotic appeal of a Fuseli. Godwin's hour of glory, with the publication of *Political Justice*, was still to come.

That summer of 1792 Mary reached the height of her intoxication. Briefly, for all her personal frustrations, she was on top of the world. Her *Rights of Woman*, despite the frowns of conservative society, had brought her national and international fame. A second English edition was already in preparation, and in the same year an American edition and a French translation came out. Saltzmann's German translation was to appear the following year. In the spring of 1792 the great Talleyrand himself, to whom the book was dedicated, called on Mary during a visit to London—and she is reported to have offered him wine out of a teacup: a nice gesture of *entente cordiale*, though more likely dictated by economic necessity. But the greatest excitement for Mary at this time was revealed in a letter to Everina dated 20th June: an excursion to Paris in the company of Joseph Johnson, Fuseli—and Mrs Fuseli. 'It is now determined on,' Mary wrote, 'and we think of going in about six weeks'. As usual, her own motives were shown to be mixed:

> I shall be introduced to many people. My book has been translated and praised in some popular prints; and Fuseli, of course, is well known; it is then very probable that I shall hear of some situation for Eliza, and I shall be on the watch. We intend to be absent only six weeks; if then I fix on an eligible situation for her she may avoid the Welsh winter.

The journey would not involve any 'extraordinary expense', she added, which she could ill afford. She was still maintaining Charles while the plans for his emigration were completed, and he was 'wearing out the clothes which were provided for his voyage'. Though she talked of finding a situation for Eliza in Paris, Mary threw out hints in this letter that it might be a good thing if her sisters also emigrated to America. She assured Everina that European women were 'particularly respected' in the New World: they could make a living by taking in pupils and might even 'marry well' (a strange argument for Mary to use!); in the meantime, Mrs Barlow would find a home for Everina and Eliza could keep house for Charles. The plan was almost too neat; and like so many of Mary's well-intentioned schemes it never materialised. Eliza, on hearing of these plans, was immediately sceptical. She wrote to Everina on 3rd July:

So the author of The Rights of Women is going to France! I dare say, her chief motive is to promote her poor Bess's Comfort! or thine, my girl, or at least I think so she will thus reason.

Eliza had a quite uncanny knack of piercing Mary's illusions: 'Well, in spite of Reason, when Mrs W. reaches the Continent she will be but a woman!' She knew full well that Mary's real reason for going to France was to be with Fuseli, even if the price she must pay for six weeks of his company was that Mrs Fuseli should go too. Yet Eliza was not ungenerous in her assessment of 'Mrs W.', though her own lot must have been all the harder to bear in the light of Mary's freedom:

> I cannot help painting her in the height of all her wishes, at the very summit of happiness. For will not ambition fill every chink of her Great Soul (for such I really think her's) that is not occupied by *Love*!

She hastened to disabuse Everina, however, of any lingering thoughts that Mary might be promoting her sisters' welfare in France:

> And you actually have the vanity to imagine that in the National Assembly Personages like M & F will bestow a thought on two females whom nature meant to 'suck fools and chronicle small beer'.

The visit to Paris was due to take place at the beginning of August, but again Mary's expectations were to be disappointed. The events of the next month are obscure, but it is clear that she did not go to France. Did Mrs Fuseli draw back and prevent it? Or was the situation considered to be too dangerous? This is a likely explanation. It is evident that the party did set out as planned but only got as far as Dover. News may then have reached them that Paris was in turmoil: the insurrection of the Commune and assault on the Tuileries palace took place on 10th August. These events would not have deterred Mary, as she later made plain, but her fellow-travellers were more cautious. Another factor in the situation was the health of Joseph Johnson, who was alway delicate and subject to attacks of asthma; this consideration would have swayed Mary more than any thought of her own safety.

Instead of attending the National Assembly with Fuseli, then, it seems likely that Mary took Johnson for a holiday—perhaps to visit her family in Wales. She was certainly away from London during that period, as she makes clear in a letter to Everina dated 14th September. She wrote that she arrived back in town 'the day before yesterday' and found that in her absence Charles had been 'well, happy and industrious'. She expressed some impatience with the Barlows' delay in taking the boy to America and observes that Mr Barlow appeared to be more interested in the 'present commotion' in France than in returning to the 'peacable shade' of America (the Barlows did in fact go to Paris soon afterwards). It is also noteworthy that she contributed almost nothing to the *Analytical Review* between July and November that year, which suggests that she was absent from her desk; although Johnson attributed this hiatus to her infatuation with Fuseli.

Her relations with the painter were rapidly approaching a climax, which may have been precipitated by the frustration of her Paris plan. In a last, desperate effort to find some *modus vivendi* that might accommodate both herself and Mrs Fuseli, Mary now proposed the expedient of a *ménage à trois*. Knowles described this episode with more frankness than Godwin:

> At length Mrs Wollstonecraft . . . had the temerity to go to Mrs Fuseli, and to tell her, that she wished to become an inmate in her family; and she added, 'as I am above deceit, it is right to say that this proposal arises from the sincere affection which I have for your husband, for I find that I cannot live without the satisfaction of seeing and conversing with him daily'. This frank avowal immediately opened the eyes of Mrs Fuseli, who being alarmed by the declaration, not only refused her solicitation, but she instantly forbade her the house.

Mary could only retreat and lick her wounds, reflecting perhaps that her honesty had cost her the few crumbs of comfort she had snatched so far. Now she was barred for ever from the nourishment of all her hopes. Knowles concludes the story with little evidence of concern (he was, of course, a Fuseli man):

> No resource was now left for Mrs Wollstonecraft, but to fly from the object which she regarded: her determination was instantly fixed; she wrote a letter to Fuseli, in which she begged pardon 'for having disturbed the quiet tenour of his life', and on the 8th of December, 1792, left London for Paris.

Mary wrote to William Roscoe on 12th November with as brave a face as she could put on it:

... I intend no longer to struggle with a rational desire, so have determined to set out for Paris in the course of a fortnight or three weeks; and I shall not now halt at Dover, I promise you; for as I go alone neck or nothing is the word...

Our friend Johnson is well—I am told the world, to talk big, married me to him whilst we were away; but you (know) that I am still a Spinster on the wing. At Paris, indeed, I might take a husband for the time being, and get divorced when my truant heart longed again to nestle with its old friends; but this speculation has not yet entered into my plan.

This was more than mere bravado. Consciously or not, Mary once again had accurately predicted her future destiny.

PART THREE: THE ROMANTIC NIGHTMARE

CHAPTER TEN

Paris in the Spring: 1793

Many things had happened in Paris since Lord Stanhope carried the congratulations of the English Revolution Society to the National Assembly in November 1789. The French Revolution club, named in honour of its English predecessor, had passed from the moderate 'Friends of the Constitution' into the hands of the extremist 'Jacobins' and was soon to become notorious as the spearhead of the Terror. The former Paris municipality of sixty districts had become a Commune with forty-eight 'sections'; and all France was a Federation. Mirabeau, the 'father' of the Revolution, was already dead and a new generation in command: Danton had risen as Minister of Justice, Robespierre as Public Prosecutor. Necker was fled to Switzerland; Lafayette to Holland, only to be captured by France's enemy, Austria. King Louis XVI, Queen Marie-Antionette and the royal household lay powerless in the Temple gaol. In the Place Louis XV (re-named Place de la Revolution) the guillotine had tasted its first blood. The *sansculottes* of Paris—still hungry, still awaiting the realisation of *liberté! egalité! fraternité!*—had erupted and, during four ghastly days and nights, summarily executed more than one thousand 'royalist' prisoners in the September massacres of 1792.

That same month a new National Convention was elected, broad enough to include the fanatical 'people's friend' Jean-Paul Marat and the English Quaker Tom Paine. Paine had been made an honorary French citizen and represented the people of Pas de Calais. Dr Priestley, too, had been elected to this Assembly but refused to accept his seat—although he had sent his son William to live in France as a token of 'solidarity' with the Revolution. Tom Paine, together with Condorcet, was also sitting on the Constitution Committee, which was preparing to draft a new constitution for the recently-proclaimed French Republic. The moderate Girondin party still held the balance of power from the Jacobins, or 'Montagnards', who occupied the upper benches of the chamber at the Salle de Manège, formerly the riding-school of the Tuileries Palace. Like a sword between them lay the knife-edge question: what should be the fate of the King? After the proclamation of the Republic in September 1792 both sides knew that the sword would soon have to be grasped. On 11th December Louis was summoned to the bar of the Assembly for interrogation on charges of conspiracy: the King's trial had begun.

Three days earlier, Mary Wollstonecraft had set out on her lone journey to France. Her eager hopes of the summer had been shattered and she had only her own desperate brand of fortitude to sustain her. To add to her depression, Joseph Johnson had recently suffered some kind of seizure and she was worried about his health. She had already postponed her departure on his account, and now she wrote to Everina[1] from Dover that if anything happened to him in her absence, 'I should never forgive myself for leaving him'. She reiterated in this letter her determination to look for a situation in Paris for one or both of her sisters.

Mary was to stay in Paris with Mme Aline Fillietaz, the recently-married daughter of Mme Bregantz who had employed Eliza and Everina at her school in Putney. This connection suggests that her intention to find a post in France for her sisters was serious and not simply her excuse to escape from London and Fuseli. But when she arrived at the *hôtel* Fillietaz the family, obviously a well-to-do one, had left their town house for the country. Mary, as so often happened, was alone with the servants. She wrote to Everina on 24th December that 'Tomorrow I expect to see Aline.' The house was very comfortable, she reported, but she was dispirited by the lack of company: 'as I wish to acquire the language as fast as I can, I was sorry to be obliged to remain so much alone.' She had seen little of Paris, she wrote, and what she had seen had not impressed her: the streets were 'so dirty'. She had, however, made the acquaintance of another Englishwoman, Helen Maria Williams:

Miss Williams has behaved very civilly to me, and I shall visit her frequently, because I *rather* like her, and I meet French company at her house. Her manners are affected, yet the simple goodness of her heart continually breaks through the varnish, so that one would be more inclined, at least I should, to love than admire her. Authorship is a heavy weight for female shoulders, especially in the sunshine of prosperity.

Helen Williams, a poetess and child prodigy who had published an 'Ode to Peace' at the age of thirteen (and been praised by Dr Johnson for it), had come to Paris with her mother and sisters to witness the 'Federation of 1790'—presumably the Fête of the Federation of 14th July. The French capital, in the early years of the Revolution, was full of foreign *voyeurs*; and those who lingered too long paid for their curiosity with their liberty, if not their lives, in the purges of the Terror. Mrs Williams and her daughters settled in Paris, and Helen later formed a life-attachment to a fellow expatriate, John Hurford Stone. Mary must also have known Stone, who had been a member of Dr Price's congregation at Newington Green.

Now, Mary evidently thought, Helen's head had been a little turned by success. She was nevertheless grateful for her friendship, and the resulting introduction to 'french company'. At the Williams' hospital table in the Rue du Bac, Mary with her halting French was flung in at the deep end to meet many of the leading Girondists: Vergniaud, President of the Assembly; General Dumouriez, fresh from his victories in the Netherlands; deputies Barbaroux and Buzot; and Jean-Pierre Brissot—'Restless, scheming, scribbling Brissot', in Carlyle's[2] critical phrase—whom Mary may even have come across in London, where according to Carlyle he had tried to form a 'social circle' in Newman Street. J. M. Roland de la Platrière, formerly king's inspector of manufactures at Lyons and now Minister of the Interior, was a regular visitor, together with his wife. The redoubtable Mme Roland (née Phlipon) must have been a woman after Mary's own heart: 'the creature of sincerity and nature, in an age of Artificiality, Pollution and Cant', said Carlyle, who saw her as 'the noblest living Frenchwoman'. Others, less kindly, suspected her of intrigue and of being the real power behind the Minister. She gave some credence to this charge in her *Memoirs*[3], describing how she shared in her husband's work 'quite naturally and as a matter of course'. A letter addressed to the Pope in the name of the Executive Council of France, she admitted, was 'sketched secretly by the hand of a woman'. Mme Roland was certainly a schemer in one respect. She was alleged to have tried to marry off Helen Williams to the Girondist deputy Bancal, and one of her letters to Bancal has been quoted to support this theory[4]:

> Either I understand nothing whatever of the human heart, or you are destined to be the husband of Mademoiselle —, if you manage properly, and if she remains here three months. Constancy and generosity can do anything with an honest and tender heart which is unpledged.

In the published letters of Madame Roland[5], however, 'Mademoiselle' is identified not as H.W. but as 'M.W.'. Could this have been Mary? It seems more likely. There was no question of Helen Williams staying in Paris for only 'three months', whereas Mary was exactly in this uncertain situation. The 'honest and tender heart' also sounds more fitting to Mary than Helen, as does Mme Roland's further advice to Bancal:

> love her enough to wish truly to relieve her sadness; remember that she cannot yet perfectly know you and appreciate you; discipline yourself to be her best friend and it is impossible that she will not in the end choose you as the first object of her affections.

It is true that Bancal did propose to Helen Williams, but not until 1796 when she was already committed to Stone. Either way, Mme Roland evidently under-estimated the 'Mademoiselle's' powers of resistance.

Mary herself was in no mood for romance during these first weeks in Paris. Not for the first time, she was putting an unhappy relationship behind her and devoting herself to study. Here in Paris there was certainly plenty to think about. In her letter to Everina on Christmas Eve she had expressed concern about the way the Revolution was going: 'my spirits are fatigued,' she wrote, 'with endeavouring to form a just opinion of public affairs. The day after tomorrow I expect to see the king at the bar, and the consequence that will follow I am almost afraid to anticipate.'

On 26th December Louis was indeed summoned to the Assembly. The hearing of evidence against him had been concluded, and he was now called on to present his defence, through his lawyer Desèze. This was perhaps the first of the 'show trials'; for the verdict was a foregone conclusion, as Mary herself assumed when she wrote that same day to Joseph Johnson[6]. She was an eye-witness, from the hotel Fillietaz on the Rue Meslay (or Meslée, as she spelt it)—only a stone's throw from the Temple prison—of the melancholy procession to the Salle de Manège:

About nine o'clock this morning, the king passed by my window, moving silently along (excepting now and then a few strokes on the drum, which rendered the stillness more awful) through empty streets, surrounded by the national guards, who, clustering round their carriage, seemed to deserve their name. The inhabitants flocked to their windows, but the casements were all shut, not a voice was heard, nor did I see anything like an insulting gesture.—For the first time since I entered France, I bowed to the majesty of the people and respected the propriety of behaviour so perfectly in unison with my own feelings. I can scarcely tell you why, but an association of ideas made the tears flow insensibly from my eyes, when I saw Louis sitting, with more dignity than I expected from his character, in a hackney coach, going to meet death, where so many of his race have triumphed.

It was curious that Mary should only now, after nearly a month in France, have 'bowed to the majesty of the people', which she had so strongly acclaimed in her *Rights of Men*. But already the reality was proving something different from the concept. She told Johnson that she would have written to him sooner 'had I not wished to wait till I could tell you that this day was not stained with blood'. Her heart was rebelling against principles that could demand such a sacrifice, and she was close enough to the slaughter to be fearful even for herself. Alone in an empty mansion, she could imagine 'eyes glare through a glass-door opposite my chair, and bloody hands shook at me'. There is an echo here of Macbeth's cry to Banquo's ghost: 'Shake not thy gory locks at me!' Was Mary even feeling a twinge of guilt at her tacit complicity in the Revolution? More likely, her fantasies were born of solitude: 'I wish I had kept the cat with me!' she confessed to Johnson, 'I want to see something alive; death in so many frightful shapes has taken hold of my fancy.—I am going to bed—and, for the first time in my life, I cannot put out the candle.'

Despite Mary's assumption that the King was 'going to meet

death' on 26th December, his trial dragged on for another three weeks. Then at last, on 15th January 1793, the question was put to the vote of the assembled deputies: Guilty or not guilty? Overwhelmingly, with only twenty-eight abstentions, the answer was 'guilty'. A second question was put: should the verdict be subject to the will of the people? By two to one, the deputies decided not—to make such an appeal would be a recipe for civil war. The third, most terrible question was reserved until the following day: what punishment should be imposed? One by one, the deputies were summoned to the bar to give judgment: death? banishment? or imprisonment? For three days and nights, the drama was played out, the speeches made. Then at last, on Sunday, 17th January, President Vergniaud rose to give the verdict: 'I declare, in the name of the Convention, that the punishment it pronounces on Louis Capet is that of Death.' The majority, out of 749 voting deputies, was only fifty-three—and a dubious fifty-three at that. As Carlyle observed: 'if we deduct from the one side, and add to the other, a certain Twenty-six, who said Death but coupled some faintest ineffectual surmise of mercy with it, the majority will be but *One*.' Though the Girondins had called for a three-quarters majority, in the event 'One' was enough. Four days later, in the Place de la Revolution, the King died on the guillotine; he was thirty-eight years old.

The Rolands, Bancal, Brissot and Tom Paine were amongst those who voted against death, and Roland at once submitted his resignation as Minister of the Interior. 'At home this Killing of a King has divided all friends,' commented Carlyle, 'and abroad it has united all enemies.' It was obvious, as Danton flung down his famous challenge, that war with England and Spain was only weeks away: 'The coalised Kings threaten us; we hurl at their feet, as gage of battle, the Head of a King.' The formal declaration of war with England came on 1st February, and with Spain on 7th March. Inevitably, from this time opinion inside France began to harden against foreign nationals, who three years earlier had been welcomed with open arms in the National Assembly under the benevolent sponsorship of the Dutch-born 'world-citizen' Jean-Baptiste de Clootz. Relations with England had deteriorated sharply since November 1792, when a British Revolutionary Club was formed in Paris, in the presence of Lord Edward Fitzgerald, and toasts were drunk to the abolition of hereditary titles in England. The company at that opening dinner also gallantly toasted 'the lady defenders of the Revolution, particularly Mrs Charlotte Smith, Miss Williams and Mrs Barbauld'[7]. Mary Wollstonecraft, curiously, was not mentioned, despite her precedence in replying to Edmund Burke; perhaps she erred, in the eyes of the revolutionaries, in applying the same standards of judgment to the new men as she had to the old.

The known British friends of the revolution were increasingly subjected to vilification in their own country; and as war fever intensified following the execution of the King, all 'radicals' were tarred with the same brush. Eliza Bishop had written to Everina on 20th January that 'Tommy Paine' had been burnt in effigy at Pembroke, and there was talk of 'immortalising Miss Wollstonecraft in a like manner'. She was obviously seriously worried about Mary, as well as being concerned with her own situation. As it happened, on that very day Mary was writing to her and Eliza passed on a transcription to Everina on 30th January. Mary wrote that she had met with 'several disappointments' regarding Eliza, but she promised not to leave Paris until something had been settled for her. She liked her host, M Fillietaz, she reported, even though he could not be termed 'polite'. She also let slip in this letter (which only exists in Eliza's transcript) an interesting piece of information which has not hitherto been noted. In a passing reference to French women she remarked on 'my favorite Mrs Schweizer ... Lavater's niece'. This was a strange coincidence! Fuseli, it may be recalled, had unsuccessfully courted Lavater's niece in 1779: but that was Anna Landolt, and Mme Schweizer has been identified as Magdalena Hess[8]. There was undoubtedly a link between them, for Eliza observed to Everina on 12th February after she had heard again from Mary: 'She talks much in favor of Lavater's niece Madam Schweizer and says she was an old favorite of Fuseli's.' Madeleine Schweizer, as she was now called, was 'notoriously frivolous and irresponsible'[9]. In this letter Eliza also referred to Mary's 'lowness of spirits' and felt that she must lately have met with 'some great disappointment'. Perhaps, until the outbreak of war with England, Mary still hoped that Fuseli might join her in Paris and renew his acquaintance with Mme Schweizer.

Eliza, it may again be noted in passing, was not nearly such a simpleton as she has sometimes been painted. Her correspondence at this period reveals surprisingly strong Republican sympathies. 'I now tremble for the Cap of Liberty,' she wrote to Everina on 10th February; and on Louis' death she observed that she was 'shocked, but not deluged in tears'. She was also more generous than she has been given credit for, and uged Everina on 30th January to send some money to Johnson so that Mary could draw on him: 'Let us feel happy to send her *all we can*, as soon as possible...' Again on 10th February she wrote: 'I mean to send her ten pounds when I can'. This was a considerable sacrifice, for her own financial position was not at all secure. By 25th February, however, after another period of silence, Eliza was convinced that Mary had returned to England: 'In short that must be the case... I am sure you must have heard from Paris since the once you mentioned, for I cannot imagine M. would double the sting of disappointment! by thus leaving me a prey to a feverish kind of anxiety'. Eliza's 'disappointment' arose from Mary's failure to find employment for her in France; despite the war situation, she still appeared to cherish this hope. When another letter from Mary did at last arrive, it evidently gave her some cause for optimism. She wrote to Everina at the end of February:

I yesterday received the *much wished* for letter; which has again bid me hope—as, Mary still says she will not leave Paris till I am settled there, or in the country, I own I should prefer the city... but these are matters I will *not quarrel* about, so I but *once* get into the Land of liberty!! and *Equality!* Yet M. says I must remain here two months longer... I believe (she) wishes to see how the war will go on in France—before she fixes me.

But a month later Eliza's hopes were finally dashed, when the British government introduced legislation which placed restrictions on travel to the Continent: 'Penalties are to be enacted against all persons who shall quit this kingdom and go to France without his *Majesty*'s licence, under the privy-seal', she informed Everina indignantly. She described Sir John Scott's Traitorous Correspondence Bill as 'slavery personified'; the next thing, she declared, would be the Bastille 'rebuilt on the banks of the Thames,'[10]. Her indignation was doubtless fed by her annoyance with Mary. 'I have ceased to wonder at M.(s) silence', she added, 'for I am sure she has been unsuccessful'.

It is doubtful if Mary had even made an application for her

sister to join her in Paris, and in continuing to hold out hopes of this she was perhaps being a little disingenuous. Eliza's earlier supposition that Mary might herself be returning to England was not far wide of the mark. She had very nearly done so, as she explained to Ruth Barlow in a letter to London written some time in February before Mrs Barlow joined her husband in Paris[11]:

> Yesterday a Gentleman offered me a place in his carriage to return to England and I knew not how to say no, yet I think it would be foolish to return when I have been at so much trouble to master a difficulty, when I am just turning the corner, and I am, besides, writing a plan of education for the Committee appointed to consider that subject.

As usual when she was separated from her family and friends, Mary was feeling homesick; although, she wrote in this letter, she was 'almost overwhelmed with civility', she was still a stranger in a strange land. The 'difficulty' she referred to was no doubt the language: 'I am exceedingly fatigued by my constant attention to words, particularly as I cannot yet get rid of a foolish bashfulness which stops my mouth when I am most desirous to make myself understood ... all the fine French phrases, ready cut and dry for use, fly away the Lord knows where'. Nevertheless, Mary had many friends in Paris—and evidently some influence. Despite her revulsion from the bloodshed she was co-operating with the Girondist regime, and no doubt her 'plan for education' was designed to rectify Condorcet's exclusion of girls beyond the primary level. To Ruth Barlow, however, she was circumspect on political matters: 'I will not now advert to public news excepting to tell you that the new constitution will soon make its appearance, and that Paris has remained perfectly tranquil ever since the death of the King'.

Her considered opinions on the state of affairs in France were reserved for Joseph Johnson. She had been commissioned by him to write a series of eye-witness reports on the situation. The first—and last—of these was despatched from Paris on 15th February, 1792; the state of war precluded any further communications. This letter on 'The Present Character of the French Nation' is included in Mary's posthumous works. It reveals something of the conflict in her mind as she saw her most cherished principles mangled in the practice. She could accept the barbarities, she wrote, and even 'bless the firm hand that lopt off the rotten limbs', if by this means the rule of liberty and virtue were to be established. But she was already aware that this was not happening: 'if the aristocracy of birth is levelled with the ground, only to make room for that of riches, I am afraid that the morals of the people will not be much improved by the change, or the government rendered less venal'. Mary had believed, with many of her contemporaries of 'the Enlightenment', that human nature was perfectible: that virtue had only to be recognised, to be accepted for its own sake; that, as she now described it, 'men would labour to become virtuous, without being goaded on by misery'. The French *sansculottes* had risen under the goad of misery; and, not surprisingly, they put bread and freedom before virtue. As Mary now perceived, this transference of power did not bring the golden age any nearer; on the contrary, it was 'fading before the attentive eye of observation' and 'almost eludes my sight'. She continued:

> ... losing thus in part my theory of a more perfect state, start not, my friend, if I bring forward an opinion, which at the first glance seems to be levelled against the existence of God! I am not become an Atheist, I assure you, by residing at Paris; yet I begin to fear that vice, or if you will, evil, is the grand mobile of action, and that, when the passions are justly poized, we become harmless, and in the same proportion, useless.

This was a startling reversal of Mary's previous convictions! Yet, dearly as these were held, she could not maintain them in the face of evidence to the contrary. Confronted suddenly with the nakedness of power, Mary did not flinch from the reality however much she hated it: 'it is the most terrific of sights,' she admitted, 'to see men vicious without warmth'. Nor could she believe that, once power was consolidated, the viciousness would pass: 'when every thing whispers to me, that names, not principles, are changed, and when I see that the turn of the tide has left the dregs of the old system to corrupt the new'. This was dangerous talk, in the Paris of 1793, but Mary went even further:

> For the same pride of office, the same desire of power are still visible; with this aggravation, that, fearing to return to obscurity after having just acquired a relish for distinction, each hero, or philosopher, for all are dubbed with these new titles, endeavours to make hay while the sun shines; and every petty municipal officer become the idol, or rather the tyrant of the

day, stalks like a cock on a dunghill.

No wonder this was the only report Mary sent; and if it had been intercepted, the writer's chances of survival must have rated very low.

For Mary had perceived, as Carlyle was to point out fifty years later, the startling truth that the fall of the monarchy meant the rise of a new aristocracy—an élite based not on nobility but on money. At present, she was only groping towards this concept:

> I must hesitatingly observe, that little is to be expected from the narrow principle of commerce which seems everywhere to be shoving aside *the point of honour* of the *noblesse*.

It was to become painfully clear to her later, through her personal encounters with the new commercial spirit. It was clearer still to Carlyle, writing with the benefit of hindsight:

> Aristocracy of Feudal Parchment has passed away with a mighty rushing; and now, by a natural course we arrive at Aristocracy of the Moneybag. It is the course through which all European Societies are, at this hour, travelling. Apparently a still baser sort of Aristocracy? An infinitely baser; the basest yet known.

The new 'aristocracy' that was spreading across Europe in the nineteenth century had itself travelled from America in the eighteenth. It was not just coincidence that the French Revolution was inspired and supported by its American predecessor. The migration of Americans to Paris was well under way by 1793. Their links with the French revolutionaries had been forged during the years of their own revolt against the English crown. Now they were eager to offer the French Republic the benefit of their experience—and, on the reverse side of the political coin, offer land in the New World to the royalists and other emigrés who began streaming out of France in their thousands after the abolition of feudal privileges in August 1789. The American genius for reconciling at one and the same time—often in one and the same person—the interests of the speculator and the liberator was already apparent in these first-generation Americans.

It was present to a marked degree in Mary Wollstonecraft's friend Joel Barlow. After serving for three years as a chaplain in the American revolutionary army, he went to Paris in 1788 to promote land settlement in the Western territory of the United States. In 1789, together with a Scotsman William Playfair he launched the Scioto company and in the space of two months sold 50,000 acres in Ohio to French emigrants[12]. At the same time, he was living in the 'red' St Antoine quarter of Paris and assisted in the capture of the Bastille! Mary had made his acquaintance through Joseph Johnson's circle in London in 1791, and he returned to Paris shortly before her in November 1792. Barlow is said to have made a fortune in Europe. Like most of his American contemporaries, his support for the Revolution was based on the principle of republicanism. Tyranny was symbolised in the crown, not in the 'capitalist'. The king must go! But when the wheels of revolution rolled on to the next stage, and the *sansculottes* rose to claim their promised land, Joel Barlow and his friends turned against it. Fleeing from the Terror in 1793, he returned to England to write a critical history of Jacobinism. In September 1792, together with the English radicals Thomas Christie, Thomas Cooper and Horne Tooke, he had been granted French citizenship.

Christie and Cooper were also in Paris during Mary's residence there. Thomas Cooper, a Manchester chemist, had accompanied James Watt—son of the inventor—to Paris in December 1791 to bring congratulations from the Manchester Constitution Society to the Jacobin Club (Wordsworth also attended the club with James Watt at this time). Thomas Christie, already known to Mary through the *Analytical Review*, was a true 'Enlightenment' man whose culture embraced science, literature and theology. Like John Hurford Stone, Christie was a disciple of Dr Price, who had given him introductions to Mirabeau and Necker in 1789. On a second visit to France in 1791 he became an intimate of Danton; and in 1792 he undertook the official English translation of the revised constitution. He was now again in Paris in the spring of 1793, after spending several months in London where he had married and acquired a partnership in a carpet factory in Finsbury Square[13]. Amongst his friends in Paris were Jean Caspard Schweizer from Zürich and his wife Madeleine; the German-born naturalist George Forster, who had sailed round the world with Captain Cook; another German, the philanthropic Count Gustav von Schlabrendorf; and an American ex-army officer, Gilbert Imlay.

Imlay, born in New Jersey probably in 1754, had fought in the American War of Independence and attained the rank of captain in the revolutionary forces. Subsequently he became a land commissioner for settlement in Kentucky, where he spent about two years in activities ranging from surveying to speculation. Unlike Joel Barlow, however, his speculative ventures seem to have ended in disaster, and he left America in 1786 heavily in debt and with summonses taken out against him. It is assumed that his next few years were spent in France, where he tried unsuccessfully to persuade the French to acquire land in New Orleans which was then held by Spain. He is believed to have come to London in 1791, and here he evidently settled into more productive work resulting in the publication of a book based on his experience of land settlement in America. This proved to be his most successful venture to date: *A Topographical Description of the Western Territory of North America*, written in the popular form of a series of letters to a friend, was received with acclamation and ran into three English editions; it was also reprinted in America and translated into German. Imlay must have felt that his true métier lay in writing, for he immediately set to work on a novel which he completed whilst still in London. *The Emigrants*, however, had a much less favourable reception when it appeared in 1793, although it later gained some recognition as a first attempt to describe the settlers' life in Kentucky. Meanwhile, Imlay had returned to France to take up new business interests.

With the coming of spring, Mary's spirits lifted and she began to feel more at home in Paris. As her confidence increased, and she moved more freely in society, she soon became absorbed into a circle in many ways similar to the one she had left in London; with the crucial difference that here the revolution was 'for real'. The talk was not of theory but of action: action that, in the rough justice of the *sansculottes*, must sometimes have seemed unpleasantly close. Yet as the blood flowed and was quenched, the talk flowed ever wider and deeper; Paris, like London, was a city of clubs, societies and journals as well as of violent uprisings. In Mary's new cricle, Joseph Johnson was replaced by Thomas Christie; and to the English faces of Tom Paine and Helen Williams was added the French presence of Brissot and the Rolands, and the Americans Barlow and Imlay. When Imlay arrived in Paris from London he carried a letter of introduction to Brissot from Thomas Cooper. Brissot had visited the United States and published an account of his travels in 1788, and he was anxious to consolidate the French links with America in order to undermine the influence of Spain. To Imlay this seemed a golden opportunity to revive his plan of interesting the French government in the acquisition of Spanish dependencies in America. At the same time he looked up his old acquaintance Thomas Christie, whom he had known in London. It is curious that he had not encountered Mary Wollstonecraft then, since they must have shared a common circle of friends, but there is no evidence of any such meeting. Now, however, in the spring of 1793, it was Thomas Christie who brought them fatally together.

It seems likely that their first meeting took place in late March or early April, soon after Imlay's arrival. A young Englishman, William Johnson, who was staying with Tom Paine, described to Godwin after her death how he became acquainted with Mary in Paris in April 1793[14]:

> At her leisure hours the family she most frequented was that of my unfortunate friend Mr Thomas Christie,* when I used to meet her several times in the week, particularly in the Evening. The society besides his family generally consisted of Mr George Forster (the friend of Captn Cook), sometimes Mr Imlay who had been lately introduced to her & appeared to pay her more than common attention, Mr Paine likewise often made one of the party.

Imlay's singling out of Mary for attention was also noticed by another member of Christie's circle. On 19th April Joel Barlow wrote to his wife in London: 'Between you and me ... I believe (Mary) has got a sweetheart, and that she will finish by going with him to A—a a wife'. On 2nd May he reported that the 'sweetheart affair goes well. Don't say a word of it to any creature'[15]. By June the prognosis was confirmed. Mary Wollstonecraft, champion of women's independence, had become the mistress of Gilbert Imlay, an adventurer with morals as dubious as his fortune. That she was ripe for such a union has already been made clear. But was this really the heart's affection, based on mutual esteem, for which she had pleaded so eloquently? 'Truly,' she had written with prophetic irony, 'the creature of sensibility was surprised by her sensibility into folly—into vice; and the dreadful reckoning falls heavily on her own weak head, when reason wakes'. By falling into the very trap against which she had most vociferously warned her sex, the author of the *Rights of Woman* was hoist with her own petard.

*Christie died in 1796, at the early age of 35, at Surinam, West Indies.

CHAPTER ELEVEN

Midsummer Madness: 1793

Mary's crime, or folly, was not that she had become the mistress of the man she loved, but that the object of her love fell so far beneath her own previous conception of what such a man should be. In committing this blunder she had none of the usual excuses arising out of ignorance or youth; for in all her years of preparation she had pondered this question more deeply than any other. Her 'ideal man' was no shadowy phantom, but a flesh-and-blood embodiment of all the virtues that flowed from reason, chastity and compassion.

Yet, from the slippery 'Neptune' through the erratic George Blood to the demonic Fuseli, her judgment of the male sex had been invariably faulty. Only Joseph Johson would seem to have been worthy of her regard, and her attachment to him was based on reason rather than emotion. It seemed almost as if the higher she aspired, the wider became the gap between theory and practice. In other spheres—in education, in religion, and to a lesser extent in politics—Mary had achieved a synthesis which eluded her in her quest for a right relationship between the sexes: a subject to which she attached supreme importance. For she was never content to view the ideal in isolation from the real. She did not expect perfection in any human being; but she did expect, from those she admired, an aspiration towards the standards of perfection which—to the eighteenth-century mind at least—could be mapped out and identified as a desirable and achievable goal. But in going even so far, she was apparently demanding too much. As she had ruefully acknowledged on more than one occasion: 'I looked for what was not to be found.'

Now, however, at the age of thirty-four, she believed that in Gilbert Imlay she had indeed found what she was looking for; in this belief, though blind to his grosser faults, she was not entirely misled. It is easy to dismiss Imlay as a callous adventurer who had taken advantage of Mary's generous and idealistic nature; but this interpretation does not altogether fit the facts. Mary was no simple girl whose head could be turned, and heart won, by a few facile compliments. It is true that she was warm-hearted, over-impulsive and starved of affection, and to that extent a gift to any man who paid her 'more than common attention' and had little scruple in exploiting the effect. But she had also a trained mind, a sensitive moral conscience, and a self-discipline wrested from adversity; and in these terms she was the hardest woman in the world to win over from her own standards to any other. Against all her instincts, she had hitherto resisted the promptings of her heart when these conflicted with her reason and had paid the price of this denial. In the case of Fuseli she had believed the two to be reconciled, only to discover a cleavage in his nature far greater than her own.

There was no such conflict in Gilbert Imlay, and what a relief this must have been. His happy acceptance of the world of sense may be the key to his attractiveness for Mary; and though he could not match her intellect, in theory at least he shared many of her ideals. He had also, like her, won some esteem as an author. He had a pleasing personality ('tall & rather awkward in his walk—very cheerful & high spirited', according to a contemporary account[1]) which had won him some success with women, if not in business—and Mary would not be inclined to hold that failure against him. All in all, then, he must have seemed at first the kindred spirit and affectionate partner she had sought for so long. There is thus no question of Mary being the 'victim' and Imlay the 'executioner'; these roles might just as easily have been reversed. Because Mary was the nobler human being and suffered more in consequence, she has rightly been accorded the lion's share of sympathy; but to the extent that she *was* superior in character, she bore the greater responsibility for her own downfall. Her affair with Imlay, therefore, was not the one tragic error of an otherwise exemplary life, as some sympathetic critics have claimed, but an essential process in her development. The tragedy, perhaps, is that a more scrupulous man could not have provided this experience. The story speaks for itself.

In setting the scene, it is necessary to envisage Mary Wollstonecraft at the centre of a revolutionary situation. Paris was a comparatively small and compact city, although it had already been enlarged in 1785 from its previous boundaries along the line of the inner boulevards and now extended north to St Martin and St Denis; south to St Jacques and St Germain; west to Passy and Chaillot; and east to St Antoine. The new city was ringed with a 'barrier' of 54 customs posts, constructed on the orders of the then Finance Minister Calonne to prevent smuggling and increase the royal revenue; and the barrier was no mere symbol but an actual wall ten feet high. When the gates to the barriers were closed—as they often were during the recurrent insurrections—it was impossible to enter or leave the city by any ordinary means. There was, therefore, amongst the half million or so inhabitants, a sense of siege as well as of solidarity; and, as the screws of the Revolution tightened, the foreign enclaves must have been drawn together in a protective alliance.

During her first few weeks in Paris Mary found the streets so 'disagreeable'—and the weather so bad—that, as she described it in a letter to Ruth Barlow, 'I half-ruin myself with coach-hires'[2]. Her lodging at No. 22 Rue Meslay was in the north-eastern Gravilliers section (the house still stands, athough sadly derelict: a gaunt, six-storey building with an inner courtyard). Nearby lived Tom Paine, in a former residence of Madame de Pompadour at No. 63 Rue du Faubourg St Denis. Thomas Christie also is said to have stayed here. Travelling a little further west, Mary could visit the Rolands on the Rue Neuve des Petits Champs, where until Roland's resignation they occupied the vast Hôtel de Calonne (after the King's trial they crossed the river to a more modest residence at No. 81 Rue de la Harpe); while just around the corner were the Schweizers, on the Chaussée D'Antin. From here, looking south, one might glimpse the Jacobin Club on the Rue St Honoré and the humble lodging of Robespierre at the house of the carpenter Duplay; and south-south-west again, the distant prospect of Madame Guillotine in the Place de la Revolution.

All this was on the north side of the river. Crossing the Pont Royal to the left bank, Helen Maria Williams held court to her admirers (amongst them, it was rumoured, Gilbert Imlay) in the Rue du Bac. Close by in the Faubourg St Germain Joel and Ruth Barlow now lodged at the Hôtel de la Grande Brétagne, Rue Jacob; as did another American of their circle, Colonel Blackden. It is more than likely that Imlay too lived here (Mary referred to 'St Germain' in her letters). A little to the east lay the Cordeliers district, stronghold of Danton and Marat; and east again, the militant St Antoine section. Here, insurrection simmered in the dissatisfied *sansculottes;* the basic demand of the Paris washerwomen for 'bread and soap' had still not been met by the intellectuals sitting in the National Convention at the Tuileries.

March 1793 was not the most propitious moment for an act of homage to the goddess of love. That very month—with the English and Spanish armies already on the march and civil war threatening in La Vendée; as Paris rocked with rumours of plots and counter-plots, and prices soared—the Convention submitted to the Montagnards' demand for a Revolutionary Tribunal and Committee of Public Safety to stamp out traitors and profiteers. Thus the machinery of 'law and order' rolled into place for the coming of the Terror. One man at least foresaw this and deserted to the enemy. General Dumouriez, hero of the Netherlands campaign and now increasingly uneasy since the death of the King, joined the Austrian armies on 4th April. The Girondins, in a desperate attempt to control the runaway horses of the Revolution, demanded the trial of Marat himself—leader of the far-left Jacobins, and to the moderates a dangerous anarchist—by the Revolutionary Tribunal. It was a fatal blunder; Marat's triumphant acquittal by the Tribunal on 24th April precipitated another. As if to consolidate its legitimacy as a government, the Convention moved from the riding-school into the Palace of the Tuileries and set up a Commission to investigate lawlessness; panic arrests of 'extremists' followed and, like lightning, Marat struck back. By 31st May, the Paris Commune was in a state of insurrection against the government. With 100,000 citizens under arms, the city barriers closed and the Tuileries Palace surrounded, the moderate party was defeated and its Commission repealed. Two days later, twenty-two Girondin deputies and ten sympathisers were expelled from the Convention by Marat's Jacobins and put under house-arrest: amongst them Brissot, Buzot, Barbaroux and

Vergniaud. The Rolands fared worse. Madame Roland was under lock and key in the Abbaye prison, and Roland had fled for his life. Now, indeed, Mary and her friends were in a city under siege. The national crisis, perhaps, precipitated a personal one.

The situation was not helped by the lack of communication with the outside world. Mary was still able to get news of her sisters through their Irish connections, but she wrote to Eliza on 13th June that 'from Mr Johnson it is, indeed, a long time since I received a line. I write with *reserve* because all letters are opened'[3]. It seemed that the censorship on the English side was even more strict than on the French, and Mary was careful not to implicate any of her English radical friends who might be under suspicion of revolutionary sympathies. She had, however, written to Johnson at the beginning of May, requesting payment of a bill of exchange for £30 to the London agents of Thomas Christie 'for value which I have received here of Mr Christie'. A similar request, for payment of £20, was made as late as July[4]. Evidently Christie was advancing money for Mary's maintenance in France, where her stay was likely to be extended far longer than she had originally planned.

But now it was becoming as dangerous to remain in Paris as it would be to return to England. As soon as the barriers were reopened after the June insurrection Mary decided to move out of the city. She had 'taken a lodging in the country', she told Eliza, 'for I could not think of staying any longer at Madame Fillietaz's'. The presence of this outspoken British subject was no doubt becoming a great embarrassment to her hosts and would soon be a threat to their own safety as well as hers. She had considered whether to flee from France to Switzerland, like so many of her fellow-countrymen, and had even procured a passport for this purpose. But Mary was never inclined to run away from a dangerous situation. She had also, by this time, more pressing personal reasons for remaining in France.

Her removal, therefore, was no more than three miles from the city centre to an isolated cottage in the woods at Neuilly. She described her changed circumstances to Eliza with more than a hint of mystery:

> I am now at the house of an old gardener writing a great book, and in better health and spirits than I have ever enjoyed since I came to France, whilst you, it always disturbs me when I think

of it, are desponding.—But do not despair, my dear girl, once more breathe on the ashes of hope; I mean not to pun on the word, and I will render your fate more tolerable, unless *my* hopes deceive me.

She assured Eliza that she had a plan for bringing all the sisters together. Eliza, in transcribing this message to Everina, added a rather sceptical postscript: 'What say you Everina now to the *continental air*? or is it *Love*? Ambition? or Pity? that has wrought the miracle?' Two weeks later, however, on 24th June, Mary wrote again to Eliza and reiterated her mysterious plan—'which promises to render the evening of your life more comfortable. I cannot explain myself in a clearer manner.' It is pretty clear, with hindsight, that she was dreaming of a golden life in America for herself, as Mrs Imlay, and for her sisters. But that was all in the future; and the remote future at that. Mary had no immediate intention of changing her own way of life: 'I am now hard at work in the country,' she continued, 'for I could not return to England without proofs that I have not been idle.' She implored Eliza to write immediately she received her letter:

... I feel quite lonely here now the communication is shut; and, as absence renders my friends more dear to me, my heart bounds, when I think of you with the emotions of youthful fondness.

There is no reason to suspect Mary of hypocrisy here. Her affections were large enough to retain the old loves along with the new. But she ended with a reminder of a different kind of reality: 'Do not touch on politics'. Here was Mary's situation in a nutshell, a familiar and recurring one: alone in a foreign land, cut off from friends and family, at work on a book, financially insecure and now with the added ingredient of personal danger. 'Do not touch on politics' was no idle warning; an incautious phrase could literally be a matter of life and death. The book on which she was working may have provided another reason for Mary's withdrawal to the country. This, her next published work, was 'an historical and moral view' of the French Revolution. Shaken by the bloody realities she had witnessed in Paris, she was evidently re-thinking her attitude and seeking to retrace the steps that had led to the present débâcle. Such a task was best accomplished alone and in secret.

No wonder, then, that Mary was feeling lonely 'now the communication is shut'. Willy-nilly, she had to find some communication closer at hand. That same month of June, 1793, she wrote another letter. It was addressed to Captain Gilbert Imlay—the first of many such[5]—and it reveals how far the affair had already progressed.

> My dear Love,
>   After making my arrangements for our snug dinner today, I have been taken by storm, and obliged to promise to dine, at an early hour, with the Miss —s, the only day they intend to pass here. I shall however leave the key in the door, and hope to find you at my fireside when I return, about eight o'clock. Will you not wait for poor Joan? whom you will find better, and till then think very affectionately of her.
>   Yours truly,
>   Mary.

The inconvenient visitors could well have been Helen Williams and her sister, and Mary evidently did not want them to know of her relationship with Imlay for she added a postscript: 'I am sitting down to dinner; so do not send an answer'. Mary's allusion to herself as 'poor Joan' must have had some private significance; it does not recur in the correspondence.

Another letter which Mary must have written at about this time, although it is undated[6], was addressed to Ruth Barlow. It suggests that Mary was already living outside Paris and that she had some private news to impart. Although Mary did not usually confide in her woman friends, Ruth Barlow—a fellow American and friend of Imlay—may have been an exception:

> A word or two which dropt from you, when I last saw you, for circumstances scarcely allowed me to speak to you, have run in my head ever since—Why cannot we meet and breakfast together, *quite alone*, as in days of yore? I will tell you how—will you meet me at the Bath about 8 o'clock either monday or tuesday? ... We may then breakfast in your favourite place and chat as long as we please before we part to return to our respective homes, for I do not wish to spend a whole day in Paris for a little time to come and when I do I must visit Madame Schweizer.

The postscript cerainly suggests some degree of intimacy: 'Remember the pills!!—and do not forget to ask Mrs Stone what is become of Schlabberndorf (sic)—give my love to Mrs

Blackden.' Mary shared with Ruth Barlow a common circle of friends in Paris, and it is evident that she was now to some extent cut off from them. The letter was therefore almost certainly written from Neuilly, where Mary was alone with her books—and Imlay; and whatever good or bad advice Mrs Barlow may have given her at their meeting, by August she was committed to him heart and soul[7]:

> You can scarcely imagine with what pleasure I anticipate the day, when we are to begin almost to live together; and you would smile to hear how many plans of employment I have in my head, now that I am confident my heart has found peace in your bosom. Cherish me with that dignified tenderness, which I have only found in you; and your own dear girl will try to keep under a quickness of feeling, that has sometimes given you pain. Yes, I will be *good*, that I may deserve to be happy; and whilst you love me, I cannot again fall into that miserable state which rendered life a burthen almost too heavy to be borne.

Now, at last, Mary had found happiness in the confidence of being loved. It never entered her consciousness that this was not a mutual and binding undertaking, no less solemn for being unconsecrated. She continued:

> God bless you! Sterne says that is equal to a kiss—yet I would rather give you the kiss into the bargain, glowing with gratitude to Heaven, and affection to you. I like the word affection, because it signifies something habitual; and we are soon to meet, to try whether we have mind enough to keep our hearts warm.

Is it possible that Mary had read Gilbert Imlay's novel *The Emigrants* and could still believe that he was interested in the 'mind' of any woman?—'The lovely Caroline's face diffused the soft effulgence of an opening rose when heaven impearls it with the morning dew,' he rhapsodised in the best—or worst—eighteenth-century idiom of the sentimental novel. Later, he described the rescue of the delectable Caroline from the Indians by his hero, Captain Arl—ton:

> When Venus lies sleeping on the couch of night, and one half of the world is cheered by the brilliancy of her charms, so looked my Caroline when Somnus had sealed up eyelides, and while Morpheus, his minister of dreams, was agitating her tender heart, her bosom disclosed the temple of bliss, while her

lips distilled nectareous sweets.

What scorn Mary would have poured on this, had the text been available when she was compiling her *Rights of Woman*! But it is doubtful if, at this stage, any evidence against Imlay could have restrained her passion. It was a compulsion of nature—not only her own nature, but 'nature' as such—that Mary Wollstonecraft should bear a child, and Imlay was the chosen instrument of this destiny. At this very moment, in fact, destiny was being fulfilled. There is a fateful postscript to her August letter: 'I will be at the barrier a little after ten o'clock tomorrow.' About this rendezvous Godwin commented—with some courage, for it must have blasted her reputation more than anything else he wrote about her—that the child which was subsequently born, and whom Mary was wont to refer to as her 'barrier girl', probably 'owed her existence to this interview'.

What else had Godwin to say about these goings-on? He informed us that when Mary first saw Imlay she did not like him and for a time avoided meeting him: 'This sentiment however speedily gave place to one of greater kindness'. It would be interesting to know what caused such a sudden change of heart. Imlay had evidently a good deal of personal charm, but charm as such had never cut much ice with Mary. There must have been more to him than that. A clue may be found in his writings. For despite its fatuities, his novel *The Emigrants* had a serious purpose in exposing what he saw as the injustices to women of the English divorce laws: a subject very close to Mary's heart, which she was to treat herself in her later novel *The Wrongs of Woman*. The sentiments expressed in Imlay's book on the Western territories were also highly congenial to her, notably his defence of the rights of the Indians and his praise of the simple life of the American settlements as compared with the decadence of Europe (his utopian ideals were said to have influenced Coleridge and Southey in their plans for a 'Pantisocracy'). Mary would certainly have echoed his hymn to liberty in spite of its florid language:

> Heavens! what charms are there in liberty! Man, born to enslave the subordinate animals, has long since enslaved himself. But reason at length, in radiant smiles, and with grateful pride, illumines both hemispheres; and FREEDOM, in golden plumes, and in her triumphal car, must now resume her lost empire.

There is no reason to suppose that Imlay was not as sincere in his love of liberty as Mary herself. What he lacked was any intellectual or moral ballast. The liberty of the libertine, which was completely foreign to her nature, was to him no more than the natural expression of the 'natural man'.

According to Godwin Mary's love affair with Imlay was kept secret, at her request, for four months. Whether Imlay had offered marriage to her during this period is not known. It does not seem likely; in any case Mary was opposed to marriage, said Godwin, because she did not wish him to be made responsible for her debts and her commitments to her family. This virtuous stance may have sprung from necessity, for Godwin also revealed that at this time Imlay 'had no property whatever'. So the arrangement suited both of them: for her, as a matter of principle; for him, as a convenience. But then, at the end of August, public events impinged on the idyll. The British fleet battered the French garrison into submission at Toulon, and in a rush of xenophobia all British subjects in France were threatened with imprisonment. On 17th September the Law against Suspects was promulgated, and the rounding-up began in earnest. Helen Maria Williams and John Hurford Stone were arrested in October and held in prison for some months. The British press assumed that Mary had shared the same fate. 'You have undoubtedly read in the papers,' Eliza wrote to Everina on 5th November, 'of her having been arrested; I hope to God she is safe, yet the contrary idea haunts and makes me forget her few faults'. A month later, however, on 4th December, she was more optimistic: 'though I read of M's being arrested I *felt it not*'; and in January 1794, though still without news, she wrote: 'I flatter myself that she is safe.' Eliza's intuition was correct, though she was unaware of the reason.

How did Mary Wollstonecraft escape? By the simple expedient of becoming the 'wife' of an American citizen. In her own eyes Mary already had this status, and it needed only a certificate from the American ambassador and a change of name to confirm it to the satisfaction of the authorities; such 'republican marriages' were commonplace in the Revolution. It was a stroke of luck for Mary that the Law against Suspects coincided with the start of her pregnancy. With her safety ensured, and respectability intact, she moved back to Paris and openly set up house with Imlay. Now Mary's cup of happiness was full—though quickly to be drained. Imlay, not surprisingly, was beset with financial problems. How, with no capital and no prospects, was he to meet his added commitments of a wife and a coming child? His hopes of a deal with Brissot (he had even proposed leading an expeditionary force to the Mississipi himself) had finally collapsed with the Girondin downfall. Now, it seems, he turned to a business acquaintance, Elias Backman, who was engaged in a profitable export trade with Scandinavia; he could not afford to miss any chance of turning an honest (or dishonest) penny, even though the conduct of this business would necessitate his absence from Paris. Shortly after settling Mary into their new lodgings Imlay was called away to Le Havre to attend to the shipping arrangements: this, at least, was his story. But the arrangements were remarkably protracted. Was he already plotting his escape?

Imlay's dilemma was brilliantly captured in Virginia Woolf's graphic phrase: 'Tickling minnows, he had hooked a dolphin'[9]. He was learning to his chagrin that Mary Wollstonecraft had very different attributes from those of the 'light' women with whom he had previously associated. He had mistakenly assumed that in acceding to his doctrine of free love she also accepted his philosophy of 'easy come, easy go'. But to Mary free love represented an advanced concept of marriage, which conferred even greater obligations on its voluntary participants than those enjoined by law—the laws of love, in her philosophy, being vastly superior to the laws of property. The coming of a child, of course, was an added complication. Imlay had not foreseen this; Mary's evident delight in her pregnancy must have been a further cause of resentment. He, Gilbert Imlay, gentleman adventurer, was being trapped into the role of family man! He did not even have the compensation of an adoring and complaisant wife to tell him what a fine fellow he was. On the contrary, Mary was at great pains to point out his shortcomings. So unequal a relationship was doomed from the start.

'Of late we are always separating,' wrote Mary ruefully after his departure for Le Havre in September 1793[10]. 'Crack! crack! and away you go!' She joked to keep up her spirits, as she explained in the same letter:

This joke wears the sallow cast of thought; for, though I began to write cheerfully, some melancholy tears have found their way into my eyes, that linger there, whilst a glow of tenderness at my heart whispers that you are one of the best creatures in the world. Pardon then the vagaries of a mind that has been almost 'crazed by care', as well as 'crossed in hapless love', and bear with me a *little* longer! When we are settled in the country together, more duties will open before me, and my heart, which now, trembling into peace, is agitated by every emotion that awakens the remembrance of old griefs, will learn to rest on yours, with that dignity your character, not to mention my own, demands.

Poor Mary! Still uncertain of her hold on Imlay, still dreaming her dreams of rural peace and domesticity, even at the climax of her bliss she was nagged by doubts and anxieties. Two months later, when he had still not returned, she wrote to confirm her supicion that she was pregnant[11]: 'Ever since you last saw me inclined to faint, I have felt some gentle twitches, which make me begin to think that I am nourishing a creature who will soon be sensible of my care.' The thought filled her with 'an overflowing of tenderness' and a consciousness of her new responsibility:

Yesterday—do not smile!—finding that I had hurt myself by lifting precipitately a large log of wood, I sat down in an agony, till I felt those said twitches again.

In the next letter, dated December, Mary was assuring Imlay that she was not angry with him and admitted the foolishness of trying to govern the temper 'by a square and compass'. Nevertheless, she continued to try to equate his feelings with her own—not altogether successfully:

I do not know why, but I have more confidence in your affections, when absent, than present; nay, I think that you must love me, for, in the sincerity of my heart let me say it, I believe I deserve your tenderness, because I am true, and have a degree of sensibility that you can see and relish.

This, though she may not yet have realised it, was a disastrous admission of 'no confidence'. If Mary was uneasy about Imlay's feelings when he was with her, her faith in his affection for her must have been based on wishful thinking rather than reality. Did she really imagine that it was possible to 'deserve' to be loved, at least by such a man?

Despite her new status as Imlay's 'wife', Mary passed her second Christmas in Paris, like her first, in solitude. 'You seem to have taken up your abode at Havre,' she observed somewhat tartly on the 29th December[12]: 'Pray sir! when do you think of coming home? or, to write very considerately, when will business permit you?' But her criticisms were still softened by a tender feeling for him. She had only to look at his slippers—'which I could not remove from my *salle* door, though they are not the handsomest of their kind'—for her anger to melt. She ended with a warning: 'Be not too anxious to get money!for nothing worth having is to be purchased.'

An affectionate letter, however, was enough to restore her spirits. Two days later she was thanking him for his 'considerate tenderness', that had made her feel 'how very dear you are to me, by charming away half my cares'. On the following day—the last of 1793—she could not resist the opportunity to send another message to Imlay by a mutual friend. Knowing how such a message would have cheered her, she endowed him with a similar quality: 'and you, with all your struggles to be manly, have some of the same sensibility.' Here, perhaps, is one key to Imlay's character and a clue to his ambivalence about Mary. His writings show that he did indeed have a high degree of sensibility and his life indicates that, like most 'manly' men, he struggled to suppress it. To Mary, this was a crime. Sensibility should be encouraged, not crushed by material considerations. 'Do not bid it begone,' she continued in this same letter, 'for I love to see it striving to master your features; besides, these kind of sympathies are the life of affection'. This was all very well, Imlay must have thought, but he also had a living to make: man cannot live by love alone. This was Mary's impracticable dream. What she really needed was a man who had sufficient means—or sufficiently simple tastes—to rise above material considerations; Imlay had neither. 'The books sent to me are such as we may read together,' she now informed him, 'so I shall not look into them till you return, when you shall read, whilst I mend my stockings'. It was a humble vision but sadly wide of the mark.

Thus ended the year 1793, at least on a note of hope. Mary had at last found a measure of happiness and, despite its precarious basis, the contentment that comes of fulfilment. In Imlay's absence she could dream of a future softened by domesticity and mutual affection, a new life in a new world—for their intention, when he had saved one thousand pounds, was to settle on a farm in America, where her brother Charles was already making his way and where she hoped also to establish Eliza and Everina in greater independence. She could not, or would not, see that in carping against Imlay's commercial activities she was also frustrating this dream. Imlay's real failing was not that he pursued his business interests so avidly, but that he pursued them unsuccessfully. The great commercial boom of the nineteenth century was just beginning, with the whole world opening out as man's oyster; in this climate his 'sensibility', as he himself saw, was a liability. The new, nineteenth-century man had no time for sentiment. Mary saw this too, but reacted in an opposite direction: if commerce rampant was incompatible with human values, then commerce must be made the servant of humanity—not its master. Was this to be the lesson of the French Revolution? It is perhaps time to take another look.

CHAPTER TWELVE
Terror and Despair: 1793–4

What had been happening to France, while Mary Wollstonecraft was pursuing the unaccustomed course of an absorbing love affair? It was perhaps fortunate that her attention was diverted from the dreadful happenings around her, or she could surely not have lived through the year of the Terror in Paris.

Almost at the same moment that Mary moved out of Paris to Neuilly and began receiving her lover, a young woman in Normandy was travelling towards the capital. Charlotte Corday left Caen, centre of the Girondin resistance, by the night coach on 9th July 1793, arriving in Paris via the Neuilly bridge on the afternoon of the 11th. Here she booked a room at the Hôtel Providence, Rue des Vieux Augustins, just south of the Pont Neuf. The next day she attended to some family business on behalf of a convent friend with Roland's successor at the Ministry of the Interior, Duperret. What else she discussed with him, if anything, is not known. But she had deeper matters on her mind: here too was a woman of destiny. Charlotte took the opportunity to visit the National Convention; she had hoped to see citizen Marat. But Marat, a sick man, was confined to his home and virtually conducting the Revolution from a hip-bath. There was nothing for it, then, but to beard the lion in his den. The next morning Charlotte crossed the bridge to the Palais Royal, now a market place, and purchased a sharp sheath-knife. The streets of Paris were dangerous for unaccompanied young women, she may have told the shopkeeper if he had raised an eyebrow; but knives were almost a commonplace, for one purpose or another, among the *citoyennes*. From here she took a coach to the Rue des Cordeliers, stopping at No. 30. Marat is unwell, his loyal helpmeet Simonne Evrard informed her: no visitors allowed. Charlotte returned to her hotel. In the evening she set out again, bearing a note purporting to give information about the Caen rebellion. This time the strategy worked—and with one stroke from the sheath-knife the dread 'people's friend' lay dying.

This heroic and futile act led Charlotte Corday, as she had anticipated, to the guillotine. She made no attempt to deny her guilt; she had consciously prepared herself for martyrdom. 'I killed one man,' she told the Revolutionary Tribunal, 'to save a hundred thousand; a villain to save innocents; a savage wild beast to give repose to my country'.[1] Alas! for one Marat dead a thousand petty tyrants rose to take his place. Charlotte's gesture was a vain one, and the terror rolled on to new depths of atrocity. France, at war on all fronts, could only choose between greater and lesser evils. The defeat of the revolution meant the defeat of France; inevitably, the revolutionary leaders fought back with increasing intolerance and brutality. 'France is become a vast Golgotha of carnage, an arena of horrors,' wrote Mme Roland from prison on 28th August[2]:

> What Rome or Babylon ever equalled Paris, polluted with debauchery and blood, and governed by magistrates who profess to trade in falsehood and calumny, and to license assassination? What people has ever depraved its nature to the point of contracting a moral necessity of beholding executions, and of glutting its eyes with scenes of cruelty; of foaming with impatience and rage when the sanguinary scenes are retarded; and of being ever ready to wreak its ferocity on whosoever shall attempt to calm and pacify its violence?

This was a terrible indictment, from a leading revolutionist. Yet nowhere in Mme Roland's noble, if rather smug, *Memoirs* was there any hint of awareness of the Girondin share of responsibility—by promising more than they could fulfil—in releasing the genie of violence. By the autumn, as Vergniaud observed, the Revolution was devouring its own children. But first, the remaining national symbol of the royalists had to be disposed of: the widowed queen Marie-Antoinette was led to the scaffold on 16th October.

Now there were only the dissidents to be dealt with. Within a week the twenty-two Girondin deputies already expelled from the Assembly and, since rounded-up into gaol, were put on trial; their execution took place on the last day of October. Amongst their number were Brissot and Vergniaud. In the provinces a similar butchery was taking place. The Revolution had now reached the stage of paranoia: he who is not with us is against us. Philippe Egalité, ducal friend of the Jacobins, went to his death on 6th November. Two days later, Madame Roland herself followed him to the block. '*O Liberté!*' she cried, glancing towards the statue of liberty which commemorated the fall of the monarchy, '*Comme on t'a jouée!*' Roland, in hiding near Rouen, on hearing the news ran himself on his own sword. So ended a historic political marriage (rather as if the Webbs, transported to the Soviet Union, had fallen under Stalin's axe). Only many years later was it discovered that Marie-Jeanne Roland's real love had been deputy Buzot, although she remained faithful to her elderly husband. Now Buzot shared a like fate. Fleeing from the avenging Jacobins he wandered, crazed by grief, through the countryside; he was found dead in a cornfield near Castillon, half-eaten by wolves.

The whole country, in the terrible winter that followed, seemed convulsed in a wave of carnage: mass executions at Lyons, mass shootings at Toulon, mass drowning at Nantes where hundreds of men, women and children were bound and flung into the Loire in the infamous 'noyades'. At Meudon, there was even a tannery of human skins: 'such of the guillotined as seemed worth flaying: of which perfectly good wash-leather was made', wrote the turncoat Montgaillard (quoted by Carlyle). The sane men of the Revolution, of whom there were still a few surviving, knew this could not go on; and one at least had the courage to say so. Camille Desmoulins, lawyer and journalist and a leader of the attack on the Bastille in 1789, in the third issue of his jounal *Vieux Cordelier* on 15th December 1793 called for the establishment of a Committee of Mercy. What had finally sickened him was not so much the butchery of the revolution, in which he had taken his share, but the consequent anarchy. In the previous month Hébert's grotesquely-named 'Feast of Reason' had attacked the church with wild orgies at the high altar of Notre Dame. France, Desmoulins declared, was treading the path of Caligula's Rome.

He also attacked the Law of Suspects, under which thousands were being gaoled and executed without charge or trial. For this temerity, he was expelled from the National Convention. So too, that same month, were the two foreigners sitting in the Convention—Tom Paine and de Clootz; and on 31st December, both were arrested. Paine was fortunate to escape the guillotine; de Clootz was not so lucky.

What, it may be wondered, were the Americans in Paris doing in the midst of these horrors? Did the ambassador—that same Gouverneur Morris who had 'married' Mary and Imlay—make any protest against the excesses carried out in the name of the Revolution? It seems unlikely. America had many commercial links with the French régime, and most Americans were doubtless carrying on their normal business activities. Joel Barlow was consolidating his fortune. Gilbert Imlay, less successfully, was dabbling in timber, grain and chemicals—even, perhaps, supplying ammunition for the national guard. Mary, who for these purposes may rank as an American, was carrying her first child. There is remarkably little of the surrounding terror in her letters to Imlay, though we are told that on hearing of Brissot's execution she 'sunk lifeless on the floor'[3]. To Godwin she later described her anguish at that moment as 'one of the most intolerable sensations she had ever experienced'. He also records an incident from the previous year when, walking into Paris from Neuilly she reached the Place de la Revolution just after an execution had taken place and 'the blood of the guillotine appeared fresh upon the pavement'. She could not restrain an outburst of indignation but was warned by a bystander to 'hide her discontents'. No doubt it was also prudent in those days not to commit subversive thoughts to paper—if only Mary had kept a secret diary, what a picture might have emerged!

However, writing to Imlay on 1st January 1794[4] she could not refrain from expressing disappointement that Desmoulins' 'counter-revolution' appeared to have failed:

The face of things, public and private, vexes me. The 'peace' and clemency which seemed to be dawning a few days ago, disappear again. 'I am fallen,' as Milton said, 'on evil days'; for I really believe that Europe will be in a state of convulsion during half a century at least. Life is but a labour of patience: it is always rolling a great stone up a hill; for, before a person can find

a resting-place, imagining it is lodged, down it comes again,
and all the work is to be done over anew!

She continued this letter on a more personal note. She could no longer conceal from the world her pregnant condition; nor, it seemed, did she wish to:

> Finding that I was observed, I told the good women, the two Mrs. — simply that I was with child: and let them stare! and —, and —, nay, all the world may know it for aught I care! Yet I wish to avoid —'s coarse jokes.

Mary was certainly not having an easy time; and it was not made any more easy by the absence of her 'husband'. Nor had she any illusions about Imlay's sense of responsibility: 'You may now tell me, that, if it were not for me, you would be laughing away with some honest fellows in London.' At least the awful suspicion had not yet dawned on her that he might even seek the company of other women! She did know, however, as she acknowledged in a postcript, that Imlay's cheerful disposition—unlike her own—'makes absence easy for you'. Mary was already realising that an equality of the sexes at the emotional level was the hardest of all to achieve: 'I do not want to be loved like a goddess, but I wish to be necessary to you', she concluded with a flash of realism. There was a world of implication, for the future of human relations, in that simple phrase.

This letter marks the beginning of the first period of real strain between Mary and her lover, culminating in an irrational emotional outburst on her part. A clue to the quarrel is provided in another letter also dated January[5]. It is evident that an acquaintance of Imlay's had made some casual remarks, perhaps making light of their relationship, that had 'cruelly hurt' her; the acquaintance is unidentified:

> — did not write to you, I suppose, because he talked of going to Havre. Hearing that I was ill, he called very kindly on me, not dreaming that it was some words that he incautiously let fall, which rendered me so.

Mary's reaction may easily be imagined, and she was obviously thoroughly ashamed of it in retrospect—especially as Imlay had been sensible enough to ignore it:

> I have just received your kind and rational letter, and would fain hide my face, glowing with shame for my folly. I would hide it in your bosom, if you would again open it to me, and

nestle closely till you had bade my fluttering heart be still, by saying that you forgave me. With eyes overflowing with tears, and in the humblest attitude, I entreat you. Do not turn from me, for indeed I love you fondly, and have been very wretched since the night I was so cruelly hurt by thinking that you had no confidence in me.

She acknowledged that the fault, on this occasion, had been hers:

It is time for me to grow more reasonable, a few more of these caprices of sensibility would destroy me. I have in fact, been very much indisposed for a few days past, and the notion that I was tormenting, or perhaps killing, a poor little animal, about whom I am grown anxious and tender, now I feel it alive, made me worse.

She urged Imlay to write and tell her that all was well again:

Write the moment you receive this. I shall count the minutes. But drop not an angry word. I cannot now bear it. Yet, if you think I deserve a scolding (it does not admit of a question, I grant), wait till you come back, and then, if you are angry one day, I shall be sure of seeing you the next.

Could the author of the *Rights of Woman* sink lower than this abject abasement to a man of so little worth? Such complexities and contradictions form the fascination of Mary Wollstonecraft's character. In her emotional palpitations she was no different from any ordinary woman: it was her honesty in recognising her weaknesses, and adapting her theories to accommodate and interpret them, that marked her out as the exception, the archetype of the 'new woman'. Some glimpses of this self-knowledge were offered to Imlay in her next letter[6] written in the calm of 'emotion recollected in tranquillity':

One thing you mistake in my character, and imagine that to be coldness, which is just the contrary. For, when I am hurt by the person most dear to me, I must let out a whole torrent of emotions, in which tenderness would be uppermost, or stifle them altogether; and it appears to me almost a duty to stifle them when I imagine *that I am treated with coldness*.

She continued with a peace offering:

My own happiness wholly depends on you; and, knowing you, when my reason is not clouded, I look forward to a rational prospect of as much felicity as the earth affords, with a little dash of rapture into the bargain, if you will look at me, when we meet again, as you have sometimes greeted your humbled, yet most affectionate Mary.

Here is Mary at her most charming, balancing reason with rapture in a brief vision of life as it should be lived. If only this mood would endure! But harsher realities kept breaking in and destroying it.

She determined now, despite the recent emotional crisis which had left her physically exhausted and fearful for her baby, to undertake the journey to Havre and join her lover. In two weeks or less, she assured Imlay,[7] she would be 'strong again'; meanwhile she would recuperate with her favourite relaxation—walking in the fresh air:

I will now sally forth (you will go with me in my heart) and try whether this fine bracing air will not give the vigour to the poor babe it had before I so inconsiderately gave way to the grief that deranged my bowels, and gave a turn to my whole system.

As her health improved, so did her spirits. A few days later she was able to joke again[8]:

I cannot boast of being quite recovered, yet I am (I must use my Yorkshire phrase; for, when my heart is warm, pop come the expressions of childhood into my head) so *lightsome*, that I think it will not *go badly with me*. And nothing shall be wanting on my part, I assure you; for I am urged on, not only by an enlivened affection for you, but by a new-born tenderness that plays cheerily round my dilating heart.

I was therefore, in defiance of cold and dirt, out in the air the greater part of yesterday; and, if I get over this evening without a return of the fever that has tormented me, I shall talk no more of illness.

She also acknowledged that Imlay too might be struggling with real problems in his business activities:

I have been seriously vexed to find that, whilst you were harrassed by impediments in your undertakings, I was giving you additional uneasiness. If you can make any of your plans answer, it is well; I do not think a *little* money inconvenient; but, should they fail, we will struggle cheerfully together—drawn closer by the pinching blasts of poverty.

When she next wrote[9] her arrangements for the journey were well advanced and her 'passport', which was needed even for internal travel in France, was secured. The prospect of a reunion after this separation of nearly three months revived all her tender feelings for him:

> You have, by your tenderness and worth, twisted yourself more artfully round my heart than I supposed possible. Let me indulge the thought that I have thrown out some tendrils to cling to the elm by which I wish to be supported. This is talking a new language for me! But, knowing that I am not a parasite plant, I am willing to receive the proofs of affection, that every pulse replies to, when I think of being once more in the same house with you.

This was indeed 'talking a new language' for the author of the *Rights of Woman*. At the same time, she had to make it quite clear that her 'clinging' was not that of a parasite-ivy—because she could give as good as she received. This may well have lessened the rapture for Imlay, who was in no mood either to be clung to or challenged. Fortunately, Mary was not in a postion to see his reaction; and soon she was 'again on the wing' and speeding happily towards her lover[10]:

> With my face turned to Havre my spirits will not sink, and my mind has always hitherto enabled my body to do whatever I wished.

On 3rd February 1794 Mary was able to write to her friend Ruth Barlow[11] that she was 'very comfortably settled' in her lodgings at Havre, 'and shall remain so, if the high price of all the necessaries of life do not ruin US'. She also reported that she was working hard to prepare her manuscript on the French Revolution for the publishers and referred to a 'Mr Codman' who would carry it to London. She was feeling the lack of her books, which had been left in Paris, and requested Mrs Barlow to send her 'the debates and decrees, from the commencement of that publication'. (She was referring to the *Journal des Débats et des Décrets* of the National Assembly, the first three volumes of which printed the proceedings of the States General from 5th May to 1st September 1789.) In March Imlay found it necessary to go to Paris on business, and Mary was again alone. But the reunion had evidently soothed her nerves, for her two letters written during this absence[12] were still in her 'lightsome' mood. She missed him, of course:

> I turned to your side of the bed, and tried to make the most of comfort of the pillow, which you used to tell me I was churlish

about; but all would not do.

However, for the time being she was content with working, walking, and dreaming of her coming child and its father—'seeing you peep over my shoulder, as I write, with one of your kindest looks—when your eyes glisten, and a suffusion creeps over your relaxing features'. In her second letter, she was apologising for having failed to enclose a requred document in the previous one:

> I had got you by the fireside, with the *gigot* smoking on the board, to lard your bare ribs, and behold, I closed my letter without taking the paper up, that was directly under my eyes!

A letter written about the same time to Everina has been preserved. Others evidently were lost or never reached their destination, so it is not known how much earlier Mary had divulged to her sisters her relationship with Imlay. She wrote on 10th March[13]:

> If any of the many letters I have written have come to your hands, or Eliza's, you know that I am safe, through the protection of an American, a most worthy man, who joins in uncommon tenderness of heart and quickness of feeling, a soundness of understanding and reasonableness of temper rarely to be met with. Having been brought up in the interior parts of America, he is a most natural unaffected creature. I am with him now at Havre, and shall remain there, till circumstances point out what is necessary for me to do.

A significant omission was any mention of the coming baby; there was perhaps an intentional ambiguity in the use of the word 'protection'. But the enthusiastic testimonial to Imlay's character must have given Everina a clue that this was not simply an arrangement of convenience. Mary also made one of her rare comments on the political situation:

> I have just sent off great part of my MS, which Miss Williams would fain have had be (me) burn, following her example—and to tell you the truth—my life would not have been worth much, had it been found. It is impossible for you to have any idea of the impression the sad scenes I have been a witness to have left on my mind.

Nevertheless, she continued:

> I am certainly glad that I came to France, because I never could have had else a just opinion of the most extraordinary event that has ever been recorded, and I have met with some

uncommon instances of friendship, which my heart will ever gratefully store up, and call to mind when the remembrance is keen of the anguish it has endured for its fellow-creatures, at large—for the unfortunate beings cut off around me—and the still more unfortunate survivors.

The Revolution was at this moment entering a new and even bloodier stage. On 31st March Danton himself, together with Camille Desmoulins, was arrested on orders of Robespierre and condemned to death by the Revolutionary Tribunal—that same tribunal which he had himself set up twelve months earlier. 'I crave pardon for it of God and man,' he cried in prison. 'They are all Brothers Cain; Brissot would have had me guillotined as Robespierre now will . . . Robespierre will follow me; I drag down Robespierre. O, it were better to be a poor fisherman than to meddle with governing of men.'[14] Too late, Danton was realising the awful logic of the revolutionary process: too late, at least, to save himself. Within a week, both he and Desmoulins were dead.

If Mary was moved by the fate of those honest revolutionaries, perhaps the last of their generation, she did not record her feelings. Her thoughts now were turned towards life rather than death: her book was finished, her 'protector' was at hand, and the birth of her first child was imminent. 'I am still very well,' she wrote to Ruth Barlow on 27th April, 'but imagine it cannot be long before this lively animal pops on us—and now the history is finished and everything arranged I do not care how soon.'[15] She also made a comment on her relationship with Imlay, which at this moment of euphoria seemed to have achieved its ideal aim: 'you perceive that I am acquiring the matrimonial phraseology without having clogged my soul by promising obedience &c. &c.' Ruth Barlow was probably one of the few people who knew the real facts about this 'republican marriage'.

The animal—a baby daughter—'popped' in the most natural way in the world on 14th May 1794. Mary took the event in her stride, as she reported to Ruth Barlow on the 20th[16]:

> Here I am, my Dear Friend, and so well, that were it not for the inundation of milk, which for the moment incommodes me, I could forget the pain I endured six days ago.—Yet nothing could be more natural or easy than my labour—still it is not smooth work–I dwell on these circumstances not only as I hope it will give you pleasure; but to prove that this struggle of

nature is rendered much more cruel by the ignorance and affectation of women. My nurse has been twenty years in this employment, and she tells me, she never knew a woman so well—adding, Frenchwoman like, that I ought to make children for the Republic, since I treat it so slightly.—It is true, at first, she was convinced that I should kill myself and my child; but since we are alive and so astonishingly well, she begins to think that the BON DIEU takes care of those who take care of themselves. But, while I think of it, as your correspondent said, let me tell you that I have got a vigorous little Girl, and you were so out in your calculations respecting the quantity of brains she was to have, and the skull it would require to contain them, that you made almost all the caps so small I cannot use them; but it is of little consequence for she will soon have hair enough to do without any.—I feel great pleasure at being a mother—and the constant tenderness of my most affectionate companion makes me regard a fresh tie as a blessing.

Mrs Barlow had evidently returned to London, for three days later Mary added a postscript to her letter which was still awaiting shipment:

23rd. The vessel being detained I add a line to say that I am now, the 10th day, as well as I ever was in my life—In defiance of the dangers of the ninth day, I know not what they are, ENTRE NOUS, I took a little walk out on the eighth—and intend to lengthen it today.—My little Girl begins to suck so MANFULLY that her father reckons saucily on her writing the second part of the R....s of Woman.

The baby, named Frances after Mary's dead friend Fanny Blood, in the best romantic tradition succeeded in uniting the parents with a new bond. Mary and Imlay lived together at Havre 'with great harmony', as Godwin described it, until August 1794.

During this period the Terror in Paris reached and passed its climax. In the month of Fanny's birth the scientist Lavoisier was brutally executed, and Condorcet the constitution-maker died in gaol. In June, in a desperate attempt to control the mounting anarchy by the discipline of a new 'religion', Robespierre instituted the Festival of the Supreme Being and ordained himself as its high priest. But this feeble gesture to a higher power than 'sansculottism' was at once cancelled out by the Law of 22 Prairial which, by extending the powers of arrest under the Law of

Suspects, acclerated the rate of executions. The guillotine was moved from its prominent site in the Place de la Revolution to the Place de la Bastille; and from there, when the local populace could stomach it no longer, to the Place du Trône, in the St Antoine section. At this time the twelve prisons of Paris were estimated by Carlyle to hold 12,000 prisoners; in the next six weeks until the fall of Robespierre over 1,3000 victims were slaughtered on the guillotine. Mary wrote to Ruth Barlow on 8th July[17]:

> On the state of things there, and the decree against the English I will not speak. The French will carry all before them—but, my God, how many victims fall beneath the sword and the guillotine! My blood runs cold, and I sicken at the thoughts of a Revolution which costs so much blood and bitter tears.

At last, on 27th July (Thermidor 9 in the revolutionary calendar), nemesis struck as the silent and cowed majority in the National Assembly turned on their oppressor and Robespierre himself was indicted. Like a wounded animal, his jaw broken while resisting arrest, the 'sea-green incorruptible' was ignominiously despatched at the national slaughter-house on the following day. The terror was finished. So too, as Carlyle perceived it, was the revolutionary ideal:

> Camille had demanded a 'Committee of Mercy', and could not get it; but now the whole Nation resolves itself into a Committee of Mercy: the Nation has tried Sansculottism, and is weary of it. Force of Public Opinion! What King or Convention can withstand it? ... Sansculottism, on the Ninth night of Thermidor suicidally 'fractured its under-jaw'; and lies writhing, never to rise more.

Ironically, those last bloody months of the Revolution were, at the personal level, the happiest Mary Wollstonecraft had ever known. Like any other mother, she boasted of her baby's progress. Not only was little Fanny 'uncommonly healthy', she told Ruth Barlow in this same letter of 8th July, but 'already, as sagacious as a child of five or six months old'. This she attributed to her 'good, that is natural, manner of nursing her'. She was proud that she was so well able to put into practice her own theories about the benefits of suckling infants: 'She has not tasted anything but my milk, of which I have abundance, since her birth'.

All was not well, however, with Imlay. Mary reported that he had been 'seriously feverish', and she put this down to his 'con-

tinual disappointments' with his business. Unlike most of his fellow-Americans in Europe, he seemed unable to turn to advantage the disturbed state of public affairs; and in this Mary wholly sympathised:
> Ships do not return, and the government is perpetually throwing impediments in the way of business. I cannot help sharing his disquietude, because the fulfilling of engagements appears to me of more importance that the making of a fortune.

It is doubtful if Imlay agreed with this conclusion, especially when he could see all his friends around him doing precisely that. In search of fortune, therefore, and with the fall of Robespierre bringing hope of a more reasonable regime, he took himself now to Paris. Mary did not accompany him, and this time she was content to remain alone. She was absorbed in her baby and amused by her provincial neighbours. 'The Havrais are very ugly without doubt—' she wrote on 17th August, 'and the house smelt of commerce from top to toe'[18]. She could even be tolerant of 'commerce', in her present relaxed mood—'nay, perhaps you will call me severe, and bid me let the square-headed money-getters alone. Peace to them!' But she ended with another warning to Imlay not to allow money-making to wither his affection: 'I hope still to see it, if you have not determined only to eat and drink, and be stupidly useful to the stupid'. Two days later, she was reiterating her need for reassurance of his love: 'unless the attachment appears to me clearly mutual, I shall labour only to esteem your character instead of cherishing a tenderness for your person'[19]. The old doubt was nagging at her, though more gently now: 'when you are from me, I not only wonder how I can find fault with you, but how I can doubt your affection'. She scarcely needed to assure him of hers, though she proceeded to do so: 'you are the friend of my bosom, and the prop of my heart'.

Mary was one of those women to whom the father of her child is more important than the offspring as such. Her love for her baby grew as Fanny's personality developed and became interesting to her. At first, she admitted, her affection was 'more the effect of reason, a sense of duty, than feeling'. But now, 'she has got into my heart and imagination, and when I walk out without her, her little figure is ever dancing before me'. The next day she wrote again about the 'little damsel': 'she certainly looks very like you; but I do not love her the less for that, whether I am angry or pleased with you'[20]. She also referred again to public affairs. She was evidently already working on the second volume of her 'French Revolution', although no trace of it has ever been discovered. 'Pray ask some questions about Tallien,' she wrote, 'I am still pleased with the dignity of his conduct'. Tallien was the former Montagnard who led the attack on Robespierre; he was then President of the National Convention. Mary praised his 'openness of heart', which she could not resist contrasting with 'a little reserve of temper' in Imlay. In other words, she suspected that he was not being entirely honest with her, and on this occasion she was realistic enough to admit the cause of this: 'You have been used to a cunning woman, and you almost look for cunning.' Imlay's previous mistresses had not been of Mary's frank and generous temper: they were mean and deceitful, no doubt, and she feared he had something of the same qualities himself although she tried to gloss this over: 'You have frankness of heart, but not often exactly that overflowing (*épanchement de coeur*), which becoming almost childish, appears a weakness only to the weak'.

In September 1794 Mary and Fanny joined Imlay in Paris. That same month, incredibly enough, he was called away to London! These coincidental departures were becoming too much for her to swallow. From this time on, the pretence of his fidelity to his 'wife' and child slipped into the realm of fantasy. Yet Mary continued to maintain the fiction for several months more. What else, after all, could she do if she was to salvage anything from the wreckage of her hopes and pride? Her family were now aware of her changed status and accepted it at its face value. Eliza appears to have received the news from Joseph Johson and found it hard to believe. Her first reference to it is in a letter to Everina dated 7th July: '... I could not even for a moment suppose Mary married! It is not true, not even in my dream will I allow it to be real.' Yet the story was confirmed by Charles, writing from America on 16th June: 'I heard from Mary six months ago by a gentleman who knew her at Paris—and since that have been informed she is married to Capt. Imlay of this country'[21]. Eliza passed on the message to Everina on 15th August, in some excitement. Was their luck really turning at last? If it were true that Mary had married an American perhaps the whole family would one day be reunited in the New World:

I would I could fancy these things matter-of-fact. I mean the poor fellow, Charles's wonderful good luck in so short a time. I own I want faith, nay doubt my senses, as I have sent you word for word, to spell and put together ... If Mary is *actually* married to Mr Imlay, it might not be impossible but she might settle there too. Yet Mary cannot be *married!* It is natural to conclude her protector is her *husband*. Nay, on reading Charles's letter, I for an instant believed it true. I would, my Everina, we were out of suspense, for all at present is uncertainty and the most cruel suspense; still, Johnson does not speak things at random, and that the very same tale should have crossed the Atlantic makes me almost believe that the once Mary is now Mrs Imlay and a mother. Are we ever to see this mother and her babe?

'I want you to see my little girl, who is more like a boy', Mary herself wrote to Everina on 20th September, a cheerful letter full of the joys of motherhood: 'She is ready to fly away with spirits, and has eloquent health in her cheeks and eyes'. Mary put this down to her 'good nursing'. Fanny had caught smallpox at Havre, where, said Mary, 'they treat the dreadful disorder very improperly'. She decided to use her own commonsense instead, and 'saved her much pain, probably her life ... by putting her twice a day into a warm bath'. Mary also boasted of her easy confinement. She rested in bed only one day, and that only 'through persuasion', and on the eighth day was 'out a-walking'. She explained that she had written to her sisters 'at least half a score times', entrusting the letters to Imlay to despatch, but had received no replies:

> I have again and again given you an account of my present situation and introduced Mr Imlay to you as a brother you would love and respect. I hope the time is not very distant when we shall all meet.

She signed this letter 'Mary Imlay' and addressed it to Everina care of 'Messrs Moore & Co, Finsbury Square, London'. This was the firm in which Thomas Christie was a partner, and with which Imlay may also have had business connections. Almost as an afterthought, Mary referred to her recently-completed volume on the French Revolution: 'You will see the last vol. I have written, it is the commencement of a considerable work'.

Mary's next series of letters to Imlay, dated from September 1794 to April 1795, were written, said Godwin, 'during a separation of many months, to which no cordial meeting ever succeeded'. There is some evidence that he was not correct in this statement, as will be seen later. The correspondence starts cheerfully enough, still full of the 'little Hercules' which Mary sought to make of her baby daughter (not so successfully as she supposed): 'Besides looking at me, there are three other things which delight her; to ride in a coach, to look at a scarlet waistcoat, and hear loud music—yesterday, at the *fête*, she enjoyed the two latter'[22]. She was now going to buy Fanny a sash, Mary reported, 'to honour J.J. Rousseau'. And why not, she added, 'for I have always been half in love with him'. Immediately, with her usual lack of tact, she contrasted this dream of Rousseau with the reality of Gilbert Imlay—'shall I talk about alum or soap? There is nothing picturesque in your present pursuits'. But her dream of romantic love had not yet quite faded:

> my imagination, then, rather chooses to ramble back to the barrier with you, or to see you coming to meet me, and my basket of grapes: With what pleasure do I recollect your looks and words, when I have been sitting on the window, regarding the waving corn!

She went on to accuse him of lack of imagination—'the mother of sentiment, the great distinction of our nature, the only purifier of the passions':

> imagination is the true fire, stolen from heaven, to animate this cold creature of clay, producing all those fine sympathies that lead to rapture, rendering men social by expanding their hearts, instead of leaving them leisure to calculate how many comforts society affords.

> If you call these observations romantic ... I shall be apt to retort, that you are embruted by trade and the vulgar enjoyments of life. Bring me then back your barrier-face, or you shall have nothing to say to my barrier-girl; and I shall fly from you, to cherish the remembrances that will ever be dear to me.

With the best will in the world, no husband with his bread and butter to earn could maintain the postures of courtship, nor would it be appropriate if he did. Mary was demanding the impossible, seeking refuge in the past because she could not face the bleak reality of her present state. The next letter was more rational[23], and she acknowledged that her temper had been 'ruffled' in the

past few days by some tiresome acquaintances. She also made an interesting comment on the situation in Paris:
> Public affairs I do not descant on, except to tell you that they write now with great freedom and truth; and this liberty of the press will overthrow the Jacobins, I plainly perceive.

This forecast proved correct. The Jacobin Club was closed in November 1794, and on 8th December seventy-three Girondin deputies who had escaped execution were readmitted to the National Convention.

It was about this time that Mary became acquainted with an expatriate Irishman, Archibald Hamilton Rowan, who had escaped from prison in Dublin where he had been sentenced on a false charge of sedition (he was a United Irishman). They first met at a festival, probably that very fête where Fanny had so enjoyed the scarlet waistcoats and loud music. Rowan described the occasion in a letter to his wife[24]:
> On the day of the celebration of one of the numerous feasts with which this country has abounded ... Mr B(ingham) who was with me, joined a lady who spoke English, and who was followed by her maid with an infant in her arms, which I found belonged to the lady. Her manners were interesting and her conversation spirited, yet not out of her sex. B(ingham) whispered to me that she was the author of the *Rights of Woman*. I started! 'What?' said I within myself, 'this is Miss Mary Wollstonecraft, parading about with a child at her heels, with as little ceremony as if it were a watch she had just bought at the jeweler's. So much for the rights of women,' thought I. But upon further enquiry, I found that she had, very fortunately for her, married an American gentleman a short time before the passing of that decree which indiscriminately incarcerated all the British subjects who were at that moment in this country. My society, which before that time, was wholly male, was now most agreeably increased, and I got a dish of tea, and an hour's rational conversation whenever I called on her.

It is clear from this letter that in her Paris circle Mary was generally accepted as the wife of Gilbert Imlay. It also indicates, if Rowan's information was correct, that the 'marriage' was registered before the passing of the Law against Suspects on 17th September 1793, and not as a result of it; in which case Fanny's birth the following May was a perfectly legitimate one, at least in the eyes of her parents. This is further evidence that there was no casual or promiscuous intention in the relationship between Mary and Imlay; almost as soon as it was entered upon the union was 'regularised', as far as this was possible in the circumstances of the time.

This letter shows too that, despite her infatuation with Imlay, Mary had lost none of her old charm. It also bore out her conviction that men could appreciate the company of rational women, who had more interesting topics of conversation than flirtation and flattery. Indeed, her obvious attraction for men did not always endear her to her own sex. Madeleine Schweizer described in her journal in 1794 an evening in the country in the company of Mary and the Baron de Wolzogen, when she drew Mary's attention to the beauties of the sunset[25]:

'Come, Mary—come, nature lover—and enjoy this wonderful spectacle—this constant transition from colour to colour!' But, to my great surprise, Mary was so indifferent that she never turned her eyes from him by whom she was at the moment captivated. I must confess that this erotic absorption made such a disagreeable impression on me, that all my pleasure vanished.

Mme Schweizer had a reputation for frivolity so her testimony may not have been unbiased; and she did acknowledge, in this same passage, that but for her 'excessive sensibility' Mary's personality would be 'exquisite'. This was the impression made on another of Mary's Paris friends, Count Schlabrendorf, who wrote in his copy of Godwin's *Memoirs* after her death[26]:

Mary was the noblest, purest and most intelligent woman I have ever met. I knew her well, even before the time of my imprisonment, during the reign of terror. Mary was, without being a dazzling beauty, yet of a charming grace. Her face, so full of expression, presented a style of beauty beyond that of merely regular features. There was enchantment in her glance, her voice, and her movement. While in prison, she often visited me; she enthralled me more and more. Not until after she had left Paris, did I realize that I loved her. Her unhappy union with Imlay prevented any closer bond with her.

Imlay, he added, 'did not appreciate her worth and became indifferent'. What a pity that Schlabrendorf had not woken to his feelings a little less tardily, since his character was so much more in tune with Mary's than that of Imlay!

Rowan, too, later confessed to his wife that Mary had 'unknowingly given me many a heart-ache'[27]. This was no cause for jealousy, however. He explained that it arose from her persistence in maintaining that 'no motive upon earth ought to make a man and wife live together a moment after mutual love and regard were gone'. Mary genuinely believed this, and it was the real cause of her own heart-ache. Her reason told her that 'mutual love and regard' no longer existed—if they ever had—between herself and Imlay. Yet mutual love and regard *must* exist, her conscience told her, for a marriage to go on . . . and the marriage *must* go on, all her instincts demanded; so love and regard, if they did not exist, must be invented by her imagination. It was an impossible equation.

Mary was further frustrated by the impossibility of sending any letters to Imlay except by personal messenger. Though the terror was relaxed, France was still at war with Britain and normal communication between the countries was barred. She was therefore dependent on the goodwill of such of Imlay's American friends as might be travelling between Paris and London. 'I have written to you three or four letters,' she reported on 28th September, 'but different causes have prevented my sending them by the persons who promised to take or forward them'[28]. She could put up with this, however, so long as she believed that Imlay would soon be returning; and she still did believe it. 'The inclosed is one I wrote to go by B——,' she continued, 'yet finding that he will not arrive, before I hope, and believe, you will have set out on your return, I inclose it to you, and shall give it in charge to ——, as Mr —— is detained, to whom also I gave a letter'. Imlay must have dreaded the arrival of his friends from Paris, turning out their pockets in a shower of reproaches! Even when her feelings were most tender towards him, some demon drove Mary to express her doubts of his integrity: 'I slept at St. Germain's in the very room (if you have not forgot) in which you pressed me very tenderly to your heart.' Why did she have to include that gratuitous parenthesis, even perhaps putting the thought into his head that it might be as well to forget? On occasions, Mary did indeed dig her own grave with a sharp-tipped quill. She admitted in her next letter that it was perhaps a mercy if some of her low-spirited ones, 'a little querulous or so', had not arrived: '*Tant mieux!* you will say, and I will not say nay: for I should be sorry that the contents of a letter, when you are far away, should damp the pleasure the sight of it would afford'[29]. Mary had the endearing quality of readily acknowledging her faults; but the acknowledgment did not cure her of repeating them. However, for the present she was buoyed up by the anticipation of his return and of easier times for both of them:

> After your return, I hope indeed that you will not be so immersed in business, as during the last three or four months past—for even money, taking into account all the future comforts it is to procure, may be gained at too dear a rate, if painful impressions are left on the mind.

These impressions, she confessed, were most acute soon after his departure. Now, 'a thousand tender recollections efface the melancholy traces they left on my mind—and every emotion is on the same side as my reason, which always was on yours'. Once again, Mary was avoiding her inner conflict by escaping into the past. It was almost as if she had to reassure herself, rather than Imlay, about the nature of her feelings. 'I feel that I love you.' she added, 'and, if I cannot be happy with you, I will seek it nowhere else.' Again, she was expressing doubts which would have been better kept hidden, if she really believed that she was going to resume her life with Imlay.

Fanny was a constant source of solace to Mary, though also something of a hindrance to her independent spirit. The nursemaid proved 'a most helpless creature', and pregnant to boot, so that Mary was 'almost a slave to the child'. But Fanny was 'a sweet little creature', 'all life and motion'; and her eyes, Mary solemnly assured Imlay, 'are not the eyes of a fool, I will swear'. A little later she was writing that the little girl was 'as gay as a lark', though this happy state of affairs also had its drawbacks—'and that in the morning too, which I do not find quite so convenient'[30]. Mary struggled hard to be a conscientious mother; but it always was a struggle, when at the same time there were so many other things to which she wished to give her mind. She was thankful when she had 'two good nurses', so that she was able to discharge her duty 'without being the slave of it'. Thus relieved, Mary was able to move freely again in congenial society, and she recovered her spirits even to the point of teasing Imlay with her new conquests:

> I have almost *charmed* a judge of the tribunal, R——, who,

though I should not have thought it possible, has humanity, if not *beaucoup d'esprit*. But let me tell you, if you do not make haste back, I shall be half in love with the author of the *Marseillaise*, who is a handsome man, a little too broad-faced or so, and plays sweetly on the violin.

This alleged rival was Colonel Rouget de Lisle, who composed the marching-song of the Revolution. 'What do you say to this threat?' she asked Imlay coyly; and perhaps fearing for his answer, hastened to anticipate it: 'My heart longs for your return, my love, and only looks for, and seeks happiness with you.' She closes this letter, dated 22nd October 1794, 'Yours most truly and tenderly, Mary'.

The next extant letter[31] is dated 26th December: for the third year in succession, Mary spent Christmas alone in Paris. Since she speaks now of being 'happier than I ever was', it seems probable that Godwin was mistaken in supposing that Imlay never returned to her. This gap of over two months in the correspondence is a strong indication that there had been a reunion in the interim. Imlay himself gave an inkling of this in a letter to Eliza in November 1794. He had evidently been in touch with Mary's sisters since his return to England, and wrote now in the guise of a considerate brother-in-law[32]:

As to your sister's visiting England, I do not think she will previous to a peace, and perhaps not immediately after such an event. However, be that as it may, we shall both of us continue to cherish feelings of tenderness for you, and a recollection of your unpleasant situation, and we shall also endeavour to alleviate its distress by all the means in our power. The present state of our fortune is rather (low) . . . I shall always be most happy to receive your letters, but as I shall most likely leave England the beginning of next week, I will thank you to let me hear from you as soon as convenient, and tell me ingenuously in what way I can serve you in any manner or respect. I am in but indifferent spirits occasioned by my long absence from Mrs Imlay and our little girl, while I am deprived of a chance of hearing from them.

As the only surviving letter of Gilbert Imlay, this is of interest for the light it throws on his character. It has generally been regarded as evidence of his hypocrisy and perfidy. But there is no real reason to suppose that it may not be taken at its face value. The rather florid style is reminiscent of his novel and was probably his natural form of expression. No doubt at the time of writing he did intend to assist Eliza—when his ship came home, which he was always hoping would happen; no doubt it was true that he missed Mary—if only for her practical good sense—and the baby; and in expressing his intention to 'leave England' very soon he may simply have been stating a fact.

It is indeed clear from Mary's letter that Imlay had been in France again, for she spoke of her fears for his safety at sea and her relief at news that he has now landed—presumably, back in England. She continues: '... return to me when you have arranged the other matters, which — has been crowding on you. I want to be sure that you are safe, and not separated from me by a sea that must be passed'. She went on in her tenderest vein with no hint of rancour or resentment:

> Come to me, my dearest friend, husband, father of my child! All these fond ties glow at my heart at this moment, and dim my eyes. With you an independence is desirable; and it is always within our reach, if affluence escapes us—without you the world again appears empty to me. But I am recurring to some of the melancholy thoughts that have flitted across my mind for some days past, and haunted my dreams.

The tone of this letter suggests that Imlay had only quite recently departed on yet another business trip and that the reunion had been happy enough on both sides to still Mary's fears.

This mood is maintained, two days later, in one of the most friendly and helpful letters Mary ever wrote to her absent spouse. If only she could have sustained this attitude—and he responded to it—how different the future might have been! Here is Mary at her best: calm, rational and affectionate, for once putting herself in Imlay's shoes rather than trying to cram his restive feet into her own. If only for its uniqueness, it is worth reproducing in full[33]:

> I do, my love, indeed sincerely sympathise with you in all your disappointments. Yet, knowing that you are well, and think of me with affection, I only lament other disappointments, because I am sorry that you should thus exert yourself in vain, and that you are kept from me. —, I know, urges you to stay, and is continually branching out into new projects, because he has the idle desire to amass a large fortune, rather an immense one, merely to have the credit of having

made it. But we who are governed by other motives, ought not to be led on by him. When we meet, we will discuss this subject. You will listen to reason, and it has probably occurred to you, that it will be better, in future, to pursue some sober plan, which may demand more time, and still enable you to arrive at the same end. It appears to me absurd to waste life in preparing to live.

Would it not now be possible to arrange your business in such a manner as to avoid the inquietudes, of which I have had my share since your departure? Is it not possible to enter into business as an employment necessary to keep the faculties awake, and (to sink a little in the expressions) the pot boiling, without suffering what must ever be considered as a secondary object, to engross the mind, and drive sentiment and affection out of the heart?

I am in a hurry to give this letter to the person who has promised to forward it with —'s. I wish then, to counteract, in some measure, what he has doubtless recommended most warmly.

Stay, my friend, whilst it is *absolutely* necessary. I will give you no tenderer name, though it glows at my heart, unless you come the moment the settling the *present* object permits. *I do not consent* to your taking any other journey, or the little woman and I will be off, the Lord knows where. But, as I had rather owe everything to your affection, and, I may add, to your reason (for this immoderate desire of wealth, which makes — so eager to have you remain, is contrary to your principles of action), I will not importune you. I will only tell you that I long to see you, and, being at peace with you, I shall be hurt, rather than made angry, by delays. Having suffered so much in life, do not be surprised if I sometimes, when left to myself, grow gloomy, and suppose that it was all a dream, and that my happiness is not to last. I say happiness, because remembrance retrenches all the dark shades of the picture.

My little one begins to show her teeth, and use her legs. She wants you to bear your part in this nursing business, for I am fatigued with dancing her, and yet she is not satisfied; she wants you to thank her mother for taking such care of her, as you only can.

Such an appeal was calculated—though not, we may be sure,

deliberately—to melt the hardest heart and move the most stubborn mind. But Imlay's shortcomings arose from his lack of acumen rather than from malevolence. Despite his absorption with commerce, and Mary's hatred of it, she had a far better head for business than he, and her advice on this occasion was no doubt based on good sense. Unfortunately, he paid no attention to it. Imlay was determined to pursue his own hunches, however disastrous they proved, and continued to lurch from one crisis to another with no tangible result. In her next letter, written only one day later, Mary was more sharply critical again[34]:

> How I hate this crooked business! This intercourse with the world, which obliges one to see the worst side of human nature! Why cannot you be content with the object you had first in view when you entered into this wearisome labyrinth? I know very well that you have imperceptibly been drawn on; yet why does one project, successful or abortive, only give place to two others? Is it not sufficient to avoid poverty?

It seemed clear to Mary, if it was not to Imlay, that he was being used by unscrupulous associates with no obvious benefit to himself. So why could he not pull out of it and be content with a modest pittance, honestly earned? If he could not do this, then she would do so herself, she now threatened:

> And let me tell you, I have my project also, and if you do not soon return, the little girl and I will take care of ourselves; we will not accept any of your cold kindness—your distant civilities—no; not we.

If Imlay imagined that, given time and the good fortune which had so far eluded him, he could placate Mary and his conscience by buying her off, he had badly misjudged her character. She stated her position even more plainly the following day (she was writing so frequently, she explained, because probably only 'one out of three of my epistles' would reach him)[35]:

> I am determined to try to earn some money here myself, in order to convince you that if you choose to run about the world to get a fortune, it is for yourself, for the little girl and I will live without your assistance, unless you are with us. I may be termed proud; be it so, but I will never abandon certain principles of action.

She was 'not of —'s opinion,' she said, referring no doubt to one of Imlay's business partners, that it was necessary for him to be absent for another 'two or three months'. For the first time now Mary voiced the suspicion that perhaps it was not only business that detained him. Was Imlay already deceiving her? Her sudden outburst suggests this:

The common run of men have such an ignoble way of thinking, that, if they debauch their hearts, and prostitute their persons, following perhaps a gust of inebriation, they suppose the wife, slave rather, whom they maintain, has no right to complain, and ought to receive the sultan, whenever he deigns to return, with open arms, though his have been polluted by half a hundred promiscuous amours during his absence.

As usual, Mary was taking the worst possible line if she really hoped to induce Imlay to return. If he were innocent, he would be bitterly wounded by her veiled accusation; if guilty, he would advisedly keep well away. Mary was not saying: 'Come home, all is forgiven!'—which was all she could say if she had proof of his infidelity and really wanted him back. But she had no such proof; Imlay's excuses were probably genuine. Now she went even further and announced that if he came back just out of a sense of duty, she did not want him either: 'if only probity, which is a good thing in its place, brings you back, never return!—for if a wandering of the heart, or even a caprice of the imagination detains you, there is an end of all my hopes of happiness. I could not forgive it if I would'. What was Imlay expected to make of this? The 'caprice of the imagination' was surely on Mary's side. He could only assume that she was determined to think the worst of him, whatever he did.

This may well have been true. Mary does give the impression that she was blackening Imlay's character in order to justify herself. Perhaps her deepest fear was not that Imlay did not love her, but that she did not love him. She could not bring herself to admit that her feeling for him was in truth no more than an infatuation with the novelty of sensual gratification; which by its nature, as she had herself warned in the *Rights of Woman*, could not last. Therefore she could only acknowledge that she did not love him, without injury to her pride, by making him unworthy of her love; this she proceeded to do until she had finally destroyed it for both of them. Of course, it was equally true that Imlay was not 'worthy' of the love of such a woman as Mary Wollstonecraft; but he had never pretended to be, and the fault lay in her own error of judgment. Mary was not 'betrayed' by Imlay; she betrayed herself.

'I have ever declared,' she wrote, 'that two people who mean to live together ought not to be long separated. If certain things are more necessary to you than me—search for them. Say but one word, and you shall never hear of me more.' Mary was almost willing Imlay to say the word that would get them both off the hook; yet, by linking it with a moral condemnation, she made it impossible for him to do so without an unacceptable loss of face. So the affair drifted miserably on, neither broken nor healed; and the agonising uncertainties were killing Mary by inches.

A new year brought no relief. Turned in upon herself again, Mary could only review the hardships of her youth and the brief respite from melancholy she had found with Imlay. 'Why have you so soon dissolved the charm?' she demanded of him on 9th January 1795, and again she called up commerce as the villain of the piece: 'My God! anything but these continual anxieties, anything but commerce, which debases the mind, and roots out affection from the heart'[36]. She reminded him of their original dream of domestic bliss: 'I should have been content, and still wish, to retire with you to a farm.' This is what Mary had set her heart on, and nothing else would do. Yet she refused to recognise that the farm itself depended on a certain amount of capital, which was something Imlay seemed quite incapable of acquiring. He had left America under a cloud of debt, and could hardly return there until his finances had been put on a sounder basis. Whether he was really trying to do this, or was a confirmed and unregenerate idler, we shall never know; at best, he seems to have been a weak and ineffectual character. By now, Mary was suffering real hardship from the absence of a bread-winner. Because week by week she had expected him to come back, she had made no arrangements 'to procure the necessaries of life'. Though the terror was relaxed, Paris was still in a state of near-anarchy; and Mary was still an alien. She pointed out to Imlay, reasonably enough, that she could not obtain these necessities without the aid of a servant, and this cost money. 'The want of wood,' she wrote, 'has made me catch the most violent cold I ever had.' She was realising at last that she could count on nothing from Imlay, and that so unsatisfactory a helpmeet was worse than none at all. She now came out into the open with this thought. 'I do not choose to be a secondary object,' she observed tartly. 'If your feelings were in unison with mine, you would not sacrifice so much to visionary prospects of future advantage.' The whole problem, of course, was that their feelings were not 'in unison', and no amount of badgering on her part would make them so.

Yet, a week later, having received two reassuring letters from Imlay, she was ready to start all over again. Forgetting her previous strictures, she confessed that 'it is pleasant to forgive those we love'[37]. 'You can scarcely conceive the effect some of your letters have produced on me,' she added, speaking no more than the truth. Imlay, with his superficial gallantry, failed to understand the devastation to her spirit when she received 'only half-a-dozen hasty lines, that have damped all the rising affection of my soul'. But the reassurance was short-lived. By the end of the month the ding-dong battle had resumed, with Imlay accusing her of complaints about petty inconveniences. 'The secondary pleasures of life,' she quoted him as saying, 'are very necessary to my comfort'; to which she retorted: 'It may be so; but I have ever considered them as secondary'[38]. Mary was indeed suffering physically from the prolonged strain and conflict of the separation; and her weakened physical state preyed in turn on her spirits. 'So many feelings are struggling for utterance,' she wrote on 9th February, 'and agitating a heart almost bursting with anguish, that I find it very difficult to write with any degree of coherence'[39]. The reason for this agitation was that Imlay had actually suggested that she and Fanny should join him! Now Mary was really put on the spot. He had cut the ground of her complaint from under her, and she could no longer conceal her own reluctance to respond to this gesture. She fell back on a prevarication. His request, she felt sure, was 'merely dictated by honour'. She also saw some prevarication on his side: 'Indeed I scarcely understand you. You request me to come, and then tell me that you have not given up all thoughts of returning to this place'. She again insisted that she wanted to be under no obligations to him 'of a pecuniary kind': 'I wanted the support of your affection; that gone, all is over!' Why was she so determined to believe that Imlay's motives were always of the most mercenary? She quotes again from his letter to her, in which he had said that 'our being together is paramount to every other consideration'. In her present mood, she could only see this as an insult. If it were true, he could not be 'running after a bubble, at the expense of my peace of mind'. She concluded with the dire statement: 'Perhaps this is the last letter you will ever receive from me.'

She had thought better of this by the following morning, however, and took up the cudgels again. She had evidently re-read his letter, and now found a reference to 'permanent views and future comfort'. Hastily, she repudiated such a rosy prospect: 'Not for me, for I am dead to hope.' Not only was her heart broken, she added for good measure, but her constitution was destroyed: 'I conceive myself in a galloping consumption, and the continual anxiety I feel at the thought of leaving my child, feeds the fever that nightly devours me.'[40] So convinced was she of her impending demise—as she had been in the worst days of her depression as a governess in Ireland—that Mary was making practical arrangements to have Fanny brought up by a German friend who had a child of the same age. To this end, she was preparing to move into the same lodgings, which would also be an economy (no doubt the real reason for the move); and, she added darkly: 'I shall entirely give up the acquaintance of the Americans.' This was probably by mutual consent. She admitted that she had made herself unpopular by criticising their commercial activities. She held Imlay's friends mainly responsible for his prolonged absence, and she returned now to her own grievance against him:

> When you first entered into these plans, you bounded your views to the gaining of a thousand pounds. It was sufficient to have procured a farm in America, which would have been an independence. You find now that you did not know yourself, and that a certain situation in life is more necessary to you than you imagined—more necessary than an incorrupted heart.

The truth about Imlay was probably that as fast as he made some money he found pleasant ways of spending it; and so the mythical goal of one thousand pounds never came any nearer. Perhaps he even realised that with Mary at his side he would have more chance of achieving it, and to this extent was anxious for her co-operation in his schemes. But this was not to be. Mary had quite decided to play the part of the martyred heroine, and in this letter she reached the nadir of self-pity. 'In the solitude of declining life,' she mused, 'I shall be remembered with regret—I was going to say with remorse, but checked my pen.' She was even willing to shoulder the burden of moral disapproval:

As I have never concealed the nature of my connection with
you, your reputation will not suffer. I shall never have a confident; I am content with the approbation of my own mind;
and, if there be a searcher of hearts, mine will not be despised.

Then she related her own personal misery to that of France in
general: 'I wish at one moment that I had never heard of the
cruelties that have been practised here, and the next, envy the
mothers who have been killed with their children.' There is no
doubting the sincerity of Mary's feelings. This was no play-acting
for Imlay's sympathy. She did not want his pity. She pitied herself
because she had the rare capacity to see her own weaknesses even
at her moments of greatest suffering. Such an awareness did not
soften the suffering, however, but rather enhanced it:

Surely I had suffered enough in life, not to be cursed with a
fondness, that burns up the vital stream I am imparting. You
will think me mad: I would I were so, that I could forget my
misery—so that my head or heart would be still.

But if Mary had near-fatal weaknesses, she also had extraordinary powers of resilience. Nine days later she was able to write
quite calmly again. The frenzy had passed, leaving her full of
sorrow but also rational enough to contain it: 'finding fault with
everyone, I have only reason enough to discover that the fault is
in myself'[41]. She turned her attention to her child, whom she was
now to start weaning; though reluctantly, 'for it is my only
solace'. Mary was not ashamed to admit that she had deep need
for physical contact, and now she had only her baby for comfort.
She had long known that her only bond with Imlay was a sensual
one, and it seems as if she had not given up hope of renewing this
at least.

'What sacrifices have you not made for a woman you did not
respect!' she commented, and this remark has usually been taken
to refer to a previous mistress of Imlay's. But its context suggests
that she was thinking of herself as that woman, with the implication that Imlay was better able to do without her than she could
do without him. He was willing to sacrifice present gratification
for the prospect of future comforts, but she sought now to bring
him back by reminding him of the gratifications of the past:

I want to tell you that I do not understand you. You say that
you have not given up all thoughts of returning here—and I
know that it will be necessary—nay is. I cannot explain

myself; but if you have not lost your memory, you will easily divine my meaning. What! is our life then only to be made up of separations?'

The answer to this was that Imlay had already offered her an alternative, and she had refused it. She did not wish to join him in England: 'a country, that has not merely lost all charms for me, but for which I feel a repugnance that almost amounts to horror'. Mary did not explain this sudden hatred of her native land, but there were good reasons for it. In a war situation she had chosen to remain in 'enemy' country; and the fact that she had escaped internment would not be a mark in her favour. Her volume on the French Revolution, published by Joseph Johnson in December 1794, was enough in itself to make her extremely unpopular: her criticisms of Marie-Antoinette, written before the queen's execution but in no way modified after it, had given considerable offence. All this was quite apart from her personal situation. Her 'republican marriage' in France would hardly stand the scrutiny of English law; and even if it had, how was the author of the *Rights of Woman* to explain her emotional dependence on a man of such little worth? English society was more than Mary could face; she could not admit this, so she found other grounds for her refusal. Her daughter would be 'freer', she said, if she were brought up in France. Also, expecting Imlay to join them there, she had made 'some plans of usefulness'. Now, with his continued absence these had vanished along with her hopes. So she had the further embarrassment of being dependent on one of Imlay's partners for her maintenance: 'With a brutal insensibility, he cannot help displaying the pleasure your determination to stay gives him.' She was in the humiliating position of having to go to this man's house and ask for money; though this was never refused, she declared that she would rather borrow from her friends than ask for more. Nor, she added, did she wish to be reminded by him of Imlay's 'eternal projects to which you have sacrificed my peace'.

This letter was dated 19th February 1795; the next was written from Havre on 7th April[42]. What had happened in the interim? Why were there no letters? Had Imlay relented and briefly returned to France? Or was one of these letters misdated? Mary refers on 7th April to the weaning of Fanny, now completed, which suggests no great interval; but other letters written from

Terror and Despair: 1793–4

Havre were also dated in April, so this date was presumably correct. Whatever the explanation, she had been persuaded to leave Paris and was now en route for England, having apparently overcome her previous repugnance. The decision had eased her inner conflict, so that she could now write quite cheerfully: 'Here I am at Havre, on the wing towards you'. Yet she was still uncertain what her reception would be: 'I cannot indulge the very affectionate tenderness which glows in my bosom, without trembling, till I see, by your eyes, that it is mutual'.

Mary knew in her heart that she had little to look forward to: 'I have indeed been so unhappy this winter, I find it as difficult to acquire fresh hopes as to regain tranquillity'. She did not even expect Imlay to meet the boat: 'I suppose I shall find you when I arrive, for I do not see any necessity for your coming to me'. She had already delayed her departure in order to bring to England 'Mr. —'s little friend', presumably a child. She admitted that the delay was 'irksome' to her 'who have not quite so much philosophy, I would not for the world say indifference, as you'. Yet she did say it! But the little dig at Imlay was softened by a concluding 'God bless you!'

Whilst waiting for her ship at Havre Mary wrote two letters to Archibald Hamilton Rowan. Imlay had evidently leased the house in which she was staying[43], for she was now planning to let it and in the meantime offered Rowan the use of it while he in his turn waited for a boat to America. The first note was dashed off at the harbour, apologising that she had not had a chance to see him before her departure. But, inevitably, as Mary stepped on board her ship ran aground; and she was obliged to return to 'an empty house', with time to write another letter[44]. It appears that Rowan was already at Havre: 'If you were to pop in, I should be glad,' she wrote, 'for in spite of my impatience to meet a friend who deserves all my tenderness, I have still a corner in my heart where I will allow you a place, *if you have no objection.*' Mary's self-confidence had taken a hard knock. But it is curious that she referred to Imlay as 'a friend', when he was generally accepted as her husband. Rowan at least believed this, as he had written in his autobiography when recalling her friendship with the Christies in Paris[45]:

There she became acquainted with Mr Imlay, also an American, who paid his addresses to her; and partly as a safeguard against prosecution by being the wife of an American, she submitted to a republican marriage, and from that time she was called Mrs Imlay. She took care of his house and commercial concerns during his absence on various speculations, and was treated as his wife by all who knew her. Expressing the hope that she would see him again in the future, and 'be introduced to your wife', Mary directed Rowan to write to her at 'Mr Johnson's'. She had no idea of her ultimate destination, since Imlay had evidently not bothered to inform her of his address.

What his real feelings were regarding Mary's return can only be speculated on. She had rejected his earlier requests to join him, in no uncertain terms. He could not be altogether blamed for taking her seriously and making alternative plans for himself. If there had indeed been a reunion in December 1794, judging from the tone of Mary's subsequent letters he may well have come away convinced that she would never again live in England. Even such a conviction, however, scarcely mitigates his callous behaviour when she did return.

CHAPTER THIRTEEN
A Revolution and its Aftermath, 1794–1795

In returning to England, against her formerly stated intention, Mary Wollstonecraft put revolution behind her. She was acknowledging her loss of faith both in her own revolt against the social conventions and in the greater cataclysm against which her personal drama was played out. She never went back to France and never completed the project which should have been her greatest work: *An Historical and Moral View of the Origins and Progress of the French Revolution; and the effect it has produced in Europe.* The historical background is adequately dealt with in the one published volume; but the progress of the Revolution stops well short of the onset of the 'terror' and does not even include the death of the king. The book cannot therefore be said to offer any comprehensive moral assessment of the whole cycle of events. Nevertheless, the volume as far as it goes—and it runs to some 500 pages—presents a remarkably well-balanced view, with a number of original observations.

No fair-minded book on the Revolution could expect to be acclaimed in the Britain of 1794. The execution of a king—and worse, a queen—had stung the many consciences that were still uneasy about their own country's act of regicide one hundred and fifty years earlier. They were only too thankful for an external enemy—sanctioned by war as well as by disapproval—to bear a worse guilt. Her contemporaries, therefore, found Mary's cool look at Marie-Antoinette—raised by her death from frivolity to martyrdom—both distasteful and offensive. (It was in this connection that Horace Walpole described Mary to Hannah More as a 'hyena in petticoats'.) She was also accused by one reviewer* of plagiarism in her historical data from the *New Annual Register* for 1791. Since her book was started at Neuilly and completed at Havre, and communication with Britain was virtually impossible during that period, this accusation may have been unfounded. We do know that Mary studied the *Journal des Débats et des Décrets* of the National Assembly which she had requested Ruth Barlow to send her, and that she was without her own books at Havre. In any case, there is no monopoly in facts, and the *Register* was surely designed to be plagiarised. It is on its interpretation of the facts that Mary's book should be judged.

Kegan Paul[1] praised her work as 'the best-balanced and most philosophical book on the Revolution, as far as it had then gone' (i.e. up to the King's removal to Paris in October 1789). This judgment takes into account what he called the 'graphic pages' of Carlyle and evidently rated her higher. An anonymous author writing in 1803 compared Mary with Gibbon as a historian: her book 'in judiciousness of general remark as an analysis of political events, and correctness of historical narrative, is not *second* to the History of the Decline and Fall of the Roman Empire'[2]. The second president of the United States of America, John Adams, was moved by his reading of the book to scribble some rather patronising comments in his own copy[3]:

> This is a Lady of masculine masterly Understanding. Her style is nervous and clear, often elegant, though sometimes too verbose. With a little Experience in Public Affairs and the Reading and Reflection which would result from it, She would have produced a History without the Defects and Blemishes pointed out with too much Severity perhaps and too little Gallantry in the Notes.

Mary's detailed reconstruction of events preceding the outbreak of the Revolution—usually set at the taking of the Bastille—is of no particular interest except to the professional historian. She traced with painstaking care the familiar road to disaster: from the 'majestic frivolity' of Louis XIV, through the 'atrocious debaucheries' of the reign of his successor, to the limited reforms of Louis XVI; the administrations of Necker, Calonne, de Brienne, and Necker again; the Convocation of Notables, followed by the convening of the States-General and

---

British Critic, VI, 1795.

leading to the establishment of a National Assembly. The facts are well known, and not in dispute.

Mary's attitude to the Revolution is clearly expressed: she accepted its necessity and, whilst deprecating the ensuing violence, acknowledged that in the circumstances this consequence was inevitable. 'If the degeneracy of the higher orders of society be such, that no remedy less fraught with horrour (sic) can effect a radical cure,' she wrote, then 'the people are justified in having recourse to coercion, to repel coercion'. She further argued, as she had previously asserted in her *Rights of Men*, that the violence of the Revolution caused a lesser degree of suffering than the preceding régime:

> if it can be ascertained, that the silent sufferings of the citizens of the world under the iron feet of oppression are greater, though less obvious, than the calamities produced by such violent convulsions as have happened in France ... it may be politically just to pursue such measures as were taken by that regenerating country ...

Later, as the terror mounted, she had to modify this assessment. But she never gave up her conviction that the seeds of revolution grew from the injustice of the prevailing social order; and that those who reaped the whirlwind had sown it themselves: 'The rich have for ages tyrannized over the poor, teaching them how to act when possessed of power, and now must feel the consequence. People are rendered ferocious by misery; and misanthropy is ever the offspring of discontent.' When, she asked, had the Parisians ever seen the execution of a convicted noble or priest? The poor, on the other hand, were punished for every trifling misdemeanour—or even 'for only being in the way of the rich'—so that for them laws were no more than 'cobwebs to catch small flies'. No wonder they turned savage!—'When justice, or the law, is so partial the day of retribution will come with the red sky of vengeance, to confound the innocent with the guilty.'

So if Mary approved of the Revolution in principle and accepted its inevitability in practice, she was clear-sighted about its nature from the start. Unlike other, more naive idealists, she did not expect an oppressed people to behave like saints when the lid was lifted; but neither did she wish the lid to be kept screwed down. She was both more realistic and more just than many of her contemporaries, who either condemned the Revolution lock, stock and barrel or threw up their caps of liberty in delight. Mary did neither. She was always balancing one good, or evil, against another and seeking to establish the point at which good was maximised and evil diminished. So she could not even cheer wholeheartedly the fall of the Bastille: 'if my pen almost bound(s) with eagerness to record the day, that levelled the Bastille with the dust ... the recollection, that still the abbey* is appropriated to hold the victims of revenge and suspicion, palsies the hand that would fain do justice to the assault ... Down fell the temple of despotism; but—despotism has not been buried in its ruins!' At the same time, she acknowledged that the actions of the 14th July marked 'the sentence of death of the old constitution'. In answer to the argument that at the time of its taking there were in fact only seven prisoners held in the Bastille, she observed that 'three of them had lost their reason' and that instruments of torture were found in the 'noisome dungeons'. This was sufficient condemnation.

Her real enthusiasm was reserved for the Declaration of Rights, and she concurred with Tom Paine's view that the first three articles contained the heart of the matter[4]:
1. Men are born, and always continue, free and equal in respect of their rights. Civil distinctions, therefore, can be founded only on public utility.
2. The end of all political associations is the preservation of the natural and imprescriptible rights of man; and these rights are Liberty, Property, Security, and Resistance of Oppression.
3. The Nation is essentially the source of all sovereignty; nor can any individual, or any body of men, be entitled to any authority which is not expressly derived from it.

These articles summed up the commonly-held eighteenth-century belief that man was naturally good and had only to cast off the shackles of an artificial society to claim this birthright of freedom and equality. The Declaration was dismissed by President Adams, in the notes already referred to, as so much pie in the sky; or, in his more elegant phrase, 'how airy and baseless a fabrick!' The only means to accomplish any part of these aims, he continued, was by forms of government 'so mixed, combined and ballanced as to restrain the passions of all orders of men'. Mary would have accepted this diagnosis, with the proviso that before

*The Abbaye prison where Mme Roland was taken on 1st June 1793 may well have been in Mary Wollstonecraft's mind when she wrote these words.

A Revolution and its Aftermath: 1794–5

such a state of co-operation could be achieved the prevailing imbalance must be corrected. Her view of the function of government belongs to the twentieth century—or possibly the twenty-first—rather than the eighteenth. The 'natural rights' which she accepted as the prerogative of all men, did not in fact exist 'naturally', but had to be established and maintained by a just society:

> Nature having made men unequal, by giving stronger bodily and mental powers to one than to another, the end of government ought to be, to destroy this *inequality* by protecting the weak.

Here again Mary was demonstrating a greater sense of realism than either the conventional 'right' or 'left' of politics. Government, she continued, should hold the balance so that 'the abilities or riches of individuals may not interfere with the equilibrium of the whole'.

How far the French National Assembly came up to these standards was a matter of some doubt. Mary was nearer to Carlyle than to Paine in her assessment of the new men in power. Paine saw them, through his rose-tinted spectacles, as being united in 'moral duty' and 'political interest':

> They have not to hold out a language which they do not themselves believe, for the fraudulent purpose of making others believe it. Their station requires no artifice to support it, and can only be maintained by enlightening mankind. It is not their interest to cherish ignorance but to dispel it.

The pity of it, in Carlyle's view, was that they *did* believe their own words—which bore so little relation to the actual condition of twenty-five million starving peasants. He dismissed the deputies as twelve hundred 'pamphleteers', who tried to regenerate a nation by 'perfecting one's theory of irregular verbs.' Mary, too, found them both unrealistic and lacking in judgment. She was strongly critical of the early proceedings of the Assembly. Why was it so slow in drafting a constitution? The new states of America, she pointed out, had mostly completed their constitutions within three weeks of gaining independence; but after three months the French Assembly had taken no action on this vital matter. She regretted, too, that it had rejected the safeguard of a second chamber and disapproved of the decision to grant the king only a 'suspensive' veto; like Mirabeau, she believed he should have retained the power of absolute veto. She regarded as inept and unjust Necker's proposal (which was adopted) to raise taxes by a national levy of one quarter of every citizen's income. Her own alternative was far more revolutionary: a tax on land, and the taking over by the Assembly of 'national property' worth 4,700 million *livres*. In her view the Assembly even bungled its most liberal measure: in guaranteeing the freedom of the press it had overlooked the necessary corollary of a law of libel, thus allowing its authority to be undermined by vicious satirical attacks on the members as 'upstarts and babbling knaves'.

Above all, Mary found the deputies ambivalent and misguided in their attitude to the king. To placate the foreign rulers who were plotting his escape they preserved the 'shadow of monarchy' whilst stripping it of all substance. The king should be made accountable for his actions like any other man, Mary maintained, not treated as 'a mere idol for state pageantry'. The Assembly's decree of 15th September, declaring that 'the person of the king is sacred and inviolable' she regarded as an act of dangerous folly, both for the king himself and for France. For his part, he would be tempted to exploit his position and thus arouse greater hostility; while for the country, the same principle of inviolability could as well be applied to the Church—one 'pious fraud' was as respecttable as the other. Time and again, in fact, the Assembly failed to act up to its own convictions and never established the principles of good government which would have provided its best guarantee against external attack.

Dealing with the events of 15th October, Mary asked why the assassins who invaded the royal apartments and murdered the Swiss guards were not brought to trial? She supported the theory that this whole exercise of marching on Versailles had been stagemanaged by the Duke of Orleans (Philippe Egalité) in revenge for his banishment by the queen; and that the 'mob' had been deliberately inflamed both by bribes and by the withholding of bread supplies. The plot should have been exposed and the perpetrators punished. The Assembly also blundered, in her view, in agreeing to move its seat from Versailles to Paris, thus becoming a prisoner of the captial—'that den of spies and assassins', as she described it. This surrender of authority to the Paris commune—which was advocated only by a vociferous minority and caused a number of resignations among the moderates—cleared the way for the later take-over by the Montagnard extremists. But too many members of the Assembly were governed by 'ambitious selfishness' and were less interested in promoting the common good than in pushing their own pet schemes for reform: if they had combined their talents, the disasters which 'disgraced the cause of freedom' would not have occurred, she said.

She attributed these faults not so much to the individual men in power, however, as to the character of the French nation as a whole, of which she did not have a very exalted view. She described them as 'a nation of women', and this was not intended as a compliment:
> More ingenious than profound in their researches; more tender than impassioned in their affections; prompt to act, yet soon weary; they seem to work only to escape from work, and to reflect merely how they shall avoid reflecting... Everything, in short, shows the dexterity of the people, in their attention to present enjoyment.

She also made the shrewd observation that Frenchmen, at all levels of society, were inspired by a desire for 'glory' (*la gloire*) rather than for the greater happiness of the people.

These national faults were of course most marked in those with most power to exercise them: in the nobility and the royal family, before the rise of the 'third estate'. Whilst 60,000 nobles ruled as despots, and 200,000 priests battened on the country like 'leeches', there was little chance of gradual reform: when 'gross selfishness' prevailed, an 'absolute change' must take place. The French aristocracy, she observed, destroyed itself through 'the ignorant arrogance of its members'. As for the king himself, he was more sinned against than sinning; the victim of an upbringing that had trained him to be a 'sensual bigot'. Nevertheless, she conceded that he was a 'tolerable scholar' and an 'ingenious mechanic'. His failings were due to weakness of character rather than malevolence:
> for ever wavering, it is difficult to mark any fixt purpose in his actions; excepting that which does him honour—the desire to prevent the shedding of blood... though the short-sighted measures of timid humanity, devoid of strength of mind, turned all his efforts to a very contrary effect.

For the queen, however—who was of course Austrian, not French—Mary could find little good to say. Admittedly, she had a superficially attractive personality, but 'her lovely face, sparkling with vivacity, hid the want of intelligence'; and, disgusted by the king's grossness of behaviour, she turned her attention elsewhere and was 'lost in pleasure and intrigue'. She also systematically robbed the country, Mary asserted, and 'would have dismembered France, to aggrandise Austria'.

Nevertheless, despite her attack on the French court as the most corrupt and vicious in Europe, Mary did not share the republicanism of Paine and her American friends. She favoured a constitutional monarchy, on the English pattern; for, notwithstanding her criticisms of the hereditary system in her *Rights of Men*, she conceded that England had led the way in social reforms and that nowhere else in Europe was liberty firmly established. She put this down to the mingling of the English aristocracy with the 'commercial' classes, whereas in France and Italy the nobility remained an aloof caste. Indeed, she had little good to say of any part of Europe: Italy, Spain and Portugal cowered under 'a contemptible bigotry'; Germany groaned beneath civil and military tyrannies; whilst Russia, 'sullen as the amphibious bear of the north', stretched out her arms and threatened all her neighbours. In short, though conditions in Europe were ripe for revolution, the people were not. France was now the bubbling crucible, watched with avid interest by friend and foe alike: 'All Europe saw, and all good men saw with dread, that the french had undertaken to support a cause, which they had neither sufficient purity of heart, nor maturity of judgment, to conduct with moderation and prudence'.

But Mary still maintained that it was the conduct of revolution rather than the principle that was at fault and refused to join its detractors: 'malevolence had been gratified by the errours they have committed, attributing that imperfection to the theory they adopted, which was applicable only to the folly of their practice'. Here she was on shaky ground. She had referred earlier to the need for gradualism and government by consent: 'the pacific progress of every revolution will depend, in a very material degree, on the moderation and reciprocity of concessions made by the acting parties'. This sounds like a recipe for reform rather than revolution; and politically, it is doubtful if Mary Wollstonecraft was a revolutionary at all, in the accepted meaning of the word. Her revolutions were all of the spirit, as she made clear in her 'lament' for France which follows a description of the deserted palace of Versailles as she must have seen it with her own eyes:

> Weeping—scarcely conscious that I weep, O France! over the vestiges of thy former oppression; which, separating man from man with a fence of iron, sophisticated all, and made many completely wretched; I tremble, lest I should meet some unfortunate being, fleeing from the despotism of licentious freedom, hearing the snap of the *guillotine* at his heels; merely because he was once noble, or has afforded an asylum to those, whose only crime is their name ... Unhappy country!—when will thy children cease to tear thy bosom?—When will a change of opinion, producing a change of morals, render thee truly free?—When will truth give life to real magnanimity, and justice place equality on a stable seat?—When will thy sons trust, because they deserve to be trusted; and private virtue become the guarantee of patriotism? Ah!—when will thy government becomes the most perfect, because thy citizens are the most virtuous!

Once again, as in the *Rights of Men*, Mary had come full circle in circumscribing a revolutionary situation from the general to the particular. She could never escape a commitment to personal responsibility; the conviction that in every crisis—to extend her theory to the twentieth century, where it is equally apt—'the buck stops here', with oneself. Carlyle echoed this view when, surveying the French Revolution fifty years later, he wrote:

> especially is it an old truth, that wherever huge physical evil is, there, as the parent and origin of it, has moral evil to a proportionate extent been.

The same principle holds good whether the crisis is one of war, or revolution—or marital breakdown. Now, in the spring of 1795, Mary's personal crisis was approaching its climax.

Her ship docked at Brighthelmstone (Brighton) on Saturday, 11th April. Always cheerful when on the move, she dashed off a note to Imlay which did not even chide him for his negligence[5].

> Here we are, my love, and mean to set out early in the morning; and, if I can find you, I hope to dine with you tomorrow. I shall drive to —'s hotel, where — tells me you have been—and, if you have left it, I hope you will take care to be there to receive us.

Now Imlay was really cornered. How could he explain to

Mary—his common-law wife and the mother of his child—that he had already formed a liaison with another woman? This was his dreadful secret, a relationship entered into when he believed Mary to be safely across the channel and, by her own declaration, never to return to England. He should have known her better than to believe that! Here was his 'family' arriving in the flesh. What was to be done? Imlay hated scenes; he liked everything to go easily and pleasantly (this, one may guess, was a major cause of his break with Mary, who could never take anything 'easily'). In desperation, he could only stave off the day of reckoning by further deception. Renting a furnished house, he installed Mary and Fanny at No. 26 Charlotte Street, Soho. Whether he joined them there is not known; nor whether any kind of reconciliation took place between them. It seems unlikely. Godwin described Mary's reception by Imlay as 'cold and embarrassed', and she could have been left in little doubt as to his changed attitude. The 'cruel explanations' which followed, said Godwin, 'only added to the anguish of a heart already overwhelmed in grief.' Mary's distress was compounded by the necessity to keep her own family at bay and prevent them from suspecting the real situation.

Writing from Paris, she had painted a rosy picture of Imlay as her generous and wealthy 'protector'. She had encouraged her sisters to believe that one day they would all be settled happily in America. Eliza, who was in a state of some distress in Wales, believed that she could now join Mary's household in London. Any such idea was quickly scotched, as Mary wrote two weeks after her arrival[6]:

> I know you will think me unkind—and it was this reflection that has prevented my writing to you sooner, not to invite you to come and live with me. But, Eliza, it is my opinion, not a readily formed one, the presence of a third person interrupts or destroys domestic happines.—accepting this sacrifice—there is nothing I would not do to promote your comfort...

(Mary's use of the word 'accepting', as it is written in the original manuscript, has usually been transcribed as 'excepting', which was obviously her meaning. She was so inured to sacrifice that the 'acceptance' may have been subconscious; more likely, it was another case of her hit or miss, phonetic spelling, based on a Yorkshire flattening of the vowels.) At the same time, she continued to promote the fiction that one day Imlay would make his fortune; and then, being 'the most generous creature in the world', he would enable her to be 'useful' to her sisters. She even went so far as to mention a likely sum being forthcoming of five or six hundred pounds, and she held out the same prospect to Everina. She also repeated to Everina her conviction that it would not do for Eliza to live with her: 'It would give me sincere pleasure to be situated near you both,' she wrote on 27th April. 'I cannot yet say where I shall determine to spend the rest of my life, but I do not wish to have a third person in the house with me'. She hastened to add that this was not in consequence of 'my present attachment', although it clearly was. Or did she, perhaps unconsciously, include Imlay in the category of undesired 'third person'?—for she and Fanny together made two without him.

Eliza, needless to say, was hurt and insulted at this news: 'Are your eyes opened at last, Everina?' she asked' 'What do you say now to our goodly prospects?—I have such a mist before my lovely eyes that I cannot see what I write'[7]. So incensed was she, in fact, that she promptly returned Mary's letter with a message scrawled across it: 'Mrs B has never received any money from America' (presumably from Charles, who like Mary repeatedly held out prospects he could not fulfil). With all her faults, Eliza had a mordant sense of humour; which was something that Mary could have done with a little more of.

To her credit, also, Eliza had shown some courage in upholding her republican sympathies in the hostile atmosphere of Upton Castle. She had finally left her post the previous December and was staying in Pembroke in order to study French with an emigré priest, M. Graux—whose personality she likened to that of Joseph Johnson and for whom she developed a great affection despite his royalist views. She helped him to master the English language and in a characteristic observation remarked to Everina that 'Mr G. understands English in the way Mary had French'. Now, however, after five months' freedom her money was running out and she had nowhere to go but to her father at Laugharne. She had been fully confident that this was only to be a stepping-stone on the way to London—if not to France or America! But, as usual, all her hopes were dashed. Charles had defaulted on his promises to provide for his sisters; Mary had likewise failed her; and even the youngest brother James seemed to be following the well-trodden Wollstonecraft path. He had returned from his ship, announced his intention of quitting the navy, and was meanwhile staying with the ever-hospitable Johnson in London with the object of going to live in France as soon as the war was over. Eliza described this plan as 'madness' and complained to Everina in March that 'apparently he has forgotten the promised "portion" to his sisters'. Eliza also passed on James's description of Imlay, whom he had met in London, as 'a fine, handsome fellow'. In her opinion, however, Imlay seemed to be 'of a piece with *nos frères*', which in this context was not intended as a compliment. By May, poor Eliza was near breaking point. Her only prospect now was to go to Ireland, and the faithful George Blood had invited her to stay with his mother at Waterford until she could find a situation. But Eliza too had an independent spirit: 'Is it not a duty to endeavour to earn my own bread?' she asked Everina, adding that she was ready to take any employment. Nevertheless Mary's apparent heartlessness continued to rankle: 'Was it greatness of mind or *Heart* that dictated the ever-memorable letter which so stupified me?' she again enquired of Everina (who by this time must have been hard put for an answer). 'The amiable Mary pined in poverty, whilst Mrs I. enjoys all her heart can sigh for.'

She could not be aware of the irony of that assessment. Eliza, like Mary, was too engrossed in her own problems to perceive the truth about her sister, although James had dropped a strong hint which she quoted to Everina: 'Mary says you returned her letter.—She appears less composed and happy than formerly. I have done everything in my power with her. I begin to place some hopes in him.' James was always Mary's favourite brother, and he was evidently an affectionate young man who had more conscience about his family than either Edward or Charles. He wrote now that he had sent their father five pounds and added: 'When writing to you and Everina there are always such contending passions struggling about my heart, that I am almost deprived of reason. I am very unhappy.' Poor James, like most young men, was longing to be free, but he was also aware of his obligations to contribute to the well-being of the whole family. Before condemning Mr Wollstonecraft and his daughters as 'scroungers' it has to be remembered that the extended family was still a real force in society and the only source of support in times of trouble. There was no 'social security' beyond the parish relief of the Poor Law, which no self-respecting citizen would wish to invoke.

Mary's real situation begins to be revealed in the letter she wrote to Imlay on 22nd May: the first we have since her return to London[8]. It is surprisingly low-keyed. Meeting him again, however unsatisfactorily, had taken the edge off her frustrated passion. 'I am no longer angry with you,' she wrote, 'nor will I ever utter another complaint.' She had been struggling to overcome her grief in diversions and 'amusements', she told him, but with little success. Nor had she yet given up hope of recapturing his affections, and she was evidently still unaware of his new attachment:

My friend, my dear friend, examine yourself well—I am out of the question, for alas! I am nothing—and discover what you wish to do, what will render you most comfortable—or, to be more explicit, whether you desire to live with me or part forever. When you can once ascertain it, tell me frankly, I conjure you, for, believe me, I have very involuntarily interrupted your peace. I shall expect you to dinner on Monday and will endeavour to assume a cheerful face to please you.

This apparent calm may have temporarily deceived Imlay and concealed from Mary's friends her inner desperation, for at about this time Eliza received a message from Johnson that 'he never saw Mary so well or so happy as at present'. The calm was, of course, more apparent than real, for such selfless detachment was quite alien to Mary's nature; so alien, in fact, that only a few days later she was seeking to end her misery for all time. 'I am nothing,' she had written, and while she lived she could not tolerate such a state; it could only be achieved in death. There is some uncertainty as to the seriousness of this suicide attempt, although Godwin states categorically that 'she formed a desperate purpose to die'. The chosen method appears to have been an overdose of laudanum, which might not have been intended to be fatal. At all events, it was Imlay who discovered her in time and who took vigorous action to save her. Had she hoped to win him back this way? She had at least succeeded in engrossing his attention. And such were Mary's powers of recovery that almost immediately she was up and about again.

The spur to her revival was Imlay's proposal that she should travel on his behalf to Scandinavia to look into his business interests there[9]. Short of marrying her—and it is doubtful if even she really wanted that—he could scarcely have hit on a better expedient. For Mary, the stimulus of travel with a purpose was always the best medicine; for him, the voyage offered a breathing-space to sort out his tangled affairs, as well as the promise of a financial return on the trip. He was only too delighted to appoint Mary as his agent and furnished her with a glowing testimonial for the purpose[10]:

> Know all men by these presents, that I, Gilbert Imlay, citizen of the United States of America, at present residing in London, do...appoint Mary Imlay, my best friend and wife, to take the sole management... of all my affairs and business which I had placed in the hands of Mr. Elias Backman, negotiant, Gottenburg, or in those of Messrs. Myburg & Co., Copenhagen, desiring that she will manage... such concerns... as she may deem most wise and prudent. For which this letter shall be a sufficient power, enabling her to receive all the money... that may be recovered from Peter Ellyson... whenever the issue of the tryal now carrying on, instituted by Mr. Elias Backman, as my agent, for the violation of the trust which I had reposed in his integrity...
>
> Respecting the cargo of goods in the hands of Messrs. Myburg & Co., Mrs. Imlay has only to consult the most experienced persons engaged in the disposition of such articles, and then placing them at their disposal, act as she may deem right and proper...
>
> Thus, confiding in the talent, zeal and earnestness of my dearly beloved friend and companion, I submit the management of these affairs entirely and implicitly to her discretion.
>
> Remaining most sincerely and affectionately hers truly.
>
> G. Imlay

It is an extraordinary document: too fulsomely personal to be offered as a business introduction; too commercial in intent to be credible as a personal affirmation. Yet no doubt Imlay did believe every word, as he composed it, and convinced himself he was doing his best for her. What on earth could Mary do with it, except file it away as more illusory evidence of Imlay's continuing affection? At any rate she accepted it and accepted the commission. By the first week in June she was already in Hull and waiting for her ship, accompanied by Fanny and the nursemaid she had brought from France. She did not trouble to inform her sisters of this change in her plans, although they were desperately worried by the rumours that had reached them. Eliza sat with her bags packed for Ireland, afraid to move until she heard that her sister was well; the suspense, she wrote to Everina on 9th June, was driving her mad. Mary had evidently written her a desperate letter which, still smarting under her disappointment, she had failed to answer, and now she was bitterly regretting it: 'I wish I had answered her letter the moment it came to Larne. But I was prevented by a dreadful headache'. Now she in turn was waiting anxiously for a letter: 'I know you would blame me if I left this (place) before I receive Mrs I's answer.' On the 13th she still had not heard from Mary. 'I know not what to think on the subject... Never was I so thoroughly unhinged.'

Mary, meanwhile, was cooling her heels in Hull, with a consequent sinking of spirits, as the ship awaited a favourable wind. The frustrating delay went on for two or three weeks, leaving her too much time to brood on her misfortunes. 'Imlay,—dear Imlay,' she wrote shortly after her arrival at the port, 'am I always to be tossed about thus? shall I never find an asylum to rest *contented* in?'[11] She reproached him for his restless spirit, so much in conflict with her own unsatisfied longing for a settled, domestic life: 'Why do you not attach those tender emotions round the idea of home, which even now dim my eyes? This alone is affection—every thing else is only humanity, electrified by sympathy.' She was, of course, addressing the wrong man: 'home' had no appeal for Imlay, and this was the real tragedy of the situation. What had started as a 'free' partnership had, for quite opposite reasons, become an intolerable burden for both sides. Mary for her part had been confident that the power of love alone was sufficient to cement their voluntary marriage into a permanent relationship; Imlay had been equally confident that, when the first rapture inevitably faded, the partnership could be amicably dissolved with a handshake and no hard feelings. The coming of Fanny had put a stop to this; Imlay's greatest crime was his unwillingness to recognise the right of his own child to a father and a home. Without children, a free marriage might have worked very well. But in what sense would this have been a 'marriage' at all? A barren partnership had little meaning for Mary.

Now she considered again, with as much detachment as she could muster, what had gone wrong between herself and Imlay. In a series of letters written between 12th and 21st June she went through the whole story[12]. She attributed Imlay's cooling affection not to his intrinsic character but to his previous, promiscuous mode of life: 'You have a heart, my friend, yet, hurried away by the impetuosity of inferior feelings, you have sought in vulgar excesses for that gratification which only the heart can bestow,' she wrote on 12th June, and contrasted this attitude with her own capacity for a love in which affection and desire were in unison, enriched by the imagination. She did not actually attribute these capacities to herself but to her concept of 'genius', yet she is clearly speaking from experience:

> These emotions, more or less strong, appear to me to be the distinctive characteristic of genius, the foundation of taste, and of that exquisite relish for the beauties of nature, of which the common herd of eaters and drinkers and child begetters certainly have no idea.

Imlay, alas, belonged to that common herd, though she could not bring herself to recognise the fact; and, in his absence, she still longed for death:

> I have looked at the sea, and at my child, hardly daring to own to myself, the secret wish, that it might become our tomb; and that the heart, still so alive to anguish, might there be quieted by death.

She implored Imlay to think again whether he could not yet live in a more settled way:

> Let our confidence in future be unbounded; consider whether you find it necessary to sacrifice me to what you term 'the zest of life'; and, when you have once a clear view of your own motives, of your own incentive to action, do not deceive me!

This reverie recalled her recent suicide attempt, and the next day she wrote to assure him that she had destroyed the farewell letter which might have implicated him, even though it 'was only written (of course warmly in your praise) to prevent any odium being thrown on you'. She still feared that she might again be overwhelmed by despair: 'Do write by every occasion!' she urged, and reminded Imlay that he was not only a husband but a father: 'For my little darling is calling papa, and adding her parrot word—Come, Come!' This too was Mary's own appeal: 'And will you not come, and let us exert ourselves? I shall recover all my energy, when I am convinced that my exertions will draw us more closely together.'

She was 'not quite well', she informed him on 14th June. She woke in the morning 'in violent fits of trembling' and everything—including the child—fatigued her. Nevertheless, she was somewhat cheered by an opportunity to visit the place where she had perhaps spent her happiest years, when the wife of a Hull physician with whom she was acquainted took her for a drive to Beverley: 'I ran over my favourite walks with a vivacity that would have astonished you,' she wrote. The town, however, she had to admit, 'did not please me quite so well as formerly. It appeared so diminutive'; and it was depressing to find many of the same people still vegetating there whilst she had been 'running over a world of sorrow, snatching at pleasure, and throwing off prejudices'.

Two days later, word came that the ship was about to sail and she was thrown into a fresh agitation: 'It would have been a comfort to me to have received another letter from you,' she wrote before embarking. 'The quitting England seems to be a fresh parting. Surely you will not forget me.' Usually Mary welcomed a change of scene, but on this occasion she was oppressed by a sense of foreboding which she struggled to shake off: 'I dread to meet wretchedness in some new shape. Well, let it come, I care not! What have I to dread, who have so little to hope for!' Yet she could still say to her faithless lover: 'God bless you; I am most affectionately and sincerely yours'.

But the order to sail proved a false alarm. At the mercy of wind and tide, the vessel rocked on its anchor for another five days; whilst the nursemaid Marguerite succumbed to sea-sickness, Mary, ever an intrepid sailor, took over her duties. The delay also brought the unexpected bonus of another letter from Imlay. This, she wrote, 'afforded me some comfort, and I will try to revive hope'. The hope, which she could not refrain from expressing yet again, was of course for a reconciliation:

> One thing let me tell you: when we meet again—surely we are to meet!—it must be to part no more. I mean not to have the sea between us; it is more than I can support.

She could hardly have believed her own words, even as she wrote them; yet only to formulate the hope was a barricade against despair. She confessed that she had never suffered such depression of spirits: 'I do not sleep, or if I close my eyes, it is to have the most terrifying dreams, in which I often meet you with different casts of countenance'. No doubt it was the hated 'commercial face' that came most often to haunt her.

On the fifth day of waiting, Mary could stand the confinement no longer and left the ship 'to take a walk, after which I hope to sleep'. She spent a night on shore and the next morning, on Sunday 21st June, the summons came that the wind had at last changed and they were ready to sail. Reluctantly, she stepped on board. She had been hoping to receive one more letter from Imlay before leaving—'it would have been kind and considerate,' she observed in a parting shot with a touch of her old spirit: 'These are attentions more grateful to the heart than offers of service. But why do I foolishly continue to look for them?' Why, indeed? The author of the *Rights of Woman*, like the French revolutionaries, was 'devouring her own children'—and eating her words. Had she forgotten her strictures on the need for independence, both of heart and mind? 'Ah!' she now cried, 'there is but one sense of it of consequence. I will break or bend this weak heart; yet even now it is full.' Mary knew now that she could not achieve the kind of independence which spelt an emotional death; and that what she was really seeking was an interdependence of equals. But it took two to achieve interdependence, and Imlay was unwilling to play. This left Mary, after all her struggle and sacrifice, still essentially alone. The realisation was enough to break even the strongest spirit. 'How am I altered by disappointment!' she had written the previous day, recalling that other voyage to Lisbon ten years earlier when 'the elasticity of my mind was sufficient to ward off weariness, and the imagination still could dip her brush in the rainbow of fancy, and sketch futurity in smiling colours'. What did the future hold now? The prospect had never seemed more bleak:

> Now I am going towards the North in search of sunbeams! Will any ever warm this desolated heart? All nature seems to frown, or rather mourn with me. Everything is cold—cold as my expectations! ... Give me, gracious Heaven! at least genial weather, if I am never to meet the genial affection that still warms this agitated bosom, compelling life to linger there.

Where there's love, Mary seems to be saying, there's hope; and where there's hope, there's life. This was all that was left of her philosophy: a small raft to cling to as she cast out to sea.

CHAPTER FOURTEEN
Journey's End: 1795

Protected from despair by so fragile an armour, it is not surprising that Mary took no pleasure in the North Sea crossing and arrived at Gothenburg on 27th June in a state of near collapse. The elements, as usual, were against her. Contrary winds prevented her landing at Arendall in Norway, as she had intended, and had she not insisted on being taken ashore off Gothenburg in the ship's boat the captain would have carried her on to Elsinore. This last stage of the journey was an alarming experience, even for Mary, whilst the French nurse Marguerite was in a state of terror. The two women and the child were rowed round the coast for more than two hours, seeking some sign of human habitation on the rocky shore where they might be landed and find accommodation. At last a cottage was located where they could spend the night before going on to Gothenburg. Here Mary experienced her first taste of Scandinavian hospitality, which she was to describe at length (together with some less agreeable aspects of the life there) in her *Letters Written During a Short Residence in Sweden, Norway and Denmark,* published the following year by Johnson after her return to London[1].

The kindliness of this Swedish family, and the beauty of the landscape, brought a temporary lifting of her spirits. She found the house spotlessly clean, the beds covered with muslin, 'coarse it is true, but dazzlingly white,' and the floor 'strewed over with little sprigs of juniper'. The visitors were fed with fish, milk, butter and cheese—'and I am sorry to add brandy, the bane of this country'. After the meal Mary was eager to explore the countryside and set off for a walk with Fanny. She took it as a good omen to find some heart's-ease among the rocks, which she picked 'to preserve it in a letter that had not conveyed balm to my heart'; while the little girl was delighted to discover some wild strawberries. 'How silent and peaceful was the scene,' she cried as she stood on the rocks guarding the seashore:

> I gazed around with rapture, and felt more of that spontaneous pleasure which gives credibility to our expectation of happiness, than I had for a long, long time before. I forgot the horrors I had witnessed in France, which had cast a gloom over all nature, and suffering the enthusiasm of my character, too often, gracious God! damped by the tears of disappointed affection, to be lighted up afresh, care took wing while simple fellow feeling expanded my heart.

But this rapture was short-lived. The next morning, walking towards the carriage which was to take them into Gothenburg, Mary fell on the rocks and became unconscious for fifteen minutes. 'The concussion is great and my brain confused,' she reported to Imlay after the journey: 'The twenty miles ride in the rain after my accident sufficiently deranged me—and here I could not get a fire to warm me or anything warm to eat—The inns are mere stables . . .'[2]. Two days later she was plunged in depression, which the friendliness of her reception in Gothenburg only exacerbated: 'I am overwhelmed with civilities,' she wrote to Imlay, 'and fatigued with the endeavours to amuse me, from which I cannot escape'[3]. She was again working up to an emotional crisis, which became explicit in her next letter[4]:

> I labour in vain to calm my mind—my soul has been overwhelmed by sorrow and disappointment. Everything fatigues me; this is a life that cannot last long. It is you who must determine with respect to futurity; and, when you have, I will act accordingly—I mean, we must either resolve to live together or part for ever; I cannot bear these continual struggles.

Yet it was she who was prolonging the struggle, by refusing to accept Imlay's quite plain intention that they should not go on living as man and wife. Nor did she really believe in her own alternative, which she had put forward before and repeated here: 'we must either live together, or I will be entirely independent'. She knew that such independence was an illusion, and in the same letter she was already suggesting another meeting. Since Imlay was due to go to Paris on business, and she planned to finish her present tour in Hamburg, she proposed that they should meet later in the summer at Basle in Switzerland. Two days later she was even more explicit. She admitted that she needed Imlay not only as a friend but as a lover; and that all her efforts to stifle her natural feelings were doomed to failure[5]:

Love is a want of my heart. I have examined myself lately with more care than formerly, and find that to deaden is not to calm the mind. Aiming at tranquility, I have almost destroyed all the energy of my soul—almost rooted out what renders it estimable.

In other words, Mary realised that to kill her capacity for love was tantamount to killing herself; at this point, she was not prepared to do that. She now had some capacity to fight back and to respect her own feelings: 'sacred emotions, that are the sure harbingers of the delights I was formed to enjoy—and shall enjoy, for nothing can extinguish the heavenly spark'. Yet, she promised, 'when we meet again, I shall not torment you . . . I will listen to delicacy, or pride'. This was an impossible promise. Pride would already have forbidden another meeting, when it was so obvious that Imlay was tired of her and that there was no other bond to take the place of a spent passion.

Nevertheless, for all her depression Mary could not fail to benefit from the stimulus of her new surroundings. 'I have a degree of vivacity,' she wrote in her next letter, 'even in my grief, which is preferable to the benumbing stupor that, for the last year, has frozen up all my faculties'[6]. She had now left Gothenburg and was travelling towards Stromstad: 'the purity of this air, and the being continually out in it, for I sleep in the country every night, has made an alteration in my appearance that really surprises me,' she reported. The colour was returning to her cheeks and she saw again 'a *physical* life in my eyes . . . that resembled the fond, credulous hopes of youth'. Arriving at Stromstad, she was disappointed not to find a letter from Imlay. However, she assured him she would not complain—'There are misfortunes so great as to silence the usual expressions of sorrow. Believe me there is such a thing as a broken heart!'—and she rather grudgingly allowed that 'could anything please me—had not disappointment cut me off from life, this romantic country, these fine evenings, would interest me'[7].

When she could forget her personal sorrows, Mary was in fact thoroughly enjoying her travels and eagerly absorbing every new impression. She must have made detailed notes of her observations, which she reproduced in her published *Letters*. On all her journeys Mary had the knack of getting on well with the local population and establishing friendly relations wherever she went. Though her own personality must have played a significant part in this goodwill, it was not of her own seeking and seemed to arise spontaneously almost in spite of herself. Her hosts were often more appreciative of her than she was of them, as witness her acid comment on the virtues of 'hospitality':

> Hospitality has, I think, been too much praised by travellers as a proof of goodness of heart, when in my opinion indiscriminate hospitality is rather a criterion by which you may form a tolerable estimate of the indolence or vacancy of a head; or, in other words, a fondness for social pleasures in which the mind not having its proportion of exercise, the bottle must be pushed about.

On Swedish food she remarked: 'Their tastes, like their compliments, seem equally a caricature of the french.' As for Swedish children, they were 'nipt in the bud, having neither the graces nor charms of their age'; and she put this down to the ignorance of their mothers, with their fondness for warm flannel and antipathy to cold water, rather than the severity of the climate. Servants seemed to be treated as no more than slaves, in particular the women who had to undertake the most menial and laborious tasks:

> In the winter, I am told, they take the linen down to the river, to wash it in the cold water; and though their hands, cut by the ice, are cracked and bleeding, the men, their fellow servants, will not disgrace their manhood by carrying a tub to lighten their burden.

On the whole Mary found the peasantry, with their 'sympathy and frankness of heart', more congenial than the upper classes; though she admitted that she would not like to live 'continually in the country', where the mental interests were so limited. She reported that travelling in Sweden was cheap, the roads were good and the inns 'tolerable'; but she disliked intensely the custom of 'sleeping between two down beds', which she found stifling, especially when taken in conjunction with windows that were never opened and closed-in stoves. Whenever and wherever possible, she escaped into the open air, revelling in the unspoilt beauties of the landscape: 'Sweden appeared to me the country in the world most proper to form the botanist and natural historian; every object seemed to remind me of the creation of things, of the first efforts of sportive nature.' She put forward the novel theory that man must first have been 'placed in the north, to tempt him to run after the sun, in order that the different parts of the earth might be peopled'. She also proffered some good advice to travellers:

> Travellers who require that every nation should resemble their native country, had better stay at home ... The most essential service, I presume, that authors could render to society, would be to promote inquiry and discussion, instead of making those dogmatical assertions which only appear calculated to gird the human mind round with imaginary circles, like the paper globe which represents the one he inhabits.

Crossing the Skagerrak straits to Norway, Mary landed at Laurvig on 14th July. She was still quite alone, having left Fanny and her nurse at Gothenburg. Marguerite had wanted to accompany her, she wrote to Imlay, being still worried about the effects of her fall. She now described this accident as 'my fainting, or rather convulsion, when I landed'[8], which suggests that she had experienced a mild fit rather than a concussion. Mary decided however that Fanny, who was cutting her teeth, should not undertake the journey; although when parted from her child she only worried the more, not without some twinges of conscience. She knew that Fanny was not getting a fair start in life—and what sort of future could she look forward to? 'Poor lamb!' she cried to the child's father, 'how can I expect that she will find protection when my naked bosom has had to brave continually the pitiless storm?' In her published *Letters* she adopted a more philosphical tone, relating Fanny's condition to that of her whole sex:

> I feel more than a mother's fondness and anxiety, when I reflect on the dependent and oppressed state of her sex. I dread lest she should be forced to sacrifice her heart to her principles, or principles to her heart ... I dread to unfold her mind, lest it should render her unfit for the world she is to inhabit. Hapless woman! what a fate is thine!

Mary acknowledged here for the first time that she herself had sacrificed her principles to her heart, but she still regarded this as the lesser evil of the two and had found no way out of the Hobson's choice. Alone now, she again berated Imlay for not writing, this time more in anger than sorrow:

> Act as you please—there is nothing I fear or care for! When I see whether I can, or cannot obtain the money I am come here about, I will not trouble you with letters to which you do not reply.

From Laurvig Mary travelled by coach, in the company of a Danish ship's captain and his mate, to Tonsberg, arriving on 17th July. Here she found she would have to remain three or four weeks in pursuit of Imlay's business interests. Fortunately, her lodging was at a quiet inn overlooking the sea, and the summer was fine and warm. She settled down fairly contentedly to do some writing. 'I have begun —,' she wrote to Imlay the day after her arrival, 'which will, I hope, discharge all my obligations of a pecuniary kind'[9]. She may have been referring here to her *Letters from Sweden* or possibly to her posthumous and unfinished novel *Maria*; the 'wrongs of woman' were certainly much in her consciousness at this time. This work was part of her cherished plan for independence, and she added: 'I am lowered in my own eyes, on acount of my not having done it sooner'. At the end of the month she at last received two letters from Imlay, which had been written on the 26th and 30th June. They brought little comfort, but the mere fact of receiving them had a calming effect. 'I will try to write with a degree of composure,' she declared, and she did succeed in expressing her inner anguish with some detachment. Her concern now was for her child; she had renounced all hope of happiness for herself[10]:

> I wish for us to live together, because I want you to acquire an habitual tenderness for my poor girl. I cannot bear to think of leaving her alone in the world, or that she should only be protected by your sense of duty. Next to preserving her, my most earnest wish is not to disturb your peace. I have nothing to expect, and little to fear, in life ... If I am destined always to be disappointed and unhappy, I will conceal the anguish I cannot dissipate; and the tightened cord of life or reason will at last snap, and set me free.

One of Mary's greatest virtues was her refusal to abandon a con-

viction when its application in practice led to suffering or even death. This was the spirit of the martyrs, but in the cause of human rather than divine love:
This heart is worthy of the bliss its feelings anticipate—and I cannot even persuade myself, wretched as they have made me, that my principles and sentiments are not founded in nature and truth.

Fidelity to 'nature and truth', wheresoever it might lead her, was Mary's *credo*. But could not Imlay, in his lesser way, have claimed the same justification for his conduct?

At least Mary's faith in the healing power of nature was borne out by the present improvement in her health. Although she was 'seriously employed' at Tonsberg she was also 'never so much in the air': 'I walk, I ride on horseback, row, bathe, and even sleep in the fields,' she confided now to Imlay, who must have thought that she was not so badly off after all. This life was indeed as near to earthly bliss as Mary could hope for. But when nature smiled, the discrepancy of her own condition became all the more painful. She longed to complete the natural order by the human trilogy of husband, wife and child. 'I could wish you to return to me poor,' she concluded this same letter, 'with the simplicity of character, part of which you seem lately to have lost, that first attached to you.' The improvement of spirits was maintained during her stay at Tonsberg. Mary found in Norway a most congenial country and people. 'The distribution of landed property into small farms, produces a degree of equality which I have seldom seen elsewhere,' she observed in her *Letters*; although Norway was still under Danish rule she found the Norwegians 'to be the most free community I have ever observed.' This liberty included freedom of the press and of religious opinions. She described the people as sensible and shrewd but uncultivated in the arts and sciences and lacking in public spirit. Her strongest criticisms were directed at the legal profession. The lawyers with whom she had to deal in her business transactions seemed to her so many 'locusts', and she was sickened by their viciousness and chicanery. Until trial by jury was established, she observed, 'little justice can be expected in Norway'. Nevertheless, the punishment of offenders was relatively mild, and the only capital crime was murder. This was a considerable advance on British practice, but even so she questioned the retention of this ultimate sanction.

Citing the case of a girl who was subsequently pardoned after killing an illegitimate child, she commented: 'a desperate act is not always a proof of an incorrigible depravity of character; the only plausible excuse that has been brought forward to justify the infliction of capital punishments'.

Besides studying the customs of the country, Mary was all the time drinking in the natural beauty around her. Teaching herself to row, she glided among rocky pools in reveries both blissful and melancholy. If she was sometimes tempted to float out into an ocean of oblivion, she was restrained by a fear of personal annihilation: the only thing, she confessed in her *Letters*, of which she felt a dread:

> I cannot bear to think of being no more—of losing myself—though existence is often but a painful consciousness of misery; nay, it appears to me impossible that I should cease to exist, or that this active, restless spirit, equally alive to joy and sorrow, should only be organized dust—ready to fly abroad the moment the spring snaps, or the spark goes out, which kept it together. Surely something resides in this heart that is not perishable—and life is more than a dream.

These thoughts on 'organized dust' were perhaps provoked by the sight of some embalmed corpses in a church she visited; a sight which filled her with horror:

> If this be not dissolution, it is something worse than natural decay—It is treason against humanity, thus to lift up the awful veil which would fain hide its weakness ... for nothing is so ugly as the human form when deprived of life, and thus dried into stone, merely to preserve the most disgusting image of death.

This led her on to ask where the 'life' had gone when it left the body: 'Where goes this breath? this *I*, so much alive? In what element will it mix, giving or receiving fresh energy?' Mary's concept of immortality was more pagan than Christian, and she scoffed at the idea of preserving the body so that it should rise again on the day of judgment—'if there is to be such a day'. It would 'require some trouble', she observed, to prepare these bodies to meet their maker: 'to make them fit to appear in the company with angels, without disgracing humanity'. Her own conviction, as stated here, was 'that we have some perfectible principle in our present vestment, which will not be destroyed just as we begin to be sensible of improvement'. She added that she did not care what habit she would next put on, 'sure that it will be wisely formed to suit a higher state of existence'.

Meanwhile, Mary was still very much alive. She reported to Imlay on 5th August that she had 'entirely recovered' her strength and that her health had seldom been better[11]. She even acknowledged that at Tonsberg she had enjoyed more tranquillity and happiness than for a long time past: 'I say happiness', she noted in parenthesis, 'for I can give no other appellation to the exquisite delight this wild country and fine summer have afforded me'. But there was still a worm in the bud: 'on examining my heart, I find that it is so constituted, I cannot live without some particular affection—I am afraid not without a passion—and I feel the want of it more in society, than in solitude'. At the same time she repeated her futile pledge that she would not inflict her feelings on Imlay: 'tenderness, rather than passion, has made me sometimes overlook delicacy; the same tenderness will in future restrain me.' But only two days later, the restraint had already snapped: 'This state of suspense, my friend, is intolerable; we must determine on something, and soon; we must meet shortly, or part for ever'[12]. Yet even as she wrote she was aware how impossible this was: 'I cannot live with you, I ought not—if you form another attachment. But I promise you mine shall not be intruded on you.' Two days later again, she received a batch of five letters from Imlay, forwarded from Stromstad. They brought no joy but only a confirmation of her worst fears. Again she could only assure him that 'you will not be tormented with any more complaints'; and this time she really seemed to mean it. 'I am disgusted with myself,' she wrote bitterly, 'for having so long importuned you with my affection'[13]. In the *Letters* written for publication Mary implied that this self-knowledge had brought her to a new stage of development:

> What a long time it requires to know ourselves; and yet almost every one has more of this knowledge than he is willing to own, even to himself. I cannot immediately determine whether I ought to rejoice at having turned over in this solitude a new page in the history of my own heart, though I may venture to assure you that a further acquaintance with mankind only tends to increase my respect for your judgment, and esteem for your character.

This claim is scarcely born out by the future conduct of either party.

From Tonsberg Mary took a short tour southwards to the villages of Potoer and Rufoer, the latter of such forbidding aspect that she described it as a 'bastille of rock'. Nevertheless, in this 'corner of the world' she found peace in observing the simplicity of the inhabitants—the 'folk'—and the majesty of the country. 'Now all my nerves keep time with the melody of nature,' she wrote. 'Ah! Let me be happy whilst I can.' Yet Mary viewed nature now with a difference. In Norway she was impressed above all by the evidence of 'human industry', and she could dismiss the vision of the 'noble savage' as 'Rousseau's golden age of stupidity'. She saw now that the world required 'the hand of man to perfect it', and she reiterated her belief in the worth and dignity of labour. Every kind of employment, she asserted, should offer a salary 'sufficient to reward industry'; no rewards should be so great as 'to permit the possessor to remain idle'. She went even further in the direction of the socialism of the future in declaring: 'It is this want of proportion between profit and labour which debases men, producing the sycophantic appellations of patron and client'.

Sailing along this wild coastline, she reflected on the state of the world as she had seen it—and as it might be in years to come:

> I anticipated the future improvement of the world, and observed how much man had still to do, to obtain of the earth all it could yield. I even carried my speculations so far as to advance a million or two years to the moment when the earth would perhaps be so perfectly cultivated, and so completely peopled, as to render it necessary to inhabit every spot; yes, these bleak shores. Imagination went still further, and pictured the state of man when the earth could no longer support him. Where was he to fly to from universal famine? Do not smile: I really became distressed for these fellow creatures, yet unborn.

Apart from the time-scale, this peep into the future was not too far out[14]. But business—Imlay's business—soon recalled her to the present. On 22nd August she again set off from Tonsberg, travelling north via Moss to the Norwegian capital of Christiania (Oslo). This part of the country was agricultural, with a much softer landscape—'the grand features of nature', Mary wrote, were 'dwindling into prettiness'. She found Moss to be a thriving trading centre, and the wealthy shop-keepers reminded her of the 'tradespeople of Yorkshire'. Here she met 'an intelligent literary man', who sought her views on the situation in France. There was great sympathy for the republican cause among the more educated Norwegians, so much so that they were willing to excuse the atrocities on the grounds of 'necessity', and Mary had great difficulty in persuading them 'that Robespierre was a monster'.

The approach to Christiania was through a charming, 'undulating valley', but Mary noted that the view was spoilt by 'the depredations committed on the rocks to make alum'. The export of alum was one of Imlay's business interests, and perhaps it was an association of ideas that caused Mary to renew her attack on 'commerce' as she found it practised in the capital city: 'What is speculation,' she asked, 'but a species of gambling, I might have said fraud, in which address generally gains the prize?' At Christiania too, she became aware of the Danish domination of Norway through the 'grand bailiffs'—usually noblemen from Copenhagen—who ruled the country and whom she described as 'political monsters'. She also found the commercial spirit of the city reflected in its architecture—or lack of it. Christiania was a 'clean, neat city' but lacking in grace. The square, wooden houses seemed to her mean and inelegant; and at the same time she was reminded of 'the meeting-house of my respected friend, Dr Price', and she wondered that the dissenters should find 'a noble pillar, or arch, unhallowed': 'Whilst men have senses', she observed, 'whatever sooths them lends wings to devotion'.

From Christiania, Mary turned south again to visit the cascades at Fredericstadt on the way back to Stromstad. The route, through magnificent pine forests, restored her to a sense of the sublime; but again she regretted that the natural beauty of the waterfall was marred by the presence of saw-mills. Crossing back into Sweden, Mary was beset by irritations and delays. The peasants were 'sluggish' and 'cunning', and she was convinced she was being cheated: she paid for horses that never arrived, was charged 'a rix dollar and a half' for a plate of fish, and found the inns noisy and dirty. Nevertheless, she enjoyed the cross-country journey to Gothenburg, with fine weather and river scenery, though she was struck with the poverty of the farms compared with those in Norway. From Gothenburg she visited the man-made cascade at Trolhette and witnessed the boring of a canal through solid rock, a feat employing 900 men and estimated to take five years to extend it for one and a half miles. She rather regretted this interference with nature, which for all its effort 'only resembled the insignificant sport of children'.

But Mary was again thoroughly out of humour, thanks to a further batch of disquieting letters from Imlay which she found waiting for her at Gothenburg. 'You tell me that my letters torture you,' she wrote on 26th August, the day after her arrival. She found it hard to believe that Imlay could be suffering from her attitude as she suffered from his: 'I will not describe the effect yours have on me ... I mean not to give vent to the emotions they produced'[15]. But she admitted that Imlay had correctly diagnosed the root of the trouble between them:

> Certainly you are right; our minds are not congenial. I have lived in an ideal world, and fostered sentiments that you do not comprehend, or you would not treat me thus.

She did not want his pity, she informed him: 'Forget that I exist; I will never remind you.' But Imlay was evidently continuing to protest his concern for her:

> You need not continually tell me that our fortune is inseparable, *that you will try to cherish tenderness* for me. Do no violence to yourself! When we are separated, our interest, since you give so much weight to pecuniary considerations, will be entirely divided. I want not protection without affection; and support I need not, whilst my faculties are undisturbed. Be not alarmed, I shall not force myself on you any more.

In defence of her 'ideal world' Mary was always under the necessity of painting Imlay and his motives in the worst possible light. Only one thing was certain in their relationship: that whatever he did would be wrong. Mary cannot be blamed for her consciousness, which sometimes bordered on self-righteousness, that her faculties were superior to his; but it was unreasonable, and irrational, of her to blame him for their total incompatibility, both of mind and heart. She had not yet learned this lesson, whatever else she had learned; and so she continued to suffer, in a lost cause.

She still could not believe that it was lost. Despite her assurances that she would trouble him no more, on 6th September she was writing again in even more extreme terms. 'Gracious God!' she cried. 'It is impossible for me to stifle something like resentiment when I receive fresh proofs of your indifference. What I have suffered this last year is not to be forgotten!'[16] Yet again she invited further punishment:

I do not understand you. It is necessary for you to write more explicitly, and determine on some mode of conduct. I cannot endure this suspense. Decide. Do you fear to strike another blow? We live together, or eternally apart! I shall not write to you again, till I receive an answer to this. I must compose my tortured soul before I write on indifferent subjects.

By this time Mary was in Copenhagen, travelling from Gothenburg via Elsinore and accompanied now by Marguerite and Fanny. Despite her 'tortured soul', she was able to record some vivid and lucid observations on Denmark and its people. Compared with Norway, and even Sweden, the countryside was flat and uninteresting, though she noted that the soil looked very fertile and there was 'a great quantity of corn land'. Copenhagen had recently suffered a great fire which destroyed much of the city, and refugees were encamped in tents on the outskirts. Mary walked through the devastated streets, appalled by the sufferings of the homeless; but even allowing for the devastation, she was not very impressed by the city:

This morning I have been walking round the town, till I am weary of observing the ravages. I had often heard the danes, even those who had seen Paris and London, speak of Copenhagen with rapture. Certainly I have seen it in a very disadvantageous light, some of the best streets having been burnt and the whole place thrown into confusion. Still the utmost that can, or could ever, I believe, have been said in its praise, might be comprised in a few words. The streets are open, and many of the houses large; but I saw nothing to rouse the idea of elegance or grandeur, if I except the circus where the king and prince royal reside.

The palace had been burnt down in an earlier fire, and now the homeless poor were sheltering in the ruins: 'Beds were thrown on the landing places of the grand stair-case where whole families crept from the cold, and every little nook is boarded up as a retreat for some poor creatures deprived of their home'. Many observed that the conflagration might well have been checked had the inhabitants been willing to permit the destruction of a number of houses, but they were more concerned to preserve their property than to extinguish the fire. She attributed this to the national character of the Danes: 'A sluggish concentration in themselves makes them so careful to preserve their property, that they will not venture on any enterprise to increase it, in which there is a shadow of hazard'. Altogether, Mary did not approve much of the Danes. The business men were 'domestic tyrants' and the women 'simply notable housewives'. The children were spoilt by 'weak, indulgent mothers, who having no principles of action to regulate their feelings, become the slaves of infants, enfeebling both body and mind by false tenderness'.

She was also horrified, on meeting a crowd which included 'well-dressed women' with their children, to discover that they had been witnessing a public execution. Until capital punishment was entirely abolished, she commented, 'executions ought to have every appearance of horrour given to them; instead of being, as they are now, a scene of amusement for the gaping crowd'. But she did not believe that even the horror of an execution was a real deterrent: 'the fear of an ignominious death, I believe, never deterred any one from the commission of a crime; because, in committing it, the mind is roused to activity about present circumstances. It is a game of hazard, at which all expect the turn of the die in their own favour; never reflecting on the chance of ruin, till it comes'. The horror was further compounded when she learned that two men had drunk a glass of the criminals' blood, which was alleged to be a remedy for apoplexy. When she objected that this was 'a violation of nature' a Danish lady reproved her severely, 'asking how I knew that it was not a cure for the disease?' She put this down as a 'remnant of exploded witchcraft', which could only be eradicated by scientific education.

For all the Danish absorption in 'property'—and Mary reiterated her view that 'an adoration of property is the root of all evil'—she found less evidence of industry and less gaiety than in Norway and attributed this to the greater liberty of the Norwegians, despite their vassal status. The lack of taste Mary observed in Denmark was accompanied by crudeness of feeling: 'Love here seems to corrupt the morals, without polishing the manners, by banishing confidence and truth, the charm as well as cement of domestic life'. She admitted that if she had visited Scandinavia before France she might have been less critical of French morals! Now she felt that the French passion for going to the theatre, which she had formerly regarded as vain and frivolous, was infinitely superior to the Scandinavian addiction to alcohol: 'Intoxication is the pleasure of savages', she remarked, and the greatest impediment to the improvement of society. The one theatre she visited in Copenhagen was of poor standard and only half full. She was agreeably surprised, however, by the public library which was well stocked and included some Icelandic manuscripts; and there were some 'good pictures' in the royal museum—but these were mixed indiscriminately with the bad, in order to 'assort the frames'. The exhibits similarly were 'huddled together without that scientific order which alone renders them useful'. Mary acknowledged that there were 'some respectable men of science' in Denmark, but very little encouragement was given to writers and artists. She blamed the parsimony of the court for this—somewhat illogically, since she had criticised the French court for its extravagance, and she acknowledged the 'good intentions' of the Danish crown prince in making economies: 'He, and the princess his wife, dine every day with the king, to save the expense of two tables'. But the 'real sovereign', she observed, was Count Bernstorff, for the king had 'lost the majesty of man', having 'neither will nor memory'. Mary actually met and talked with Bernstorff, whom she found well-meaning, though apparently more anxious not to do wrong than to do any active good. She observed that when Lavater had visited him, he 'found lines in his face to prove him a statesman of the first order'—an assessment based on diplomacy rather than physiognomy, for Lavater 'had a knack of seeing a great character in the countenance of men in exalted stations, who have noticed him, or his works'.

Mary acknowledged that the Danes seemed happy and well-satisfied with their lot. She also noted that one of the best streets in Copenhagen contained many hospitals provided by the government, and she was assured they were well-run. She voiced a doubt, however, whether such institutions anywhere, whether hospitals or work-houses, were 'superintended with sufficient humanity'. Mary's gloomy view of Denmark was undoubtedly coloured by the depressed mood in which she had left Gothenburg, and she admitted as much in quitting the country: 'I may be a little partial, and view every thing with the jaundiced eye of melancholy—for I am sad—and have cause. God bless you!' This was to Imlay in her published *Letters*.

On leaving Denmark Mary was headed for home—and there was little to cheer her in this prospect. She planned to travel through Germany to Switzerland, with the fast-receding hope that Imlay would join her there. This necessitated a crossing of the Great Belt and the Little Belt to Sleswig, en route for Hamburg. The sea was rough, but Mary was never deterred by the elements: 'as neither I nor my little girl are ever attacked by sea sickness,' she observed 'I enter a boat with the same indifference as I change horses; and as for danger, come when it may, I dread it not sufficiently to have any anticipatory fears'.

She found Holstein an agreeable, if rather dull, piece of country, with thriving and industrious towns and no signs of the brutal poverty that had so depressed her in Sweden. Indeed, the king of Denmark's German dominion—as it still was—appeared to her 'far superior to any other part of his kingdom which had fallen under my view; and the robust rustics to have their muscles braced, instead of the *as it were* lounge of the danish peasantry'. The only distasteful sight was a military camp. 'I viewed, with a mixture of pity and horrour, these beings training to be sold to slaughter, or be slaughtered,' she wrote; and the thought gave rise to a philosophical speculation on the purpose of existence:

> it is the preservation of the species, not of individuals, which appears to be the design of the Deity throughout the whole of nature. Blossoms come forth only to be blighted; fish lay their spawn where it will be devoured: and what a large portion of the human race are born merely to be swept prematurely away. Does not this waste of budding life emphatically assert, that it is not men, but man, whose preservation is so necessary to the completion of the grand plan of the universe?

The pleasant approaches to Hamburg were marred on arrival by the impossibility of finding a suitable lodging. This minor irritation recalled Mary to her greater sorrows, and the 'cruelest of disappointments' she had suffered when she returned from France the previous spring: 'Know you of what materials some hearts are made?' she asked rhetorically in her *Letters*; and, writing here for publication, she could not resist an extravaganza of sentiment that had little relation to the actual facts of the case:

> I play the child, and weep at the recollection—for the grief is

still fresh that stunned as well as wounded me—yet never did drops of anguish like these bedew the cheeks of infantine innocence—and why should they mine, that never were stained by a blush of guilt? Innocent and credulous as a child, why have I not the same happy thoughtlessness?

The author of the *Rights of Woman* was no innocent and credulous child, and if she had behaved like one she had only herself to blame—as she was quick to blame other women for childish and irresponsible behaviour.

The following day the party moved out of their uncomfortable room in Hamburg to the pleasant suburb of Altona, where lodgings had been arranged for them by 'a gentleman from whom I received many civilities during my journey'. This gentleman, whom Mary had found 'intelligent and friendly', was perhaps the 'Captain' to whom she made reference in the letter she now wrote to Imlay from Hamburg on 25th September. She did not like this city—'an ill, close-built town, swarming with inhabitants'—and Imlay's continued silence only increased its repugnance for her[17]:

> I have just finished a letter to be given in charge to Captain—. In that I complained of your silence, and expressed my surprise that three mails should have arrived without bringing a line for me. Since I closed it, I hear of another, and still no letter. I am labouring to write calmly—this silence is a refinement on cruelty. Had Captain — remained a few days longer, I would have returned with him to England. What have I to do here? I have repeatedly written to you fully. Do you do the same, and quickly. Do not leave me in suspense. I have not deserved this of you.
> I cannot write, my mind is so distressed.

Imlay's failure to keep Mary informed even of his business activities confirms the suspicion that he had sent her to Scandinavia to get rid of her, rather than in the capacity of his 'agent'. This role, even when she was in a position to carry it out, was in any case an irksome one for her. She was forced to consort with the kind of profiteers and speculators she most despised. The blatantly commercial character of Hamburg, which as a free port was dedicated wholly to trade, reminded her of all Imlay's worst failings: 'Ah! shall I whisper to you—that you—yourself, are strangely altered, since you have entered deeply into commerce', she wrote in her *Letters*: 'Nature has given you talents, which lie dormant, or are wasted in ignoble pursuits.—You will rouse yourself, and shake off the vile dust that obscures you, or my understanding, as well as my heart, deceives me, egregiously—only tell me when?' The answer, of course, was: never. Commerce was part and parcel of Imlay's nature, and it had always been so. It was not he who was 'strangely altered', but Mary; and her understanding did indeed deceive her, 'egregiously'.

Yet apart from this one blind spot Mary's faculties were as alert as ever. Altona had become the haven for a number of eminent refugees from the French Revolution. 'It is scarcely possible to stir out,' Mary wrote, 'without meeting interesting countenances, every lineament of which tells you that they have seen better days.' Madame de Genlis, whose views she had challenged in the *Rights of Woman*, was living there under an assumed name. Madame Lafayette left the day she arrived and joined the General in Vienna where he was interned by the Austrians. In her *Letters* Mary described a duke who had gone into partnership with his cook, and observed that this was a not uncommon situation: 'Many noble instances of the attachment of servants to their unfortunate masters, have come to my knowledge both here and in France, and touched my heart, the greatest delight of which is to discover human virtue'. A former president of the French parliament was the keeper of the inn where Mary stayed, on the recommendation of an acquaintance of Imlay's who was also in Altona at that time. This was St John de Crevecoeur, author of *An American Farmer's Letters*, with whom she often dined together with 'the gentleman whom I have already mentioned'. Mary was never slow to point out to Imlay that other men enjoyed her company, even if he did not; this was no more than the truth. She was evidently on good terms with de Crevecoeur, who shared her critical attitude to commerce, and Mary welcomed him as an ally in her fight to win back Imlay to an imagined lost innocence. What she saw in Hamburg, she wrote, only confirmed her opinion of the 'baleful effect' of speculation on the moral character:

> A man ceases to love humanity, and then individuals, as he advances in the chase after wealth; as one clashes with his interest, the other with his pleasures: to business, as it is termed, every thing must give way; nay, is sacrificed; and all the endearing charities of citizen, husband, father, brother, become empty names.

This was a clear dig at Imlay himself. Mary was now

preparing to return to England. Imlay had at last written, and it was obvious that he had no intention of joining her at Basle as she had originally hoped. In her published account, she made light of the change of plan:

> though Switzerland is the country which for several years I have been particularly desirous to visit, I do not feel inclined to ramble any farther this year; nay, I am weary of changing the scene, and quitting people and places the moment they begin to interest me.

To Imlay himself, however, she wrote on 27th September with all the clarity of despair[18]:

> You had perpetually recurred to your promise of meeting me in the autumn. Was it extraordinary that I should demand a yes, or no? Your letter is written with extreme harshness, coldness I am accustomed to, in it I find not a trace of the tenderness of humanity, much less of friendship. I only see a desire to heave a load off your shoulders.

At last, if only briefly, Mary did see Imlay clearly. Yet she continued to assure him that she would never be a burden on him: 'I will write to Mr Johnson to procure me an obscure lodging and not to inform anybody of my arrival. There I will endeavour in a few months to obtain the sum necessary to take me to France...' Even at this eleventh hour, she could not believe that it was really all over between them. Nor could she refrain from reminding Imlay of how much—on her side—the relationship had meant:

> Of me you have no cause to complain, but for having had too much regard for you—for having expected a degree of permanent happiness when you only sought for a momentary gratification.
>
> I am strangely deficient in sagacity. Uniting myself to you, your tenderness seemed to make me amends for all my former misfortunes. On this tenderness and affection with what confidence did I rest!—but I leaned on a spear that has pierced me to the heart. You have thrown off a faithful friend, to pursue the caprices of the moment. We certainly are differently organised; for even now, when conviction has been stamped on my soul by sorrow, I can scarcely believe it possible. It depends at present on you, whether you will see me or not. I shall take no step, till I see or hear from you.

This was calculated (though not deliberately) to touch any

heart—but Imlay's. The appeal fell on stony ground, as she must have known it would. One week later, Mary and her child were in Dover: unmet and unprovided for, with no further message from Imlay and with a hardening of her suspicion that he had indeed forsaken her in favour of a new liaison. In the circumstances, Mary's letter of 4th October is remarkable for its dignity and calm[19]:

> You say, I must decide for myself. I have decided, that it was most for the interest of my little girl, and for my own comfort, little as I expect, for us to live together; and I even thought that you would be glad, some years hence, when the tumult of business was over, to repose in the society of an affectionate friend, and mark the progress of our interesting child, whilst endeavouring to be of use in the circle you at last resolved to rest in; for you cannot run for ever.
>
> From the tenour of your last letter, however, I am led to imagine that you have formed some new attachment. If it be so, let me earnestly request you to see me once more, and immediately. This is the only proof I require of the friendship you profess for me. I will then decide, since you boggle about a mere form.

Imlay must have believed that in hinting at his 'new attachment' he had played his trump card: no self-respecting woman could accept that situation and still wish to maintain her own relation with him. But he had reckoned without the force of Mary's passion, which was really a passionate attachment to her own principles. Imlay was the father of her child; therefore, they should live together as the family they in fact were, whether the tie had been cemented by a legal ceremony or not. The legal tie, the 'mere form', was the least important factor. This was a simple, perhaps naive, concept; yet by any moral reasoning, a valid one. Why, then, could Imlay not accept it?

'I am labouring to write with calmness,' Mary continued, 'but the extreme anguish I feel, at landing without having a friend to receive me, and even to be conscious that the friend whom I most wish to see, will feel a disagreeable sensation as being informed of my arrival, does not come under the description of common misery'. This, for Mary, was an extreme under-statement. In landing at Dover, she had reached the end of the road. She could go no further to meet Imlay; while he had taken not a single step towards her. There was still time, if he wished to do so—but only just: 'Do not keep me in suspense,' she pleaded:

I have fortitude enough to determine to do my duty; yet I cannot raise my depressed spirits, or calm my trembling heart. That being who moulded it thus, knows that I am unable to tear up by the roots the propensity to affection which has been the torment of my life—but life will have an end!

Should you come here (a few months ago I could not have doubted it) you will find me at —. If you prefer meeting me on the road, tell me where.

We do not know which of these alternatives, if either, Imlay chose to take. The next time we hear of Mary, by hook or by crook she had made her way to London.

ic # PART FOUR: TOWARDS HUMANITY

CHAPTER FIFTEEN

Death of a Romantic: 1795–1796

On Saturday, 24th October 1795, *The Times* newspaper reported an incident which had occurred two weeks earlier:

On Saturday fortnight a Lady, elegantly dressed, took a boat from one of the stairs in the Strand, and ordered the waterman to row to Putney, where landing, she paid him 6s. and immediately going upon Putney Bridge, threw herself from the frame of the centre arch into the Thames: fortunately she was picked up by a fishing-boat, and being carried to an inn at Fulham, was soon restored by the skill of the one of the medical persons belonging to the Humane Society. She told her place of abode, and added, that the cause of this, which was the second act of desperation she had attempted on her life, was the brutal behaviour of her husband. In about two hours afterwards, her coach came, with her maid, and a proper change of apparel, when she was conveyed home, perfectly recovered.

This account does not entirely tally with Godwin's description in his *Memoirs* of Mary's second suicide attempt, nor does it sound altogether in character; but the similarities are too great to be coincidental. If the 'elegantly dressed' lady was indeed Mary Imlay, the desperate act took place on 10th October, less than a week after her return to London. What had happened in this short interval to precipitate the crisis? The answer is not hard to find.

Faced with the inescapable fact of her presence, Imlay could do no less than provide a lodging for Mary and their child. He did not, however, join them. He had already procured a furnished house for his London mistress—who has never been identified except as 'an actress'—and here he sought refuge from Mary's importunities. No doubt she was in a sufficiently agitated state for him to justify a period of rest and seclusion for her, and if this had been forthcoming the crisis might have been averted. Unfortunately, however, a cook at the house gave way under Mary's questioning and blurted out the truth that Imlay was living with another woman. The distraught Mary rushed to confront Imlay with his perfidy, and the ensuing scene must have been the most painful for both of them in the whole sorry story. Even Godwin could not or would not divulge the details: 'What was the particular nature of their conference I am unable to relate,' he observed; but undoubtedly it was 'the wretchedness of the night which succeeded this fatal discovery' that drove Mary over the brink of despair. Imlay is said to have tried to pass off the other woman as his legal wife, whom he claimed to have married before he met Mary, but this subterfuge deceived nobody. Joseph Farington recorded in his diary[1] that Imlay 'pretended he had been married before, and proposed to Mrs Imlay to live in the same house with his first wife (who in fact is only his mistress)'. The story was therefore common gossip, and whether true or false it was a near-lethal blow to Mary.

Assuming the *Times* report to be correct, her interview with Imlay must have taken place on Friday, 9th October, and her 'suicide note' was written the following day[2]. It is a strange mixture of nobility and petulance, of tragedy and melodrama. 'I write to you now on my knees,' she began, imploring Imlay to send the child to Paris to be cared for. She bequeathed her clothes to her faithful nursemaid Marguerite, and ordered the cook's wages to be paid—that same cook who had been the instrument of the present disaster: 'do not mention the confession which I forced from her,' Mary added, 'a little sooner or later is of no consequence'. She then turned her attention to Imlay:

> Nothing but my extreme stupidity could have rendered me blind so long. Yet, whilst you assured me that you had no attachment, I thought we might still have lived together.
>
> I shall make no comments on your conduct, or any appeal to the world. Let my wrongs sleep with me! Soon, very soon, I shall be at peace. When you receive this, my burning head will

be cold.

I would encounter a thousand deaths, rather than a night like the last. Your treatment has thrown my mind into a state of chaos; yet I am serene. I go to find comfort, and my only fear is, that my poor body will be insulted by an endeavour to recall my hated existence. But I shall plunge into the Thames where there is least chance of my being snatched from the death I seek.

God bless you! May you never know by experience what you have made me endure. Should your sensibility ever awake, remorse will find its way to your heart; and, in the midst of business and sensual pleasure, I shall appear before you, the victim of your deviation from rectitude.

Did Mary really intend that she should drown, or was this only a theatrical gesture? The *Times* report, with its quite false suggestion of home comforts (if Mary was the 'lady' in question) implies that the attempt was little more than frivolous. This is confirmed by an entry in the records of the Royal Humane Society for 1796 which may refer to the same incident: 'An Unfortunate Desponding Lady—Her Life happily saved;—*which brought about a change of circumstance, and a serene state of mind*'. A more serious account is given by Farington:

... she took a boat and was rowed to Putney, where going on shore & to the Bridge, she threw herself into the water. Her cloaths buoyed her up and she floated, & was taken senseless abt 200 yards from the Bridge, and by proper applications restored to life.

The inn to which Mary was carried may well have been the Swann Inn, east of Putney Bridge, where meetings of the Fulham Bridge Commissioners were held; it has since been destroyed. The bridge from which she jumped, a wooden toll bridge, was burnt down in 1871 and replaced by the present stone bridge[3]. Godwin himself provided the most convincing evidence that Mary Imlay was determined to die. She first made for Battersea Bridge but finding it 'too public' for her purpose she continued further up the river[4]:

It was night when she arrived at Putney, and by that time it had begun to rain with great violence. The rain suggested to her the idea of walking up and down the bridge, till her clothes were thoroughly drenched and heavy with the wet, which she did for half an hour without meeting a human being. She then leaped from the top of the bridge, but still seemed to find a difficulty in sinking, which she endeavoured to counter-act by pressing her clothes closely round her. After some time she became insensible; but she always spoke of the pain she underwent as such, that, though she could afterwards have determined upon almost any other species of voluntary death, it would have been impossible for her to resolve upon encountering the same sensations again.

Against all the odds, Mary survived. But it had been so close a thing that even Imlay was shaken. He arranged for a physician to attend her and prevailed on his friends the Christies—who had returned to London the previous year—to take her into their own house in Finsbury Square. Mary was not very grateful for this belated concern[5]:

I have only to lament that, when the bitterness of death was past, I was inhumanly brought back to life and misery. But a fixed determination is not to be baffled by disappointment; nor will I allow that to be a frantic attempt which was one of the calmest acts of reason.

Here Mary seems to be threatening to do it again, if things did not improve. But Imlay could not bring himself to visit her, making the incredible excuse (in view of all that had gone before) that to do so would be 'indelicate'. In truth he was almost as distraught by the impossible situation as she was: 'You say "that you know not how to extricate ourselves out of the wretchedness into which we have been plunged",' she continued in the same letter, adding rather tartly: 'You are extricated long since'. Mary, with her amazing resilience, was in fact recovering from the shock rather more quickly than Imlay, and in the next paragraph she seemed to have accepted the new situation:

But since your new attachment is the only sacred thing in your eyes, I am silent—Be happy! My complaints shall never more damp your enjoyment; perhaps I am mistaken in supposing that even my death could, for more than a moment ... I never wanted but your heart. That gone, you have nothing more to give, for if I had only poverty to fear I should not shrink from life.

Irrationally, Mary refused Imlay's offers of material help, even on Fanny's behalf, as 'an insult'; at the same time she threatened that 'When I am dead, respect for yourself will make you take care of the child'.

At this point Imlay—who could be as unpredictable as Mary herself—apparently changed his tune to the extent of assuring her that his present attachment was—in Godwin's words—'merely a casual, sensual connection'. Whereupon Mary, turning the tables again, promptly proposed that they should live together in a *ménage à trois* (had she forgotten her disastrous intervention in the Fuseli household?). She was determined, said Godwin—and this was another sign of her reviving health and spirits—to bring the issue to a head. She acknowledged that Imlay could not be expected to 'abruptly break off' his present connection: 'I consent then, for the present, to live with you, and the woman to whom you have associated yourself.' This was an astounding *volte face*, and Mary justified it in the interests of their child: 'I think it important that you should learn habitually to feel for your child the affection of a father.' It was a feeble argument, as Mary very well knew, and even as she offered it she was anticipating the alternative: 'But, if you reject this proposal, here we end. You are now free. We will correspond no more. We will have no intercourse of any kind. I will be to you as a person that is dead.'[6]

This account, it should be made clear, is Godwin's interpretation of the events of that melancholy autumn, but it has the ring of truth. Amazingly enough, Imlay at first appeared to accept Mary's proposition. They even went to look at a house together like any conventional couple. But he soon had second thoughts and—wisely, no doubt—drew back.

By her own terms, Mary should now have acknowledged that this was indeed the end. 'I will be to you' she had declared, 'as a person that is dead'. And for a time at least, she tried to keep her word—'existing', said Godwin, 'in a living tomb', seeing nobody but Mrs Christie. But Mary could never entirely forget Imlay, and she continued to nag him with letters which, however justified, were certainly unwise. 'I am compelled at last to say that you treat me ungenerously', she wrote in November, 'But let the obloquy now fall on me'[7]. The London of her circle was no doubt buzzing with malicious gossip, and not a few people outside her circle were only too delighted to see the author of the *Rights of Woman* humbled in the dust. In spirit, however, despite all her tribulations Mary was not humbled. She still held herself superior—and rightly so—to the hypocrisies of society:

My child may have to blush for her mother's want of prudence, and may lament that the rectitude of my heart made me above vulgar precautions; but she shall not despise me for meanness. You are now perfectly free. God bless you!

In Imlay's view, no doubt, women should have the sense not to saddle themselves—and him—with illegitimate babies[8]. Mary had proved the troublesome exception, and he could not forgive her for it; especially as in her own eyes this 'want of prudence' was not a crime but a virtue. If only she could have behaved as other women and treated the affair with circumspection! But it was not in Mary's nature to do so; and she was still wounded, even at this late stage, by Imlay's attempts to minimise their former relationship. 'I have been hurt by indirect enquiries, which appear to me not to be dictated by any tenderness to me,' she wrote again in the same month. 'You ask, "If I am well or tranquil?" They who think me so, must want a heart to estimate my feelings'[9]. She was also 'mortified' by his offers of financial assistance, especially after he had blatantly set up house with his new mistress: 'considering your going to the new house, as an open avowal that you abandon me, let me tell you that I will sooner perish than receive anything from you.' Yet even Imlay's 'open avowal' did not finally convince her that he had gone for good. She insisted on having it spelt out in black and white: 'But let me see, written by yourself—for I will not receive it through any other medium—that the affair is finished'. When at last he did visit her, she refused to believe that he had come in her interests: 'Even your seeing me, has been to oblige other people, and not to soothe my distracted mind'. As so often before, Mary was behaving unreasonably—though not without gross provocation—and deliberately sabotaging any attempt to salvage some small comfort from the wreckage of her hopes. She admitted as much when she wrote in the same letter apropos her financial difficulties: 'But this even pleases me; an accumulation of disappointments and misfortunes seems to suit the habit of my mind'.

As soon as she was fit to do so Mary moved out of the Christies' house and took a lodging nearby in Finsbury Place. As ever, Joseph Johnson was at hand with sympathy and encouragement, which extended to practical help in extricating her from the painful involvement with Imlay. 'Mr Johnson having forgotten to desire you to send the things of mine which were left at the house, I have to request you to let Marguerite bring them to me', Mary wrote at the time of her removal. 'I shall go this evening to the lodgings, so you need not be restrained from coming here to transact your business. And, whatever I may think or feel, you need not fear that I shall publicly complain'[10]. Her only wish now, she continued, was 'to hide myself'; she would be 'silent as the grave in which I long to forget myself'. But, she assured Imlay, 'You have nothing to fear from my desperation'. At last, it seemed, Mary had succeeded in putting the past behind her and was looking towards a possible future. In this mood of resolution she even requested Imlay to return her letters; he at least made no bones about this. Probably he was glad to be rid of such an embarrassing dossier on his own shortcomings. In acknowledging the letters, Mary described them as 'a register of sorrow'; and though she declared that she had 'thrown them aside', even to see them again must have revived all her former melancholy[11]:

> The grief I cannot conquer ... I labour to conceal in total solitude. My life therefore is but an exercise of fortitude, continually on the stretch, and hope never gleams in this tomb. I am buried alive.

Then she turned her attention to Imlay's covering letter:

> You tell me that I shall judge more coolly of your mode of action some time hence. Is it possible that passion clouds your reason as much as it does mine? And ought you not to doubt whether those principles are so 'exalted', as you term them, which only lead to your own gratification? ... *Do you judge coolly*, and I trust you will not continue to call those capricious feelings 'the most refined', which would undermine not only the most sacred principles, but the affections which unite mankind. You would render mothers unnatural—and there would be no such thing as a father!

Was there ever a more tragic misunderstanding than this conflict of passion and principle, which both saw as being totally misconceived in the other?

Imlay had not unnaturally assumed that his return of Mary's letters meant an acknowledgment that their relationship was at an end. He was weary of the whole affair and, one may guess, past caring about the rights or wrongs of it. All he wanted was to escape from an onerous commitment, and in November he took himself and his new mistress to Paris[12]. Though Mary wrote him three further letters which have survived, they have the dying fall of a waning vision; a vision that had become, in her own words 'a frightful dream'[13].

As love faded, the erstwhile romantic hero was revealed as no more than a rather inadequate human being, though Mary continued to cherish the hope that Imlay would outgrow this immature phase: 'You will not be satisfied to act the part of a boy, till you fall into that of a dotard', she wrote to him on 8th December[14]. But what of the romantic heroine? Did Mary see herself equally clearly? Not yet, it seems: 'In a comfortless old age, you will remember that you had one disinterested friend, whose heart you wounded to the quick'. But the heroine could not play her part alone, and she maintained that Imlay's aberration was only a temporary one: 'I know that your mind, your heart, and your principles of action are all superior to your present conduct. You do, you must, respect me—and you will be sorry to forfeit my esteem'. It was her own self-esteem that Mary was protecting by refusing to admit, when the facts were staring her in the face, that Imlay was as unworthy as his conduct had time and again proved him to be. Even while acknowledging that the parting was 'for ever', she continued to 'expostulate' with him, flinging back at him his own words before she returned to England[15]:

'Business alone has kept me from you. Come to any port and I will fly down to my two dear girls with a heart all their own.' With these assurances is it extraordinary that I should believe what I wished? Imlay, believe me, this is not romance, you have acknowledged to me feelings of this kind.

At this recollection, her own feelings gushed back in a last surge of hope:

Tearing myself from you it is my own heart I pierce, but the time will come when you will lament that you have thrown away a heart that even in the moment of passion you cannot despise. I would owe everything to your generosity, but for God's sake keep me no longer in suspense! Let me see you once more!

The response to this appeal was, predictably, totally negative.

At the same time Mary had painfully been piecing together the threads of her former life. If she was to support herself and her child unaided, as she had resolved, she must get back to writing. Her first task was to prepare for the press her Scandinavian journal, *Letters written during a short residence in Sweden...*, which Johnson was ready to publish. She also sketched out during this period a 'comedy', based partly on her own experiences, which she submitted unsuccessfully to two theatre managers. When Godwin found the draft amongst her papers he judged it too 'crude and imperfect'—and also too indiscreet?—to be preserved, and burnt it.

In reviewing her past life, and steeling herself for the future, Mary recalled another painful episode—her unrequited passion for Fuseli. She had already tried to resume her acquaintance with him when she came back to England the previous spring and evidently met with a stony reception. She had since heard nothing from him, and now in this end-of-year stocktaking she wrote to request the return of her letters, at the same time rebuking him for his coldness towards her[16]:

> When I returned from France, I visited you, Sir, but finding myself after my late journey in a very different situation, I vainly imagined you would have called upon me. I simply tell you what I thought, yet I write not, at present, to comment on your conduct or expostulate. I have long ceased to expect kindness or affection from any human creature, and would fain tear from my heart its treacherous sympathies.

Considering their relative positions, Mary's somewhat imperious tone was hardly likely to endear her to Fuseli any more than her previous criticisms had. Yet she went on to appeal to his sympathies:

> I am alone. The injustice, without alluding to hopes blasted in the bud, which I have endured, wounding my bosom, have set my thoughts adrift into an ocean of painful conjectures. I ask impatiently what—and where—is truth? I have been treated brutally; but I daily labour to remember that I still have the duty of a mother to fulfil.

Fuseli was evidently acquainted with Mary's story and felt under no obligation to offer his sympathy, let alone support. There was no good reason why he should, except gratuitously; and Fuseli was never noted for his generosity. Now at last Mary got to the real point of her letter:

> I have written more than I intended.—for I only meant to

request you to return my letters: I wish to have them, and it must be the same to you. Adieu!

Unlike Imlay, Fuseli ignored this request; and the earlier letters have never been found[17].

The barrier between Mary and Imlay (so different from that happy, far-off 'barrière' in Paris!) was unexpectedly lifted, about two weeks after his return to London, by a chance (or not so chance) encounter at the house of Thomas Christie, with whom Imlay still had business connections. One evening when he was there, in company with some other friends, Mrs Christie heard Mary's voice in the entrance-hall and ran out to intercept her. But May, characteristically, refused to be deterred. She felt that she had nothing to be ashamed of in her conduct and, in Godwin's words, 'that it was not consistent with conscious rectitude, that she should shrink, as if abashed, from the presence of one by whom she deemed herself injured'. She had Fanny with her (which is rather surprising on an evening visit, if the interview had not been deliberately stage-managed) and firmly led the child to her father's knee. What else could Imlay do, in the presence of company, but retire as gracefully as possible to another room and hear her out? Evidently the interview did not go badly, and the upshot was an arrangement that he should dine at her lodging the following day. Here he must have made some effort to repair the damage of his absence, for Mary instantly soared again into the seventh heaven of hope: 'the gentleness of his carriage', wrote Godwin, 'was to her as a sunbeam, awakening the hope of returning day'. The hope was, of course, a delusion; but even after the delirium expired she dwelt, as Godwin phrased it, 'upon the air-built and insubstantial prospect of a reconciliation'.

Yet the inconsistencies were not all on one side. According to Godwin, it was at Imlay's insistence that Mary retained his name. She agreed to do so, he said, not for the sake of convention but because she was 'unwilling to cut the Gordian knot'. Nevertheless, she was prevailed upon to leave London the next day to visit an old friend, Mrs Cotton, at Sonning in Berkshire. Here she stayed for the rest of the month of March; and from here, after some further discouraging communication from Imlay, she wrote her last letter to him. This time, it was really the end of the road[18]:

You must do as you please with respect to the child. I could wish that it might be done soon, that my name may be no more mentioned to you. It is now finished. Convinced that you have neither regard nor friendship, I disdain to utter a reproach, though I have had reason to think that the 'forbearance' talked of has not been very delicate. It is, however, of no consequence. I am glad you are satisfied with your own conduct.

I now solemnly assure you, that this is an eternal farewell. Yet I flinch not from the duties which tie me to life.

That there is 'sophistry' on one side or other, is certain; but now it matters not on which. On my part it has not been a question of words. Yet your understanding or mine must be strangely warped, for what you term 'delicacy', appears to me to be exactly the contrary. I have no criterion for morality, and have thought in vain, if the sensations which lead you to follow an ancle or step, be the sacred foundation of principle and affection. Mine has been of a very different nature, or it would not have stood the brunt of your sarcasms.

The sentiment in me is still sacred. If there be any part of me that will survive the sense of my misfortunes, it is the purity of my affections. The impetuosity of your senses, may have led you to term mere animal desire, the source of principle; and it may give zest to some years to come. Whether you will always think so, I shall never know.

It is strange that, in spite of all you do, something like conviction forces me to believe that you are not what you appear to be.

For this letter alone, Mary may be forgiven much. Here, as the affair ended, she touched on the very heart of the matter and crystallised the essential incompatibility that had torn the lovers apart and very nearly torn them to pieces. Only in the last sentence did her vision waver, as she hesitated to expunge the ideal image of the man she had imagined Imlay to be. Perhaps one reason why she could see herself more clearly than she ever saw him was that her own ideals came closer to reality than his, even at their best, had ever done. Her 'criterion for morality' was not, like his, a dominance of sensation over reason—or, in reverse, of reason over sensation—but an equilibrium of thought and feeling: in her own words, of 'principle and affection'. Imlay could not see the connection between them; Mary could not envisage either in the absence of the other.

Godwin compared Mary's letters to Imlay with Goethe's *Werther*, perhaps hoping thereby to confer on them the respectability of a classic. But he was paying her no compliment, nor was the comparison a very perceptive one. *Werther*, first published in 1774, and in English translation in 1779, enjoyed an extravagant success as a novel of 'sensibility'. In fact, it displays all the worst excesses of *Stürm und Drang* romanticism. Whereas Werther's 'sentiment' was irrational and totally self-centred, Mary struggled heroically to reconcile reason and emotion: and this not simply in her own interest, but for the greater good of society. So her failure, when it came, was all the more devastating. Not only her personal life was shattered, but her philosophy. She had 'thought in vain', she declared in her final appeal to Imlay, if 'principle and affection' could not be built on a surer foundation than fleeting sensation.

Now, at last, she was seeing clearly that her needs lay elsewhere than within Imlay's limited perspective. Looking elsewhere, she could face the 'eternal farewell' and accept that there had been faults on both sides—'but now it matters not on which'. This was an extraordinary reversal of mood from the despairing cry: 'Let me see you once more!' In a few short weeks, it seems, Mary's incalculable resilience had been restored. Was she already aware that the future did after all hold some promise of happiness, and that 1796 was to prove a very different year from the one she had just—and only just—lived through? If so, the change must have taken place during her stay in Berkshire.

Up to the time of this final letter to Imlay, Mary still saw herself as the ill-used heroine of a broken romance. On 26th January she had written again to her former acquaintance Alexander Hamilton Rowan[19]. He had now returned to America and was operating a calico mill at Wilmington, Delaware, in partnership with Charles Wollstonecraft. Mary apologised for her long silence—'But what can I say to you?' She had nothing good to tell:

> I am unhappy—I have been treated with unkindness—and even cruelty, by the person from whom I had every reason to expect affection—I write to you with an agitated hand—I cannot be more explicit—

She asked for news of Charles. She had not written to him either, 'because I hate to explain myself'. Had Mary divulged her predicament to Eliza and Everina? There is no surviving correspondence to indicate it, but the sisters were already putting two and two together when she returned empty-handed from France the previous spring. Writing to Everina in August from Waterford, where she was staying with Mrs Blood, Eliza was in her usual state of gloom. Not only Mary but Charles was failing to offer her any better future than another stint as a governess. He had sent an 'unpleasant account of himself and America and it struck me *forcibly* that he does not wish us to go over'. She made no reference to Mary, who was then in Scandinavia.

Mary herself reiterated to Rowan her idea of settling in France—'because I wish to leave my little Girl there'; admitted that she had 'taken some desperate steps'; but assured him that she was now 'writing for independence'. This composure broke down in the postscript, however, when she confessed: 'for me there is nothing good in store, my heart is broken'. Yet at the same time she could take trouble to write a recommendation for a young man—'a clerk to Mr Imlay'—who was seeking a better situation in America. 'The state of public affairs here', she added, 'are not in a posture to assuage private sorrow'.

Nevertheless, the year had opened with some encouraging portents for Mary. Her *Letters from Sweden*, published by Johnson in January, received more favourable notice than any of her previous books—perhaps because it was less overtly 'political' in tone. It appeared, incidentally, with the name of Mary Wollstonecraft on the title page, although she was publicly known as Mrs Imlay and habitually used her 'married' name in private correspondence. In preparing the edition Mary added an Appendix to her eyewitness accounts of the countries she had visited, in which she apologised for the deficiencies in her observation at times when her attention was absorbed by 'private business and cares'. In retrospect, her impression of Sweden was summed up by the word 'poverty'; and of Denmark, by 'slavery'; though she acknowledged that conditions in both countries were steadily improving. She ended with a caution to those who sought to hasten the process of reform, based no doubt on her experiences not only in Scandinavia but in France:

> An ardent affection for the human race makes enthusiastic characters eager to produce alteration in laws and governments prematurely. To render them useful and perma-

nent, they must be the growth of each particular soil, and the gradual fruit of the ripening understanding of the nation, matured by time, not forced by an unnatural fermentation. This did not mean that Mary had renounced her radicalism. On the contrary, she still believed that the march of progress was as inevitable as the rising of the sun:

> And, to convince me that such a change is gaining ground, with accelerating pace, the view I have had of society, during my northern journey, would have been sufficient, had I not previously considered the grand causes which combine to carry mankind forward, and diminish the sum of human misery.

Subsequent editions of the *Letters* appeared in America, Holland, Portugal and Germany; and later English editions in 1802 and 1889.* The original edition inspired a poem from a Scottish professor of moral philosophy ('The Wanderer in Norway', by Thomas Brown); and the poet Southey wrote of the book that it 'made me in love with a cold climate'. But the crowning accolade came from William Godwin:

> The narrative of this voyage is before the world, and perhaps a book of travels that so irresistably seizes on the heart, never, in any other instance, found its way from the press. The occasional harshness and ruggedness of character, that diversify her Vindication of the Rights of Woman, here totally disappear. If ever there was a book calculated to make a man in love with its author, this appears to me to be the book.

This passage was written retrospectively as part of Godwin's *Memoirs* of Mary; but the impression he recorded obviously sprang from his first reading of the book, which he has noted took place at the end of January. By a happy coincidence (surely *this* meeting could not have been planned!), he had met the author in person only a week or two previously in the house of their mutual friend Mary Hays at No. 30 Kirby Street, Hatton Garden. He would be 'happy to meet Mrs Wollstonecraft', he wrote in accepting the invitation[20]. Godwin evidently did not concur in the myth of 'Mrs Imlay'; but this was not due to malice, for he continued that he had never 'said a word of harm' about Mary, although she 'has frequently amused herself with depreciating me'. But this time he found a personality very different from the one he remembered as an intellectual sparring-partner at Johnson's

---

* A facsimile edition was published by the Centaur Press in 1970.

dinner table. At their first meeting, it may be recalled, Mary and Godwin had parted 'mutually displeased with each other'. They could find little to agree on, and Mary had talked too much. Now, however, he observed in his *Memoirs*, 'Affliction had tempered her heart to a softness almost more than human'; she was, in short, 'improved'.

Godwin, too, was changed for the better. In 1791 he had been a little-known political journalist with radical sympathies. Now he was the famous author of *Political Justice*, hero of the treason trials of 1794, and one of the most sought-after 'lions' on the London scene. Mary on her side, no doubt, was also more favourably impressed. She could not have failed to contrast his sober sincerity and firmness of principle with the irresponsible dilettantism of Gilbert Imlay. Yet the ghost of Imlay still beckoned her to destruction. Though both Godwin and Mary were agreeably surprised by the other, the meeting passed off, in Godwin's phrase, 'with no particular effect'. For Mary it must have provided a pleasing respite in a scarcely tolerable existence, and she returned from the dinner party to her 'living tomb' in Finsbury Place. It was after this meeting that she wrote her 'heart-broken' letter to Rowan and her last, despairing appeal to Imlay.

The decisive change in her attitude came about during her month in Berkshire with Mrs Cotton. Their neighbour here was Sir Harry East of Hall Place, and Mary's acceptance in this social circle must have done something to restore her morale. But social life as such was never very important to her, and that alone was certainly not sufficient grounds for her almost miraculous recovery. Was she corresponding with Godwin during this period? There is no evidence of this. Yet it seems likely that some contact was maintained. Why else should Mary—who never acted without reason, if only the obscure reason of the heart—have moved suddenly, on her return to London, from Finsbury Place to Cumming Street, Pentonville, a step in the direction of Godwin's residence in Chalton Street, Somers Town? How else, when she unexpectedly encountered Gilbert Imlay riding his horse along the 'New Road' (Euston Road), could she have preserved her equanimity, so that she was able to walk with him for some distance without experiencing—in Godwin's words—'any oppressive emotion'? This was the final meeting with Imlay and a surprisingly uneventful one. There was neither vituperation, nor remorse, nor tears. Mary's attention, like Imlay's, was turned in another direction. He was no longer the romantic hero; she was no longer the tragic heroine. In March 1796, 'Mary Imlay' died of natural causes.

CHAPTER SIXTEEN

The Consummation of Compromise: 1796–1797

Mary's return to London at the end of March 1796 signalled the start of a new life. Her move from Finsbury Place to Cumming Street took her out of the Christie–Imlay orbit of international intrigue and back into the more placid English waters of Joseph Johnson and William Godwin. But it was not just a return to the past. Mary could never be the same again: Fanny Imlay was a living proof of that. Yet Mary could no longer regard herself in any sense as Imlay's wife. She was still adrift, though at least it could be said that her feet had touched bottom and the waters of despair had receded sufficiently for her to take a few faltering steps towards the shore. But in which direction, and to what country? She was still undecided and unwilling to put down roots in a city where she had endured so much unhappiness both before and after her disastrous sojourn in France. So her lodging at No. 1 Cumming Street was a furnished one, intended only as a temporary resting place, and her possessions from her former 'home' in Store Street remained at a repository. She had evidently abandoned a previous plan to return to Paris, and, according to Godwin, was contemplating a tour in Switzerland (which she had looked forward to visiting the previous summer with Imlay) or Italy. But one can imagine that her enthusiasm for either scheme was no more than half-hearted. Mary had had enough of foreign travel. What she longed for above all was security and stability; she knew from bitter experience that she could find these neither in isolation nor in casual attachments.

After two weeks' deliberation, she reached a decision. On 14th April her footsteps led her not to the continent of Europe but to Somers Town; a small move in physical terms, but one with resounding reverberations. Mary Wollstonecraft called on William Godwin at his house in Chalton Street: a breach of social etiquette which Godwin belittled in his *Memoirs* but which nevertheless must have startled him at the time. Godwin was in many ways the archetype of the ideal bachelor. Then forty years old, he lived alone in simple austerity, unperturbed by the notoriety of *Political Justice*, devoting himself to study and writing, and relaxing in the company of friends of both sexes. Kindly and tolerant, untrammelled by the storms of passion or the cares of family, he employed his freedom not in selfish pleasures or idle dissipation but to improve himself and benefit society; in short, a perfect 'enlightenment' man. This was the Godwin of 1795, riding high on the fame of *Political Justice*, at the apex of his career. But the truth about him was more complex than that.

All his life he had longed for esteem, as Mary had longed for affection. This was the difference between them, but also the bond. Like Mary, Godwin had his principles. Esteem was not to be won at the price of his conscience. Brought up according to the strict faith of his father, an East Anglian Calvanist minister—whom he despised as narrow-minded and intellectually complacent—William adopted the Sandemanian heresy whilst a student at Hoxton Academy and himself became a minister of that faith. By the time he was 24, influenced like Mary by Rousseau and the revolutionary *philosophes*, doubt had already set in and he resigned his ministry at Stowmarket in favour of a literary career in London. Poverty drove him to return briefly to a ministry at Beaconsfield, but Godwin could not live hypocritically: in 1787 he finally renounced his religion and declared himself an atheist. By this time he had published a biography (*Life of Chatham*, 1783), a volume of sermons (*Sketches from History*, 1784) and three novels (not surviving), none of which brought him much reward either in money or reputation. His first real break came in 1785 when he was taken on by the *New Annual Register*, edited by his former tutor Dr Kippis, to contribute the historical sections. Godwin's struggle to establish himself as an independent writer was as great as Mary's and only made more bearable by the fraternity of congenial 'cronies' which is rarely enjoyed by a woman. Godwin shared a house for a time with a publisher's indexer, James Marshal, who remained a lifelong friend; amongst other friends were the poet George Dyson and Thomas Holcroft, playwright and passionate radical.

At the same time, Godwin like Mary was concerned with the reform of education, even to the point of drawing up plans for his own school at Epsom[1]. He did not succeed in launching this venture, but the views expressed in his 'prospectus' showed a marked similarity to her 'thoughts on education':

> Modern education not only corrupts the heart of our youth, by the rigid slavery to which it condemns them, it also undermines their reason, by the unintelligible jargon with which they are overwhelmed . . . and the little attention that is given to accommodating their pursuits to their capacities.

He believed that virtue came naturally to children and that vices were implanted by society: 'The vices of youth spring not from nature, who is equally the kind and blameless mother of all her children; they derive from the defects of education'. Mary did not share this blithe optimism: she saw that virtue was an acquired rather than a natural characteristic of man, and must therefore be inculcated. But they concurred in believing that the best teaching was by example rather than precept.

In *Political Justice*, Godwin developed this theme to the point of attacking all systems of state education as mind-bending and coercive: 'No creature in human form will be expected to learn anything, but because he desires it and has some conception of its utility and value'. Mary took an opposite view on this. Knowing how girls were handicapped by the lack of even a defective education, she wanted a free and universal state system. According to Godwin, the girls were better off in their state of pristine ignorance. He maintained that at universities and other large centres of education the knowledge taught was 'a century behind the knowledge which exists among the unshackled and unprejudiced members of the same political community'. There was no doubt a good deal of truth in this, at a time when the universities and grammar schools were in a state of open corruption. But the dissenting academies had proved that reform was possible, without destroying the whole institution of schooling. It was Godwin's besetting weakness to wish to throw away the baby with the bathwater.

In comparing his development with that of Mary Wollstonecraft this striking difference emerges again and again. Where Godwin was the theorist, she was the practitioner. Mary wrote about education from her experience as a schoolmistress and a governess; Godwin only thought about it (although he did 'adopt' a young relative, Thomas Cooper, in order to supervise his education—with little more success than Mary achieved with her 'daughter' Ann). She wrote about the rights of men and the rights of women after suffering the absence of these rights in her own life and that of her family; she described the French Revolution from the very heart of its challenge and terror. When she departed from direct experience into the realm of speculation—as in her observations on marriage in the *Rights of Woman*—her theories were least convincing. The same could be said of Godwin's views on marriage as expressed in *Political Justice*. Both, at that stage, were arguing from theory rather than practice; and though here again Mary was the reformer and Godwin the abolitionist, both theories subsequently proved faulty.

Godwin's rejection of marriage might have been regarded as pathological if it had not been so naive. He was too reasonable a man to be a fanatic, and his most extreme views—which were later moderated—arose from ignorance rather than conviction. In fact, like Mary he was an idealist in his attitude to the relations of the sexes; but his ideal drove him to a different conclusion. Mary believed in marriage based on mutual affection and esteem; Godwin believed that mutual affection and esteem were incompatible with marriage. Both rejected an institution in which either partner was regarded as the 'property' of the other. But Godwin went much further in renouncing—and denouncing—any claim to the exclusive affection of another human being:

> It is absurd to expect that the inclinations and wishes of two human beings should coincide through any long period of time. To oblige them to act and to live together, is to subject them to some inevitable portion of thwarting, bickering and unhappiness. This cannot be otherwise, so long as man has failed to reach the standard of absolute perfection.

This, like so many of Godwin's assertions, was superficially true. But how would man ever come any nearer to 'perfection' without a process of trial and error? On the alleged comforts of matrimony, Godwin was equally scornful:

The Consummation of Compromise: 1796–7 293

> The supposition that I must have a companion for life, is the result of a complication of vices. It is the dictate of cowardice, and not of fortitude.

This statement had more validity, for a man who was determined to devote his life to the pursuit of knowledge and had the ability to do so. But Godwin claimed to speak for the good of society, and not just that of the exceptional individual. His offer to 'share' the woman of his choice (should he have one) with other men was even more unrealistic and must have caused some merriment in the coffee houses:

> ... it may happen that other men will feel for her the same preference that I do. This will create no difficulty. We may all enjoy her conversation, and we shall all be wise enough to consider the sensual intercourse a very trivial object.

This was indeed a blue-print for utopia; none the worse for that, but hardly to be taken seriously by 'practical' men. Godwin did, however, acknowledge the existence of 'brutal lust and depravity', and he was probably right in asserting that over-insistence on a puritanical monogamy only exacerbated this tendency: '... it really happens in this, as in other cases, that the positive laws which are made to restrain our vices irritate and multiply them'. Godwin's real objection to marriage was because it was part of the legal system he abhorred. Again, he had no time for reform of the law; he simply wanted to abolish it:

> Marriage is law, and the worst of all laws. Whatever our understandings may tell us of the person from whose connection we should derive the greatest improvement, of the worth of one woman, and the demerits of another, we are obliged to consider what is law, and not what is justice.
>
> Add to this that marriage is an affair of property, and the worst of all properties. So long as two human beings are forbidden by positive institution to follow the dictates of their own mind, prejudice is alive and vigorous.

But there was no law against good judgment, which was really all Godwin was asking for in the regulation of personal relations! This could be exercised inside or outside the law, and so his strictures were largely irrelevant to the abuses he wished to correct. He would have been better employed in devising a system of education which gave the same weight to emotional as to intellectual development. That his own education was deficient in this respect is shown in his fatuous statement that though the abolition of marriage might mean that children did not know their own fathers, and surnames would eventually become unnecessary, this would be 'of no importance'. He was apparently blind to the problems of identity, not to mention incest, that such anonymity would produce. Or perhaps there was no problem, since he also believed that when an 'optimum population' had been reached procreation would cease and men would miraculously become immortal in one generation! When this happy state was achieved, there would be 'no war, no crimes, no administration of justice as it is called, and no government'; and, one might add, no human race.

Meanwhile, however, he was prepared to ameliorate the imperfect human condition. In their passion for social justice Mary and Godwin were at one, but again they differed as to the method of achieving it. Godwin was more cautious than she in his attitude to the French Revolution. Though he had many friends among the English revolutionists in the Corresponding Society, he never actually joined the Society himself. He never visited France. His opposition to violence was more thoroughgoing than hers, extending as it did to all forms of 'coercion' even under the law. Like her, however, he acknowledged that in the circumstances of the French Revolution some violence was inevitable: 'the last struggles of expiring despotism . . ., if it had survived, would have produced mischiefs, scarcely less atrocious in the hour of their commission, and infinitely more calamitous by the length of their duration'. In England, however, he believed that if men were shown the better way they would voluntarily practise it; that the rich had only to see that it was actually in their interest to promote justice and they would give up their privileges. Godwin was not being so naive here as he may sound and in the long term may even be proved right. He saw that there were many disadvantages in being rich; that the esteem of the community was a more satisfying thing than the possession of material goods; and above all, that 'the progress of truth is the most powerful of all causes'. The pursuit of wealth, he believed, would be replaced by the love of liberty, equality, art and knowledge. Mary had expressed similar views in sketching her vision of a social order based on cooperation rather than oppression.

Compared with Mary, of course, Godwin had been little more

than an armchair strategist. From the comfort and safety of Somers Town, he could 'roar you like any sucking dove'. He admitted himself that he was 'bold and adventurous in opinion, but not in life'[2]. This could be seen either as a failure of courage or a virtuous prudence, when set against Mary's dauntless but often foolhardy activity. Yet he was not just a paper tiger. He saw himself, indeed, as something of a lion: 'It required some provocation and incitement to call me out; but there was the lion, or whatever combative animal may more justly prefigure me, sleeping, and that might be awakened'[3]. When the necessary provocation came, Godwin did not fail to respond. The 'treason trials' of 1794 were an affront to his every principle of political justice; and worse, the life and liberty of some of his own friends were at stake. The threat was in a real sense a personal one. If Thomas Holcroft could be on trial today, why not William Godwin tomorrow?

The twelve accused were held in gaol, in defiance of *habeas corpus*, from May to October and then charged at the Old Bailey with treasonable conspiracy. They included the founder of the London Corresponding Society, Thomas Hardy; Horne Tooke, lawyer and politician; Thomas Thelwall, possibly the only one among them who advocated violent revolution; and Holcroft, who had given himself up in order to expose the weakness of the government's case. Leading the prosecution was the Attorney-General, the infamous Sir John Scott. On 20th October the *Morning Chronicle* printed an Open Letter, 'Cursory Strictures on the Charge delivered by Lord Justice Eyre to the Grand Jury'. It was published anonymously, but amongst those in the know its authorship was not in doubt. Godwin argued that under English law the prosecution must prove the actual commission of a crime and not merely a treasonable intent. His letter was reprinted as a pamphlet and widely disseminated. In thus alerting public opinion to the threats to liberty implicit in the charges, Godwin's intervention undoubtedly influenced the verdict. All the accused were acquitted. Godwin had saved them from transportation (the fate of their Scottish colleagues in the convention trials the previous year) if not from death. The gentle lion had roared to some purpose.

Godwin's attack on the treason trials was akin to Mary's defence of Dr Price in her reply to Edmund Burke, although the risks to his own safety were greater. Had the verdict gone another way he might well have been indicted too. *Political Justice* had already put him under suspicion, and it was only Pitt's mistaken belief that working men would not spend three guineas on a book (in fact they clubbed together to buy it) that had saved him from the fate of Tom Paine. Oddly enough, Dr Price was a common factor in the 'radicalisation' of both Mary and Godwin (who had started his political life as a Tory). Unknown to each other, they may both have been present at the famous sermon to the Revolution Society in November 1789. Godwin was certainly there; and he was subsequently concerned with the publication of Paine's *Rights of Man*, which in turn sowed the seeds of his own major work.

Godwin started to write *Political Justice* in September 1791, and he gave up his post with the *New Annual Register* and other literary work in order to complete the book in sixteen months. The gamble paid off handsomely, for he received a generous advance and a total sum of one thousand guineas for the manuscript from his publisher, Robinson. One can only wonder at this extraordinary act of faith, for as Godwin observed in his preface he was addressing a public that was 'panic struck' by the doctrines he was advancing in the book: 'All the prejudices of the human mind are in arms against it'. Nor did he trim his sails to the wind. *Political Justice* (1793) is a far more revolutionary manifesto than either Paine's *Rights of Man* or Mary's *Rights of Men*. Perhaps this was not immediately recognised because he chose to wage his revolution with the weapons of reason and persuasion rather than the more conventional blood-and-thunder of the left. Or perhaps it was regarded as no more than a visionary's pipe-dream, with no practical application and therefore not to be taken seriously. For despite its rational basis, *Political Justice* is a work of faith rather than politics. Its validity rests on a view of human nature that with hindsight appears naive and which even in the author's own day was never verified by any demonstrable experience. Nevertheless, the book was an enormous success amongst the intelligentsia and the quiet philosopher was suddenly the most sought-after man in London. As Hazlitt put it: 'He blazed as a sun in the firmament of reputation . . . wherever liberty, truth, justice was the theme, his name was not far off'.

Godwin's head was in no way turned by this success. He continued on his sober way, following up *Political Justice* with an even more successful novel. This book, *Caleb Williams* (1794), established Godwin's reputation with a far wider public. Editions were published in America, France and Germany; and the novel was made into a popular play under the title *The Iron Chest*. By modern standards the story is long-winded and rambling and the characters unconvincing, but the great merit of *Caleb Williams*, which lifted it out of its own age and gives it a timeless quality, is the nobility of its hero. Caleb represented, and represents, the helplessness of the good man in a corrupt society: 'But of what use are talents and sentiments in the corrupt wilderness of human society?' he cried after the death of his master, Falkland. 'It is a rank and rotten soil, from which every finer shrub draws poison as it grows'. This was a sentiment that found many echoes; not least in the heart of Mary Wollstonecraft. She must have been a little surprised, on her return from France, to find what had happened to Godwin in her absence. Her former shabby acquaintance at Joseph Johnson's, with a head too large for his body and a nose too long for his face—the ex-minister who continued to look the part long after he had ceased to play it—was suddenly transformed into the darling of progressive society. What was even more remarkable, on all the evidence he deserved his place. Was there after all one man in England who was worthy of her regard? On 14th April 1796, she set off to find out.

The fateful visit evidently gave pleasure to both parties. 'From that time', Godwin observed in his *Memoirs,* 'our intimacy increased, by regular, but almost imperceptible degrees'. It was more odd, perhaps, that during the same month Godwin was visited by Imlay and returned the visit[4]. Was Mary the object of their mutual interest? They could have had little else in common. Godwin was a prudent man and may have wished to verify in person that Mary was not in law the wife of Gilbert Imlay. At all events, the outcome was evidently an 'all clear' for him to pursue his advances. On 22nd April he recorded that he entertained 'a party of twelve persons ... Amongst this party were Dr Parr and his two daughters, Mr and Mrs Mackintosh, Mr Holcroft, Mrs Wollstonecraft and Mrs Inchbald'. Dr Parr was an old friend with whom Godwin frequently stayed at his Warwickshire vicarage; James Mackintosh, like Mary, had attacked Burke's attitude to the French Revolution though he later changed sides.

Godwin consistently described Mary as 'Mrs Wollstonecraft', though she was still publicly known as Mrs Imlay. After she came back to London from Berkshire Mary Hays had informed him that 'Mrs Imlay is returned ... I am sorry to add, her health appears in a still more declining state. It does not signify what is the cause, but her heart, I think, is broken'. The fictitious 'Mrs Imlay' was no doubt a form of propriety to cover the inconvenient existence of Fanny Imlay. But Godwin cared little for propriety, and Mary's bid for freedom, unsuccessful though it had proved, was no doubt a mark in her favour.

For despite his antipathy to marriage, Godwin was no misogynist. He enjoyed female company and some of his best friends were women. Mary Hays had won his regard by requesting a copy of *Political Justice* from him, at the same time praising the 'originality, force and genius' of *Caleb Williams*[5]. An author of some repute in her own right, she had expressed a similar admiration for Mary's *Rights of Woman*—'a work full of truth and genius'—and remained a loyal friend, even though Mary had commented unfavourably on her own book of essays which she had submitted to Joseph Johnson in November 1792. This piece of constructive criticism is worth quoting as a guide to young authors[6]:

> ... I do not approve of your preface—and I will tell you why. If your work should deserve attention, it is a blur on the very face of it. Disadvantages of education, etc., ought, in my opinion, never to be pleaded with the public in excuse for defects of any importance, because if the writer has not sufficient strength of mind to overcome the common difficulties which lie in his way, nature seems to command him, with a very audible voice, to leave the task of instructing to those who can. This kind of vain humility has ever disgusted me—and I should say to an author who humbly sued for forbearance, If you have not a tolerably good opinion of your own production, why intrude it on the public? We have plenty of bad books already, that have just gasped for breath and died.

If the young author happened to be a woman, a further warning was needed:

> An author, especially a woman, should be cautious lest she too hastily swallows the crude praises which partial friend and polite acquaintance bestow when the supplicating eye looks for

them. In short, it requires great resolution to try rather to be useful than to please ... Indeed, the preface, and even the pamphlet, is too full of yourself ... till a work strongly interests the public true modesty should keep the author in the background—for it is only about the character and life of a *good* author that curiosity is active—a blossom is but a blossom.

The essays were published in 1793 and Mary Hays later wrote a successful novel, *Emma Courtney*, as well as compiling a *Female Biography* of eminent women.

Godwin, in every other respect a modest and diffident man, had a proper pride in his intellectual brilliance and basked in the admiration of women who were discerning enough to appreciate it. His objections to marriage, in truth, were largely determined by circumstance. In his youth he had been too poor to contemplate the burden of a family. 'He was very averse to marriage', his daughter Mary Shelley wrote of him. 'Poverty was a strong argument against it'[7]. When circumstances became more favourable, so did Godwin's attitude. But his uncompromising standards, and his public disparagement of the institution, strictly limited his choices. Mary Wollstonecraft, with a corresponding attachment to freedom rooted in principle, provided the ideal complement to his views although he did not yet see her in this light. In April 1796, she still had three serious rivals. Mary Hays was not one of these. Her admiration for both Godwin and Mary was genuinely disinterested; her own heart was engaged elsewhere. For Mrs Inchbald, however, Godwin cherished a tender affection. Elizabeth Inchbald was as good as she was charming. Left, like Mary, with a child to support, she spurned the temptation of a masculine 'protector' and lived in a state of spartan independence. Her dramatic novel *A Simple Story* (1791)—which Godwin read and criticised in manuscript—was a popular success, without recourse to the Gothic excesses of Mrs Radcliffe's *Romance of the Forest* published the same year. Mrs Inchbald enjoyed Godwin's company along with that of Holcroft, Horne Tooke and other radical thinkers who accepted her as an equal; but she singled him out no more than the rest.

A more ardent relationship, at least on his side, was his friendship with Mrs Maria Reveley, another intelligent and attractive member of his circle. But Mrs Reveley was happily married to a successful architect and had no intention of jeopardising her security by compromising herself with an anarchist philosopher. According to Godwin's biographer Woodcock, Mr Reveley became jealous and discouraged Godwin's attentions. This left him with the only unmarried woman in whom he took any serious interest, Amelia Alderson. The daughter of Godwin's old Norwich friend, Dr Alderson, Amelia had many things going in her favour. Apart from her political sympathies with Godwin, she was endowed with a lively charm and was diversely talented in music, painting and writing. On her frequent visits to London she was chaperoned by Mrs Inchbald. who was sufficiently disturbed to remark: 'now you are come, Mr Godwin never comes near me'[8]. Godwin must really have been infatuated, for he was said by Hazlitt to have discarded his sober minister's dress in favour of 'a green coat, crimson waistcoat and pointed red morocco shoes' in order to impress her. Unfortunately, however, Amelia did not take the philosopher as seriously as he deemed proper. She was in any case considerably younger than he and was more prone to flirtation than to serious thoughts of matrimony.

Thus, though Godwin had a highly satisfactory social circle there was little prospect of his achieving a closer bond with any of his existing acquaintances; and he had evidently reached a stage when such a bond was becoming necessary to him, for all his disclaimers about the value of personal affections. So there was no serious obstacle to the progress of his relationship with Mary Wollstonecraft; a progress which developed astonishingly smoothly and which he described himself as 'friendship melting into love'. Whether the melting process was facilitated by a greater warmth on one side than the other we can only guess. Godwin in his *Memoirs* was scrupulously impartial—and not altogether convincing:

> The partiality we conceived for each other, was in that mode, which I have always regarded as the purest and most refined style of love. It grew with equal advances in the mind of each. It would have been impossible for the most minute observer to have said who was before, and who was after. One sex did not take the priority which long-established custom has awarded it, nor the other overstep that delicacy which is so severely imposed. I am not conscious that either party can assume to have been the agent or the patient, the toil-spreader or the prey, in

The Consummation of Compromise: 1796–7   301

the affair.

In the light of their respective characters and previous behaviour, there is little doubt that the initiative came from Mary. She was rapidly recovering her former zest for life and renewing her old enthusiasms, both professional and personal. She had gone back to her employment with Joseph Johnson (that most magnanimous of men!), reviewing Mrs Inchbald's *Nature and Art* in the May issue of the *Analytical Review* and Fanny Burney's *Camilla* in August. At a deeper level, her imagination was working on the raw material of her own tragic experiences which were to be transmuted into fiction.

During the month of July Godwin was away in Norfolk visiting his mother—with whom he maintained an affectionate relationship—and the friendship was put to its first test of absence. Both parties, perhaps, were surprised to find how much they missed each other. Mary, in particular, must have dreaded a return to that empty desolation which had driven her to attempted suicide the previous year. Godwin, we may suppose, was restless and uneasy. The even tenor of his ways had already been shaken to the point of no return; never again could he be content with the self-imposed limits of his bachelor existence. But could he successfully pit himself against the mighty Wollstonecraft? How would he compare with that renowned lady-killer, Gilbert Imlay? Godwin was not at all sure yet that he wanted to commit himself to Mary. But he had to admit that he was pretty nearly hooked. He had even fallen so low as to address some sentimental verses to her. Acknowledging these on 1st July, just before he went away, Mary wrote in a teasing vein. Don't rhapsodise about my perfections, she said in effect, but tell me what your own feelings are: 'give me a bird's eye view of your heart'[9]. This Godwin scarcely knew himself, as she was well aware: 'I have observed that you compliment without rhyme or reason, when you are almost at a loss what to say'.

From the haven of his mother's house at Norwich, Godwin made a last attempt to evade his fate—by proposing to Amelia Alderson! At least, his diary entry 'propose to Alderson' has been assumed to mean that he asked her father for her hand. If this is so, his suit was refused—yet he continued to see Miss Alderson after his return to London. At the same time, he was writing to Mary in terms of such warmth as to make the proposal theory a little far-fetched, unless the philosopher in him had completely given way to the courtier; as witness his letter of 13th July:

> Now, I take all my Gods to witness—do you know how many they are?—but I detest & obescrate them all—that your company infinitely delights me, that I love your imagination, your delicate epicurism, the malicious leer of your eye, in short, every thing that constitutes the bewitching tout ensemble of the celebrated Mary. But to write!
>
> Alas, I have no talent, for I have no subject. Shall I write a love letter? May Lucifer fly away with me, if I do! No, when I make love, it shall be with the eloquent tones of my voice, with dying accents, with speaking glances (through the glass of my spectacles), with all the witching of that irresistible, universal passion. Curse on the mechanical, icy medium of pen & paper. When I make love, it shall be in a storm, as Jupiter made love to Semele, & turned her at once to a cinder. Do these menaces terrify you?

There was perhaps smoke rather than fire in this epistle, which owed more to literature than to life, though Godwin assured Mary that he would be back in London in a week's time, 'to depart no more'. This was what she wanted to hear, and she admitted her pleasure when she wrote back on 21st July; but she was also piqued because he did not call on her immediately he returned. During his absence she had moved her lodging again, to No. 16 Judd Place West—which was even nearer to Chalton Street. This time her rooms were unfurnished, and she brought her own furniture out of store. Mary was now reconciled to staying in England—'probably without exactly knowing why this change had taken place in her mind', Godwin ingenuously observed. Yet the past still threatened to engulf her in waves of black despair. If her experience with Imlay had not hardened her heart—no power on earth could do that—at least it had sharpened her defences. She was now more ready to strike at the first whiff of danger, and she scented this in Godwin's continued attentions to Amelia Alderson. Early in August she started a deliberate campaign to thwart this relationship. She knew that if there was one thing the philosopher could not stand it was to be laughed at, and in her notes of 4th and 6th August she seems to be deliberately taunting him with his ineffectiveness as a lover. She had it from Miss Alderson's own lips that he, Godwin, was 'ready to devour her—in your little parlour', she teased him; immediately destroying this carnivorous image by further informing him that 'Miss Alderson was wondering, this morning whether you *ever* kissed a maiden fair'. Here, with uncharacteristic guile, she was killing two birds with one well-directed stone—aimed at discrediting Amelia and rousing William to the point of decision. Few men could resist such a challenge, and Godwin was no exception.

From subsequent correspondence, it is evident that on Saturday 13th August Godwin made an unequivocal declaration of passion to Mary. She, in her direct way, assumed that he would immediately suit his actions to his words. What passed between them during the next few days was painful and humiliating for both parties; yet paradoxically, this common acknowledgment of 'mortification' served to weld them more closely together. Godwin explained the situation in his letter of 17th August:

> I swear to you that I told you nothing but the strict & literal truth, when I described to you the manner in which you set my imagination on fire on Saturday. For six & thirty hours I could think of nothing else. I longed inexpressibly to have you in my arms. Why did not I come to you? I am a fool. I feared still that I might be deceiving myself as to your feeling, & that I was feeding my mind with groundless presumptions. I determined to suffer the point to arrive at its own denouement. I was not aware, that the fervour of my imagination was exhausting itself. Yet this, I believe, is no uncommon case.

This was in answer to Mary's letter of the same date. She had waited in vain for a lover who never showed up and then had gone to meet one who was reluctant to receive her:

> I have not lately passed so painful a night as the last. I feel that I cannot speak clearly on the subject to you, let me then briefly explain myself now I am alone. Yet, struggling as I have been a long time to attain peace of mind (or apathy) I am afraid to trace emotions to their source, which border on agony.
>
> Is it not sufficient to tell you that I am thoroughly out of humour with myself? Mortified and humbled, I scarcely know why—still, despising false delicacy I almost fear that I have lost sight of the true. Could a wish have transported me to France or Italy, last night, I should have caught up my Fanny and been off in a twinkle, though convinced that it is my mind, not the place, which requires changing ...

I would not be unjust for the world—I can only say that you appear to me to have acted injudiciously; and that full of your own feelings, little as I comprehend them, you forgot mine—or do not understand my character ...

Mary knew that another experience such as she had had with Imlay would kill her. She could not bear to have her love aroused again, only to be dashed with indifference. But unlike Imlay, Godwin both understood her character and laboured to meet her needs. He assured her that in no way had she lost sight of true delicacy: 'I see nothing in you but what I respect & adore'. 'I know the acuteness of your feelings', he continued, '& there is perhaps nothing upon earth that would give me so pungent a remorse, as to add to your unhappiness'. Godwin's honest nature, however, compelled him to admit that 'I find in you one fault, & but one':

You have the feelings of nature, & you have the honesty to avow them. In all this you do well. I am sure you do. But do not let them tyrannise over you. Estimate every thing at its just value. It is best that we should be friends in every sense of the word; but in the mean time let us be friends.

Suffer me to see you. Let us leave every thing else to its own course. My imagination is not dead, I suppose, though it sleeps.

Even at this late stage, Godwin was still reluctant to commit himself to more than friendship with any woman. On the very brink of a deeper relationship, he had drawn back. No wonder Mary was upset. Yet it was no simple decision. He was fighting for what he conceived to be his own highest principles; at the same time he was uncomfortably aware that stronger forces than 'reason' could take possession of him. Above all, he did not want to lose Mary. 'Send me word that I may call on you in a day or two', he finally appealed: 'Do you not see, while I exhort you to be a philosopher, how painfully acute are my own feelings? I need some soothing, though I cannot ask it from you'.

The appeal fell, of course, on fertile ground. Reassured that his apparent coldness was not due to indifference, Mary was at once his friend again: 'I like your last—may I call it *love* letter? better than the first', she wrote back the same day:

...it has calmed my mind—a mind that had been painfully active all the morning, haunted by old sorrows that seemed to come forward with new force to sharpen the present anguish—Well! well—it is almost gone—I mean all my unreasonable fears—and a whole train of tormenters, which you have routed—I can scarcely describe to you their ugly shapes so quickly do they vanish—and let them go, we will not bring them back by talking of them. You may see me when you please.

Even before he received this letter, Godwin had perceived what a fool he had been to doubt either her love or his own and had dashed off a yet more repentant note:

Intent upon an idea I had formed in my own mind of furtive pleasure, I was altogether stupid & without intelligence as to your plan of staying, which it was morally impossible should not have given life to the dead.

Perhaps you will not believe that I could have been so destitute of understanding. It seems indeed incredible...

I have now only left to apologise for my absurdity, which I do even with self-abhorrence. The mistake being detected, it is for you to decide whether it is too late to repair it.

It did not take long for Mary to decide. On 21st August Godwin was able to record in his diary: 'chez moi, toute'. The union of Mary and Godwin had been consummated.

This 'friendship melting into love' took its course with a remarkable lack of strain on either side. The philosopher adapted himself to his new role with an ease that must have surprised himself. He discovered that his commitment to Mary, far from compromising his principles, actually strengthened them with the added dimension of personal experience. This was because her vision of the good society broadly coincided with his own, and there was no real conflict of interest between them. He could, therefore, give free rein to his natural capacity for affection, hitherto suppressed in the interests of 'reason', without destroying the foundations of his rational judgment. 'I had never loved till now', he wrote in his *Memoirs*, 'or, at least, had never nourished a passion to the same growth, or met with an object so consummately worthy'. In making this adjustment, he had of course performed a complete *volte-face* from his denigration of the personal affections in *Political Justice*—but that had always been the weakest part of his case. He had not withdrawn his objections to marriage, and the need did not arise since Mary was perfectly willing to accept him as a lover without binding him as a husband. There was at this time no question of marriage between them. Godwin's natural reticence, and Mary's wish to avoid further notoriety, kept their relationship secret from even their closest friends. That which is 'of all things most sacredly private', declared Godwin, should not be required 'to blow a trumpet before it, and to record the moment when it has arrived at its climax'. So Mary remained 'Mrs Imlay' in the eyes of the world; and Godwin remained the most confirmed bachelor in England. Each partner maintained a separate establishment and continued to work independently. Godwin must indeed have counted himself a lucky man, enjoying the best of both worlds—intellectual independence and emotional surrender—with none of the drawbacks that may mar either state in isolation from the other.

What of Mary? Some inkling of her situation is given in a letter she wrote to Archibald Hamilton Rowan at Wilmington, Delaware, on 12th September[10]:

> ...I feel an inclination to inform you of the present state of my mind. It is calmer. I have been used ill; and very wretched has the cruellest of disappointments, that of discovering I was deceived by a person in whom I trusted with all the confidence of the most perfect esteem, made me.

She sent this letter via Godwin's young cousin, Thomas Cooper, who was just then emigrating and for whom she wished to provide some introductions. At the same time she dropped a hint which was probably not lost on Rowan:

> The bearer of this, Mr Cooper, is a very ingenious young man, for whom an intimate friend of mine, Mr Godwin, has a particular affection. By showing him any attention you would oblige Mr G. as well as myself...

It has been argued that Mary did not really love Godwin at all and only accepted him to fill the aching void created by Imlay's desertion; that he was a poor substitute for Imlay but the best she could get; or even that for Mary Wollstonecraft any man was better than none. There was some truth in all these assertions, though not much. It was inevitable that Imlay, as the first lover, should have made the deepest impression on her sensibilities. But Godwin was not a substitute for anybody: he was in every respect superior to Imlay and superior to the majority of his peers. He won the admiration of many women of distinction, as Mary had won the admiration of many men. It is true that Mary was more susceptible, and more passionate, than he; but she was just as critical, and almost as fastidious. She had turned away several suitors before succumbing to the spurious charms of Imlay. She was still turning them away, and as late as December 1796 it was being rumoured that she was to marry the painter John Opie, who had recently divorced his runaway wife. Joseph Farington recorded in his diary on 11th November:

> I told Opie it had been reputed that he was going to be married to Mrs Wolstencraft (sic), but that could not be as she is already married to Mr Imlay an American. He replied that would not have been an obstacle if he had had any such intention, as Mrs Wollstencraft had herself informed him that she never was married to Imlay, but lived under his protection as an American to avoid a prison and had a Child by him.

On 18th December Amelia Alderson repeated the same rumour to Mary[11]:

> I hear in a letter received from town, that you are to marry Opie. I mean *Law willing*—that he would be most happy to marry you, I firmly believe; but I doubt yr willingness to marry *him*—I wish I did *not* for many reasons, all of which, if I explained them you would find affectionate towards you.

Miss Alderson was no doubt worried by Mary's anomalous social position and would like to have seen it regularised, even if this meant admitting that her previous 'marriage' was a fiction. Like Mary Hays, Amelia had become devoted to Mary since their first introduction by Godwin the previous summer. She had expressed something of this feeling in a letter dated 28th August[12]:

> I remember the time when my desire of seeing you was repress'd by fear—but as soon as I read your letters from Norway the cold awe which the philosopher had excited was lost in the tender sympathy call'd forth by the *woman* ... I *saw* you, & you are one of the few objects of my curiosity who in gratifying have not disappointed it also—You & the *Lakes of Cumberland* have exceeded my expectations.

A flattering unction, indeed! As so often happened, Mary's personal charm melted all criticism. That there was a great tenderness from the start in her relationship with Godwin is shown in the notes they exchanged on 22nd August immediately after its consummation. Mary wrote:

> I am sometimes painfully humble.—Write me, but a line,

just to assure me, that you have been thinking of me with affection, now and then—Since we parted—

To which Godwin replied:

Humble! for heaven's sake, be proud, be arrogant! You are — but I cannot tell what you are. I cannot yet find the circumstance about you that allies you to the frailty of our nature. I will hunt it out.

Since Mary and Godwin lived separately, only visiting each other surreptitiously in the evenings, they continued to communicate by means of letter. Compared with the *Letters to Imlay*, the note is pitched in a minor key. Stresses do emerge from time to time, but they are the routine stresses of daily life rather than the *angst* of the soul in torment. This does not make them any the less readable. They may even give a more accurate picture of Mary's real character than the distortions which emerged under the pressure of excessive emotion. For the first time, she achieved a perfect equilibrium. Her 'wayward heart' was at last stabilised by the certainty of an inflowing affection as great as that which poured out. 'I am glad that you force me to love you more and more', she wrote on 30th September, 'in spite of my fear of being pierced to the heart by every one on whom I rest my mighty stock of affection. Your tenderness was considerate, as well as kind . . .' Nor was this 'affection' in any way inferior to the romantic raptures she had experienced—or imagined—with Imlay. She summed up the difference herself, on 4th October:

I would describe one of those moments, when the senses are exactly tuned by the rising tenderness of the heart, and according reason entices you to live in the present moment, regardless of the past or future—It is not rapture.—It is a sublime tranquillity.

With this statement Mary renounced her former romanticism—which lives always in the past or future because the present is unbearable—and accepted the given reality. It marked the consummation not only of love, but of compromise.

One proof of this was her acceptance of criticism from Godwin. When Imlay had criticised her she had flown off the handle or had sought to justify herself, because her hold on his affections was in any case precarious. She knew that when Godwin criticised her this did not mark a diminution of affection, but rather expressed his concern that she should achieve the best she was capable of. She acknowledged the force of his criticisms, on 4th September:

> I allude to what you remarked, relative to my manner of writing—that there was a radical defect in it—a worm in the bud—&c. What is to be done, I must either disregard your opinion, think it unjust, or throw down my pen in despair; and that would be tantamount to resigning existence; for at fifteen I resolved never to marry for interested motives, or to endure a life of dependence.

Mary could say this because she knew that Godwin would take her seriously and not scoff at her cherished independence, but love her all the more for it. She could even acknowledge to him that her conduct had not always been above reproach:

> I know that many of my cares have been the natural consequence of what, nine out of ten would (have) termed folly—yet I cannot coincide in the opinion, without feeling a contempt for mankind. In short, I must reckon on doing some good, and getting the money I want, by my writings, or go to sleep for ever.

Mary could say this because she knew that Godwin was the tenth man, who could see something divine in her folly and yet not divest her of her necessary humanity. For this reason too, she could also boast a little:

> And, for I would wish you to see my heart and mind just as it appears to myself, without drawing any veil of affected humility over it, though this whole letter is a proof of painful diffidence, I am compelled to think that there is something in my writings more valuable, than in the products of some people on whom you bestow warm elogiums—I mean more mind—denominate it as you will—more of the observations of my own senses, more of the combining of my own imagination—the effusions of my own feelings and passions than the cold workings of the brain on the materials procured by the senses and imagination of other writers—

Mary was always her own best critic, because she knew that nothing she wrote—however extravagant it might appear—was written without the best of all reasons for committing thoughts to paper: that she had felt it thus herself. What she felt for Godwin she recorded with scrupulous honesty, and it leaves little doubt that she was as deeply in love with him as she had ever been with

Imlay: 'When the heart and reason accord', she wrote on 13th September, 'there is no flying from voluptuous sensations, I find, do what a woman can—Can a philosopher do more?' Mary was so sure of herself now that she could even afford to speak lightly of her emotions, a thing she had never dared to do in the past.

Although there was now the certainty of a mutual and equal affection for both Mary and Godwin, their semi-detached manner of living brought disadvantages as well as blessings. If their secret was to remain a secret, their movements must be carefully circumscribed. 'You once talked of giving me one of your keys', Mary wrote on 30th September. 'I then could admit myself without tying you down to an hour, which I cannot always punctually observe in the character of a woman, unless I tacked that of a wife to it'. (Was this a hint that Mary at least was not averse to a more conventional union?) There was the further embarrassment of having to deceive their friends about their true relationship. Even as Mary was writing this letter she was forced to conceal it: 'Miss Hays entering, in the midst of the last sentence, I hastily laid my letter aside, without finishing, and have lost the remain—Is it sunk in the quicksand of Love?'

Mary Hays was probably less easily deceived than some of Godwin's cronies, who were more interested in his political opinions than his private life. But Miss Hays, with a heart as unrequited as Mary's had been in the past, was sensitive to every emotional nuance. She knew there was something between Mary and Godwin, and Mary knew that she knew. As early as 10th September she was warning Godwin of this:

> I am almost afraid on reflection that an indistinct intuition on our affection produced the effect on Miss H that distresses me—She has owned to me that she cannot endure to see others enjoy the mutual affection from which she is debarred—I will write a kind note to her today to ease my conscience, for when I am happy myself, I am made up of milk and honey, I would fain make everybody else so—

Deception was always irksome to Mary, and doubly so when she was eager to share her newly found happiness, not to conceal it as something shameful. In an undated letter to Mary Hays, she dropped the broadest possible hint short of a full revelation[13]:

> I have not called on you, it is true, or sent the book; but I have still the same regard for you, and was merely prevented by rain,

business and engagements. Mr Godwin has been ill, and as I am a tolerable nurse, and he in a little want of one, I have frequently been with him, as well to amuse as to see that the things proper for him were got.

Miss Hays was also a friend of Godwin's, and Mary was careful to ensure that she did not burst in on them uninvited: 'He is much better, but I believe had rather not see any company for a few days'. For good measure, she added that 'Mrs Christie is also in town, only for two or three days and I have had business to do for her—Thus you have a full and true account of my moments'. Since in her letter to Godwin of 30th September, Mary spoke of going 'into the city round by Finsbury Square' (the London home of the Christies) this letter probably belongs to the same period. A postscript asked Miss Hays to send her 'the Monk' when she has finished it. This presumably refers to Matthew Lewis's notorious Gothic novel of that name, first published in England in 1795.

Mary was evidently using Miss Hays as a book critic for the *Analytical Review*. In a later letter, probably written towards the end of the year or early in 1797, she sent her *A Gossip's Story** to review, at the same time offering some sound advice[14]:

In reviewing, will you pardon me? you seem to run into an error which I have laboured to cure in myself: you allude to things in the work which can only be understood by those who have read it, instead of, by a short summary of the contents, or an account of the incident on which the interest turns, enabling a person to have a clear idea of a book, which they have never heard of before.

She also referred to Mary Hays' own 'novel'—presumably *Emma Courtney*, published in 1797—which she had given another friend to read: 'She had read your novel, and was *very much* pleased with the *main* story; but did not like the conclusion'. This friend was Mrs Mary ('Perdita') Robinson, a former actress and mistress of the Prince of Wales, who had won her way back to respectability on her personal and literary merits. Mary arranged for Miss Hays to visit her; Mrs Robinson's hospitality was also extended to little Fanny, as Mary acknowledged in an undated letter which she signed 'Mary Imlay'[15]:

As you were so obliging as to offer to send the carriage for little *Fannikin*, I promised to call for her. In the evening, if one of your servants will put Marguerite in her way, she and Fanny

---
* by Jane West, published in 1797.

may return at an early house (sic). You will smile at having so much of the womanish mother in me; but there is a little philosophy in it, *entre nous*; for I like to rouse her infant faculties by strong impressions.

It is interesting to note that as Mary had progressed from education into politics, so now she was moving away from politics and towards the arts. Godwin shared these broad interests, and it was a tribute to the maturity of both parties that they could maintain so many independent friendships without jeopardising their own special relationship. While Godwin continued his association not only with Mary Hays but also with Mrs Inchbald and Amelia Alderson, Mary was receiving visits from the poet Dyson and the painter Opie. She also counted amongst her friends the actress Sarah Siddons and novelist Eliza Fenwick. On 28th September Mary was requesting Godwin to 'drink tea with M. Hays'; on 3rd November she observed: 'Opie called this morning—But you are the man—Till we meet joy be with thee—'. Mary was at this time entertaining her friend Mrs Cotton, and finding the visit something of a strain: 'She talks of a *few* days. Mon Dieu! Heaven and Earth!' Here was another drawback to a clandestine relationship: it must endure the invasion of privacy, with no compensating recognition.

Social acceptance was of no great importance to Mary, but these continued, minor irritants were beginning to fray at her nerves. Almost imperceptibly at first, she was edging Godwin towards an unconditional commitment. Yet she sensed that, for all their present happiness, he was not yet ready for this: 'I was endeavouring to discover last night', she wrote on 7th October, 'what it is in me, of which you are afraid. I was hurt at perceiving that you were—but no more of this—mine is a sick heart; and in a life, like this, the fortitude of patience is the most difficult to acquire'. Mary's love for Godwin was sufficiently secure for her to accept the blame herself for her sense of dissatisfaction. But was she hinting here that spontaneous feeling alone was not enough to maintain her precarious stability? The following month, on 10th November, she reverted to her 'wifely' role: 'I send you your household linen—.I am not sure that I did not feel a sensation of pleasure at thus acting the part of a wife, though you have so little respect for the character'. She did not, it will be noticed, say '*we* have so little respect . . .'

Godwin blandly ignored all such innuendo. He was still convinced they had chosen the better way. But could such an ambiguous situation really continue indefinitely? For Godwin, it probably could. Not so for Mary. She disliked ambiguity, whether in social or personal matters, and she found her own communications with Godwin impaired by the restraints of secrecy: 'I wish you would always take my ye for a ye; and my nay for a nay', she wrote on 19th November. 'It torments me to be obliged to guess, or guard against, false interpretations—and, while I am wishing, I will add another—that you could distinguish between jest and earnest, to express myself elegantly.' It was an ominous sign that Mary could no longer take Godwin's teasing criticism in the spirit in which it was given. She was beginning to take herself over-seriously again. 'I never play with edged tools,' she declared now, 'for when I am really hurt or angry I am dreadfully serious'. To which Godwin replied, not unreasonably: 'How can I always distinguish between your jest & earnest, & know when your satire means too much & when it means nothing?' This had been Imlay's problem too, and he had soon lost patience with it. The difference between the two men was never more clearly demonstrated than in Godwin's modest addendum: 'But I will try'.

Mary was not altogether soothed, but her touchiness was partly explained by poor health. During late November and December she was plagued by a troublesome cough and a general lowness of spirits. She struggled not to feel resentment that Godwin was going out and enjoying himself without her, even though this arrangement had been part of their compact. When she did manage to go to the theatre on 7th December it was evidently with a woman friend—'I was a fool not to ask Opie to go with me', she remarked, chiding Godwin for the poor seats he had obtained for them: 'in a corner, in the third row, quite as bad as the Gallery'. It rankled that she had observed Godwin with Mrs Inchbald, 'at your ease enjoying yourselves'. This rift, trivial as it was, seems to have had a disproportionate effect on their relationship. Godwin was baffled by Mary's continued displeasure; Mary was baffled by the continued indisposition that gave rise to her ill-humour. 'I like the note before me better than six preceding ones', he wrote on 13th December. 'I own I had the premeditated malice of making you part with me last night unwillingly. I feared Cupid had taken his final farewel'. Godwin could not know the reason for Mary's capriciousness, because she did not know it herself. But by 20th December she had a horrid suspicion, which at the end of the year hardened into certainty. Incredibly, for a second time Mary Wollstonecraft was in the situation of becoming an unmarried mother.

Mary's immediate reaction to her suspected pregnancy was the very natural one of wishing it away; and when it was confirmed—for she would never have acted on the wish—of resenting the cause of it. This explains her temporary coldness towards Godwin and her envy of his greater freedom. All her old self-pity for her own sex flooded back; although she could hardly fail to see now that the 'injustice' of her present situation was natural rather than man-made. Godwin had not deliberately 'trapped' her—far from it. It had probably never entered his mind that she might be 'caught' in this way. This in itself, however, was a further cause for dissatisfaction with him. He ought to have understood, without having it spelt out for him—she had thrown out enough hints. On 20th December she introduced the metaphor of 'the womb of time'; on the 23rd she reported, 'Of myself I am still at a loss what to say'. A week later, after a further deterioration of relations, Godwin was still blind to the real situation:

> You treated me last night with extreme unkindness: the more so, because it was calm, melancholy, equable unkindness. You wished we had never met; you wished you could cancel all that had passed between us. Is this—ask you own heart—Is this compatible with the passion of love? Or, is it not the language of frigid, unalterable indifference?

To which Mary replied, with almost superhuman restraint:

> This does not appear to me just the moment to have written me such a note as I have been perusing.
>
> I am, however, prepared for any thing. I can abide by the consequences of my own conduct, and do not wish to envolve any one in my difficulties.

This was a brave statement. But Godwin knew that, willy-nilly, he *was* 'envolved'. Mary's following letter, on 1st January 1797, confirmed his understanding of the situation:

> I am not well.—I have a fever of my spirits that has tormented me these two nights' past. You do not, I think, make sufficient allowance for the peculiarity of my situation. But

women are born to suffer.
I cannot bear that you should do violence to your feelings, by writing to Mr. Wedgewood. No; you shall not write—I will think of some way of extricating myself.
You must have patience with me, for I am sick at heart—Dissatisfied with every body and every thing.

Godwin had offered to request a loan from his friend Thomas Wedgwood, for Mary was harassed by financial as well as emotional problems. Her work for Johnson was intermittent, she received no support for herself or Fanny from Imlay despite his promised 'bond', and she continued to bestow what little money she had on her family and needy friends. In February that year her sister Everina had stayed with her for a few days before taking up a new post as governess to the Wedgwood family at Etruria in Staffordshire; no doubt Mary's influence with Godwin had helped to obtain this congenial situation for her. One may imagine they both sped the departing guest with some relief, as Mary wrote to Godwin on 6th March:

Everina goes by the mail, this evening. I shall go with her to the coach and call at Johnson's in my way home. I will be with you about nine, or had you not better *try*, if you can, to while away this evening. Those to come are our own. I suppose you will call this morning to say adieu! to Everina.

How much Everina knew, or suspected, of her sister's new relationship with Godwin is not clear; it is unlikely that Mary had confided in her. Writing to her sister on 22nd March, she gave no hint of what was to come. She was full of her money worries, with no indication how they might be resolved[16]:

The scarcity of money makes all the tradesmen send in their bills, and I have had some sent to me which I could hardly avoid paying. The mantua-maker called so often for your bill, three pound four, and seemed in such distress to pay her rent I was obliged to let her have it, and I then gave to young Cristall all the money I had. I am continually getting myself into scrapes of this kind. I must get some in a day or two, Johnson teazes me, and I will then send you a guinea. My pecuniary distress I know arises from myself—or rather, from my not having had the power of employing my mind and fancy when my soul was on the rack. I was obliged to let my father have all my money, but I imagine that Mr. I— would have paid, at least the first half-year's interest of the bond given to me for Fanny. A year, however, is nearly elapsed, and I hear nothing of it, and have had bills sent to me which, I take it for granted, he forgot to pay. Had Mr. I. been punctual, I should, after the first year, the amount of which is due to me, have put by the interest for Fanny, never expecting to receive the principal, and not chusing to be under any obligation to him. But more than enough of this subject. Johnson is either half ruined by the present public circumstances, or grown strangely mean, at any rate he torments me, and Charles neglecting to answer his and my request, respecting a provision for my father, makes me very uneasy.

Mary's sense of desperation is revealed in her singularly ungrateful remarks about Joseph Johnson. Did Johnson know of her relation to Godwin? From Mary Shelley's later account of this period in her life it seems unlikely: 'Mr Johnson in particular, had stood between her and any of the annoyances and mortifications of debt. But this must cease when she married'[17]. As long as Mary remained an independent woman she could be sure of his support, but even the long-suffering Johnson would baulk at coming to the rescue of another man's wife! Yet married she must be, if she and her children were not to suffer indefinite hardship. Godwin could not fail to see that she was in an impossible situation; and only he could get her out of it. He accepted his commitment without further ado and, over-riding Mary's objections, asked Thomas Wedgwood for £50 to settle her debts before marrying her. At the same time he felt obliged to offer some explanation for his apparent inconsistency[18]:

> Nothing but a regard for the happiness of the individual, which I had no right to injure, could have induced me to submit to an institution which I wish to see abolished, and which I would recommend to my fellow-men never to practise, but with the greatest caution.

At least, in abandoning a cherished principle, Godwin went down fighting.

The marriage took place at St Pancras Old Church on 29th March, with Godwin's friend James Marshal as the only witness apart from the clerk. The world was variously astounded, shocked, dismayed and amused. Fuseli, on hearing the news, summed up the occasion with a sly paradox: 'the assertrix of female rights has given her hand to the *Balancière* of political justice'[19]. To him, perhaps, it seemed an inversion of the sexes. But the parties to the contract were well satisfied that the rights of woman and the rights of man had at last coalesced.

CHAPTER SEVENTEEN
Femme Godwin: 1797

That Mary's choice of William Godwin as a husband was based on a conscious tempering of emotion with reason is made clear in the letter she wrote to Amelia Alderson shortly after their marriage[1]. She was not to be trapped a second time into throwing prudence—and principle—to the winds:

> My conduct in life must be directed by my own judgement and moral principles: it is my wish that Mr Godwin should visit and dine out as formerly, and I shall do the same; in short, I still mean to be independent, even to the cultivating sentiments and principles in my children (should I have more) which he disavows.

This time, the marriage was to be based on companionship and identity of interest, rather than on passion:

> The wound my unsuspecting heart formerly received is not healed. I found my evenings solitary, and I wished, while fulfilling the duty of a mother, to have some person with similar pursuits, bound to me by affection; and beside, I earnestly desired to resign a name which seemed to disgrace me.

It was certainly high time that Mary renounced the name of Imlay. But she was careful to point out that she had not taken this step for the sake of the greater security it might offer. Nor was she still hankering after the dream of bliss that had threatened to destroy her:

> Condemned, then, to live my hour out, I wish to live as rationally as I can; had fortune or splendour been my aim in

life, they have been within my reach, would I have paid the price. Well, enough of the subject, I do not wish to resume it.

Miss Alderson, who was made of more worldly stuff, was not altogether deceived by Mary's high moral tone. Her comment on the affair to her friend Mrs Taylor in Norwich was decidedly flippant[2]:

> Heigho! what charming things would sublime theories be, if one could make one's practice keep up with them; but I am convinced it is impossible, and am resolved to make the best of everyday nature.

Godwin, meanwhile, was breaking the news to Mary Hays (if she had not already guessed it)[3]:

> My fair neighbour desires me to announce to you a piece of news, which it is consonant to the regard that she and I entertain for you, you should rather learn from us than from any other quarter.

He even suggested that Miss Hays was the cause of his own changed attitude to matrimony:

> She bids me remind you of the earnest way in which you pressed me to prevail upon her to change her name, and she directs me to add, that it has happened to me, like many other disputants, to be entrapped in my own toils: in short, we found there was no way so obvious for her to drop the name of Imlay, as to assume the name of Godwin.

The pretence that Mary had ever been Imlay's legal wife was now openly abandoned, and the shock of discovering that they had been on visiting terms with a 'fallen woman' was more than some members of her circle could tolerate. Mrs Inchbald and Mrs Siddons promptly broke off relations, to the sorrow of both Mary and Godwin. They could scarcely be blamed, for as women of the theatre their own reputations could all too easily be sullied. Godwin's mother—who was perhaps unfamiliar with the finer nuances of the situation—took a very different view. To her, William's marriage signified that he was on the road to salvation[4]:

> Your broken resolution in regard to matrimony incourages me to hope that you will ere long embrace the Gospel, that sure word of promise to all believers, and not only to you, but your other half, whose souls should be both one ... you are certainly transformed in a moral sense, why is it impossible in a spiritual sense, which last will make you shine with the radiance of the

sun for ever.

This hope was to be disappointed. Godwin must have felt that one compromise of principle was quite enough: not even Mary's influence could persuade him to abandon his atheist conviction.

Nor were the compromises all on one side. Mary was willing for Godwin to practise his belief that too much 'co-habitation' was a recipe for disaster. After their marriage they occupied a joint residence at 29 The Polygon, Somers Town, but Godwin maintained his own apartments nearby in Evesham Buildings. 'We were both of us of the opinion', Godwin records[5], 'that it was possible for two persons to be too uniformly in each other's society'. This arrangement was thought a little odd by some acquaintances. 'In order to give the connection as little as possible the appearance of such a vulgar and debasing tie as matrimony', Mrs Barbauld wrote to her friend Mrs Beecroft[6], 'the parties have established separate establishments, and the husband only visits his mistress like a lover when each is dressed, rooms in order, &c'. In fact, Godwin's rooms served mainly as a retreat for his literary studies, and in making this arrangement he differed very little from any other man who spends his working day in an office. The same necessity for a measure of solitude applied to Mary, who now that she was happily settled was hard at work again. As far as any human beings can, Godwin and Mary had achieved an ideal mode of living. 'No two persons', Godwin wrote, 'ever found in each other's society, a satisfaction more pure and refined'. On a basis of mutual trust and consideration, they seemed to be experiencing the best of both worlds: combining, as Godwin put it, 'the novelty and lively sensation of a visit, with the more delicious and heart-felt pleasures of domestic life'. Mary had no reason to fear Godwin's absences, as she had feared Imlay's. This nice blend of independence and affection was exactly what her own nature demanded and had never hitherto found. No wonder that she seemed like a woman reborn.

It might have been expected that this rebirth would be reflected in her writing, to which she was now applying herself with a concentration that for the first time could be described as wholehearted. Yet the results are disappointing. Her main work during 1797 was an uncompleted novel, *The Wrongs of Woman; or Maria*, which was published posthumously. It is paradoxical that Mary's best-balanced book—her history of the French

Revolution—was written during her feverishly insecure association with Gilbert Imlay, whilst in her year of serene happiness with William Godwin she produced what is arguably her worst. The past was still nagging at Mary, and until she had expunged it from her consciousness she could not rest easy in the present, for all its surface calm.

To describe *The Wrongs of Woman* as Mary Wollstonecraft's worst book does not mean that it was a failure in terms of the literature of her day. Despite the melodramatic plot and thin characterisation it marked a departure from the conventions of the Gothic and the sentimental novel and a step towards the realism of the late nineteenth century in both the subject matter and its treatment. But in technique Mary remained as deficient in her second novel as she had been in her first; and the faults are more glaring because the concept was more ambitious. *Maria* was only a more mature version of the young girl in *Mary, a Fiction*; and both were puppets manipulated by the thoughts and feelings of the real Mary who stood behind them. She could not even invent an original name for her heroines! She failed as a novelist because she could never wholly lose herself in a fictitious character or situation; fact, in her experience, being stranger and more compelling than fiction. The plot of *The Wrongs of Woman* does show some advance, being richer in incident and more dramatically conceived than that of *Mary*, but the drama soon lapses into melodrama as Mary consciously distorted it into an instrument of propaganda.

The message of the book, as spelt out in the preface, is the helplessness of women before the law: 'the misery and oppression, peculiar to women, that arise out of the partial laws and customs of society'. *Maria* is seen as the symbol of her whole sex, and her plight as a general condition: 'Was not the world a vast prison, and women born slaves?' To this thesis Mary sacrificed all credibility. For if Maria's fate could happen to some women it did not happen to all; it was the exception rather than the rule. The point was, however, that it *might* happen; and if it did, there was no protection for the victim of injustice. This was a valid point, but it would have been better argued as the sequel to the *Rights of Woman* which Mary had promised her readers in that volume but which she never wrote. Too much water had flowed under the bridge since those days of innocent optimism for her ever to repeat that exercise in unproven assertion! Now Mary could only write from experience; and since her experience had been a bitter one, *Maria* was a bitter book. In her preface she disclaimed any such personal prejudice:

> ... surely there are a few, who will dare to advance before the improvements of the age, and grant that my sketches are not the abortion of a distempered fancy, or the strong delineations of a wounded heart.

Unfortunately, to many readers this must seem a fair description of *The Wrongs of Woman*.

The book opens with the heroine, Maria Venables, being imprisoned in a private asylum and bereft of her infant daughter, by a tyrant husband who seeks by this means to seize her fortune. Maria, like Mary's sister Eliza, had married as an escape from an unhappy family situation only to find herself in the power of a brutal and depraved husband. It might be said that in acting so foolishly she deserved her fate. But, as Mary had argued in the *Rights of Woman*, girls were not taught to think independently or to analyse their emotions. Maria was the victim of her upbringing; and once caught in the trap of matrimony she had no redress against abuse. She could not even buy her freedom; for if a wife had money of her own the husband could appropriate it:

> A wife being as much a man's property as his horse or his ass, she had nothing she can call her own. He may use any means to get at what the law considers as his, the moment his wife is in possession of it ... he can rob her with impunity, even to waste publicly on a courtezan; and the laws of her country—if women have a country—afford her no protection from the oppressor, unless she have the plea of bodily fear.

The alienation of the wanderer is recalled in Mary's bitter comment: 'if women have a country ...' Maria shares this feeling: she has not even a home, after the ultimate humiliation of being 'offered' by her husband to his creditors. In desperation she runs away; or, in the eyes of the law, 'absconds'. This was an offence for which anyone caught harbouring the runaway could be punished. Hunted from pillar to post, at every point of refuge Maria encounters other injured wives who add their tales of woe to the catalogue of 'the wrongs of woman'. These were not imaginary wrongs. Every instance could doubtless have been verified by actual cases known to the author. Mary only weakened her polemic by squeezing the facts into an unconvincing fictional pattern.

One would think, from the evidence presented, that no woman in the eighteenth century escaped seduction and betrayal. Every minor character who appears has a story more horrendous than the last. The most extreme case is that of Jemima, Maria's attendant in the asylum, who is the most vividly realised character in the book. Her story is told with such indignation and compassion that it could have stood alone as the main plot. If Mary had concentrated on Jemima, she might have created a character of truly heroic stature. This was not to be. The servant could not yet steal the mistress's clothes and play the heroine—especially when that heroine was, in essentials, Mary herself! Jemima, for all the sympathy she evokes, was kept in her station. The child of a seduced servant girl who died soon after her birth, Jemima was reared as a drudge, suffered the inevitable rape by her master at the age of sixteen, and was flung 'out to starve. Deprived of all affection she was, in her own graphic phrase, 'an egg dropped on the sand': 'a pauper by nature, hunted from family to family, who belonged to nobody'. She survives only by becoming the mistress of an elderly man who, though depraved, treats her kindly and gives her a smattering of culture. In his household, for a brief spell, she enjoys some comfort and security. But after his death, having no legal claim on his estate she is again reduced to penury and is forced to take employment as a washer-woman. In the course of this heavy work she suffers an injury which drives her into hopsital and thence to the workhouse. Here we are given a glimpse into the abominable degradation of paupers and their exploitation by unscrupulous officials. The workhouse overseer, Jemima relates, has 'farmed the poor of several parishes', and with the proceeds he purchases the asylum where Maria is held. When he offers Jemima the chance of employment as an attendant on the inmates she has little option but to accept. She justifies her connivance in the iniquitous business by asking: 'Who ever risked anything for me? Who ever acknowledged me to be a fellow-creature?'

There is little doubt that every sordid episode of Jemima's history could and did happen in real life. In telling her story Mary was inveighing against social injustice as powerfully as she had done in the *Rights of Men*. To be poor in the eighteenth century was hardship enough; to be poor and a woman a further handicap;

but to be a poor woman, like Jemima, with no family support, was to court almost certain disaster. Yet even when a woman was not poor she still suffered injustice—simply by being a woman. Maria herself was the exemplar of this. Her higher social status won her the right to be a wife rather than a mistress—but what advantage was this when the wife could be held prisoner with no protection from the law? Not every husband, of course, was a tyrant like Venables; the real answer to her dilemma was that she should never have married him in the first place. Even this, however, given the choices open to Maria, was easier said than done. Her family background as described in the novel is very similar to that of the Wollstonecrafts; as their own history had shown, it required the strength of character of a Mary to resist the temptation of matrimonial status to which Eliza had succumbed.

In addition to Jemima's story Mary introduced another subplot which had little to do with social justice but was very much concerned with her personal situation. This was a quite blatant attempt to justify her own conduct with Imlay. After Maria is finally captured by her husband's agents whilst attempting to flee to France with her infant daughter, and confined in the asylum, she becomes romantically involved with another inmate who has been wrongfully detained, Henry Darnford. Despite the adverse conditions the relationship soon develops into a clandestine love affair and Maria, like Mary, is enslaved by her passion. Darnford bears many resemblances to Gilbert Imlay. He has lived in America, but soon wearying of 'the land of liberty and vulgar aristocracy, seated on her bags of dollars' he returns to London. Here he dissipates his wealth, gets into bad company, is robbed and then, for no clear reason, taken into custody in the asylum. The lovers exchange their life stories, agree that love is superior to marriage, and resolve to escape together. With Jemima's connivance the stratagem suceeds, whereupon Venables brings an action against Darnford for 'seduction and adultery'. Darnford (like Imlay) promptly finds urgent business in France and leaves Maria to face the music alone. Even before his departure there is a hint of disillusionment in Maria's remark that 'there was a volatility in his manner which often distressed her; but love gladdened the scene'. (Was the 'asylum' in which the lovers were imprisoned a symbol of the madness of Mary's own love affair?) However, Maria refused to blame Darnford for what has happened and pleads guilty to the charge of adultery whilst denying that of seduction. She even conducts her own defence, seizing the occasion for an attack on the injustice of matrimonial law. She was not attacking marriage as such, she explained, but only the partiality of the law in favour of the male partner:

> I exclaim against the laws which throw the whole weight of the yoke on the weaker shoulders, and force women, when they claim protectorship as mothers, to sign a contract which renders them dependent on the caprice of the tyrant whom choice or necessity has appointed to reign over them.

In inveighing against the abuses of marriage, rather than against the institution as such, Maria was on strong ground. But she weakened her case when she went on to defend her own illicit union:

> I protest equally against any charge being brought to criminate the man whom I consider as my husband. I was six-and-twenty when I left Mr Venables' roof; if ever I am to be supposed to arrive at an age to direct my own actions, I must by that time have arrived at it. I acted with deliberation. Mr Darnford found me a forlorn and oppressed woman, and promised the protection women in the present state of society want...

Because her legal husband had impugned her honour, she maintained, she was no longer subject to her marriage vows: 'I believed myself, in the sight of heaven, free—and no power on earth shall force me to renounce my resolution'.

No court of law could accept 'the sight of heaven' as a reliable witness. The flesh-and-blood witness to Maria's testimony—'the man whom I consider as my husband'—was conspicuously absent; and her case was lost, as Mary's had been, by the failure of her own 'higher' law rather than by the injustice of man's law. The judge in his summing up argues that divorce must not be made easier because, although a few might suffer, the 'sanctity of marriage' was for the good of the whole community. This was not far from Mary's own opinion, allowing for her more liberal definition of 'marriage'. She had believed in the sanctity of her union with Imlay, and, however badly he behaved, she had not wished to 'divorce' him: for the sake of the child, she had pleaded, let us stay together. In this respect she was in a worse position than the legal wife, for however badly a husband behaved he must take responsibility for his children. In a 'free marriage' no less than a tied one, the yoke fell on the 'weaker shoulders'. The remedy for injustice, therefore, was not freedom but the cultivation of those human qualities making for an equal partnership—within whatever framework—for which Mary had pleaded so eloquently in her *Rights of Woman*. She knew this very well: yet her heroine's conduct (and her own) must be defended. These were the horns of the dilemma which now impaled her.

It is at this point that the narrative of *The Wrongs of Woman* peters out. Mary could no more resolve Maria's predicament than she had been able to resolve her own. For this was not, like so many of her books, a hurried work. According to Godwin she wrote and re-wrote the manuscript, but she could never find a satisfactory conclusion. Her notes indicate that in one version Maria obtains a legal separation from Venables only to find herself deserted by Darnford; learning at the same time that her lost child is dead, she takes an overdose of laudanum. In an alternative draft, the child is restored and she resolves to live on for her sake. Either way the story was dangerously close to reality, and Mary could not evade this. In a genuine work of fiction the situation could have been resolved either in a happy ending or in tragedy; but this would have meant falsifying the facts on which it was based. Mary had set out to tell the truth about women; she only succeeded in telling the truth about herself.

It might seem a little odd that no mitigating character appears in *The Wrongs of Woman* to represent William Godwin. This may be explained partly by the fact that she had already started to plan the book before their relationship began. It may also be, as has already been suggested, that she found it necessary to exorcise the past before she could fully accept the present. Mary had many ghosts to lay, and it is not surprising that she remained to some extent a haunted woman. Hence, perhaps, the intense trouble she took over this book—far more than its merit as a mere 'story' could justify—and her anxiety to have it approved not only by Godwin but by other critics to whom she submitted the manuscript. One of these was George Dyson, and her personal involvement is again shown in her reluctance to accept his criticisms[7]:

> I have been reading your remarks and I find them a little discouraging. I mean I am not satisfied with the feelings which seem to be the result of the perusal. I was perfectly aware that

some of the incidents ought to be transpossed (sic) and heightened by more harmonious shadings and I wished to avail myself of yours and Mr G's criticism before I began to adjust my events into a story, the outline of which I had sketched in my mind at the commencement; yet I am vexed and surprised at your not thinking the situation of Maria sufficiently important, and can only account for this want of—shall I say it? delicacy of feeling by recollecting that you are a man—

Mary was blaming the reader, rather than her own faulty technique, for her failure to produce the desired effect; and if *Maria* was not convincing to her male readers the message had certainly misfired. She was using the novel as a vehicle for propaganda, as she now proceeded to explain:

These appear to me (matrimonial despotism of heart & conduct) to be the peculiar wrongs of woman; because they degrade the mind. What are termed great misfortunes may more forcibly impress the mind of common readers, they may have more of what might justly be termed *stage effect* but it is the delineation of finer sensations which, in my opinion, constitutes the merit of our best novels, this is what I have in view; and to shew the wrongs of different classes of women equally oppressive, though from the differences of education, necessarily various.

But how could 'the delineation of finer sensations', which she rightly saw as the unique function of the novel, be expressed in terms of 'classes of women'?

In *The Wrongs of Woman* Mary had put the cart squarely before the horse, breaking the first rule of fiction by arguing from the general to the particular rather than vice versa. No wonder the animal refused to budge! The book was a failure because, despite all her efforts, she was unable to come to terms with her material: the 'wrongs', on both sides, proved intractable.

Yet there were indications in some minor pieces Mary wrote at this period that new attitudes were developing out of her immediate experience in the last few months of her life. It is a pity that she did not have time to extend this perspective further. Her 'Essay on Poetry', first published in the *Monthly Magazine* in April 1797 (and included in *Posthumous Works* under the title 'On Poetry and our Relish for the Beauties of Nature'), in its small way makes an original contribution to the ferment of the Romantic movement—and not all on the side of romanticism. It was a plea not for a return to the 'nature' of primitive societies, but for a re-direction of the town dweller's attention so that he may apprehend nature by direct sensation rather than indirectly from books. At the same time, he will look on the beauties of nature with the eye of reason and thus retain his separate identity. This was the difference in Mary's attitude from that of the Romantic poets for whom 'nature' was all-powerful and all-absorbing. She could worship nature with the best of them, and she maintained a clear distinction between the creation and its creator: natural beauty represented the 'temple', but the informing spirit dwelt elsewhere. In Mary's hierarchy the Supreme Being still reigned supreme:

> How solemn is the moment, when all affections and remembrances fade before the sublime admiration which the wisdom and goodness of God inspires, when he is worshipped in a *temple not made with hands* and the world seems to contain only the mind that formed, and the mind that contemplates it.

This passage may be compared with Wordsworth's 'Tintern Abbey', written in 1798:

> ... Therefore am I still
> A lover of the meadows and the woods,
> And mountains; and of all that we behold
> From this green earth; of all the mighty world
> Of eye and ear, both what they half create
> And what perceive; well pleased to recognise
> In nature and the language of the sense,
> The anchor of my purest thoughts, the nurse,
> The guide, the guardian of my heart, and soul
> Of all my moral being.

The early Romantics rejected the eighteenth-century goddess of reason in favour of the cult of sensibility—'the language of the sense'. Mary had already passed beyond this second stage. She had learnt from experience that 'sensibility' as the sole criterion of conduct could be both irrational and anti-social. In the present state of society, she now wrote:

> the understanding must bring back the feelings to nature, or the sensibility must have such native strength, as rather to be whetted than destroyed by the strong exercises of passion.

Here she distinguished between two kinds of 'sensibility': that based on sensation and that based on reason. The former, which she had seen at work in Gilbert Imlay, produced the libertine; the latter, which was her own kind, could be represented by William Godwin. Yet she was enough of a Romantic to maintain that 'genius' was only another word for 'exquisite sensibility'; and she rejected Dr Johnson's too rational definition of genius as 'a strong mind, accidentally led to some particular study in which it excels'.

Another fragment which might have revealed how Mary's mind was continuing to develop is unfortunately very brief. According to Godwin, these jottings, entitled simple 'thirty-two hints', were intended to be incorporated in a second volume of the *Rights of Woman*. There is little obvious connection. The 'hints' display none of the feverish indignation of the former book, and few of them are concerned directly with the status of women. There is a philosophical detachment which was quite foreign to the earlier work. The main drift of Mary's thought now, in so far as it emerges, seems to have been to dispute Kant's dictum that 'the understanding is sublime, the imagination beautiful'. She took a contrary view: 'The deductions of reason destroy sublimity'. She acknowledged that reason may be 'the mother of wisdom'; but wisdom is not necessarily the final arbiter; 'some flights of the imagination seem to reach what wisdom cannot teach'. At the same time she issued a warning that to renounce the supremacy of reason does not mean the abandonment of thought. Thought is still the vital process through which imagination must work: 'When we say that a person is an original'. she observed, 'it is only to say in other words that he thinks'. A little later, however, she seems to contradict this when she said: 'A writer of genius makes us feel; an inferior author reason'. She went on to analyse the nature of feeling and to enquire whether 'pleasure' must always be equated with self-love. She concluded not:

> Some principle prior to self-love must have existed: the feeling which produced the pleasure, must have existed before the experience.

This was not very logical. She might equally well have argued that it was the 'experience' which produced the 'feeling'. But in even probing these areas of consciousness, she was reaching out towards twentieth-century existentialism.

Mary never quite achieved the reconciliation of reason and emotion, of 'principle' and 'pleasure', towards which her life and works bore testimony. In one respect only did she come near to a perfect expression of her theories, and this was in her attitude to children. Also included in her *Posthumous Works* are the enchanting 'Lessons for Fanny', which Mary had planned as the first of a series of readers 'for my unfortunate girl'. She was aware that she must make amends to her child, as best she could, for the unpropitious circumstances of her birth. It was a tragedy for Fanny no less than for herself that she did not live long enough to fulfil this aim. In considering the needs of children Mary displayed all her best qualities: sympathy without sentimentality, understanding without condescension, training without harshness, and imagination underpinned by reason.

The fourteen lessons which were printed are simple but effective. Starting from single words, they built up skilfully into sentences which serve both to illustrate the use of words and to teach simple rules of behaviour. Lesson III is purely descriptive:

The bird sings. The fire burns. The cat jumps. The dog runs. The bird flies. The cow lies down. The man laughs. The child cries.

There may have been some significance in Mary's choice of a verb for the man and the child, but Fanny was not to know this. The mother is strangely absent, but the role assigned to the father is noticeable in the lessons. In Lesson VIII, for instance:

Always you ran to papa, and putting both your arms round his leg, for your hands were not big enough, you looked up at him and laughed. What did this laugh say, when you could not speak? Cannot you guess by what you now say to papa? Ah! it was: Play with me, papa—play with me!

Here Mary seems to be compensating Fanny for the loss of her real father by creating the image of a complete family circle. With Godwin, happily, the image can become a reality; and now she can even project her vision into the future to include the coming baby (Lesson IX):

When you were a baby, with no more sense than William, you put everything in your mouth to gnaw, to help your teeth to cut through the skin. ... William presses his gums against my finger. Poor boy! he is so young he does not know what he is doing. When you bite anything, it is because you are hungry.

Mary was careful always to give a reason for her precepts. Here is the delightful little cookery lesson (X):

Betty is making an apple-pye. You love an apple-pye; but I do not bid you make one. Your hands are not strong enough to mix the butter and flour together; and you must not try to pare the apples, because you cannot manage a great knife. Never touch the large knives: they are very sharp, and you might cut your finger to the bone. You are a little girl, and ought to have a little knife.

Kindness to animals is illustrated in the example of the puppy which falls off a stool (XIII): 'Run and stroke him. Put a little milk in a saucer to comfort him'. This is immediately followed by a practical warning: 'Do not forget to put the bason (sic) in a corner, less (sic) somebody should fall over it'. Mary takes pains to teach her little girl that she should always think before she acts; and in this context, 'thinking' means to take thought for others—as in Lesson XIV. Here the child is praised for remembering not to make a noise when 'papa' is resting:

So you came to me, and said to me, very softly, Pray reach me my ball, and I will go and play in the garden, till papa wakes.

Better still is the child's second thought:

You are going out: but thinking again, you came back to me on your tip-toes. Whisper—whisper: 'Pray mama, call me, when papa wakes; for I shall be afraid to open the door to see, lest I should disturb him.'

In these halcyon months of 1797, as Godwin played father to Fanny and his baby grew in her womb, Mary reached her pinnacle of fulfilment. It is a measure of her contentment that the coming child was envisaged as 'William'. Fanny had always been 'her' baby; but 'William' belonged equally to both parents. Despite their semi-detached style of living, the bond between Godwin and Mary was now cemented by custom as well as sentiment. They were acquiring the habits of a conventional married couple—so much so that Mary even expected the philosopher to unstop the drains and attend to the bills like any ordinary husband; and like any ordinary husband, Godwin was slow to respond. 'I wish you would desire Mr Marshall to call on me', she wrote on 11th April:

Mr Johnson, or somebody, has always taken the disagreeable business of settling with trades-people off my hands—I am, perhaps as unfit as yourself to do it—and my time appears to me, as valuable as that of any other persons accustomed to employ themselves.

The only rift in the lute, in fact, was the chronic shortage of money. Insecurity could still cause Mary to snap at the hand that stroked her: 'I am tormented by the want of money', she wrote in this same letter, 'and feel, to say the truth, as if I was not treated with respect, owing to your desire not to be disturbed'. Godwin was 'pained' by this and other accusations of lack of consideration, which in any case were quite unjustified. Mary had hurled similar charges at Imlay, with considerably more reason; but Godwin, unlike Imlay, understood the cause of these outbursts. After what must have been a quite serious quarrel, he wrote on 20th April:

> I found a wounded heart, &, as that heart cast itself upon me, it was my ambition to heal it. Do not let me be wholly disappointed.

How different was this from Imlay's reaction! But for all Godwin's efforts Mary's 'wounded heart' was never completely healed; and even if that cure had been accomplished, it is likely that her habit of making hyper-critical judgments would still have been a thorn in his wide. She acknowledged this herself, after another disagreement, on 21st May:

> I am sorry we entered on an altercation this morning, which probably has led us both to justify ourselves at the expence of the other. Perfect confidence, and sincerity of action is, I am persuaded, incompatible with the present state of reason. ...
> There is certainly an original defect in my mind—for the cruelest experience will not eradicate the foolish tendency I have to cherish, and expect to meet with, romantic tenderness.

On 3rd June Godwin set out from London with his friend Basil Montagu to visit the Wedgwood family at Etruria in Staffordshire. Montagu, a natural son of the Earl of Sandwich, had recently been widowed and was now courting Josiah Wedgwood's daughter Sarah. They travelled via Beaconsfield, Oxford and Stratford-upon-Avon, visiting Dr Parr at his Warwickshire rectory and seeing the ruins of Dr Priestley's burntout house in Birmingham. The tour lasted for nearly three weeks, and his letters show that Godwin thoroughly enjoyed this 'bachelor' excursion. But he was a conscientious correspondent, describing every detail of the itinerary and expressing himself with a wit and gaiety that might have surprised some readers of

Political Justice. They would have been even more surprised by his tender concern for Mary, Fanny and 'little W'. Now revealed for the first time, this was as 'new' a Godwin as the 'new' Mary; in fact more so, because the old Mary could still break through and overwhelm the new, whereas Godwin never shrank back into his former self.

At first, as she wrote on 6th June, Mary experienced his pleasure almost as keenly as if she were sharing it with him:

> I find you can write the kind of letter a friend ought to write, and give an account of your movements. I hailed the sunshine, and moon-light and travelled with you scenting the fragrant gale.—

She missed him, but not too much:

> I am not fatigued with solitude.—Yet have not relished my solitary dinner. A husband is a convenient part of the furniture of a house, unless he be a clumsy fixture. I wish you, from my soul, to be rivetted in my heart; but I do not desire to have you always at my elbow—though at this moment I did not care if you were. Yours truly and tenderly, Mary.

This sentiment accorded perfectly with Godwin's own mood: 'You cannot imagine how happy your letter made me', he wrote on 10th June:

> No creature expressed, because no creature feels, the tender affections, so perfectly as you do; &, after all one's philosophy, it must be confessed that the knowledge, that there is some one that takes an interest in our happiness something like that which each man feels in his own, is extremely gratifying.

The temporary separation, at least for him, gave a new dimension to their relationship:

> One of the pleasures I promised myself in my excursion, was to increase my value in your estimation, & I am not disappointed. What we possess without intermission, we inevitably hold light; it is a refinement in voluptuousness, to submit to voluntary privations. Separation is the image of death; but it is Death stripped of all that is most tremendous, & his dart purged of its deadly venom.

Mary was not so sure about this: even the 'image of death' could poison her veins with the 'deadly venom' of insecurity. Nor could she entirely banish a twinge of resentment that Godwin should be gadding about enjoying himself while she was tied at home by his baby. After all, her own sister was now at Etruria; if anyone should go there, it was surely she. Mary did not actually say these things, but they were implicit in the tone of some of her letters.

When Godwin arrived at his destination Everina at first refused to see him. She may have imagined, perhaps, that the headstrong Mary had embroiled herself with another Imlay; if so, she must soon have realised her error. A few days later Godwin reported that, 'for Everina', she was 'in high spirits'. She enjoyed being shown round 'Mr Wedgwood's manufactory' with Godwin and Montagu as the only woman in the party. Commenting on Everina's initial coldness, Mary remarked on 10th June: 'I supposed that Everina would assume some airs at seeing you—She has very mistaken notions of dignity of character'. It was certainly a little hard on Mary that she was not there to present this very real husband in person to her incredulous sister. But she was not seriously upset, and could even make a joke about her condition:

> I do believe I shall be glad to see you!—on your return, and I shall keep a good look out—William is all alive—and my appearance no longer doubtful—you, I dare say, will perceive the difference. What a fine thing it is to be a man!

Resentment was a very minor factor in Mary's relationship with Godwin. She had bitterly resented Imlay's freedom of movement, because he had grossly abused it. She rejoiced in Godwin's freedom, as she rejoiced in her own: no less and no more. It would not be abused, she knew, because on both sides it was bounded by a genuine affection. She added now: 'Take care of yourself—now I have ventured on you, I should not like to lose you'.

This calm detachment, however, was not always maintained. Godwin knew Mary well enough to take fright himself if he did not hear for a few days. He had not received the latter reassurance when he wrote to her in some agitation on 12th June. What was her mood? Was she well? Could anything have happened to her or the baby?—

> How many possible accidents will the anxiety of affection present to one's thoughts? Not serious ones I hope: in that case, I trust I should have heard. But headaches; but sickness of the heart, a general loathing of life & of me. Do not give place to this worst of diseases! The least I can think is, that you recollect me with less tenderness and impatience than I reflect

on you.

Such concern was worthy of Mary herself. But almost as he wrote the words, Godwin received her letter. He decided not to withdraw his unfounded speculations. Perhaps he thought—and justly so—that it would do Mary no harm to know that she did not hold a monopoly of sensibility. He added only one sentence: 'I am not sorry to have put down my feelings as they were'.

Starting out for home three days later, Godwin's spirits soared, and he resumed his lighthearted chronicle of the hazards and diversions of the journey. Now it was Mary's turn to feel affronted (what a thing it was to live in the age of sensibility, with every nuance of feeling charted like a temperature on a graph!). The trouble now was that he had not informed her of the date when he would be back, and he seemed to be deliberately dawdling on the way in order to delay it. The last straw was his amusing account of a detour to Coventry—to witness Lady Godiva on her horse! That he and Montagu arrived too late and found the ceremony over did nothing to mollify Mary. 'Your latter letters might have been addressed to any body', she complained on 19th June:

> ... whatever tenderness you took away with you seems to have evaporated in the journey, and new objects—and the homage of vulgar minds, restored you to your icy Philosophy.

She could not understand how the journey from Coventry to Cambridge should have taken so long, and he had offered no explanation. This cast her down again to a nadir of self-doubt: 'unless you suppose me a stick or a stone, you must have forgot to think—as well as to feel, since you have been on the wing. I am afraid to add what I feel—'

Before condemning Mary's fears as groundless, it has to be remembered that 'little W' was well on the way to maturing, and although Mary took her pregnancy lightly she was in constant need of reassurance that Godwin loved her no less for this. She remembered, no doubt, how the child who should have cemented her bond with Imlay had actually served to frighten him away. She was also irked by the restrictions imposed by her condition, which added to her sense of isolation when Godwin was away. Writing again on 25th June she recalled the stimulating company she had enjoyed in the old days at Joseph Johnson's. But that circle had since broken up and now she found 'Mr J's house and spirits were so altered, that my visiting him depressed instead of exhilarating my mind'. She reminded Godwin of her need 'to see new faces, as a study'. He had evidently criticised her for calling on Thomas Holcroft during his absence—not on grounds of propriety but because Holcroft was his friend rather than hers, and they had agreed to maintain separately the friendships that had existed before their marriage. 'I think you are right in principle', Mary now rejoined, 'but a little wrong in the present application'. As she pointed out 'it is not convenient for me, at present to make haphazard visits'.

She whiled away some of her solitary hours at home by sitting for her portrait to John Opie. The result, which now hangs in the National Portrait Gallery, finally nails the lie of Horace Walpole's 'hyena in petticoats'. Admittedly it shows a somewhat idealised Mary, but all the salient features are there, and it may be taken to be an accurate representation of her character in maturity[8]. The thoughtful, serene and slightly wistful face reveals little of the storm and stress which had wracked her—and even less of feminism triumphant. If Mary was now 'emancipated', it was an emancipation from the separateness of selfhood in acknowledgment of the oneness of life. This is what the portrait suggests, although its truth is belied by the unresolved conflicts in *The Wrongs of Woman* and the uneasiness in her letters to Godwin as late as July 1797. Opie, perhaps, had captured and elucidated the potential rather than the actual Mary.

The month of August passed, as far as we know, in tranquillity. Mary had no worries about her coming confinement. In accordance with her belief that a woman in labour should be ministered to by one of her own sex she had engaged a midwife from the Westminster hospital to attend her at the birth. She had sailed through her first labour and might expect the second to be even easier. In fact, said Godwin, she was planning to come down to dinner the day after the birth. Her pains started on the morning of Wednesday 30th August, and she informed Godwin blithely: 'I have no doubt of seeing the animal today'. She requested books and papers to while away the time, sent for Mrs Blenkinsop, and in the afternoon retired to her bedroom to prepare for the birth. Mrs Blenkinsop assured her that 'Everything is in a fair way' and that the event would certainly take place that day. A little later, Godwin received another reassuring bulletin:

Mrs Blenkinsop tells me that I am in the most natural state, and can promise me a safe delivery— But that I must have a little patience.

These were the last words Mary ever wrote. 'A little patience', her own mother had cried on her deathbed, 'and all will be over!' Was there some conscious foreboding in this echo from the past?

If so, Godwin did not sense it. He too was taking the impending birth with equanimity. He had gone out as usual in the morning to study in his own rooms, and he did not think it necessary to return during the day. Mary had requested that he should not attempt to see her until she could present the baby to him. He came back to The Polygon in the evening and settled in the parlour to await the expected summons. At eleven o'clock he was still waiting, with mounting anxiety. The baby—a girl—was born soon afterwards, but it was two o'clock the next morning before he learned with dismay from Mrs Blenkinsop that the placenta had not completely come away. He immediately sent for the hospital obstetrician, Dr Poignard, who set to work to extract the remaining tissue. This was an agonising process for Mary, and several times she fainted away from pain and loss of blood. She had 'never known what bodily pain was before', she told Godwin on the following Tuesday, after the doctor had assured her that all the tissue had been removed and the worst was now over. But Godwin was still uneasy, and he called in their old friend Dr George Fordyce for his opinion. When he too reported that Mary was doing well Godwin breathed again, and by the Friday he felt able to go about his normal business. Mary was rallying, and he was sure she was out of danger. On the Sunday, ten days after the birth, he was so encouraged by her progress that he went out visiting several friends and did not return until dinner time. This was certainly a mistake on his part. He ought to have known that, as she fought to regain her strength, Mary would desperately need his moral support. He came back to find her shivering and in a state of anxiety about his absence.

In the evening the shivering grew worse. Her teeth chattered, he recorded, and 'the bed shook under her'. It seemed that both doctors were wrong, that a portion of the placenta still remained and was poisoning her system. She was forbidden to nurse her baby, and puppies were brought to draw off the milk: this, says Godwin, 'occasioned some pleasantry of Mary with me and the other attendants'. In all her enthusiasm for suckling she could never have envisaged this! But she was still desperately ill. Dr Fordyce was again called, bringing a second doctor with him. The possibility of an operation was discussed, and Godwin was ordered to ply Mary with wine as a crude anaesthetic should this be necessary. But in fact nothing more could be done for her. She was in the grip of puerperal fever, and all the doctors in England were helpless to cure it. Dr Fordyce and his colleague were joined by the surgeon Mr Carlisle. Friends converged on The Polygon, eager to offer their services. Mrs Fenwick was in constant attendance on Mary. Mr Fenwick, together with Basil Montagu, James Marshal and George Dyson, stood by to take messages and run errands. No effort was spared to save Mary; and no effort could avail. On Thursday 7th September Carlisle warned Godwin that the end was near. Yet Mary lingered on, raising and dashing his hopes, for another three days. Carlisle put her chances of recovery at 'one in a million'. The odds proved too great. On Sunday, 10th September 1797, Godwin faithfully recorded the conclusion to his *Memoirs* of Mary Wollstonecraft: 'She expired at twenty minutes before eight'.

Mary was buried in St Pancras churchyard[9] on 15th September. Godwin did not attend the funeral. It has generally been assumed that he was too shattered to do so, but this is scarcely in keeping with his character. He had married in a church, for Mary's sake. What would it profit her now, if he should commend her soul to a God in whom he did not believe? She carried in her own heart the comfort of a 'Supreme Being'. Godwin's only comfort was his memory of her life.

CHAPTER EIGHTEEN
Post-mortem

In the aftermath of Mary's death there is little good to relate. For Godwin the year of 'private disaster' coincided with 'the triumph of reaction in England'[1]. (Joseph Johnson was fined £50 and sentenced to nine months' imprisonment in 1797 for the crime of selling a seditious pamphlet by Gilbert Wakefield.) Despite the success of his novel *St Leon* in 1799, Godwin's public influence continued to decline and his personal convictions were blurred by compromise. (The anarchist philosopher of *Political Justice* was to end his days as a pensioner of the state.) Yet, in compromising, Godwin did not necessarily change for the worse. That the paramount influence in this change was Mary herself is made clear both from his conduct after her death and from his subsequent writings.

In 1798, said Woodcock in his biography of Godwin, he was planning a book on 'First Principles of Morals', which would correct the 'errors' in *Political Justice*: 'The part to which I allude is essentially defective', he observed, 'in the circumstance of not yielding a proper attention to the empire of feeling'. His change of heart was made even more explicit the following year in the introduction to *St Leon*:

> Not that I see cause to make any change respecting the principles of justice, or anything else fundamental in the system there delivered; but that I apprehend domestic and private affections inseparable from the nature of man, and from what may be styled the culture of the heart, and am fully persuaded

that they are not incompatible with a profound and active sense of justice in the mind of him that cherishes them.

The link between 'private affections' and social justice had long been clear to Mary. In admitting that the two were 'not incompatible' Godwin went a further step towards her conviction that they were indeed indivisible and that the one was little good without the other. They did not have time enough in their brief life together to demonstrate this principle in practice. Godwin was still dazed by the novelty of his newfound happiness when it was snatched away.

'I firmly believe that there does not exist her equal in the world', he wrote to Thomas Holcroft[2] on the day of Mary's death. 'I know from experience we were formed to make each other happy. I have not the least expectation that I can now ever know happiness again'. This was a natural reaction to bereavement, but in the event Godwin soon sought some degree of consolation in a second marriage. He had not only his own grief to contend with but also the problem of caring for the infant Mary and the orphaned Fanny Imlay. 'I must preserve myself', he wrote to Mary's friend Mrs Cotton on 14th September 1797[3], 'if for no other reason, for the two children'. The following day, writing to thank the surgeon Carlisle for his devoted attendance[4], he displayed a touch of Mary's own tendency towards self-dramatisation—and self-pity:

I am here, sitting alone in Mr Marshal's lodgings, during my wife's funeral. My mind is extremely sunk and languid. But I husband my thoughts, and shall do very well. I have been but once since you saw me, in a train of thought that gave me alarm. One of my wife's books now lies near me, but I avoid opening it. I took up a book on the education of children, but that impressed me too forcibly with my forlorn and disabled state with respect to the two poor animals left under my protection, and I threw it aside.

Godwin echoed Mary's language as well as her attitudes in speaking of the children as 'animals' and describing his own mental condition as 'sunk and languid'. Yet this letter does not give the impression of a man totally prostrated—not sufficiently so, surely, to justify his absence from his wife's funeral except as a matter of principle.

Writing again to Mrs Cotton on 24th October[5], he reiterated his concern for the two infants left in his care:

I am the most unfit person for this office; she was the best qualified in the world. What a change. The loss of the children is less remediless than mine. You can understand the difference.

By that curiously clumsy phrase 'less remediless', Godwin seemed to imply that the children would recover more quickly than he from the shock of their mother's death, but in this he proved to be mistaken. The damage to Fanny and Mary, from whatever cause, was never righted. If her mother had lived, would Mary Godwin have eloped with the poet Shelley at the age of sixteen, leaving a trail of destruction in her wake? Would Fanny Imlay, feeling more unwanted than ever, have sought refuge from a harsh world in an overdose of laudanum? Would Shelley's deserted wife Harriet have flung herself into the Serpentine? It might all have happened, inevitably, from the intrinsic character of the protagonists; or, in happier circumstances, some part of the tragedy might have been averted. How far Mary Wollstonecraft might have influenced her growing daughters for better or worse, had she been spared to direct their upbringing, can only be guessed at. In her absence, she has often been blamed for sowing the dragon-seed of 'emancipation' and 'free love'. Yet the negative aspects of Mary's philosophy were part of a historical process in which she was equally the victim; it is in her positive qualities that she was uniquely herself. This is apparent in the striking differences of attitude between the personal testimonies of her friends and the criticism of those who never knew her. It might be argued, of course, that friends would naturally be prejudiced in her favour. Yet their esteem was based on a devotion to her principles as much as to her person. As Mrs Fenwick wrote to Everina on 12th September[6], in breaking the news of her death:

I know of no consolation for myself, but in remembering how happy she had lately been, and how much she was admired, almost idolised, by some of the most eminent and best of human beings.

She added a request from Godwin that Eliza too should be informed: 'He tells me that Mrs Godwin entertained a sincere and earnest affection for Mrs Bishop'. Mrs Fenwick also quoted to Everina Mary's final testimony to Godwin: 'Her description of him, in the very last moments of her recollection, was, "He is the kindest, best man in the world".'

A similar view of Mary was expressed by Mary Hays in a letter to Hugh Skeys describing her last days[7]. Never, wrote Miss Hays, could she have pictured 'a mind so tranquil, under affliction so great':

> She was all kindness and attention, and cheerfully complied with everything that was recommended to her by her friends. In many instances she employed her mind with more sagacity on the subject of her illness than any of the persons about her. Her whole soul seemed to dwell with anxious fondness on her friends; and her affections, which were at all times more alive than perhaps those of any other human being, seemed to gather new disinterestedness upon this trying occasion. The attachment and regret of those who surrounded her appeared to increase every hour, and if her principles are to be judged of by what I saw of her death, I should say that no principles could be more conducive to calmness and consolation.

Mary Hays was also the author of the anonymous obituary of Mary which appeared in the *Monthly Magazine* in September 1797. 'This extraordinary woman', she wrote, '... commanding the respect and winning the affections of all who were favoured with her friendship and confidence, or who were within the sphere of her influence, may justly be considered as a public loss'. The following month she acknowledged her authorship in a letter to the magazine, 'as a public testimony of respect and affection for my late admirable friend'. Mary Hays also provided the best personal description we have of Mary[8]:

> Her person was above the middle height, and well proportioned; her form full; her hair and eyes brown; her features pleasing; her countenance changing and impressive; her voice soft, and, though without great compass, capable of modulation. When unbending in familiar and confidential conversation, her manners had a charm that subdued the heart.

Mary's friends may well have expressed their regard in somewhat exaggerated terms. A tribute from a more surprising quarter was that which appeared in the *Gentleman's Magazine* (October 1797):

> Her manners were gentle, easy and elegant; her conversation intelligent and amusing, without the least trait of literary pride, or the apparent consciousness of powers above the level of her sex; and, for soundness of understanding and sensibility of heart, she was, perhaps, never equaled. Her practical skill in

education was even superior to her speculations upon that subject; nor is it possible to express the misfortune sustained, in that respect, by her children. This tribute we readily pay to her character, however adverse we may be to the system she supported in politicks and morals, both by her writings and practice.

But for that final sentence, one might almost suppose this notice to have been written by Godwin himself. He was already engaged on his *Memoirs*, a labour of love whereby he sought to vindicate in her own right the author of *A Vindication of the Rights of Woman*. But when the book was published in January 1798 it precipitated a critical backlash that must have stunned him. So virulent was the attack, indeed, that he felt obliged to issue a second edition a few months later in which he 'corrected' the frankness of some of his earlier statements. The tragic manner of Mary's dying had temporarily silenced criticism, but now it was her life rather than her death that excited attention—most of it unfavourable[9]. The vicious hostility of the *Anti-Jacobin Review* (July 1798), which actually described her as 'the concubine of Mr Imlay', was only to be expected. The *Monthly Magazine* (July 1798), though less eager to criticise, countermanded Mary Hays' glowing obituary with a smug self-righteousness:

It is not for us to vindicate Mary Godwin from the charge of multiplied immorality, which is brought against her by the candid as well as the censorious; by the sagacious as well as the superficial observer: her character, in our estimation, is far from being entitled to unqualified praise; she had many transcendent virtues.

Even the *Analytical Review* (March 1798) was hard put to defend her 'singular opinions'; and worse, the fact that she 'reduced them into practice'. *The Critical Review* (April 1798) was more generous in acknowledging Mary's 'great genius' and 'original habits of thinking', but at one with its contemporaries in regarding her doctrines as pernicious. This ambiguity ran right through the criticisms of Mary's life and works: acknowledgment of her 'genius' was coupled with condemnation of the 'error' into which it led her.

Only Mary Hays, it seems, dissented from this view. In the biographical memoir which she contributed to the *Annual Necrology 1797–8*, whilst acknowledging that Mary's conduct had been 'in many instances imprudent' she exonerated her from blame: 'The qualities of her heart and the attainments of her understanding appear to have been eminently her own, her errors and her sufferings arose out of the vices and prejudices of others'. This assessment, appearing in 1800 and drawn largely from Godwin's *Memoirs* of 1798, offered a generous and courageous defence of a controversial character. That Miss Hays subsequently omitted Mary Wollstonecraft from her six-volume *Female Biography*, published in 1803, need not be regarded as a slight on her memory. It is a singularly unbalanced collection of 'brief lives' and Mary was in good company: also excluded were Fanny Burney, Mrs Barbauld, Mrs Inchbald and Mrs Radcliffe, to name only a few of her contemporaries. The exception was Madame Roland, to whom the author devoted more than two hundred pages. Incidentally, in her article in the *Annual Necrology* Mary Hays stated that Mary never actually met Madame Roland in Paris: 'Various accidents, which she was accustomed to mention with regret, prevented her from being introduced to Madame Roland'. It has generally been assumed, perhaps without foundation, that the two were on terms of personal friendship.

Another champion rose to defend Mary in 1803, when *A Defence of the Character and Conduct of the Late Mary Wollstonecraft Godwin* was published anonymously. The author has been identified as Sir Charles Aldis, and from his warm tribute to her personality one would assume that he had known her in the life. Yet if this is the same Charles Aldis, physician and surgeon, who features in the *Dictionary of National Biography* he was born in 1775 or 1776 and was therefore no more than twenty-two at the time of her death. He had no apparent connection with any of her circle, and his interest in the author of the *Rights of Woman* remains a mystery. His case for the defence rested on Mary's 'genius', which he claimed exempted her from the 'common rules'. Mary herself would not have desired any such exemption, since she saw her *Rights of Woman* as a model for the whole sex; to this end she believed that the 'common rules' must be changed. This was her real crime in the eyes of society; had she contented herself with merely breaking the rules, rather than seeking to change them, she could have been dismissed as just another eccentric. Nevertheless, in this respect her defender was surely right and she was mistaken. The 'common rules' are drawn up by and for the common man and woman, and serve their interests best. To break the norms of society, and suffer the consequences, is both the privilege and the penalty of genius. The penalty—without the privileges—must also be suffered by the close associates of such 'originals'. Godwin had a foot in both camps, although he was nearer to the norm than Mary in accepting the constraints of society when these clashed seriously with his principles—his prompt amendment of his *Memoirs* is an immediate witness to this. Yet he was also sufficiently strong in principle to be able to shrug off unjustified criticism without serious upset. A worse injury—or so they believed—was done to Mary's sisters, who had little defence against calumny. Eliza and Everina had refused to give Godwin any assistance in compiling his *Memoirs*. They claimed, that they had 'found difficulties in getting situations because of their relationship to Mary Godwin'; Hugh Skeys, however, attributed this to 'their own infirmities of temper'[10]. Whatever the cause, they were not having an easy time. In an undated letter which must almost certainly have been written in 1798 (a postscript mentions Mary's posthumous works *The Wrongs of Woman* and *The Cave of Fancy*)[11], Everina commiserated with Eliza on the 'illiberal' treatment she had received owing to her relationship to 'poor Mary'. Whether this was also the cause of Everina's leaving the Wedgwoods is not known—it seems unlikely in view of the liberal character of that family—but she was now living in very inferior conditions with some relatives in Ireland. 'Let the present storm pass over . . . and the prejudice against me may die away, and I may be able to settle myself in Dublin', she wrote. This 'prejudice' seems to have been against her Englishness rather than her family name, for she spoke also of 'those bloodthirsty wretches, the United Irishmen'. Eliza and Everina certainly had little joy from their sister's fame, or notoriety, but Mary had done them one good turn in teaching them the value of education. The last we hear of them is that they had opened their own school in Dublin.

Godwin meanwhile had lost no time in putting his new philosophy into practice. Already in April 1798, less than six months after Mary's death, he was courting Miss Harriet Lee of Bath, a schoolmistress and author of *The Errors of Innocence* (1786). Could any repudiation of his former self be more absolute than that expressed in his letter to Miss Lee in June 1798[12]?—

The sentiments of mutal and equal affection, and of parental love, and these only, are competent to unlock the heart and expand its sentiments—they are the Promethean fire, with which, if we have never been touched, we have scarcely attained the semblance of what we are capable to be.

Miss Lee, however, remained unimpressed, and Godwin struggled on alone. A housekeeper, Louisa Jones, was engaged to look after the children, and this lady at least would not have been averse to a more permanent role; but Godwin was wise enough to resist that pressure. The following summer, however, the chance of a more suitable match seemed to come his way with the widowing of his old friend Maria Reveley. His admiration for her preceded his union with Mary and had only been contained by the presence of her husband. Now that obstacle had been removed, surely the way was clear? It seemed logical to the philosopher to suppose so and, with unabashed frankness, he started to press his suit within a month of Mr Reveley's death. But time had wrought changes in Maria too, and again poor Godwin was repulsed. It was doubly humiliating for him that less than a year later she married another man, John Gisborne. Even the flirtatious Amelia Alderson finally eluded Godwin by becoming the second Mrs Opie in May 1798.

It is not surprising, in the circumstances, that when the widowed Mrs Clairmont moved into a neighbouring house in The Polygon and threw him a well-directed straw, he clutched at it with the fervour of a drowning man; particularly as the straw was dipped in honey.

'Is it possible that I behold the immortal Godwin?' she is reputed to have called across the balcony. Greater men than Godwin would have risen to this bait. They were married at Shoreditch Church on 21st December, 1801. It was to prove a sad day for Godwin and even sadder for his daughters. Mrs Clairmont brought to the union a son and daughter of her own and soon made it clear that they had first claim on the family's limited resources. She was a 'harsh stepmother'; and whilst her own daughter Jane was offered an education, 'household drudgery was from an early age discovered to be the life-work of Fanny and Mary Godwin'[13].

Mary Wollstonecraft's daughters shared many of their mother's characteristics, but individually they were of very different temperaments. It might have been supposed that the 'love child', Fanny, would have the sunnier nature, but this was not so. As a small child she had been healthy and active, but she does not seem to have benefited in the long term from the hardiness of her early upbringing. In her letter to Mary of 28th August 1796 Amelia Alderson had commented on the child's 'strong, well-formed limbs and florid complexion'[14]; yet Fanny had inherited the negative rather than the positive aspects of her mother's disposition. Godwin compared her unfavourably with her half-sister in a letter to an unknown correspondent which was written when Mary Godwin was fifteen[15]:

> Of the two persons to whom your enquiries relate, my own daughter is considerably superior in capacity to the one her mother had before. Fanny, the eldest, is of a quiet, modest, unshowy disposition, somewhat given to indolence, which is her greatest fault, but sober, observing, peculiarly clear and distinct in the faculty of memory, and disposed to exercise her own thoughts and follow her own judgment. Mary, my daughter, is the reverse of her in many particulars. She is singularly bold, somewhat imperious, and active of mind. Her desire of knowledge is great, and her perseverance in everything she undertakes almost invincible. My own daughter is, I believe, very pretty; Fanny is by no means handsome, but in general prepossessing.

Despite Godwin's scrupulous fairness in his treatment of the girls, this description may well have been coloured by a father's partiality. A more favourable account is given by Kegan Paul[16]. After her mother, he wrote, Fanny was 'the most attractive character with whom we meet in the whole enormous mass of Godwin's mss'. He described her at the age of twenty-two: 'a young woman of marked individuality, and most lovable nature ... Well-educated, sprightly, clever, a good letter-writer, and an excellent domestic manager, she had become not only a dear child, but a favourite companion to Godwin, was useful to, and not unkindly treated by Mrs Godwin'. Yet he too acknowledged that there was a dark side to her nature:

> The extreme depression to which her mother had been subject, and which marked other members of the Wollstonecraft family, seized hold of Fanny Godwin also from time to time; the outward circumstances of her life cannot be called happy, and

though she put the best face on them to others, she was, to herself, often disposed to dwell on them and intensify them in a way which may fairly be called morbid. She made at times a luxury of her sorrows.

It was in just such a mood that Fanny, setting off on a journey to visit her aunts in Ireland, stopped at Swansea on 9th October 1816 and found she could go no further. She left by her bedside in the Mackworth Arms an empty laudanum bottle and a note from which the signature had been torn away:

> I have long determined that the best thing I could do was to put an end to the existence of a being whose birth was unfortunate and whose life has only been a series of pain to those persons who have hurt their health in endeavouring to promote her welfare. Perhaps to hear of my death will give you pain, but you will soon have the blessing of forgetting that such a creature ever existed as ...

Who was to blame for this tragedy? Her mother for bringing her into the world in the first place? Her real father, Imlay, for ignoring her inconvenient existence? Her aunts for telling her the facts about her birth? This latter has generally been accepted as the most likely explanation, as Kegan Paul believed:

> It may be that alone, and possibly, with the full particulars of her own birth, and her mother's story, but lately known to her through her recent intercourse with her aunts, the morbid feelings to which she was occasionally subject gained the mastery over her reason, usually so sound, and led her to seek a lasting rest.

But if Fanny had ever read Godwin's *Memoirs* she must already have been well aware of her origins. Another theory was that Fanny had been adversely affected by the scandal of Mary Godwin's elopement with Shelley two years earlier, which was said to have prejudiced her chances of employment. Her aunt Everina, it appears, had considered her as a teacher in her own school but decided against it. This hardly seems adequate grounds for suicide. According to Mrs Godwin, both Mary and Fanny and her own daughter Jane had been infatuated with Shelley and she maintained that 'the eldest killed herself on his account'[17]. Shelley's own epitaph on Fanny is ambiguous:

> Her voice did quiver as we parted,
> Yet knew I not that heart was broken

from which it came, and I departed
Heeding not the words then spoken.
Misery—O Misery,
This world is all too wide for thee.

Yet Crabb Robinson—who described Fanny in his diary as 'a very plain girl and odd in manners and opinions'—claimed that she 'fully approved of and vindicated her sister's conduct in living with Shelley'[18]. Certainly her own letter to Mary and Shelley of 29th May 1816 is warm and friendly: 'Believe, my dear friends', she wrote, 'that my attachment to you has grown out of your individual worth and talents, and perhaps because I found the world deserted you, I loved you the more'[19]. But she also let slip a cruel jibe of Mrs Godwin's: 'I understand from Mamma that I am your laughing-stock and the constant beacon of your satire'. This may well have been a spiteful invention on the part of her step-mother. Both Godwin and his wife were horrified by the elopement and refused to receive the guilty pair. 'I wish papa had not begun this letter', Fanny added, 'it is so cold'. Yet, she assured them, 'he speaks of you with great kindness and interest. I hope the day will not be long ere you are reconciled'.

Most probably, it was a combination of circumstances that overwhelmed poor Fanny. She had inherited all her mother's sensibility, but most of the toughness and charm that went with it had passed to her younger sister. Shelley's first wife Harriet—who evidently saw no grounds for jealousy in Fanny—commented that 'the beauty of her mind overbalances the plainness of her countenance'[20]. It was this inherent nobility, perhaps, that led her to tear the signature from her suicide note, in the hope of sparing her family some pain. The gesture was a futile one, as she was identified from her clothing. Nevertheless, Godwin with his new-found respectability did his best to hush up the affair and clung to the story that Fanny really had gone to visit her aunts in Ireland. After Mary's elopement he could not face another scandal in the family. (He was not to be spared for long. Only a month after Fanny's death, Harriet Shelley drowned herself; the circle of tragedy was complete. Yet when Mary and Shelley were legally married Godwin was pleased to recognise the *fait accompli*, and even boasted to his brother of the 'good match'.)

It is evident that during the last months of her life Fanny's thoughts were much with her mother. Whatever version of

Mary's character Eliza and Everina had given her during their visit to London that summer, she was beginning to form an independent opinion. In reaching her own conclusions she was influenced by a curious incident which she described to her sister in her letter of 29th May already quoted, and which throws more light on one of Mary's early attachments:

> My feelings and tone of mind have undergone a considerable revolution for the better since I last wrote to you—I have unexpectedly seen Mr George Blood brother of Fanny Blood, my mother's friend. Everything he has told me of my mother has increased my love and admiration of her memory, he has given me many particulars of the days of her youth and inner(?) life. George Blood seems to have loved and venerated her as a superior being, to have been most devotedly attached to her memory ever since her death and to have ventured to hope that her daughters were not unworthy of her—this has in some degree roused me from my torpor. I have determined never to live to be a disgrace to such a mother. I have found that if I will endeavour to overcome my faults, I shall find beings to love and esteem me.

Far from being ashamed of her mother, Fanny seemed to be oppressed by the sense of her own unworthiness of such a parent. It may well have been her inability to live up to Mary's memory, rather than to live it down, that led her to believe her own life was not worth living. Her description of George Blood himself goes a good way to explain the attraction for Mary of the boy whose heart, as she used to say, was 'dancing in his eyes':

> George Blood is not a man of superior intellect but has great warmth of feeling and great goodness of heart. The manner in which he has spoken of my mother has been a great balm to my heart, and has endeared him much to me. He had not been in London for 26 years and our mother then bid him adieu at the coach-door. He also met her at Lisbon at the time of Fanny Blood's death.

In the interim, George had married in Ireland and lost his own wife in childbirth. It is small wonder that his thoughts turned to Mary and her daughters when he returned to London after so long an absence. He must have been disappointed to find the younger chick already flown—and, it might seem, in danger of repeating her mother's unhappy experience.

But Percy Bysshe Shelley was of a different order from Imlay, despite his desertion of Harriet (whom he had married in the first place to please her rather than himself). The young Mary too was made of tougher stuff than either her mother or her sister. She was blessed not only with good looks and intelligence but with a resilience that carried her through the loss in infancy of three of her four children and the shock of Shelley's untimely death at the age of twenty-nine. Yet her father believed her to be a true Wollstonecraft, rather than a Godwin, with all the disadvantages that implied. As he wrote to her in 1827[21]:

> How differently are you and I organized! In my seventy-second year I am all cheerfulness, and never anticipate the evil day with distressing feelings till to do so is absolutely unavoidable. Would to God you were my daughter in all but my poverty! But I am afraid you are a Wollstonecraft. We are so curiously made, that one atom put in the wrong place in our original structure will often make us unhappy for life ...

Mary Shelley was certainly deeply in sympathy with the mother she had never known and eagerly absorbed the golden opinions of those who had. Her own description of Mary, said Kegan Paul, was gleaned as much from Mrs Reveley as from Godwin himself:

> Mary Wollstonecraft was one of those beings who appear once perhaps in a generation, to gild humanity with a ray which no difference of opinion nor chance of circumstances can cloud. Her genius was undeniable. She had been bred in the hard school of adversity, and having experienced the sorrows entailed on the poor and the oppressed, an earnest desire was kindled within her to diminish these sorrows. Her sound understanding, her intrepidity, her sensibility and eager sympathy, stamped all her writings with force and truth, and endowed them with a tender charm that enchants while it enlightens. She was one whom all loved who had ever seen her.

Yet, after her first act of defiance of the conventions, Mary Shelley made no attempt to follow in her mother's footsteps. She was more of a Godwin than her father supposed and had all his capacity for compromise. Her creative gifts were undeniable, and in *Frankenstein* (written when she was only nineteen) she showed powers of imagination that surpassed both her parents. But it seems as if, after Shelley's death, the mantle of her brilliant inheritance was too great a burden to be borne alone; she had seen too much of the suffering caused by dissent. She prayed that her son would 'think like other people', and this desire for conformity even extended to politics. 'I have no wish to ally myself with the Radicals', she wrote in her diary[22]:

> they are full of repulsion to me—violent without any sense of justice—selfish in the extreme—talking without knowledge—rude, envious and insolent—I wish to have nothing to do with them.

She did not, presumably, include either her mother or Shelley in this sweeping condemnation.

'She was one whom all loved who had ever seen her', Mary Shelley had written of her mother. The odd man out in this eulogy was Gilbert Imlay. What he thought, or said, about Mary's death is, like so much about him, unknown. There is a blank of thirty years between his farewell to Mary on the New Road in 1796 and his burial in St Brelade's churchyard on the island of Jersey on 24th November 1828, at the age of seventy-four. What he had been up to—and where—in the intervening years nobody knows. But there is an indication in his last recorded action that the leopard had not changed his spots[23]. In June 1828 he had filed a lawsuit to recover £50 from a bankrupt merchant, William Goff, who was agent for the steam packet *Ariadne* plying between Jersey and the mainland of England. Imlay was evidently still some kind of trader, and in the absence of any overt evidence about his activities in Jersey it might reasonably be assumed that he was involved in the widespread smuggling that went on in those days. Such records as are available give no indication that he bought any land or property on the island, and he left no will. There is no evidence that he ever married or had any lawful heirs. Yet somebody cared enough about him to inscribe an epitaph on his gravestone! This is no longer visible in the churchyard but was reproduced by Richard Garnett in *The Atheneum* in 1903[24]:

> Stranger intelligent! should you pass this way
> Speak of the social graces of the day—
> Mention the greatly good, who've serenely shone
> Since the soul departed its mortal bourne;
> Say if statesmen wise have grown, and priests sincere
> Or if hypocrisy must disappear
> As phylosophy extends the beam of truth,
> Sustains rights divine, its essence, and the worth

Sympathy may permeate the mouldering earth,
Recal the spirit, and remove the dearth,
Transient hope gleams even in the grave,
Which is enough dust can have, or ought to crave.
Then silently bid farewell, be happy,
For as the globe moves round, thou will grow nappy.
Wake to hail the hour when new scenes arise,
As brightening vistas open in the skies.

Could anyone have composed this inflated nonsense but Imlay himself? It bears all the marks of the pretentious sentiment and woolly aspiration that had at first attracted and then repelled Mary Wollstonecraft.

A very different epitaph, on a very different character, was that to Joseph Johnson which was inscribed on his grave in All Saints churchyard, Fulham (no longer visible). In his later years Johnson lived at Acacia Cottage (a wing of the former Bolingbroke House), Purser's Cross. He died on 20th December 1809, at the age of 72, following an attack of pleurisy. This epitaph was written by no less a man than Henry Fuseli and was reproduced by Knowles in his biography:

A man equally distinguished by probity, industry, and disinterestedness in his intercourse with the public, and every domestic and social virtue in life; beneficent without ostentation, ever ready to produce merit and relieve distress; unassuming in prosperity, not appalled by misfortune; inexorable to his own, indulgent to the wants of others; resigned and cheerful under the torture of a malady which he saw gradually destroy his life.

Mary's testimonial to Johnson would have confirmed this estimate of his character—surely the most attractive, next to Godwin, of all the men in this history—even more fervently. About Mary herself, however, Fuseli had less to say. He had been informed of her death in a note signed 'J.J.' and presumably written by Johnson: 'One who loved you, & whom I respected, is no more. Mrs Godwin died this morning'[25]. Fuseli's comment, according to Knowles, was simple: 'Poor Mary!' He could have afforded a little more magnanimity. His own status was now assured. He rose to become Professor of Painting at the Royal Academy in 1799 and Keeper in 1804. Like so many of Mary's associates, he lived on into his eighties; he died at Putney Hill in

1825 whilst on a visit to the Countess of Guildford.

And what of that dashing cleric whom Mary was alleged to have loved, Joshua Waterhouse? His later career was unedifying, and his ending was bizarre in the extreme[26]. In 1798 he was elected, by some dubious manoeuvres, to the mastership of St Catherine's College, Cambridge, only to be removed from the post a few months later. In 1806 he became vicar of Little Stukeley, Huntingdon; and here, on 3rd July 1827, at the age of 81, he was found dead in a brewing-tub with his throat cut. His murderer was a dismissed servant, Joshua Slade, who was rumoured to have been his illegitimate son. This seems highly unlikely, since the youth was only eighteen when he was executed for the murder on 1st September 1827. He at first denied his guilt but later, after an unsuccessful suicide attempt, confessed. The *Cambridge Chronicle* reported (7th September 1827):

> He was naturally a youth of strong comprehensive mind, but sunk in the most deplorable state of ignorance.... Because the life of Mr Waterhouse was stained with some immoralities, Slade imagined there could be little or no sin in destroying such a person. He later changed his attitude and repented.

Had Mary still lived, her pity for this young victim of 'justice' must have outweighed her horror and mortification at the revelations of the case. Waterhouse had never married, and over the years he had changed from a gay bachelor about town to an eccentric, miserly recluse. But his amorous adventures must have been extensive, for after his death there was found in his kitchen a sack full of 'love letters', amongst them, some from Mary Wollstonecraft. This treasure trove was described thus in a contemporary account[27]:

> Mr W. used to say that he had love letters enough, of one kind or another, to cook the marriage feast, whenever it should take place; and that the rev. gentleman was not far wrong in his conjecture may be guessed from the fact, that at the time of his death, these melting epistles were numerous enough to fill an entire sack. Amongst the many fair ones to whom the singular rector of Stukeley paid his addresses was the once-famous Mary Wollstonecraft ... How far the rev. gentleman sped in his wooing with this intellectual amazon we have not been able to ascertain; but, like all his other attachments, his passion for the author of the *Rights of Woman* was destined to envince the

truth of the poet's observation,
    The course of true love never did run smooth
The observation, in the circumstances of the kitchen miscellany, seems hardly apt; but the real truth about Waterhouse's affairs, and Mary's part in them, will never be known. His letters were said to have been sent to Cambridge and sold, but no trace of them has ever been found.

It is a somewhat surprising thought that had Mary Wollstonecraft been granted the full span of life that so many of her associates enjoyed, she would have seen the dawn of the Victorian age. Her youngest sister Everina was still alive in 1834[28]. (The Abinger collection contains a letter dated 29th September that year from her niece Elizabeth Berry in Australia.) William Godwin, already a Victorian, died in 1836; Maria Gisborne (Reveley) a year previously. Mary's girlhood friend Jane Gardiner (née Arden) lived on until 1840; Mary Hays until 1843. Amelia Opie (née Alderson) visited the Great Exhibition of 1851 when she was 82, two years before her death. Even Mary's father, that pitiful wreck, lingered on into the nineteenth century; he was buried at Laugharne on 2nd April 1803[29]. Yet the century contrived largely to ignore Mary. Kegan Paul, though sympathetic, felt it expedient to coat her with large dollops of whitewash in his life of Godwin published in 1876. The first objective biography, by Elizabeth Robins Pennell, did not appear until 1884—close on a hundred years after her death. An account of the *History and Antiquities of Beverley* (1829) by G. Oliver could not omit her connection with the town. After stating erroneously that Mary was born at Beverley in 1768, the author went on to describe her as 'a lady of very superior literary attainments, which can scarcely be said to have been applied to the most laudable purposes; for there were certain peculiarities of system both in her writings and her conduct, against which every true friend of religion and morals must conscientiously protest'. This tone was echoed by Anne Elwood in her *Memoirs of the Literary Ladies of England* (1843). Despite the author's obvious sympathy for her subject, and a determined effort to extenuate her union with Imlay, she felt obliged to give judgment against her:

> It is to be lamented that Mary Wollstonecraft, whom nature, when she so lavishly endowed her with virtues and talents, evidently meant should be a bright pattern of perfection to her

sex, should, by her erroneous theories and false principles, have rendered herself instead, rather the beacon by which to warn the woman of similar endowments with herself, of the rocks upon which enthusiasm and imagination are too apt to wreck their possessor.

On the level at which it is presented, this is a fair summing up. But Mrs Elwood, like most of Mary's critics, failed to comprehend the social content of her rebellion. They saw her behaviour in terms of personal caprice rather than as an essential element in the struggle for social justice.

It is certainly difficult to find a place for Mary Wollstonecraft in the Victorian age. She seems almost to leap straight from the eighteenth century into the twentieth, where she would perhaps have felt more at home. By then her pioneering vision was beginning to find practical expression: in the women's suffrage campaigns; in the extension of state education; and in the growth of the labour and co-operative movement. Yet neither in the women's movement nor in education was her pattern immediately followed. The first wave of twentieth-century feminists, intent on political and economic emancipation, ignored the emotional imbalance between the sexes which Mary had well-nigh crucified herself to rectify. The system of public education practised the same repressive doctrines as the orthodox private schools. Only since World War Two have both feminism and education displayed a more human face. The third movement—the rise of organised labour in industrial societies from penury to comparative affluence—is part of a general historical process in which any one individual can only have played a limited role. Yet if Robert Owen rather than Karl Marx is seen as the rightful father of socialism (and even Marxists have acknowledged the need for 'socialism with a human face'), the influence of Mary Wollstonecraft in this field, too, is greater than she has been credited with. Not only Owen himself, but the early French socialists Saint-Simon and Fourier are also said to have been affected by her writings[30].

For evidence of Robert Owen's opinion we are indebted to Fanny Imlay, who wrote to Mary Shelley on 29th July 1816[31]:

So much for Mr Owen, who is indeed, a very great and good man. He told me the other day that he wished our mother was living, as he had never met with a person, who thought so exactly as he did, or who would have so warmly and zealously entered into his plans.

This almost suggests that Owen actually knew Mary, but such an acquaintance hardly seems possible. He did not meet Godwin until 1813, although he had already started to put into practice some of the principles of *Political Justice* in his New Lanark mills and was to carry them further in the New Harmony community in America which he founded in 1825. Thus Mary's influence did live on through the nineteenth century, but in the New World rather than the old. To establish just such a community had been her own American dream, which she had hoped to realise with Gilbert Imlay; and her brother Charles after his emigration did in fact spend some time at the community founded by Thomas Cooper in Pennsylvania. Imlay too, through his novel *The Emigrants*, can claim some share in this quest for an ideal society.

For Mary, the ideal was always rooted in reality; and reality meant the sentient, living being of which she was so palpably conscious in herself. For her, the 'new harmony' signified a rightful balance between personal and social relations, in which neither element should be improperly sacrificed to the other. If the search for this balance is peculiarly a woman's task—which is not proven, but at least it was this woman's task—therein lies her real contribution to the emancipation both of her own sex and of society in general; for, as she never tired of pointing out, the two are inseparable.

Mary Wollstonecraft could not have foreseen that the greatest means to women's emancipation was to be not education, not the opening up of the professions, not the vote nor a seat in parliament—but contraception. She would however have understood it, better perhaps than some more recent feminist campaigners. She would have appreciated too the dramatic improvement in status that has come about, in England at least, from a change in the numerical balance of the sexes, males now outnumbering females in the child-bearing years so that the traditional role of the supplicant has been reversed. Never has the position of woman been stronger. How will she use her newly-won power and freedom? Will she do better than the men? That remains to be seen. Too much power—whether of a nation, a class or a sex—can be as damaging as too little, as Mary often pointed out. Her maxim that the two sexes mutually corrupt and improve each other—and society—is more than ever relevant today, when it can actually be practised on equal terms. Mary Wollstonecraft died too soon to see the vindication of her prophecies, herself a victim of ignorance and prejudice. If her message still speaks to us, her sacrifice to nature—and human nature—was not in vain.

Notes and References

Chapter 1
1. Information from Claire Tomalin, *The Life and Death of Mary Wollstonecraft* (1974).
2. Deed poll, Middlesex Record Office (Pinner 1758/4/84).
3. Godwin's estimate. (*Memoirs*, 1798).
    Eleanor Flexner (*Mary Wollstonecraft*, 1972) gives details of the will showing that Mary's father received less cash but inherited the Primrose Street property. Flexner also states that the family moved to Essex in 1761; but Eliza's baptism at St Botolph's, Bishopgate, in 1763 would appear to cast doubt on this.
4. Godwin, *op. cit.* There is a Whalebone Inn at Chadwell Heath on Chapman & André's map of 1771, with Pigtail Farm adjacent.
5. *Ibid.*
6. A.C. Edwards, *History of Essex* (1965).
7. Flexner (*op. cit.*) found evidence that by this time the family had moved from Walkington into Beverley and were living in the street known as Wednesday Marketplace.
8. Beverley Corporation Apprentices Register.
9. *Shelley and his Circle*, ed. K.N. Cameron, vol. II (1961).
10. *Ibid.*
11. *Op. cit.*
12. *Shelley and his Circle*, vol. II, SC 186.
13. *Selected Letters of Josiah Wedgwood*, ed. Ann Finer & George Savage (1965).
14. Edward Wollstonecraft was married at St Botolph's, Aldgate, on 21st June 1778 (register at Guildhall Library). This fact, not noted by the Carl Pforzheimer Library, suggests that their dating of correspondence with Jane Arden in May/June 1778 is incorrect. In the second of these letters (SC 186) Mary writes that Edward had been married for some time and was 'now a father'.

Chapter 2
1. Godwin, *Memoirs*.
2. SC 186. This letter may be later than May/June 1778 (see Note 14, Ch.1).
3. SC 187.
4. *Gentleman's Magazine*, August 1795.
5. SC 188.
6. SC 190, dated June/August 1780.
7. SC 189, dated April /June 1780. There are some grounds for supposing that this letter came after SC 190 above.
8. Abinger collection.
9. SC 191.
10. Middlesex Record Office. Flexner (*op. cit.*) deduces that the family moved to another address in Enfield (there is a second entry for Edward John Wollstonecraft in the rate book for the second quarter of 1781).
11. There is an entry in the parish burials register for Elizabeth Woolstingcroft dated April 1782. If this is indeed Mrs Wollstonecraft, as seems likely, Mary's letter to Jane Arden referring to her mother's death (SC 191), tentatively dated January/May 1781, must have been written more than a year later. Godwin put the year of death at 1780 and subsequent biographers adhered to this until Flexner, *op. cit.*
12. Tomalin (*op. cit.*) has pointed out that a wife is named in his will at the Public Record Office.
13. The poor rate books show an entry for Francis Blood from 1780 to 1784. (Fulham records, PAF/1/29, in Shepherd's Bush public library.)
14. SC 191. See Note 11 above.
15. SC 192, dated October/January 1782–3.
16. This problem was tragically solved by the baby's death. (Burials register, St Mary Magdalene's, Bermondsey, 4th August 1784. Noted in Tomalin, *op. cit.*)
17. *Shelley and his Circle*, vol. II.

Chapter 3
1. Abinger collection.
2. A lease in the name of Mary Wollstonecraft is recorded for the years 1785 and 1786. (Middlesex Record Office, LTA 2424/5.)
3. Letter to Godwin, 24th November 1797 (Abinger collection).
4. Godwin, *Memoirs*.
5. *Ibid*. This comment appeared in a revised, second edition of the *Memoirs* which was published later in 1789.
6. Elizabeth Nitchie, 'An Early Suitor of Mary Wollstonecraft', *P.M.L.A.*, LVIII, 1943.
7. Abinger collection.
8. Godwin, *op. cit.*

Chapter 4
1. Godwin, *Memoirs*.
2. Abinger collection.

Notes and References 361

3 Ralph M. Wardle, *Mary Wollstonecraft: a critical biography* (1951).
4 Sir H. C. Maxwell-Lyte, quoted in H.R. James, *Mary Wollstonecraft, a sketch* (1932).
5 Lord Kingsborough built a model town providing houses for his workers, a church and a school, and established local industries (Flexner, *op. cit.*). The family history is given in some detail in Tomalin, *op. cit.*—including the fact that Lord and Lady Kingsborough, who had married very young, were only a few years older than Mary herself.
6 Quoted in W. Clark Durant, Supplement to Godwin's *Memoirs* (1927).
7 *Letters written . . . in Sweden, etc.* (1796).
8 *Shelley and his Circle*, vol. IV (1970).
9 Letter I in the series to Johnson included in *Posthumous Works*, vol. IV.
10 Mary's influence was held to blame for Margaret's later action in leaving her husband Lord Mountcashel for another man. (See Tomalin, *op. cit.*)
11 Letter II.

Chapter 5
1 Abinger collection.
2 *Ibid.*
3 *Shelley and his Circle*, vol. IV.
4 Godwin, *Memoirs*.
5 See W. Lyon Blease, *The Emancipation of English Women* (1910).

Chapter 6
1 Abinger collection.
2 The second edition (1791) was illustrated with six engravings by William Blake; this edition, with introduction by E. V. Lucas, was re-issued in 1906. Blake also illustrated Mary's translation of *Elements of Morality* (3 vols, 1790–91) with fifty copper engravings.
3 Letter IV, *Posthumous Works*, IV.
4 Abinger collection.
5 Mary had arranged for Everina to go to France to learn the language in February 1788. Tomalin (*op. cit.*) states that she stayed with 'a family of well-to-do shopkeepers'.
6 Confusion has been caused by the listing of this book in some bibliographies as *The French Reader*; there is also some uncertainty about the authorship (see Wardle, *op. cit.*).
7 Ralph M. Wardle, 'Mary Wollstonecraft, Analytical Reviewer', *P.M.L.A.*, LXII, 1947.
8 Information in Tomalin, *op. cit.*
9 Note to Godwin, Abinger collection.
10 John Knowles, *The Life and Writings of Henry Fuseli* (1831).
11 Quoted in W. Clark Durant, Supplement to Godwin's *Memoirs*.
12 Note to Godwin, *op. cit.*
13 Letter IV.
14 Letter VI.
15 Letter VIII.

16 Letter IX.
17 Letter XI.
18 Letters XII and XIII.
19 Letter XV.

Chapter 7
1 Quoted in C. C. O'Brien, introduction to Burke's *Reflections on the Revolution in France* (Pelican edn, 1968).
2 *Ibid.*
3 H. N. Brailsford, *Shelley, Godwin and their Circle* (1913).
4 *Ibid.*

Chapter 8
1 W. Lyon Blease, *op. cit.*
2 'Sophia', *Woman not Inferior to Man* (1739); reprinted by Brentham Press (1975).
3 This question is not discussed in Robert Halsband's *Lady Mary Wortley Montagu* (1956). He does however refer to *The Nonsense of Common Sense*, a political journal founded by her, which in January 1738 devoted an issue to the feminist cause.
4 This vindictive onslaught (could it have been the work of Alexander Pope?) evoked a further riposte by Sophia, *Woman's Superior Excellence over Man*. All three essays were published in one volume by Jacob Robinson in 1743.
5 See Tomalin, *op. cit.*, for a more detailed discussion of women in the French Revolution.
6 Wardle, *op. cit.*
7 Blease, *op. cit.*
8 Brailsford, *op. cit.*
9 Godwin's estimate. Flexner (*op. cit.*) publishes letters from Mary to William Roscoe which indicate that the period of composition was three months. Mary acknowledged that 'had I allowed myself more time I could have written a better book' (3rd January 1792).
10 Quoted in Anne Elwood, *Memoirs of the Literary Ladies of England* (1843).
11 *Ibid.*

Chapter 9
1 Abinger collection.
2 *Ibid.*
3 Information on Upton Castle from R. Fenton, *A Historical Tour through Pembrokeshire* (2nd edn, 1903).
4 G. M. Trevelyan, *English Social History*, vol. 3 (Pelican edn, 1964).
5 Horace Walpole's phrase in a letter to Hannah More.
6 Quoted in *The Literary Diary of Ezra Stiles*, ed. F. D. Dexter (1901).
7 *Farington Diary*, ed. James Grieg, vol. I (1922).
8 Quoted in Eudo C. Mason, *The Mind of Henry Fuseli* (1951). Biographical

Notes and References

information about Fuseli is mainly from this source. See also: Frederick Antal, *Fuseli Studies* (1956).
9 *Angelica* (1954).
10 Mason, *op. cit.*
11 Allan Cunningham, *Lives of the Painters*, vol. II (ed. Mary Heaton, 1879).
12 Quoted in Mason, *op. cit.*
13 Quoted in Knowles, *op. cit.*
14 Mason, *op. cit.*
15 Quoted in Mason, *op. cit.*
16 *Tracks in the Snow* (1946).
17 *Splendours and Miseries* (1943).
18 Note to Godwin, *op. cit.*
19 Letter of 6th October 1791 (Roscoe collection, Liverpool City Libraries, quoted in Flexner, *op. cit.*). In this same letter Mary speaks of 'sitting for the picture'. Could this have been by Fuseli?—if so, it has never been identified; there is an unattributed portrait of Mary Wollstonecraft in the Walker Art Gallery, Liverpool.
The correspondence with Roscoe confirms Mary's close relationship with Fuseli: 'I love the man and admire the artist' (February 1792).

Chapter 10
1 Abinger collection.
2 Thomas Carlyle, *The French Revolution* (Everyman edn, 1906).
3 *The Private Memoirs of Madame Roland*, ed. E. G. Johnson (1901).
4 John G. Alger, *Englishmen in the French Revolution* (1899).
5 *Lettres de Madame Roland* (to Bancal; Paris 1835).
6 *Posthumous Works*, vol. IV.
7 Alger, *op. cit.*
8 Mason, *op. cit.*
9 *Ibid.*
10 Eliza did not exaggerate. Scott, who became Attorney General in 1793, was described (*D.N.B.*) as the 'best hated man in England' for his Traitorous Correspondence Act (1793); Habeas Corpus Suspension Act (1794); and Treasonable Practices and Seditious Meetings Acts (1795).
11 *Shelley and his Circle*, vol. IV.
12 Information in Wardle, *op. cit.*
13 Christie's 'enlightenment' did not extend to his personal morality. Tomalin (*op. cit.*) describes his liaison with a Frenchwoman who bore him a daughter in London in July 1792; six weeks later he married Rebecca Thomson, the 'carpet heiress'.
14 Letter of 13 November 1797, quoted in *Shelley and his Circle*, vol. I.
15 Quoted in Flexner, *op. cit.*

Chapter 11
1 Wardle, *op. cit.*
2 February 1793, in *Shelley and his Circle*, vol. IV.
3 Abinger collection.

4 *Shelley and his Circle*, vol. I.
5 Mary's letters to Imlay, numbered I to LXXVII, were included by Godwin in *Posthumous Works*, vols. III and IV. An edition of *Letters to Imlay* was published in 1879, with preface by C. Kegan Paul; and again in 1908, edited by Roger Ingpen. All quoted references are from Kegan Paul's edition, unless otherwise stated.
6 Durant (*op. cit.*) dated this letter late in 1794; but the signature 'M. Wollstonecraft' makes that unlikely.
7 Letter II.
8 In his introduction to a recent reprint of *The Emigrants* (Florida, 1964), Robert C. Hare suggests that this novel, and possibly also Imlay's *Topographical Description of the Western Territory*, was actually written by Mary. He points out certain similarities in the plot with that of *The Wrongs of Woman*, with a feminist bias that was uncharacteristic of Imlay. But *The Emigrants* was reviewed in *The British Critic* in July 1793 and must have been completed before the lovers met in Paris that April. A possible explanation is that Mary read the manuscript and contributed information about the English divorce laws; she may also have been responsible for the preface, which resembles her own style of writing in some respects. It seems highly improbable that she had any part in Imlay's previous book.
9 *The Common Reader*, 2nd series (1932).
10 Letter IV.
11 Letter V.
12 Letter VII.

Chapter 12

1 Quoted in Carlyle, *op. cit.*
2 *The Private Memoirs of Madame Roland.*
3 Amelia Alderson to Mrs John Taylor, quoted in Wardle, *op. cit.*
4 Letter X.
5 Letter XI.
6 Letter XII.
7 Letter XIII.
8 Letter XV.
9 Letter XVI.
10 Letter XVII.
11 B. P. Kurtz & C. C. Autrey (ed), *Four New Letters of Mary Wollstonecraft and Helen Maria Williams* (Berkeley, 1937).
12 Letters XVIII and XIX.
13 Abinger collection.
14 Quoted in Carlyle, *op. cit.*
15 Kurtz & Autrey, *op. cit.*
16 *Ibid.*
17 Quoted in Durant, *op. cit.*
18 Letter XX.
19 Letter XXI.

20 Letter XXII.
21 Abinger collection.
22 Letter XXIII.
23 Letter XXIV.
24 Quoted in Durant, *op. cit.*
25 *Ibid.*
26 *Ibid.*
27 *Ibid.*
28 Letter XXV.
29 Letter XXVI.
30 Letter XXVII.
31 Letter XXVIII.
32 Quoted in Durant, *op. cit.*
33 Letter XXIX.
34 Letter XXX.
35 Letter XXXI.
36 Letter XXXII.
37 Letter XXXIII.
38 Letter XXXIV.
39 Letter XXXV.
40 Letter XXXVI.
41 Letter XXXVII.
42 Letter XXXVIII.
43 The house in Havre where Fanny was born has been identified as that of an English soap-merchant, John Wheatcroft (Tomalin, *op. cit.*).
44 Both letters quoted in Durant, *op. cit.*
45 *Ibid.*

Chapter 13

1 *William Godwin, his friends and contemporaries* (1876).
2 *A Defence of the Character and Conduct of the late Mary Wollstonecraft* (1803).
3 Quoted in Durant, *op. cit.*
4 *The Rights of Man* (Everyman edn, 1969).
5 Letter XXXIX.
6 Abinger collection.
7 *Ibid.*
8 Letter XL. Flexner (*op. cit.*) quotes a hitherto unpublished letter from Mary to Schlabrendorf dated 13 May 1796, but which must surely belong to 1795 (the original has been lost). It is signed 'Mary Imlay' and is full of her sense of betrayal and 'cruel disappointment'. The whole tone is consonant with her desperate mood on returning to England and discovering Imlay's deception.
9 Elias Backman, referred to in this document, has been identified as an exporter from Gothenberg, with whom Imlay had been associated in France (Wardle, *op. cit.*).
10 Abinger collection.

11 Letters XLII.
12 Letters XLIV to LI.

Chapter 14
1 The *Letters* were addressed to Imlay but written for publication. Mary's personal letters written to Imlay from Scandinavia are included in *Letters to Imlay* and are numbered here accordingly.
2 Letter LII.
3 Letter LIII.
4 Letter LIV.
5 Letter LV.
6 Letter LVI.
7 Letter LVII.
8 Letter LVIII.
9 Letter LIX.
10 Letter LX.
11 Letter LXI.
12 Letter LXII.
13 Letter LXIII.
14 Mary here anticipated Malthus, whose *Essay on the Principles of Population* did not appear until 1798.
15 Letter LXIV.
16 Letter LXV.
17 Letter LXVI.
18 Letter LXVII.
19 Letter LXVIII.

Chapter 15
1 11 November 1795.
2 Letter LXIX. Kegan Paul dates this letter 'November'.
3 Information from *History of Fulham* (Fulham Historical Society, 1970). Tomalin (*op. cit.*) identifies the inn where Mary was taken as the Duke's Head.
4 Godwin, *Memoirs*. The heavy rainfall was obviously a factor. Somerset House meteorological station recorded 0.21 inches of rain during the night of 10 to 11 October 1795, the date of the *Times* version of the incident. (*Trans. Roy. Soc.*, v.86, 1976; met. suppl, p.20. Information supplied by Ealing central reference library.)
5 Letter LXX.
6 Godwin, *Memoirs*.
7 Letter LXXI.
8 Birth-control was not unknown in the eighteenth century, even among 'respectable' women (see Tomalin, *op. cit.*).
9 Letter LXXII.
10 Letter LXXIII.
11 Letter LXXIV.
12 According to Godwin, Imlay was gone for three months. If so, Kegan Paul's dating of Mary's subsequent letters is incorrect.

Notes and References

13 Letter LXXV.
14 *Ibid.*
15 Letter LXXVI.
16 Knowles, *op. cit.*
17 Tomalin (*op. cit.*) states that Mary's letters to Fuseli were bought and destroyed by Sir Percy Shelley.
18 Letter LXXVII.
19 Quoted in Durant, *op. cit.*
20 *Ibid.*

Chapter 16
1 George Woodcock, *William Godwin* (1946). Biographical information about Godwin, unless otherwise stated, is from this source.
2 Godwin, 'Autobiographical notes', quoted in Woodcock.
3 Godwin, Diary.
4 R. G. Grylls, *William Godwin and his World* (1953). It is of course possible that the entry 'Imlay' referred to 'Mrs Imlay'.
5 Letter of 14 October 1794, quoted in A. F. Wedd (ed), *The Love Letters of Mary Hays* (1925).
6 Wedd, *op. cit.*
7 Quoted in Kegan Paul, *William Godwin* etc.
8 Quoted in Wardle, *op. cit.*
9 Ralph M. Wardle, (ed). *Godwin & Mary: letters of William Godwin and Mary Wollstonecraft* (1967). All quoted letters are from this source.
10 Quoted in Durant, *op. cit.*
11 Abinger collection.
12 *Ibid.*
13 Quoted in Wedd, *op. cit.*
14 *Ibid.*
15 Quoted in *Shelley and his Circle*, vol. IV.
16 Abinger collection.
17 Kegan Paul, *op. cit.*
18 Quoted in Woodcock, *op. cit.*
19 Letter to William Roscoe, 25 May 1797.

Chapter 17
1 Quoted in *Amelia: the tale of a Plain Friend*, by Jacobine Menzies-Wilson and Helen Lloyd; 1937.
2 *Ibid.*
3 Quoted in Wardle, *op. cit.*
4 *Ibid.*
5 Godwin, *Memoirs.*
6 Quoted in Wardle, *op. cit.*
7 Quoted in *Shelley and his Circle*, Vol. IV.
8 Another portrait by John Opie entitled 'Mary Wollstonecraft Godwin' (Tate Gallery) has been disputed, although Flexner (*op. cit.*) believes it to be authentic. There is certainly a strong similarity in the features and eyes,

but the general impression is of an older woman; the hair is grey and slightly frizzy. Flexner deduces that it was painted before 1790, when 'powdering' was still in fashion; Durant (*op. cit.*) on the contrary believes it was painted in 1795 and is a spurious representation. Neither explanation is satisfactory. Mary disliked powdered hair, and before 1790 she was neither famous nor acquainted with Opie. Yet in essentials the portrait *is* Mary, and a glimpse of auburn beneath the grey adds to its authenticity. The mystery is further compounded by Mary's reference to her 'picture' in her letter to William Roscoe in October 1791 (see Note 19, chapter 9).

9 Godwin too was buried here in 1836; both were re-interred in the Shelley family tomb at St Peter's, Bournemouth, in 1851. A memorial stone to Mary, Godwin and his second wife Mary Jane has been placed in the former churchyard at Old St Pancras church, now a public garden.

Chapter 18

1 Brailsford. *op. cit.*
2 Quoted in Kegan Paul, *William Godwin*, etc.
3 *Ibid.*
4 *Ibid.*
5 *Ibid.*
6 *Ibid.*
7 *Ibid.*
8 *Annual Necrology 1797–8:* London 1800.
9 A selection is printed in Durant, *op. cit.*
10 Kegan Paul, *op. cit.*
11 Abinger collection.
12 Quoted in Kegan Paul, *op. cit.*
13 *Ibid.*
14 Abinger collection.
15 Kegan Paul *op. cit.*
16 *Ibid.*
17 Quoted in *Mary Shelley*, by Eileen Bigland; 1959.
18 12th February 1817; ed. Edith J. Morley; 1938.
19 Abinger collection.
20 Quoted in Grylls, *op. cit.*
21 Quoted in Kegan Paul, *op. cit.*
22 Quoted in Bigland, *op. cit.*
23 Information about Imlay's residence supplied by Mr Raymond Falla, local history librarian, St Helier.
24 Quoted in Durant, *op. cit.*
25 Abinger collection.
26 See Nitchie, *op. cit.*
27 *Narrative of the Murder of the late Rev. J. Waterhouse,* by T. Lovell; 1827.
28 Flexner (*op. cit.*) has added a good deal of new information on the family history:
Eliza died in Dublin between 1827–32; Everina died in London in 1843. Mary's eldest brother Edward died in 1812; his son and daughter

(Elizabeth Berry) emigrated to Australia.
James died on naval service in the West Indies in 1806.
Charles served in the US army and died in 1817.
29 *Shelley and his Circle*, Vol. IV.
30 *A Study of Mary Wollstonecraft and the Rights of Woman*, by Emma Rauschenbusch-Clough; 1898.
31 Abinger collection.

Bibliography

Books by Mary Wollstonecraft

Thoughts on the Education of Daughters: with reflections on female conduct, in the more important duties of life (1787).

Mary: a fiction (1788).

Original Stories from Real Life; with conversations calculated to regulate the affections, and form the mind to truth and goodness (1788).

Of the Importance of Religious Opinions: translated from the French of Mr Necker (1789).

Elements of Morality for the use of children: with an introductory address to parents: translated from the German of the Rev. C. G. Salzmann (in three volumes, 1790–91).

A Vindication of the Rights of Men (1790).

A Vindication of the Rights of Woman (1792).

An Historical and Moral View of the Origin and Progress of the French Revolution; and the effect it has produced in Europe (Vol. I, 1794).

Letters written during a short residence in Sweden, Norway and Denmark (1796).

Posthumous Works, ed. William Godwin (1798).
Vols. *i* and *ii*: *The Wrongs of Woman, or Maria: a fragment; Lessons for Children.*
Vols. *iii* and *iv*: *Letters to Imlay.*
Vol. *iv*: *Letters to Johnson; The Cave of Fancy; Essay on Poetry and our relish for the beauties of nature; Fragments.*

Books about Mary Wollstonecraft

Carl Pforzheimer Library. *Shelley and his Circle.* Vols. I & II. (ed.) Kenneth N. Cameron, New York, 1961; Vols. III & IV, New York, 1970.

Flexner, Eleanor. *Mary Wollstonecraft*, New York, 1972.

Godwin, William. *Memoirs of the author of A Vindication of the Rights of Woman*, 1798; (ed.) W. Clark Durant, with supplementary material, 1927.

James, H. R. *Mary Wollstonecraft*, 1932.
Jebb, Camilla. *Mary Wollstonecraft*, 1912.
Kegan Paul, C. (ed.). *Letters to Imlay*, 1879.
Kurtz, B. P. & Autrey, C. C. *Four New Letters of Mary Wollstonecraft and Helen M. Williams*. Berkeley, California, 1937.
Linford, Madeleine. *Mary Wollstonecraft*, 1924.
Nixon, Edna. *Mary Wollstonecraft: her life and times*, 1971.
Pennell, Elizabeth. *Mary Wollstonecraft Godwin*, 1885.
Preedy, George. *This Shining Woman*, 1937.
Rauschenbusch-Clough, Emma. *A Study of Mary Wollstonecraft and the Rights of Woman*, 1898.
Stirling Taylor, G. R. *Mary Wollstonecraft: a study in economics and romance*, 1911.
Tomalin, Claire. *The Life and Death of Mary Wollstonecraft*, 1974.
Wardle, R. M. *Mary Wollstonecraft: a critical biography*, 1951.
—— (ed.) *Godwin and Mary* (letters), 1967.

General

Alger, J. G. *Englishmen in the French Revolution*, 1899.
Ayling, S. G. *The Georgian Century 1714–1837*, 1966.
Bigland, Eileen. *Mary Shelley*, 1959.
Blease, W. Lyon. *The Emancipation of English Women*, 1910.
Brailsford, H. N. *Shelley, Godwin and their Circle*, 1913.
Burke, Edmund. *Reflections on the Revolution in France*, 1790; (ed.) Conor Cruise O'Brien, Penguin edn., 1969.
Carlyle, Thomas. *The French Revolution*, 1837.
Dobinson, C. H. *Jean-Jacques Rousseau*, 1969.
Dobson, H. Austin. *Four Frenchwomen*, 1893.
Elwood, Anne. *Memoirs of the Literary Ladies of England*, 1843.
Farington, Joseph. *Diary*, Vol. I; (ed.) Grieg, 1922.
Furst, Lilian R. *Romanticism in Perspective*, 1969.
Godwin, William. *Political Justice*, 1793.
Grylls, Rosalie G. *William Godwin and his World*, 1953.
Kegan Paul, C. *William Godwin, his friends and contemporaries*, 1876.
Knowles, J. *The Life and Writings of Henry Fuseli, R. A.*, 1831.
Lea, F. A. *Shelley and the Romantic Revolution*, 1945.
Loomis, S. *Paris in the Terror*, 1964.
Paine, Tom. *The Rights of Man*, 1791; Everyman edn. 1969.
Roland, Mme. *Letters to Bancal*, Paris, 1835.
—— *Private Memoirs*, (ed.) E. G. Johnson, 1901.
Rousseau, J. J. *Emile*, 1762.
Trevelyan, G. M. *English Social History*, Vol. III; Penguin edn., 1964.
Wedd, A. F. (ed.). *The Love Letters of Mary Hays*, 1925.
Willey, B. *Eighteenth Century Background*, 1961 edn.
Woodcock, G. *William Godwin*, 1946.

Index

Alderson, Amelia: 300–3, 307, 312, 318–19, 346–7, 355
Aldis, Charles (Sir): 232, 344
Allen, John Bartlett: 10
Analytical Review: 81, 91, 96–8, 130, 157, 167, 311, 343
Anderson, George: 92
'Ann': 153–4, 163
Arden, Jane: 6–11, 14–21, 152, 355
Arden, John (Dr): 6, 8–9, 14

Backman, Elias: 195, 244
Bancal, (M.): 174
Barbaroux, (M.): 173, 188
Barbauld, Anna Laetitia: 92, 177, 320, 344
Barlow, Joel: 162, 165, 167, 179, 181–4, 188, 202
Barlow, Ruth: 162, 167, 179, 183–4, 187–8, 191–2, 206, 208–10, 232
Bernstorff, (Count): 263
Bishop, Meredith: 20, 23–8, 31
Blake, William: 92, 153, 360n6,2
Blenkinsop, (Mrs): 336–7
Blood, Caroline: 95
the Blood family: 10, 20, 22–3, 35, 37, 41–2, 44, 46, 48, 56, 95
Blood, Fanny: 10–11, 17–18, 20, 24, 27, 30–40, 44, 47, 70–2, 209
Blood, George: 20, 35–9, 41–2, 44–6, 49–51, 53, 55, 66, 73, 86–7, 94–6, 147–8, 153, 162, 185, 350
Bonnycastle, John: 92
Bregantz, (Mme): 93–4, 172
Brissot, Jean-Pierre: 173, 176, 183, 188, 201–2
Burgh, James (Mrs): 32, 45–6, 95
Burke, Edmund: 103; (*Reflections on the French Revolution*) 104–20; 127, 150
Buzot, (M.): 173, 188, 201

Carlisle, (Mr): 338

The Cave of Fancy: 62, 74–7, 81
Chesterfield, (Lord): (*Letters to his Son*) 138–41
Christie, Thomas: 81, 182–4, 187, 189, 213, 229, 276, 278, 282, 362n10,13
Christie, Thomas (Mrs): 277, 282, 311
Church, (Mr): 36, 38, 53
Clairmont, Jane: 346, 348
Clairmont, (Mrs): 346–9
Clare, (Mrs): 10, 27, 31
Cooper, Thomas: 182–3, 292, 306, 357
Cowper, William: 92, 140
Cotton, (Mrs): 282, 287, 312, 340
Cristall, (Mr): 94

Darwin, Erasmus: 92
Dawson, (Mrs): 13–16, 18, 35, 56, 64, 127
de Crevecoeur, St John: 266
A Defence of the Character and Conduct of the Late Mary Wollstonecraft Godwin: 344
de Genlis, (Mme): (*Letters on Education*) 133; 266
de Stael, (Mme): 133
de Wolzogen, (Baron): 216
Dumouriez, (General): 173, 188
Dyson, George: 291, 312, 326, 338

East, Harry (Sir): 287
Elements of Mortality (cf: Saltzmann, C. G.): 88
'Essay on Poetry': 327–8

Farrington, Joseph: 274, 307
The Female Reader; or Miscellaneous Pieces in Prose and Verse: 90–1
Fenwick, Eliza: 312, 341
Fillietaz, Aline (Mme): 172, 189
Fillietaz, (M.): 177
Fordyce, George (Dr): 92, 127, 337–8
Fordyce, James: (*Sermons to Young Women*) 130–1

Index

Forster, George: 184
Fuseli, Henry: 92, 154–66, 177, 185, 277, 281–2, 316, 353, 362n19.
Fuseli, Sophia (née Rawlins): 158–9, 165–7

Gabell, Ann: 101
Gabell, Henry: 48, 54–5, 59, 61, 69, 73, 100
George III: 17, 110–11
Godwin, Mary (cf: Shelley, Mary): 299, 316, 337, 341, 346–52, 356
Godwin, William: 7, 8, 10–12, 15, 19, 28–9, 32, 34, 40–1, 44, 46, 49, 53, 58, 68, 70, 81–2, 92–3, 106, 129, 153, 158–9, 161, 164–5, 167, 184, 193–4, 202, 209, 213, 219, 240, 273–5, 277, 281–2, 284, 286, 316, 329, (last years) 339*ff*; 367n17,9
Gregory, John (Dr): (*A Father's Legacy to his Daughters*) 130–1; 140

Hays, Mary: 128, 286, 298–9, 307, 310–12, 319, 342–4, 355
Hewlett, John (Rev.): 34, 43–4, 53
An Historical and Moral View of the ... French Revolution ...: 228, 231–9, 320–1
Holcroft, Thomas: 291, 295, 297, 299, 336, 340

'Imlay', Frances (Fanny 'Godwin'): 209*ff*, 226–8, 240–53, 261*ff*, 274, 276, 282, 311, 315, 330–1, 340–1, 346–50, 356
Imlay, Gilbert: 182*ff*, 240*ff*, 273*ff*, 282*ff*, 287, 308, 316, 324, 352–3, 357, 363n11,8
Inchbald, Elizabeth: 92, 297, 299, 312–13, 319, 344

Johnson, Joseph: 34, 44, 50, 56, 59*ff*, 73, 81–2, 91–3, 96–100, 105, 150–2, 156, 159, 166, 168, 172, 175, 179, 185, 188–9, 212, 228, 243, 249, 267, 278, 281, 286–7, 289, 298, 315–16, 331, 339, 353
Johnson, Samuel (Dr): 34, 73, 91, 140
Johnson, William: 184
Jones, Louisa: 346

Kingsborough, (Lady): 45, 47, 49, 51–2, 57–8, 82, 360n5

Kingsborough, (Lord): 49, 51, 53, 57–8, 360n5
King(sborough), Margaret: 49, 58, 96, 360n10
King(sborough), Mary: 49

Leavenworth, Mark (Mrs): 153
Lee, Harriet: 345–6
'Lessons for Fanny': 330–1
Letters Written during a Short Residence in Sweden, Norway and Denmark: 249*ff*, 281, 285–6
Louis XVI: 171–6

Macaulay, Catherine: 127, (*Letters on Education*) 128; 137
Mackintosh, James: 297
'Marguerite': 244, 247, 249, 274, 279
Maria (cf: *The Wrongs of Woman*)
Marie-Antoinette: 171, 200, 228, 231, 237–8
Marshal, James: 291, 316, 337–8, 340
Mary: a fiction: 58, 62, 68–74, 82, 321
Memoirs of Mary Wollstonecraft: 7–8, 11, 19, 28, 40, 44, 53, 68, 81–2, 158–9, 161, 216, 273–5, 286–90, 297, 300, 338, 343, 345, 348
Montagu, Basil: 332–5, 338
Morris, (Gouverneur): 202

Necker, Jacques: (*De l'Importance des Opinions Religieuses*) 87–8
'Neptune': 46, 51, 53, 55, 185

Ogle, George: 53–4, 57, 73
Opie, John: 163, 307, 312–13, 336, 346, 367n17,8
Original Stories from Real Life: 82–5, 88, 153
Owen, Robert: 356–7

Paine, Thomas: (*Common Sense*) 86; 92, 104, (*The Rights of Man*) 105*ff*; 119, 150, 171–2, 176–7, 183–4, 187, 202, 234, 238
Parr, (Dr): 297, 332
Piozzi, (Mrs) (cf: Thrale): 133
Poignard, (Dr): 337
Posthumous Works: 81, 179, 327, 330
Price, Richard (Dr): 32–4, 38–9, 46, 52, 73, 86–7, 103–6, 109, 114, 173, 296
Priestley, Joseph (Dr): 92, 150, 332
Prior, John (Rev.): 45, 47, 55

Index

Reveley, Maria (née Gisborne): 299–300, 346, 351, 355
Rights of Woman (cf: *A Vindication of the Rights of Woman*)
Robinson, Mary ('Perdita'): 311
Roland de la Platrière, J. M.: 173, 176, 189, 199, 201
Roland, Marie-Jeanne (née Phlipon): 173–4, 176, 189, 200–1, 234*n*, 344
Roscoe, William: 162, 167–8
Rousseau, Jean Jacques: 56, 138–43, 214
Rowan, A. Hamilton: 215, 217, 229–30, 284–5, 306

Saltzmann, C. G. (Rev.): (*Moralisches Elementarbuch*) 88–90; 147
Schlabrendorf, (Count): 216–7
Schweizer, Madeleine: 177, 182, 187, 216
A Sermon written by the late Samuel Johnson ... for the Funeral of his Wife: 91
Shelley, Harriet: 349, 351
Shelley, Mary (cf: Godwin, Mary)
Shelley, Percy Bysshe: 341, 348–9, 351
Siddons, Sarah: 312, 319
Skeys, Hugh: 24, 32–3, 37–8, 42, 46, 53, 55, 95, 342
Stone, John Hurford: 173–4, 194

Talleyrand-Perigord, (M.): 128–9, 165
Thoughts on the Education of Daughters: 44, 54, 62, 68, 85, 158
Thrale, (Mrs) (cf: Piozzi)
Tooke, Horne: 92, 182, 295

Vergniaud, (M.): 173, 176, 200–1
A Vindication of the Rights of Men: 105, 120–1, 147, 151, 175, 233, 239, 323
A Vindication of the Rights of Woman: 3, 67, 86, 89, 92, 114, 121, 128–9, 133, 142–7, 151, 161, 165, 193, 321, 326, 344

Walpole, Horace: 232
Waterhouse, Joshua: 34–5, 38, 46, 57, 66, 73, 354–5
Wedgwood, Thomas: 315–16
Williams, Helen Maria: 172–4, 187, 191, 194, 207
Wollstonecraft, Charles: 4, 6, 20, 94, 149, 162–3, 167, 197, 241–2, 284–5, 316, 357, 368*n*28
Wollstonecraft, Edward (Ned): 4, 11, 20, 24–7, 31, 94, 242, 358*n*14, 368*n*28
Wollstonecraft, Edward (pére): 4–11, 19, 61, 149, 242, 355, 358*n*3
Wollstonecraft, Elizabeth (née Dixon): 7–8, 18–19, 359*n*11
Wollstonecraft, Eliza(beth) (Bess): 4–5, 18–33, 36, 42, 45–8, 57–9, 61, 81, 93–4, 101, 147–9, 152, 162, 165, 177–8, 188–90, 194, 207, 212, 220, 240–3, 285, 324, 341, 345, 358*n*3, 368*n*28
Wollstonecraft, Everina: 4–5, 19–20, 23–4, 26–7, 30, 36, 45, 47–8, 50–4, 56–8, 60–1, 82, 87, 93–4, 100–1, 147–9, 153, 162–3, 165–7, 172, 174, 177–8, 190, 194, 207, 212–13, 241–2, 285, 315, 334, 341, 345, 348, 355, 360*n*6,5, 368*n*28
Wollstonecraft, Henry: 4
Wollstonecraft, James: 4–5, 20, 94, 148, 154, 241–2, 368*n*28
Wollstonecraft, 'Lydia': 19
Wollstonecraft, Mary: (childhood) 4*ff*; (in Bath) 14*ff*; (at Waltham Green) 20*ff*; (at Newington Green) 31*ff*, 41*ff*; (in Lisbon) 38*ff*; (in Ireland) 46, 48*ff*; (in London) 59*ff*, 81*ff* (journalist); (in France) 168*ff*; (Imlay) 185*ff*; ('Mrs' Imlay) 194*ff*; (birth of Fanny) 209; (in England) 240*ff*; (in Scandinavia) 245*ff*; (in Germany) 264*ff*; (return to London) 269*ff*; (suicide attempt) 273–5; (Wm. Godwin) 286*ff*; (marriage) 316; (birth of Mary) 337; (death) 338.
(on children) 50, 62*ff*, 134–5, 152, 330; (on education) 82–3, 134–5; (on education of girls) 62*ff*, 132; (on equality) 136*ff*, 145; (on friendship) 145; (on love) 65–6, 76–7, 132–3, 145, 251; (on matrimony) 22, 28, 66–7, 131–2, 136, 144, 152, 318; (on morality) 90, 137*ff*; (on natural creation) 83–4; (on power) 180; (on the established Church) 112–16; (on rights and duties of women) 129*ff*, 133*ff*; (on sensibility) 329
The Wrongs of Woman, or Maria: 86, 193, 254, 320*ff*

Young Grandison: 91